GLOBE FEARON
LITERATURE

AMERICAN LITERATURE

be
earon
arning Group

pany, New Jersey
earsonlearning.com

■ *Custom Printed* ■

PROGRAM REVIEWERS

Kathy Babigian, Coordinator, Tioga Literacy Center, Fresno, California
Pat Bartholomew, M.A., Reading Specialist, Milton, Ohio
Jennifer Dilks-Mundt, English Teacher, Brant Rock, Massachusetts
Ann Fitzgerald, M.A., Education Director, Southshire Community School,
   North Bennington, Vermont
Pat Miller, M.A., Reading/English/Language Arts Supervisor, Prince Georges County
   Public Schools, Maryland
Artie P. Norton, English Teacher, Suffern, New York
Timothy Rasinski, Professor of Curriculum and Instruction, Kent State University, Kent, Ohio
Cynthia Saska, M.A., Professor of English, University of Texas, San Antonio, Texas
Margaret-Mary Sulentic, Ph.D., Assistant Professor of Literacy, Department of Curriculum
   and Instruction, University of Southern Mississippi, Hattiesburg, Mississippi
Dr. Helen W. Taylor, Director of Programs K-12 Curriculum and Instruction, Portsmouth City
   Public Schools, Virginia

CONSULTANTS

Dr. Virginia Bryg; Josephine Gemake, Ph.D.; Alfred Schifini, Ph.D.; Deborah Walker; Robert
   Wandberg, Ph.D.

ABOUT THE COVER

3rd and Rhode Island, LeDetroit Park, Hilda Wilkinson Brown. From the Hilda Wilkinson Brown
Collection. Courtesy of Lillian Thomas Burwell. This oil painting shows a simple scene of a street in
Detroit. This is a reflection of Brown's ideals. She was described as a "traditional woman, an
idealist in manner and mores of the then womanhood." How is Brown's painting a representation
of traditional American values?

ISBN 0-13-024708-1

Printed in the United States of America
   3 4 5 6 7 8 9 10   08

1-800-321-3106
www.pearsonlearning.com

Preview

UNIT 1   *Voices of Colonial America*

UNIT 2 *Writers in a Growing Nation*

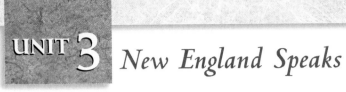

UNIT 3 *New England Speaks*

UNIT 4 A Nation Expresses Itself

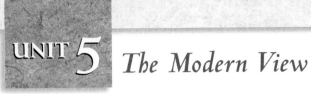

UNIT 5 The Modern View

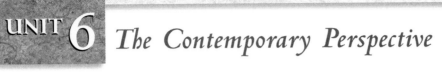

UNIT 6 The Contemporary Perspective

References

HOW TO USE THIS BOOK

Welcome to *Globe Fearon Literature*. As you read this textbook, you will learn about many new worlds. By reading literature you can experience the past and the future, and you can learn about people—how they feel and how they think.

To get the most out of this book, you will need to become an active reader. Active readers think about reading materials before they begin, during, and after they read.

TIPS FOR IMPROVING YOUR READING

Before You Read

- Think about the title of the selection. What does it tell you about the topic? What do you already know about the topic?
- Determine the genre of the selection. For example—if the selection is a poem, ask yourself, "How will this be different from reading an essay or short story?"
- Set a purpose for reading. What do you think you will learn by reading this selection?

As You Read

- Predict what you think will happen next. Then pause occasionally and ask yourself if your predictions were correct.
- Form questions about what you are reading. For example, ask yourself, "What idea is the author trying to convey?"
- When you encounter a word you are unfamiliar with, use the help that Globe Fearon Literature gives you. Difficult words are defined at the bottom of the page they appear on.

After You Read

Consider the following questions:

- Did the selection end the way you anticipated?
- What did you learn from reading this selection?
- How does this selection relate to others you have read?

THE BOOK IS ORGANIZED TO HELP YOU

Your literature book has been organized into units. Each unit is introduced with a piece of fine art and a quote. Look at these pages. What do you think this unit will be about?

The "Focus On" feature gives you some tips to help you understand specific genres of literature, such as fiction or poetry. You will notice that each Model selection has blue notes in the margin. These are study hints to help you read actively. The notes relate back to the "Focus On" feature. The notes will help you identify key elements of the genre. Later, you can look for similar elements in other selections as you read independently.

Before each selection, you will be introduced to a reading skill, a literary skill, and a writing activity. The reading skill will help you understand what you are reading. The literary skill will call your attention to elements of literature. The writing activity will help you relate the literature to your own life.

You will notice that words in boldface type sometimes appear at the bottom of a page. These are words that may help your understanding of a selection. The entries show pronunciations and definitions of the words. These words are also listed in the glossary, which includes a pronunciation key, at the back of this book. In addition, you may find footnoted words in a selection. These words appear at the bottom of a page with the appropriate superscript numbers. (Example: [1]signal corps) This notation indicates additional information rather than a dictionary definition, and these footnoted words do not appear in the glossary.

There are review questions at the end of each selection. These questions help you think about what you have just read. They will also help you relate this selection to others that you may have read.

Globe Fearon Literature was created for you. Reading literature can be one of the most rewarding experiences you can ever have. There are new worlds to explore and exciting people to meet. It's all here. So, let's begin. . .

Voices of Colonial America

In this our western world
Be Freedom's flag unfurl'd
Through all its shores!
May no destructive blast
Our heaven of joy o'ercast,
May Freedom's fabric last
While time endures.
　　　　　—Philip Freneau

The Landing of the Pilgrims, 1620. 19th century, Anonymous.
The Granger Collection

Learn About

The Boating Party, Mary Cassatt. National Gallery of Art, Washington, DC/Index/Bridgeman Art Library

READING FOCUS

Identify Cause and Effect A cause is what makes something happen. An effect is what happens as a result of an event. Each event can have many causes, and a cause can have many effects.

A writer who explores the questions "What happened?" and "Why did it happen?" must use cause and effect in his or her text. As you read Bradstreet's poem, think about the events and emotions she describes. What has caused her to feel the way she does? What are the effects of her feelings?

TONE

When you speak, your voice carries a meaning beyond the words you use. For example, if you say to someone, "I'm going shopping," your tone of voice will reflect whether you feel hope, dread, excitement, or boredom. It is not just the words you speak, but your tone of voice that reveals your feelings about the shopping trip.

Beneath the surface of their words, writers show their feelings and attitudes, too. **Tone** is the literary term used to describe a writer's feeling and attitude toward the subject matter and toward the reader. Is the writer's tone playful or serious, respectful or rude, personal or impersonal, loving or angry, light or grim—or any of many other possible attitudes?

As you read "To My Dear and Loving Husband," ask yourself:

1. What is the writer's tone?
2. How early in the poem do you recognize the tone?

WRITING CONNECTION

Write a paragraph describing your favorite movie. Write a second paragraph describing a movie you did not like. Read your paragraphs and pay close attention to the tone of each one. How do the tones of your paragraphs differ?

To My Dear and Loving Husband

by Anne Bradstreet

Portrait of Mr. and Mrs. Thomas Mifflin (Sarah Morris), John S. Copley. Philadelphia Museum of Art

If ever two were one, then surely we;
If ever man were loved by wife, then thee;
If ever wife was happy in a man,
Compare with me, ye women, if you can.
5 I prize thy love more than whole mines of gold,
Or all the riches that the East doth hold.
My love is such that rivers cannot quench,
Nor ought but love from thee give recompense.
Thy love is such I can no way repay,
10 The heavens reward thee manifold, I pray.
Then while we live in love let's so persever
That when we live no more we may live ever.

---

quench (KWENCH) satisfy thirst or other need
ought (AWT) anything (variation of *aught*)
recompense (REHK um pens) repayment
manifold (MAN uh fohld) in many ways
persever (pur SEV ur) continue to uphold; keep on trying
  (Today the word is spelled *persevere* and pronounced *pur suh VEER.*)

Review the Selection

UNDERSTAND THE SELECTION

Recall

1. To whom is Anne Bradstreet writing?

2. Above what does she prize her husband's love?

3. What does she pray rewards her husband?

Infer

4. How does Anne Bradstreet feel about her husband?

5. How does Bradstreet's love compare with the love of other wives?

6. How does she think her husband feels about her?

7. How long does Bradstreet want their love to last?

Apply

8. How do you think Anne Bradstreet's husband felt when he read her poem?

9. How might her husband have responded to the poem?

10. Bradstreet chose poetry to communicate her feelings. What would you write to communicate love?

Respond to Literature

Anne Bradstreet was a Puritan. Why is it surprising that this poem was written by a Puritan?

THINK ABOUT TONE

Tone is the literary term used to describe the writer's attitude toward his or her readers, toward his or her characters, and toward the subject matter of the piece. Tone contributes greatly to the effectiveness of a work. If the reader misunderstands a writer's tone, he or she will miss much of the meaning of the work.

1. Does this poem sound like a casual conversation? Explain your answer.

2. Why do you think the writer chose poetry as the genre rather than a letter?

3. What do the comparisons used in lines 5 through 10 tell the reader about the depth of the writer's emotion?

4. How does the tone contribute to the mood of the poem?

5. What effect would a touch of humor have had on the poem?

READING FOCUS

Identify Cause and Effect You have paid attention to what caused the writer to feel the way she does and the effects of those causes. Name at least one cause and one effect in this poem.

DEVELOP YOUR VOCABULARY

You cannot understand the meaning of a literary work unless you understand the meanings of the words the author uses. Sometimes the **context**—the words surrounding the unfamiliar term—will suggest a meaning. When it does, you should confirm your guess by looking up the word in a dictionary.

Another place to check for the meaning of unfamiliar words is in the book itself. Sometimes, as in this book, you can find the meaning of unfamiliar words in footnotes at the bottom of the page. They also may be given at the end of a selection or in a special glossary at the end of the book.

Review the meanings of the following words from "To My Dear and Loving Husband." Write an original sentence using each word.

1. quench   **4.** manifold
2. ought   **5.** persevere
3. recompense

RHYTHM

Rhythm is the repetition of a pattern of sounds. It occurs in natural speech; rhythm is the "swing," or sense of movement, that the ear hears when successive syllables are stressed or unstressed.

Most poetry has very strong rhythm because the poet writes into a poem a pattern of strongly stressed syllables alternating with a pattern of unstressed syllables. Such a pattern is called **meter**. Not all poems have meter, but that does not mean that they lack rhythm. In non-metrical poetry, rhythm is irregular and comes from the natural rise and fall of syllables. The effect is sometimes enhanced by the repetition of words or word patterns.

As you read this selection, ask yourself:

1. How does the poet use rising and falling sounds to create rhythm?
2. What two phrases does the author repeat three times? How do they affect the reader?

WRITING CONNECTION

Write down the lyrics of your favorite song. Then explain how the songwriter used rhythm to create an effect.

READING FOCUS

Understand the Speaker's Purpose
People speak and write to communicate their ideas to others. They may want to describe, to entertain, to inform, or to persuade.

Diction and tone are two elements of a text that can help you determine the speaker's purpose. Look at the speaker's diction, or word choice. Ask yourself what it tells you about the speaker's tone, or attitude, toward both the subject and the audience.

Song Concerning a Dream of the Thunderbirds

by the Teton Sioux

Friends, behold!
Sacred I have been made.
Friends, behold!
In a sacred manner
I have been influenced
At the gathering of the clouds.
Sacred I have been made.
Friends, behold!
Sacred I have been made.

Red Thing That Touches In Marching, 1832. George Catlin. The Granger Collection

---

thunderbird (THUN dur burd) in the mythology of certain North American tribes, an enormous bird supposed to produce thunder, lightning, and rain

Review the Selection

UNDERSTAND THE SELECTION

Recall

1. To whom is the writer speaking?

2. What change did the writer undergo during the dream?

3. Where was the writer when the change took place?

Infer

4. When do you think the Sioux might sing this song?

5. Who was present at the gathering of the clouds?

6. What do you think the Sioux believe caused thunder, lightning, and rain? Why?

7. Why do you think the Sioux visualized a thunderbird as a large bird?

Apply

8. Assume you are a Sioux living in the 18th century. When might you have asked a thunderbird for help?

9. Predict what might happen after the Sioux sang this song.

10. Do you think the Sioux still tell the legend of the thunderbird? Why?

Respond to Literature

How do you think "Song Concerning a Dream of the Thunderbirds" is representative of the literature of Native Americans?

THINK ABOUT RHYTHM

Rhythm is the repetition of a pattern of sounds. Even natural speech has a rhythm of stressed and unstressed syllables. A two-syllable word with the stress on the second syllable will create a rising sound. A two-syllable word with the stress on the first syllable will create a falling sound. Words with a mixed pattern will create a rising and falling rhythm.

1. Describe the use of repetition in this poem.

2. Why do you think the song begins and ends with the same two lines?

3. What two-syllable, six-letter word accented on the second syllable does the writer repeat?

4. What two-syllable, six-letter word accented on the first syllable does the writer repeat?

5. What kind of rhythm do these accented words create?

READING FOCUS

Understand the Speaker's Purpose You have studied this song to determine the speaker's purpose, or reason for the song. What is the purpose of the line "Friends, Behold!"? What is the purpose of the repetition of the word *sacred*?

DEVELOP YOUR VOCABULARY

Synonyms are words that mean the same or nearly the same. For example, you might use either *strange* or *weird* to describe something odd. Writers try to use synonyms to make their writing more interesting. Paragraphs that use the same words over and over make dull reading.

Following is a list of words you might use in writing about the meaning of the poem, "Song Concerning a Dream of the Thunderbirds." For each, write a synonym.

1. holy
2. interesting
3. invitation
4. metaphor
5. big
6. influenced

Write a short description of the poem in which you use some of your synonyms for the words in the list.

Patrick Henry, after Alonzo Chappel. Archive Photos

READING FOCUS

Recognize Fact and Opinion Statements of fact can be proven true or false. Opinions are statements of belief. They cannot be proven true or false.

Patrick Henry tries to persuade his listeners of something. Therefore, he must give them reasons to believe what he says. As you read, look for statements of fact that his listeners can prove or disprove. Look for statements of opinion that his listeners will have to consider.

THEME AND THESIS

Theme is the main or central idea in a literary work. It is usually a broad, abstract idea, expressed directly or indirectly.

Theme in drama, poetry, and fiction is usually expressed indirectly. It may not be apparent until after the reader has finished reading the work and thought about it. Then readers draw their own conclusions about the meaning of the work.

In nonfiction, on the other hand, theme is usually expressed directly. The reader knows it immediately because theme and the subject matter of the work are usually identical.

Writers of nonfiction not only announce their theme, they often make a statement that tells just what position they will try to prove or support. This statement is called the **thesis statement**.

As you read Patrick Henry's speech, ask yourself:

1. What is the theme, or central idea, of Henry's speech?
2. Does he make a thesis statement? If so, what is it?

WRITING CONNECTION

Choose a newspaper editorial. Write down its theme, or central idea. Then look for the thesis statement and write it down.

Speech in the Virginia Convention

by Patrick Henry

No man thinks more highly than I do of the patriotism, as well as abilities, of the very worthy gentlemen who have just addressed the house. But different men often see the same subject in different lights; and, therefore, I hope it will not be thought disrespectful to those gentlemen if, entertaining as I do opinions of a character very opposite to theirs, I shall speak forth my sentiments freely and without reserve. This is no time for ceremony. The question before the house is one of awful moment to this country. For my own part, I consider it as nothing less than a question of freedom or slavery; and in proportion to the magnitude of the subject ought to be the freedom of the debate. It is only in this way that we can hope to arrive at the truth, and fulfill the great responsibility which we hold to God and our country. Should I keep back my opinions at such a time, through fear of giving offense, I should consider myself as guilty of treason towards my country, and of an act of disloyalty toward the Majesty of Heaven, which I revere above all earthly kings.

Mr. President, it is natural to man to indulge in the illusions of hope. We are apt to shut our eyes against a painful truth, and listen to the song of that siren till she transforms us into beasts. Is this the part of wise men, engaged in a great and arduous struggle for liberty? Are we disposed to be of the numbers of those who, having eyes, see not, and, having ears, hear not, the things which so nearly concern their temporal salvation? For my part, whatever anguish of spirit it may cost, I am willing to know the whole truth, to know the worst, and to provide for it.

I have but one lamp by which my feet are guided, and that is the lamp of experience. I know of no way of judging of the future but by the past. And judging by the past, I wish to know what there has been in the conduct of the British ministry for the last ten years to justify those hopes with which gentlemen have been pleased to solace themselves and the House. Is it that insidious smile with which our petition has been lately received?

Trust it not, sir; it will prove a snare to your feet. Suffer not yourselves to be betrayed with a kiss. Ask yourselves how this gracious reception of our petition comports with those warlike preparations

---

awful (AW full) extreme; grave
magnitude (MAG nuh tood) importance; significance
siren (SY run) in Greek and Roman mythology, a sea nymph represented as part bird and
    part woman who lured sailors to their death by singing

which cover our waters and darken our land. Are fleets and armies necessary to a work of love and reconciliation? Have we shown ourselves so unwilling to be reconciled that force must be called in to win back our love? Let us not deceive ourselves, sir. These are the implements of war and subjugation; the last arguments to which kings resort. I ask gentlemen, sir, what means this martial array, if its purpose be not to force us to submission? Can gentlemen assign any other possible motive for it? Has Great Britain any enemy, in this quarter of the world, to call for all this accumulation of navies and armies? No, sir, she has none. They are meant for us: they can be meant for no other. They are sent over to bind and rivet upon us those chains which the British ministry have been so long forging. And what have we to oppose to them? Shall we try argument? Sir, we have been trying that for the last ten years. Have we anything new to offer upon the subject? Nothing. We have held the subject up in every light of which it is capable; but it has been all in vain. Shall we resort to entreaty and humble supplication? What terms shall we find which have not been already exhausted? Let us not, I beseech you, sir, deceive ourselves. Sir, we have done everything that could be done to avert the storm which is now coming on. We have petitioned; we have remonstrated; we have supplicated; we have prostrated ourselves before the throne, and have implored its interposition to arrest the tyrannical hands of the ministry and Parliament. Our petitions have been slighted; our remonstrances have produced additional violence and insult; our supplications have been disregarded; and we have been spurned, with contempt, from the foot of the throne! In vain, after these things, may we indulge the fond hope of peace and reconciliation.

There is no longer any room for hope. If we wish to be free—if we mean to preserve inviolate those inestimable privileges for which we have been so long contending—if we mean not basely to abandon the noble struggle in which we have been so long engaged, and which we have pledged ourselves never to abandon until the glorious object of our contest shall be obtained—we must fight! I repeat it, sir, we must fight! An appeal to arms and to the God of hosts is all that is left us! They tell us, sir, that we are weak; unable to cope with so formidable an adversary. But when shall we be stronger? Will it be the next week, or the next year? Will it be when we are totally disarmed, and when a British guard shall be stationed in every house? Shall we gather strength by irresolution and inaction? Shall we acquire the means of effectual resistance by lying supinely on our backs and hugging the delusive phantom of hope, until our enemies shall have

---

array (uh RAY) an orderly arrangement of troops
petitioned (puh TISH und) made a formal request of someone in authority
adversary (AD vur ser ee) opponent; enemy
delusive (dih LOO siv) misleading; unreal
phantom (FAN tum) something that seems real but does not exist

Patrick Henry Speaking Against the Stamp Act in the Virginia House of Burgesses in 1765, 19th century.
The Granger Collection

bound us hand and foot? Sir, we are not weak if we make a proper use of those means which the God of nature hath placed in our power. Three millions of people, armed in the holy cause of liberty, and in such a country as that which we possess, are invincible by any force which our enemy can send against us. Besides, sir, we shall not fight our battles alone. There is a just God who presides over the destinies of nations, and who will raise up friends to fight our battles for us. The battle, sir, is not to the strong alone; it is to the vigilant, the active, the brave. Besides, sir, we have no election. If we were base enough to desire it, it is now too late to retire from the contest. There is no retreat but in submission and slavery! Our chains are forged! Their clanking may be heard on the plains of Boston! The war is inevitable—and let it come! I repeat it, sir, let it come. It is in vain, sir, to extentuate the matter. Gentlemen may cry, Peace, Peace—but there is no peace. The war is actually begun! The next gale that sweeps from the north will bring to our ears the clash of resounding arms! Our brethren are already in the field! Why stand we here idle? What is it that gentlemen wish? What would they have? Is life so dear, or peace so sweet, as to be purchased at the price of chains and slavery? Forbid it, Almighty God! I know not what course others may take; but as for me, give me liberty or give me death!

---

inevitable (in EV ih tuh bul) certain to happen
extenuate (ik STEN yoo ayt) to lessen the seriousness of
resounding (rih ZOUND ing) loud, echoing, or prolonged sound
brethren (BRETH run) brothers; fellow members of a group

Review the Selection

UNDERSTAND THE SELECTION

Recall

1. On what does Patrick Henry depend in order to predict the future?

2. Whom does Henry think the British plan to attack?

3. What does Henry say are his only alternatives?

4. What was the population of the colonies at this time?

Infer

5. What position had those who spoke before Patrick Henry taken?

6. Does Henry trust the British? Explain.

7. With what does Henry equate defeat in the coming revolution?

Apply

8. If you had been a delegate to the Virginia Convention, would you have supported Henry? Explain.

9. Do you think Patrick Henry's speech changed the minds of some delegates? Why or why not?

10. Would Henry's argument have been more effective as a letter? Explain.

Respond to Literature

Why do you think this speech was of interest to people in other colonies?

THINK ABOUT THEME AND THESIS

Theme is the main or central idea in a literary work. It is a comment on life or on a situation in life. Nonfiction writers state their theme directly. They may also make a **thesis statement**—an announcement of the position that will be proved or supported in the work.

1. What is the theme of Patrick Henry's speech?

2. Summarize Henry's thesis statement.

3. List three arguments that Henry makes in support of his thesis, or position.

4. How do you think his listeners would have reacted if he had started his speech with the paragraph beginning: "Gentlemen may cry peace, but there is no peace!"

5. What action does Henry recommend as the inevitable result of Britain's refusal to listen to the colonists' pleas and petitions?

READING FOCUS

Recognize Fact and Opinion You looked carefully at Henry's speech to distinguish between fact and opinion. Name three opinions and the facts that Henry used to support each opinion.

DEVELOP YOUR VOCABULARY

Rhetoric is the art or science of using words effectively in speaking or writing. A rhetorical question is a question that does not require an answer from the listener. It is a technique used by speakers and writers in order to make a point. The author is actually making a statement. It is phrased as a question only for dramatic effect.

Patrick Henry uses this technique extensively. For example he asks, "Do wise men pretend that all is well when their eyes and ears tell them it is not?" This is a rhetorical question. The answer is so obvious that Patrick Henry does not answer it. However, he answers in detail the rhetorical question, ". . . what is the purpose of this military array?" He presents his answer as arguments to support his position.

Find three other rhetorical questions in this selection. Review the meanings of the vocabulary words from this selection. Then answer each of the three rhetorical questions in original sentences that make use of a word from the vocabulary list.

Focus ON NONFICTION

What is nonfiction? **Nonfiction** is the branch of literature that communicates information and ideas. It presents factual information. Nonfiction often offers an interpretation of the facts it presents. It can also propose opinions and theories. Nonfiction is written in prose, or ordinary language.

Forms of Nonfiction   Nonfiction can be broken down into four categories, or forms. The four forms are exposition, persuasion (or argumentation), description, and narration.

Exposition is writing that explains. There are a number of writing methods used in exposition. One is definition, writing that explains the meaning of a term, such as _democracy_. Another is classification, writing that groups things or ideas according to their similarities or differences. Breaking down nonfiction into four forms involves classification. Still another method of exposition is comparison and contrast. This is writing that explains how one thing is like or unlike another thing. Writing that shows the similarities and differences between baseball and stickball is an example of comparison and contrast. A fourth type of exposition is analysis. Analysis is writing that examines the different parts of something and tells how they fit together to form a whole. Explaining the parts of a steam engine and how they work together is an example of analysis.

Persuasion (or argumentation) is writing that attempts to convince a reader or listener by showing that a statement is either true or false. While expository writing aims merely to explain, persuasion seeks to influence the reader or listener. An editorial in the newspaper urging people to vote in the next election is an example of persuasion.

Description is writing that paints word pictures of the details, qualities, or appearances of something. Specific details make the word picture come alive. The details are the result of careful observation, with attention to shapes, sizes, colors, tastes, sounds, and textures.

Narration is writing in which an event or a series of events is told. While description is concerned with how things look, narration is concerned with what happens when events occur.

Rarely will only one element of nonfiction be used in a single piece of writing. Most writing makes use of two or more.

Organization of Nonfiction

Most nonfiction follows a three-part organization. There is an introduction, a body, and a conclusion.

The **introduction** may state a problem or give background or examples. In expository and persuasive writing, the author may make a **thesis statement**. This is an announcement of what is to be proved or supported in the writing. The central idea, or general topic of discussion, in exposition and persuasion is the *theme*. Writers of description use details to create a *dominant impression*. The **body** of the work is used to develop or discuss the ideas of the work. Narration is organized chronologically; that is, in the order in which events have occurred. Other kinds of writing are organized in some kind of logical order. The **conclusion** rounds out the work. It may do so by restating the thesis, by summarizing the main ideas in the body, by answering a question that was raised, or by urging the reader to future action.

Types of Nonfiction

Many different kinds of literature fall into the category of nonfiction. Biography, autobiography, diaries, memoirs, journals, and letters tell about people's lives. Reports, articles, news stories, and essays deal with facts, theories, and ideas. There are many different kinds of essays. Orations, like those made by Patrick Henry and George Washington, are essays that are spoken rather than written.

from

Farewell Address

by George Washington

Friends and Citizens:

The period for a new election of a citizen to administer the executive government of the United States being not far distant, and the time actually arrived when your thoughts must be employed in designating the person who is to be clothed with that important trust, it appears to me proper, especially as it may conduce to a more distinct expression of the public voice, that I should now apprise you of the resolution I have formed, to decline being considered among the number of those out of whom a choice is to be made.

I rejoice that the state of your concerns, external as well as internal, no longer renders the pursuit of inclination incompatible with the sentiment of duty or propriety, and am persuaded, whatever partiality may be retained for my services, that, in the present circumstances of our country, you will not disapprove my determination to retire.

Here, perhaps, I ought to stop. But a solicitude for your welfare, which cannot end but with my life, and the apprehension of danger, natural to that solicitude, urge me, on an occasion like the present, to offer to your solemn contemplation, and to recommend to your frequent review, some sentiments which are the result of much reflection, of no inconsiderable observation, and which appear to me all-important to the permanency of your felicity as a people. These will be offered to you with the more freedom, as you can

---

inclination (in kluh NAY shun) a particular disposition or bent of mind

George Washington, after Gilbert Stuart. The Granger Collection

only see in them the disinterested warnings of a parting friend, who can possibly have no personal motive to bias his counsel. Nor can I forget, as an encouragement to it, your indulgent reception of my sentiments on a former and not dissimilar occasion.

Interwoven as is the love of liberty with every ligament of your hearts, no recommendation of mine is necessary to fortify or confirm the attachment.

The unity of government which constitutes you one people is also now dear to you. It is justly so, for it is a main pillar in the edifice of your real independence, the support of your tranquility at home, your peace abroad; of your safety; of your prosperity; of that very liberty which you so highly prize. But as it is easy to foresee that, from different causes and from different quarters, much pains will be taken, many artifices employed to weaken in your minds the conviction of this truth; as this is the point in your political fortress against which the batteries of internal and external enemies will be most constantly and actively (though often covertly and

insidiously) directed, it is of infinite moment that you should properly estimate the immense value of your national union to your collective and individual happiness; that you should cherish a cordial, habitual, and immovable attachment to it; accustoming yourselves to think and speak of it as of the palladium of your political safety and prosperity; watching for its preservation with jealous anxiety; discountenancing whatever may suggest even a suspicion that it can in any event be abandoned; and indignantly frowning upon the first dawning of every attempt to alienate any portion of our country from the rest, or to enfeeble the sacred ties which now link together the various parts.

For this you have every inducement of sympathy and interest. Citizens, by birth or choice, of a common country, that country has a right to concentrate your affections. The name of American, which belongs to you in your national capacity, must always exalt the just pride of patriotism more than any appellation derived from local discriminations. With slight shades of difference, you have the same religion, manners, habits, and political principles. You have in a common cause fought and triumphed together; the independence and liberty you possess are the work of joint counsels, and joint efforts of common dangers, sufferings, and successes.

While, then, every part of our country thus feels an immediate

---

tranquility (tran KWIL uh tee) calmness; peacefulness

and particular interest in union, all the parts combined cannot fail to find in the united mass of means and efforts greater strength, greater resource, proportionably greater security from external danger, a less frequent interruption of their peace by foreign nations; and, what is of inestimable value, they must derive from union an exemption from those broils and wars between themselves, which so frequently afflict neighboring countries not tied together by the same governments, which their own rival ships alone would be sufficient to produce, but which opposite foreign alliances, attachments, and intrigues would stimulate and embitter. Hence, likewise, they will avoid the necessity of those overgrown military establishments which, under any form of government, are inauspicious to liberty, and which are to be regarded as particularly hostile to republican liberty. In this sense it is that your union ought to be considered as a main prop of your liberty, and that the love of the one ought to endear to you the preservation of the other.

These considerations speak a persuasive language to every reflecting and virtuous mind, and exhibit the continuance of the Union as a primary object of patriotic desire.

In contemplating the causes which may disturb our Union, it occurs as matter of serious concern that any ground should have been furnished for characterizing parties by geographical discriminations, Northern and Southern, Atlantic and Western; whence designing men may endeavor to excite a belief that there is a real difference of local interests and views. One of the expedients of party to acquire influence within particular districts is to misrepresent the opinions and aims of other districts. You cannot shield yourselves too much against the jealousies and heartburnings which spring from these misrepresentations; they tend to render alien to each other those who ought to be bound together by fraternal affection.

The author makes his first point; he warns against party politics.

I have already intimated to you the danger of parties in the State, with particular reference to the founding of them on geographical discriminations. Let me now take a more comprehensive view, and warn you in the most solemn manner against the baneful effects of the spirit of party generally.

The author supports his first point.

This spirit, unfortunately, is inseparable from our nature, having its root in the strongest passions of the human mind. It exists

The author states his
second point; he warns
against tyrannical
leaders.

under different shapes in all governments, more or less stifled, controlled, or repressed; but, in those of the popular form, it is seen in its greatest rankness, and is truly their worst enemy.

The alternate domination of one faction over another, sharpened by the spirit of revenge, natural to party dissension, which in different ages and countries has perpetrated the most horrid enormities, is itself a frightful despotism. But this leads at length to a more formal and permanent despotism. The disorders and miseries which result gradually incline the minds of men to seek security and repose in the absolute power of an individual; and sooner or later the chief of some prevailing faction, more able or more fortunate than his competitors, turns this disposition to the purposes of his own elevation, on the ruins of public liberty.

Without looking forward to an extremity of this kind (which nevertheless ought not to be entirely out of sight), the common and continual mischiefs of the spirit of party are sufficient to make it the interest and duty of a wise people to discourage and restrain it.

The author supports his
second point.

It is important, likewise, that the habits of thinking in a free country should inspire caution in those entrusted with its administration, to confine themselves within their respective constitutional spheres, avoiding in the exercise of the powers of one department to encroach upon another. The spirit of encroachment tends to consolidate the powers of all the departments in one, and thus to create, whatever the form of government, a real despotism. A just estimate of that love of power, and proneness to abuse it, which predominates in the human heart, is sufficient to satisfy us of the truth of this position. The necessity of reciprocal checks in the exercise of political power, by dividing and distributing it into different depositaries, and constituting each the guardian of the public weal against invasions by the others, has been evinced by experiments ancient and modern; some of them in our country and under our own eyes. To preserve them must be as necessary as to institute them. If, in the opinion of the people, the distribution or modification of the constitutional powers be in any particular wrong, let it be corrected by an amendment in the way which the Constitution designates. But let there be no change by usurpation; for though this, in one instance, may be the instrument of good, it

---

encroach (en KROHCH) to intrude upon the rights of others
consolidate (kun SOL uh date) to unite
usurpation (you sir PAY shun) illegal seizure; taking over

is the customary weapon by which free governments are destroyed. The precedent must always greatly overbalance in permanent evil any partial or transient benefit, which the use can at any time yield.

It is substantially true that virtue or morality is a necessary spring of popular government. The rule, indeed, extends with more or less force to every species of free government. Who that is a sincere friend to it can look with indifference upon attempts to shake the foundation of the fabric?

Promote then, as an object of primary importance, institutions for the general diffusion of knowledge. In proportion as the structure of a government gives force to public opinion, it is essential that public opinion should be enlightened.

Observe good faith and justice towards all nations; cultivate peace and harmony with all.

The author states his third point; he warns against foreign entanglements.

The great rule of conduct for us in regard to foreign nations is in extending our commercial relations, to have with them as little political connection as possible. So far as we have already formed engagements, let them be fulfilled with perfect good faith. Here let us stop. Europe has a set of primary interests which to us have none; or a very remote relation. Hence she must be engaged in frequent controversies, the causes of which are essentially foreign to our concerns. Hence, therefore, it must be unwise in us to implicate ourselves by artificial ties in the ordinary vicissitudes of her politics, or the ordinary combinations and collisions of her friendships or enmities.

The author supports his third point.

Our detached and distant situation invites and enables us to pursue a different course. If we remain one people under an efficient government, the period is not far off when we may defy material injury from external annoyance; when we may take such an attitude as will cause the neutrality we may at any time resolve upon to be scrupulously respected; when belligerent nations, under the impossibility of making acquisitions upon us, will not lightly hazard the giving us provocation; when we may choose peace or war, as our interest, guided by justice, shall counsel.

Why forego the advantages of so peculiar a situation? Why quit our own to stand upon foreign ground? Why, by interweaving our destiny with that of any part of Europe, entangle our peace and prosperity in the toils of European ambition, rivalship, interest, humor or caprice?

It is our true policy to steer clear of permanent alliances with any portion of the foreign world; so far, I mean, as we are now at liberty to do it; for let me not be understood as capable of patronizing infidelity to existing engagements. I hold the maxim no less applicable to public than to private affairs, that honesty is always the best policy. I repeat it, therefore, let those engagements be observed in their genuine sense. But, in my opinion, it is unnecessary and would be unwise to extend them.

Taking care always to keep ourselves by suitable establishments on a respectable defensive posture, we may safely trust to temporary alliances for extraordinary emergencies.

The author begins his conclusion. He restates his thesis and summarizes his main points.

In offering to you, my countrymen, these counsels of an old and affectionate friend, I dare not hope they will make the strong and lasting impression I could wish; that they will control the usual current of the passions, or prevent our nation from running the course which has hitherto marked the destiny of nations. But, if I may even flatter myself that they may be productive of some partial benefit, some occasional good; that they may now and then recur to moderate the fury of party spirit, to warn against the mischiefs of foreign intrigue, to guard against the impostures of pretended patriotism; this hope will be a full recompense for the solicitude for your welfare, by which they have been dictated.

Though, in reviewing the incidents of my administration, I am unconscious of intentional error, I am nevertheless too sensible of my defects not to think it probable that I may have committed many errors. Whatever they may be, I fervently beseech the Almighty to avert or mitigate the evils to which they may tend. I shall also carry with me the hope that my country will never cease to view them with indulgence; and that, after forty five years of my life dedicated to its service with an upright zeal, the faults of incompetent abilities will be consigned to oblivion, as myself must soon be to the mansions of rest.

Relying on its kindness in this as in other things, and actuated by that fervent love towards it, which is so natural to a man who views in it the native soil of himself and his progenitors for several generations, I anticipate with pleasing expectation that retreat in which I promise myself to realize, without alloy, the sweet enjoyment of partaking, in the midst of my fellow-citizens, the benign influence of good laws under a free government, the ever-favorite object of my heart, and the happy reward, as I trust, of our mutual cares, labors, and dangers.

Review the Selection

UNDERSTAND THE SELECTION

Recall

1. What decision did Washington disclose to his audience?

2. What did he say was more dangerous to liberty than geographical loyalties?

3. What two things did he say were essential to popular government?

Infer

4. Why did Washington choose this time to make the remarks he did?

5. Did he owe his first loyalty to Virginia or America?

6. Why did he believe education was indispensable?

7. Why did he believe we should avoid permanent alliances with Europe?

Apply

8. Which of Washington's warnings do you think is most effectively stated?

9. What opinion do you think he held of the framers of the Constitution?

10. Do you think Washington would have approved of today's voting system?

Respond to Literature

List Washington's warnings about dangers to democracy. How do his themes reflect Washington's time?

THINK ABOUT NONFICTION

An **oration** is a speech that is intended to inspire listeners to action. In Washington's day, oratory was a highly regarded and eagerly enjoyed mode of communication. It was especially prevalent in courtrooms, on the political stump, and at religious gatherings.

1. How many parts did George Washington's address have? Name the parts.

2. What action did George Washington hope his listeners would take?

3. Does Washington make a thesis statement in his speech? If so, what is it?

4. Summarize the three main points about which Washington cautioned his listeners.

5. Patrick Henry made a very emotional speech in defense of liberty. How would you characterize the tone of Washington's "Farewell Address"?

DEVELOP YOUR VOCABULARY

A word can sometimes be used as either a noun or a verb. For example, in the title of this selection, "Farewell Address," the word *address* is a noun meaning "speech." However, in the sentence "I will address this package to Jim J. Johnson," the word *address* is a verb meaning "to write the destination on." The meanings are clearly not the same.

The following words are also found in this selection. Each word can be used either as a noun or as a verb. If you are not certain of the meanings of each of the words, check the definitions in a dictionary.

Write a sentence using each word as a noun. Then write a sentence using each as a verb.

1. triumph
2. result
3. form
4. favor
5. counsel
6. offer
7. defeat
8. change
9. benefit
10. quarrel

Learn About

Abigail Adams, 1766, Benjamin Blyth.
The Granger Collection

READING FOCUS

Make Inferences Many times you figure out how a person feels about something without being told directly. You make inferences, or use the information given to understand something not stated. As you read this selection, you will be able to make inferences about how Abigail Adams feels about living in the White House. Look for the descriptions that help you make the inferences.

DESCRIPTION

Description is one of the four main forms of writing. Writers use it when they want to paint a picture in words or help the reader know what something looks, sounds, tastes, or feels like.

Details make a description come alive. Writers carefully choose the details they use in order to create a main focus for the description. This focus is called the dominant impression. The dominant impression contributes to the mood of the description and helps the reader to experience a scene or a sensation as the writer wishes. The description becomes real to the reader.

To understand a writer's dominant impression, notice not only the details selected but also the choice of words. Description is especially effective when it makes precise use of words and phrases.

As you read the selection, ask yourself:
1. On what details does Abigail Adams focus?
2. What is the dominant impression in her letter?

WRITING CONNECTION

Look at the artwork in this unit. Describe one person pictured. Create a dominant impression for your description.

Letter to Her Daughter from the New White House

by Abigail Adams

Washington, 21 November, 1800

My Dear Child:

I arrived here on Sunday last, and without meeting with any accident worth noticing, except losing ourselves when we left Baltimore and going eight or nine miles on the Frederick road, by which means we were obliged to go the other eight through woods, where we wandered two hours without finding a guide or the path. Fortunately, a straggling black came up with us, and we engaged him as a guide to extricate us out of our difficulty; but woods are all you see from Baltimore until you reach the *city*, which is only so in name. Here and there is a small cot, without a glass window, interspersed among the forests, through which you travel miles without seeing any human being. In the city there are buildings enough, if they were compact and finished, to accommodate Congress and those attached to it; but as they are, and scattered as they are, I see no great comfort for them. The river, which runs up to Alexandria[1], is in full view of my window, and I see the vessels as they pass and repass. The house is upon a grand and superb scale, requiring about thirty servants to attend and keep the apartments in proper order, and perform the ordinary business of the house and stables; an establishment very well proportioned to the President's salary. The lighting of the apartments, from the kitchen to parlors and chambers, is a tax indeed; and the fires we are obliged to keep to secure us from daily

---

extricate (EK strih kayt) to set free; release; disentangle
cot (KOT) cottage or small house
interspersed (in tur SPURST) scattered among other things
[1]**Alexandria:** A city in northeastern Virginia

agues is another very cheering comfort. To assist us in this great castle, and render less attendance necessary, bells are wholly wanting, not one single one being hung through the whole house, and promises are all you can obtain. This is so great an inconvenience, that I know not what to do, or how to do. The ladies from Georgetown[2] and in the city have many of them visited me. Yesterday I returned fifteen visits—but such a place as Georgetown appears—why, our Milton is beautiful. But no comparisons—if they will put me up some bells and let me have wood enough to keep fires, I design to be pleased. I could content myself almost anywhere three months; but, surrounded with forests, can you believe that wood is not to be had because people

---

ague (AY gyoo) violent fever
[2]**Georgetown:** A section of Washington, DC

cannot be found to cut and cart it? Briesler entered into a contract with a man to supply him with wood. A small part, a few cords only, has he been able to get. Most of that was expended to dry the walls of the house before we came in, and yesterday the man told him it was impossible for him to procure it to be cut and carted. He has had recourse to coals; but we cannot get grates made and set. We have, indeed, come into a *new country*.

You must keep all this to yourself, and, when asked how I like it, say that I write you the situation is beautiful, which is true. The house is made habitable, but there is not a single apartment finished, and all withinside, except the plastering, had been done since Briesler came. We have not the least fence, yard, or other convenience, without, and the great unfinished audience room I make a drying-room of, to hang up the clothes in. The principal stairs are not up, and will not be this winter. Six chambers are made comfortable; two are occupied by the President and Mr. Shaw; two lower rooms, one for a common parlor, and one for a levee room. Upstairs there is the oval room, which is designed for the drawing room, and has the crimson furniture in it. It is a very handsome room now; but, when completed, it will be beautiful. If the twelve years, in which this place has been considered as the future seat of government, had been improved, as they would have been if in New England, very many of the present inconveniences would have been removed. It is a beautiful spot, capable of every improvement, and, the more I view it, the more I am delighted with it.

Since I sat down to write, I have been called down to a servant from Mount Vernon,[3] with a billet from Major Custis, and a haunch of venison, and a kind, congratulatory letter from Mrs. Lewis, upon my arrival in the city, with Mrs. Washington's love, inviting me to Mount Vernon, where, health permitting, I will go before I leave this place. . . .

Affectionately, your mother,
Abigail Adams

---

procure (proh KYUUR) to obtain or secure
recourse (REE kawrs) a turning back for aid, safety, etc.
habitable (HAB it uh bul) fit to be lived in
levee (LEV ee) a morning reception held by a person of high rank
billet (BIL it) a brief letter
[3]**Mount Vernon:** Home of George Washington, located in northern Virginia

Review the Selection

UNDERSTAND THE SELECTION

Recall

1. From what city was Abigail Adams writing?

2. What surrounded the White House?

3. What home did Mrs. Washington invite Abigail Adams to visit?

Infer

4. What elected position did Abigail Adams's husband hold?

5. How was the White House heated at that time?

6. Why did Adams ask her daughter to keep the negative comments about the White House a secret?

7. In what year did Americans begin to consider building the White House?

Apply

8. List three personal qualities you think apply to Mrs. Adams.

9. If you were in Mrs. Adams's situation, how would you spend your time?

10. How would Mrs. Adams's description of the White House differ today?

Respond to Literature
Why might the national capital have been located where it is?

THINK ABOUT DESCRIPTION

Writers use description to paint a picture for the reader. Effective writers do not list every feature of the object being described. They select those that will support their sense of what is important.

1. List five features of the White House that Mrs. Adams selected for her description.

2. What are some reactions that Mrs. Adams had to the house?

3. What was the dominant impression created in your mind by her description of these features?

4. If Mrs. Adams were describing the White House for a newspaper article, what dominant impression do you think she would try to create? Why would her description to a newspaper be different from the description written to her daughter?

5. If she were describing the White House today, how do you think her description would differ?

READING FOCUS
Make Inferences How does Abigail Adams feel about being in the White House? Find three descriptions that helped you make inferences about her feelings.

DEVELOP YOUR VOCABULARY

Language is always changing. People invent new words, and others drop from current usage. New words form as the need for them arises. Sometimes old words acquire new meanings. These new meanings become part of common usage along with the original meanings of the words. At other times, the commonly used meaning of a word changes entirely. The original meaning may become lost, or **archaic**. The word may remain in the language but assume an entirely new meaning.

Using a dictionary, look for the meaning of each of the following words as they were used in Mrs. Adams's letter. Remember, these may be unusual or archaic meanings today. Then compare that meaning with the usual, or common, meaning of the words today. Write an original sentence using each word in its older meaning. Then, write an original sentence using its contemporary meaning.

1. expended
2. attend
3. design
4. audience
5. tax

Learn About

NARRATION

Narration is one of the four main forms of composition. It is the primary form of novels, short stories, and narrative poems, as well as of biography, autobiography, and news reports. In short, narration is the form used in fiction and nonfiction storytelling.

Stories, whether true or fictional, are about events—the birth of a new island in the Pacific, the rescue of a lost child, the appearance of Peter Rabbit in Mr. MacGregor's garden, your first birthday party. To make a good narrative, the events should have a beginning, a middle, and an end. This is part of the normal development of the plot.

The unique feature of narration is chronology. Events happen in time, and every story is told in some kind of time order. The most common time order is straightforward—from beginning to end.

As you read the next selections, ask yourself:

1. What kind of narrative writing is Franklin presenting?
2. In what order is he telling his stories?

WRITING CONNECTION

Write a paragraph in which you tell of an important event in your life. Give your paragraph a beginning, a middle, and an end.

READING FOCUS

Make Generalizations As you read, you often make generalizations, or use the information given to understand a broader idea. What generalizations can you make from Franklin's writings about his personality and about the values of the time?

from
The Autobiography

by Benjamin Franklin

[*This excerpt reveals events from Franklin's teen-age years.*]

When about 16 years of age I happened to meet with a book, written by one Tryon, recommending a vegetable diet. I determined to go into it. My brother, being yet unmarried, did not keep house, but boarded himself and his apprentices in another family. My refusing to eat flesh occasioned an inconveniency, and I was frequently chid for my singularity. I made myself acquainted with Tryon's manner of preparing some of his dishes, such as boiling potatoes or rice, making hasty pudding, and a few others, and then proposed to my brother, that if he would give me, weekly, half the money he paid for my board, I would board myself. He instantly agreed to it, and I presently found that I could save half what he paid me. This was an additional fund for buying books. But I had another advantage in it. My brother and the rest going from the printing-house to their meals, I remained there alone, and, despatching presently my light repast, which often was no more than a bisket or a slice of bread, a handful of raisins or a tart from the pastry-cook's, and a glass of water, had the rest of the time till their return for study, in which I made the greater progress, from that greater clearness of head and quicker apprehension which usually attend temperance in eating and drinking. . . .

I believe I have omitted mentioning that, in my first voyage from Boston, being becalm'd off Block Island[1], our people set about catching cod, and hauled up a great many. Hitherto I had stuck to

---

boarded (BAWRD id) had rooms and meals provided regularly for pay
chid (CHYD) scolded
hasty pudding (HAYS tee PUUD ing) cornmeal mush
tart (TAHRT) small, filled pastry; small pie
temperance (TEM pur uns) self-restraint in conduct, appetite, etc.
becalm'd (bih KAHLMD) to make motionless from lack of wind
[1]**Block Island:** an island off the coast of Rhode Island

my resolution of not eating animal food, and on this occasion consider'd, with my master Tryon, the taking every fish as a kind of unprovoked murder, since none of them had, or ever could do us any injury that might justify the slaughter. All this seemed very reasonable. But I had formerly been a great lover of fish, and, when this came hot out of the frying-pan, it smelt admirably well. I balanc'd some time between principle and inclination, till I recollected that, when the fish were opened, I saw smaller fish taken out of their stomachs; then thought I, "If you eat one another, I don't see why we mayn't eat you." So I din'd upon cod very heartily, and continued to eat with other people, returning only now and then occasionally to a vegetable diet. So convenient a thing it is to be a *reasonable creature*, since it enables one to find or make a reason for everything one has a mind to do.

[*This excerpt deals with Franklin's early career.*]

My brother had, in 1720 or 1721, begun to print a newspaper. It was the second that appeared in America, and was called the New England Courant. The only one before it was the Boston News-Letter. I remember his being dissuaded by some of his friends from the undertaking, as not likely to succeed, one newspaper being, in their judgment, enough for America. At this time (1771) there are not less than five-and-twenty. He went on, however, with the undertaking, and after having worked in composing the types[2] and printing off the sheets, I was employed to carry the papers thro' the streets to the customers.

He had some ingenious men among his friends, who amus'd themselves by writing little pieces for this paper, which gain'd it credit and made it more in demand, and these gentlemen often visited us. Hearing their conversations, and their accounts of the approbation their papers were received with, I was excited to try my hand among them; but, being still a boy, and suspecting that my brother would object to printing anything of mine in his paper if he knew it to be mine, I contrived to disguise my hand, and, writing an anonymous paper, I put it in at night under the door of

---

resolution (rez uh LOO shun) decision as to future action
unprovoked (un pruh VOHKT) not to stir up an action
slaughter (SLAWT ur) the killing of animals for food
principle (PRIN suh pul) a fundamental truth or rule of conduct
inclination (in kluh NAY shun) a liking or preference
[2]**composing the types** setting a piece of writing into type
anonymous (uh NON uh mus) written by a person whose name is withheld

the printing-house. It was found in the morning, and communicated to his writing friends when they call'd in as usual. They read it, commented on it in my hearing, and I had the exquisite pleasure of finding it met with their approbation, and that, in their different guesses at the author, none were named but men of some character among us for learning and ingenuity. I suppose now that I was rather lucky in my judges, and that perhaps they were not really so very good ones as I then esteem'd them.

Encourag'd, however, by this, I wrote and convey'd in the same way to the press several more papers which were equally approv'd; and I kept my secret till my small fund of sense for such performances was pretty well exhausted, and then I discovered it, when I began to be considered a little more by my brother's acquaintance, and in a manner that did not quite please him, as he thought, probably with reason, that it tended to make me too vain. And, perhaps, this might be one occasion of the differences that we began to have about this time. Though a brother, he considered himself as my master, and me as his apprentice, and accordingly, expected the same services from me as he would from another, while I thought he demean'd me too much in some he requir'd of me, who from a brother expected more indulgence. Our disputes were often brought before our father, and I fancy I was either generally in the right, or else a better pleader, because the judgment was generally in my favor. But my brother was passionate, and had often beaten me, which I took extreamly amiss; and, thinking my apprenticeship very tedious, I was continually wishing for some opportunity of shortening it, which at length offered in a manner unexpected.

One of the pieces in our newspaper on some political point, which I have now forgotten, gave offense to the Assembly. He was taken up, censur'd, and imprison'd for a month, by the speaker's warrant, I suppose, because he would not discover his author. I too was taken up and examin'd before the council; but, tho' I did not give them any satisfaction, they content'd themselves with admonishing me, and dismissed me, considering me, perhaps, as an apprentice, who was bound to keep his master's secrets.

During my brother's confinement, which I resented a good

---

apprentice (uh PREN tis) a person under legal agreement to work for a specified time under a master craftsperson in return for instruction and, formerly, support

demean'd (dih MEEND) lowered in status or character; degraded

Young Franklin as an Apprentice in James' Printshop. Corbis Bettmann

deal, notwithstanding our private differences, I had the management of the paper; and I made bold to give our rulers some rubs in it, which my brother took very kindly, while others began to consider me in an unfavorable light, as a young genius that had a turn for libelling and satyr. My brother's discharge was accompany'd with an order of the House (a very odd one), that *"James Franklin should no longer print the paper called the New England Courant."*

There was a consultation held in our printing-house among his friends, what he should do in this case. Some proposed to evade the order by changing the name of the paper; but my brother, seeing inconveniences in that, it was finally concluded on as a better way, to let it be printed for the future under the name of BENJAMIN FRANKLIN; and to avoid the censure of the Assembly, that might fall on him as still printing it by his apprentice, the contrivance was that my old indenture should be return'd to me, with a full discharge on the back of it, to be shown on occasion, but to secure to him the benefit of my service, I was to sign new indentures for the remainder of the term, which were to be kept private.

---

libelling (LY bull ing) tending to expose a person to public ridicule in a
   written statement
satyr (SA tyr) a literary work in which vices, stupidities, etc. are held up
   to ridicule and contempt

A very flimsy scheme it was; however, it was immediately executed, and the paper went on accordingly, under my name for several months.

At length, a fresh difference arising between my brother and me, I took upon me to assert my freedom, presuming that he would not venture to produce the new indentures. It was not fair in me to take this advantage, and this I therefore reckon one of the first errata of my life; but the unfairness of it weighed little with me, when under the impressions of resentment for the blows his passion too often urged him to bestow upon me, though he was otherwise not an ill-natur'd man: perhaps I was too saucy and provoking.

When he found I would leave him, he took care to prevent my getting employment in any other printing-house of the town, by going round and speaking to every master, who accordingly refus'd to give me work. I then thought of going to New York, as the nearest place where there was a printer; and I was rather inclin'd to leave Boston when I reflected that I had already made myself a little obnoxious to the governing party, and, from the arbitrary proceedings of the Assembly in my brother's case, it was likely I might, if I stay'd, soon bring myself into scrapes; and farther, that my indiscrete disputations about religion began to make me pointed at with horror by good people as an infidel or atheist. I determin'd on the point, but my father now siding with my brother, I was sensible that, if I attempted to go openly, means would be used to prevent me. My friend Collins, therefore, undertook to manage a little for me. He agreed with the captain of a New York sloop for my passage, under the notion of my being a young acquaintance of his, that had got a naughty girl with child, whose friends would compel me to marry her, and therefore I could not appear or come away publicly. So I sold some of my books to raise a little money, was taken on board privately, and as we had a fair wind, in three days I found myself in New York, near 300 miles from home, a boy of but 17, without the least recommendation to, or knowledge of any person in the place, and with very little money in my pocket.

My inclinations for the sea were by this time worne out, or I might now have gratify'd them. But, having a trade, and supposing myself a pretty good workman, I offer'd my service to the

---

errata (air RAH ta) a printer's term for "errors"

printer in the place, old Mr. William Bradford, who had been the first printer in Pennsylvania, but removed from thence upon the quarrel of George Keith. He could give me no employment, having little to do, and help enough already; but says he, "My son at Philadelphia has lately lost his principal hand, Aquila Rose, by death; if you go thither, I believe he may employ you." Philadelphia was a hundred miles further; I set out, however, in a boat for Amboy, leaving my chest and things to follow me round by sea.

In crossing the bay, we met with a squall that tore our rotten sails to pieces, prevented our getting into the Kill, and drove us upon Long Island. In our way, a drunken Dutchman, who was a passenger too, fell overboard; when he was sinking, I reached through the water to his shock pate, and drew him up, so that we got him in again. His ducking sobered him a little, and he went to sleep, taking first out of his pocket a book, which he desir'd I would dry for him. It proved to be my old favorite author, Bunyan's Pilgrim's Progress, in Dutch, finely printed on good paper, with copper cuts, a dress better than I had ever seen it wear in its own language. I have since found that it has been translated into most of the languages of Europe, and suppose it has been more generally read than any other book, except perhaps the Bible. Honest John was the first that I know of who mix'd narration and dialogue; a method of writing very engaging to the reader, who in the most interesting parts finds himself, as it were, brought into the company and present at the discourse. De Foe in his Cruso, his Moll Flanders, Religious Courtship, Family Instructor, and other pieces, has imitated it with success; and Richardson has done the same in his Pamela, etc.

When we drew near the island, we found it was at a place where there could be no landing, there being a great surf on the stony beach. So we dropt anchor, and swung round towards the shore. Some people came down to the water edge and hallow'd to us, as we did to them; but the wind was so high, and the surff so loud, that we could not hear so as to understand each other. There were canoes on the shore, and we made signs, and hallow'd that they should fetch us; but they either did not understand us, or thought it impracticable, so they went away, and night coming on, we had no remedy but to wait till the wind should abate; and, in the meantime, the boatman and I concluded to sleep, if we could; and so crowded into the scuttle, with the Dutchman, who was still wet, and the spray beating over the head of our boat, leak'd thro' to us, so that we were soon almost as wet as he. In this manner we lay all night, with very little rest; but, the wind abating the next day, we made a shift to reach Amboy before night, having been thirty hours on the water, without victuals, or any drink but a bottle of filthy rum, and the water we sail'd on being salt.

In the evening I found myself very feverish, and went in to bed; but, having read somewhere that cold water drank plentifully was good for a fever, I follow'd the prescription, sweat plentiful most of the night, my fever left me, and in the morning, crossing the ferry, I proceeded on my journey on foot, having fifty miles to Burlington, where I was told I should find boats that would carry me the rest of the way to Philadelphia.

It rained very hard all the day; I was thoroughly soak'd, and by noon a good deal tired; so I stopt at a poor inn, where I staid all night, beginning now to wish that I had never left home. I cut so miserable a figure, too, that I found, by the questions ask'd me, I was suspected to be some runaway servant, and in danger of being taken up on that suspicion. However, I proceeded the next day, and got in the evening to an inn, within eight or ten miles of Burlington, kept by one Dr. Brown. He entered into conversation with me while I took some refreshment, and, finding I had read a little, became very sociable and friendly. Our acquaintance continu'd as long as he liv'd.

At his house I lay that night, and the next morning reach'd Burlington, but had the mortification to find that the regular boats were gone a little before my coming, and no other expected to go before Tuesday, this being Saturday; wherefore I returned to an old woman in the town, of whom I had bought gingerbread to eat on the water, and ask'd her advice. She invited me to lodge at her house till a passage by water should offer; and being tired with my foot travelling, I accepted the invitation. However, walking in the evening by the side of the river, a boat came by, which I found was going towards Philadelphia, with several people in her. They took me in, and, as there was no wind, we row'd all the way; and about midnight, not having yet seen the city, some of the company were confident we must have passed it, and would row no farther; the others knew not where we were; so we put toward the shore, got into a creek, landed near an old fence, with the rails of which we made a fire, the night being cold, in October, and there we

---

sociable (SOH shuh bul) enjoys the company of others

remained till daylight. Then one of the company knew the place to be Cooper's Creek, a little above Philadelphia, which we saw as soon as we got out of the creek, and arriv'd there about eight or nine o'clock on the Sunday morning, and landed at the Market-street wharf.

I have been the more particular in this description of my journey, and shall be so of my first entry into that city, that you may in your mind compare such unlikely beginnings with the figure I have since made there. I was in my working

Benjamin Franklin, after J.S. Duplessis. The Granger Collection

dress, my best cloaths being to come round by sea. I was dirty from my journey; my pockets were stuff'd out with shirts and stockings, and I knew no soul nor where to look for lodging. I was fatigued with travelling, rowing, and want of rest, I was very hungry; and my whole stock of cash consisted of a Dutch dollar, and about a shilling in copper. The latter I gave the people of the boat for my passage, who at first refus'd it, on account of my rowing; but I insisted on their taking it. A man being sometimes more generous when he has but a little money than when he has plenty, perhaps thro' fear of being thought to have but little.

Then I walked up the street, gazing about till near the market-house I met a boy with bread. I had made many a meal on bread, and, inquiring where he got it, I went immediately to the baker's he directed me to, in Second-street, and ask'd for bisket, intending such as we had in Boston; but they, it seems, were not made in Philadelphia. Then I asked for a three-penny loaf, and was told they had none such. So not considering or knowing the difference of money, and the greater cheapness nor the names of his bread, I made him give me three-penny worth of any sort. He gave me, accordingly, three great puffy rolls. I was surpriz'd at the quantity, but took it, and, having no room in my pockets, walk'd off with a roll under each arm, and eating the other. Thus I went up Market-street as far as Fourth-street, passing by the door of Mr. Read, my future wife's father; when she, standing at the door, saw me, and thought I made, as I certainly did, a most awkward, ridiculous appearance. Then I turned and went down Chestnut-street and part of Walnut-street, eating my roll all the way, and, coming round, found myself again at Market-street wharf, near the boat I came in, to which I went for a draught of the river water; and, being filled with one of my rolls, gave the other two to a woman and her child that came down the river in the boat with us, and were waiting to go farther.

Thus refreshed, I walked again up the street, which by this time had many clean-dressed people in it, who were all walking the same way. I joined them, and thereby was led into the great meeting-house of the Quakers near the market. I sat down among them, and, after looking round awhile and hearing nothing said, being very drowsy thro' labor and want of rest the preceding night, I fell fast asleep, and continued so till the meeting broke up, when one was kind enough to rouse me. This was, therefore, the first house I was in, or slept in, in Philadelphia.

[*The following excerpt relates events that occurred several years later.*]

It was about this time I conceiv'd the bold and arduous project of arriving at moral perfection. I wish'd to live without committing any fault at any time; I would conquer all that either natural inclination, custom, or company might lead me into. As I knew, or thought I knew, what was right and wrong, I did not see why I might not always do the one and avoid the other. But I soon found I had undertaken a task of more difficulty than I had imagined. While my care was employ'd in guarding against one fault, I was often surprised by another; habit took the advantage of inattention; inclination was sometimes too strong for reason. I concluded, at length, that the mere speculative conviction that it was our interest to be completely virtuous, was not sufficient to prevent our slipping; and that the contrary habits must be broken, and good ones acquired and established, before we can have any dependence on a steady, uniform rectitude of conduct. For this purpose I therefore contrived the following method.

In the various enumerations of the moral virtues I had met with in my reading, I found the catalogue more or less numerous, as different writers included more or fewer ideas under the same name. Temperance, for example, was by some confined to eating and drinking, while by others it was extended to mean the moderating every other pleasure, appetite, inclination, or passion, bodily or mental, even to our avarice and ambition. I propos'd to myself, for the sake of clearness, to use rather more names, with fewer ideas annex'd to each, than a few names with more ideas; and I included under thirteen names of virtues all that at that time occurr'd to me as necessary or desirable, and annexed to each a short precept, which fully express'd the extent I gave to its meaning.

These names of virtues, with their precepts, were:

1. TEMPERANCE. Eat not to dullness; drink not to elevation.
2. SILENCE. Speak not but what may benefit others or yourself; avoid trifling conversation.
3. ORDER. Let all your things have their places; let each part of your business have its time.
4. RESOLUTION. Resolve to perform what you ought; perform without fail what you resolve.
5. FRUGALITY. Make no expense but to do good to others or yourself; i. e., waste nothing.
6. INDUSTRY. Lose no time; be always employ'd in something useful; cut off all unnecessary actions.
7. SINCERITY. Use no hurtful deceit; think innocently and justly, and, if you speak, speak accordingly.
8. JUSTICE. Wrong none by doing injuries, or omitting the benefits that are your duty.
9. MODERATION. Avoid extreams; forbear resenting injuries so much as you think they deserve.
10. CLEANLINESS. Tolerate no uncleanliness in body, cloaths, or habitation.
11. TRANQUILLITY. Be not disturbed at trifles, or at accidents common or unavoidable.
12. CHASTITY. Rarely use venery but for health or offspring, never to dulness, weakness, or the injury of your own or another's peace or reputation.
13. HUMILITY. Imitate Jesus and Socrates.

---

precept (PREE cept) rule of conduct; aphorism
frugality (froo GAL uh tee) careful economy; thrift
tranquility (tran KWIL uh tee) calmness, peacefulness
chastity (CHAS tuh tee) decency; modesty
humility (hyoo MIL uh tee) humbleness; the absence of pride

My intention being to acquire the *habitude* of all these virtues, I judg'd it would be well not to distract my attention by attempting the whole at once, but to fix it on one of them at a time; and, when I should be master of that, then to proceed to another, and so on, till I should have gone thro' the thirteen. . . .

I enter'd upon the execution of this plan for self-examination, and continu'd it with occasional intermissions for some time. I was surpris'd to find myself so much fuller of faults than I had imagined; but I had the satisfaction of seeing them diminish. . . .

In truth, I found myself incorrigible with respect to Order; and now I am grown old, and my memory bad, I feel very sensibly the want of it. But, on the whole, tho' I never arrived at the perfection I had been so ambitious of obtaining, but fell far short of it, yet I was, by the endeavour, a better and a happier man than I otherwise should have been if I had not attempted it. . . .

It may be well my posterity should be informed that to this little artifice, with the blessing of God, their ancestor ow'd the constant felicity of his life, down to his 79th year, in which this is written. What reverses may attend the remainder is in the hand of Providence; but, if they arrive, the reflection on past happiness enjoy'd ought to help his bearing them with more resignation. To Temperance he ascribes his long-continued health, and what is still left to him of a good constitution; to Industry and Frugality, the early easiness of his circumstances and acquisition of his fortune, with all that knowledge that enabled him to be a useful citizen, and obtained for him some degree of reputation among the learned; to Sincerity and Justice, the confidence of his country, and the honorable employs it conferred upon him; and to the joint influence of the whole mass of the virtues, even in the imperfect state he was able to acquire them, all that evenness of temper, and that cheerfulness in conversation, which makes his company still sought for, and agreeable even to his younger acquaintance. I hope, therefore, that some of my descendants may follow the example and reap the benefit.

Poor Richard, 1733.

AN

Almanack

For the Year of Chriſt

1733,

Being the Firſt after LEAP YEAR:

And makes ſince the Creation	Years
By the Account of the Eaſtern *Greeks*	7241
By the Latin Church, when ☉ ent. ♈	6932
By the Computation of *W. W.*	5742
By the *Roman* Chronology	5682
By the *Jewiſh* Rabbies	5494

Wherein is contained

The Lunations, Eclipſes, Judgment of the Weather, Spring Tides, Planets Motions & mutual Aſpects, Sun and Moon's Riſing and Setting, Length of Days, Time of High Water, Fairs, Courts, and obſervable Days.

Fitted to the Latitude of Forty Degrees, and a Meridian of Five Hours Weſt from *London*, but may without ſenſible Error, ſerve all the adjacent Places, even from *Newfoundland* to *South-Carolina*.

By RICHARD SAUNDERS, Philom.

PHILADELPHIA:

Printed and ſold by *B. FRANKLIN*, at the New Printing-Office near the Market.

Poor Richard's Almanack, Title Page, First Edition, 1733. Benjamin Franklin.
The Granger Collection

from
Poor Richard's
Almanack

by Benjamin Franklin

1. Tart words make no friends; a spoonful of honey will catch more flies than a gallon of vinegar.

2. Early to bed and early to rise, makes a man healthy wealthy and wise.

3. The sleeping Fox catches no Poultry.

4. Beware of little expences; a small Leak will sink a great Ship.

5. Fish & Visitors smell after 3 days.

6. Lost time is never found again.

7. The worst wheel of the cart makes the most noise.

8. Be slow in choosing a Friend, slower in changing.

9. At the working man's house Hunger looks in, but dares not enter.

10. A slip of the foot you may soon recover, but a slip of the tongue you may never get over.

Review the Selection

Recall

1. Which foods did Franklin not eat?

2. Where did he finally settle after leaving Boston?

3. "Early to bed and early to rise makes a man" what?

Infer

4. In the first excerpt, why did Franklin have extra money to buy books?

5. Why did Franklin seek employment outside of Boston?

6. Why did Franklin leave New York City so quickly?

7. Why do you think ". . . visitors smell after three days"?

Apply

8. How difficult would it be for you to stay on a vegetable diet? Why?

9. Predict what might have happened if Franklin had stayed in Boston.

10. If you were making the trip from Boston to Philadelphia today, how would you travel?

Respond to Literature
How do you think Franklin's works reflect the lifestyle of the colonists?

THINK ABOUT NARRATION

Narration is writing in which events are related in chronological order. It is used in fiction (novels and short stories), poetry (narrative poems), and nonfiction (biography, autobiography, and news stories).

1. What type of nonfiction are Franklin's stories?

2. Do you think a serious sermon on the subject of excusing one's own actions would have been more effective than the humorous ending of the first excerpt? Explain your answer.

3. Do you think Franklin's account of his struggle with self-improvement would have been more or less effective if he had been writing of someone else's struggle? Explain your answer.

4. Explain the difference between a short story and an autobiography.

5. Why would a story in Franklin's newspaper be called a narrative?

READING FOCUS
Make Generalizations Write two generalizations about the values of Franklin's time. Then write two generalizations about Franklin's personality. Be sure to support your generalizations with details from the selection.

A **root** is a word or word part that is used to form other words. The addition of various prefixes or suffixes to the root word usually yields a variety of words. The root usually carries the central meaning of the word. For example, the root word *temper* is used to form the word *temperance*. *Temper* means "to regulate or mix properly." *Temperance* means "to regulate or have self-restraint in conduct, expression, or appetite." Many times you can use the root word to help you understand the meaning of a larger word. This is especially true if you know the meanings of various prefixes and suffixes.

Find the root in each of the following words. Use the root to figure out the meaning of each word. Check each meaning in a dictionary. Then write an original sentence for each word.

1. resolution
2. becalmed
3. unprovoked
4. tranquility
5. inclination
6. accountable
7. frugality
8. moderation

Learn About

POINT OF VIEW

Essayists and storytellers choose a point of view from which to write. **Point of view** is the position from which an author writes.

In nonfiction, three points of view are used. If writers make themselves the speaker, they have used the first-person point of view. You can recognize first person by a writer's use of *I* and *me.*

If the writer addresses the reader directly, the choice is the second-person point of view. You can recognize second person by the use of the pronoun *you.*

If writers position themselves outside the material altogether, they have used the third-person point of view. You can recognize third person by a writer's use of the pronouns *he, she* or *it.*

As you read "What Is an American?" ask yourself:

1. Which point of view did Crèvecoeur use?
2. Would his essay have been as effective if he had chosen a different point of view?

WRITING CONNECTION

Write three sentences, using first-person point of view, about your participation in an after-school activity. Rewrite the sentences, using third-person point of view.

READING FOCUS

Compare and Contrast To compare two things, you look at what they have in common. To contrast two things, you look at ways in which they differ.

You have your own opinions about what it means to be an American. As you read, think about your own views. Compare and contrast them with those of Crèvecoeur.

50 ■ Unit 1

What Is an American?

by Jean de Crèvecoeur

What then is the American, this new man? He is either a European, or the descendant of a European; hence that strange mixture of blood which you will find in no other country. I could point out to you a family whose grandfather was an Englishman, whose wife was Dutch, whose son married a French woman, and whose present four sons have now four wives of different nations.

He is an American who, leaving behind him all his ancient prejudices and manners, receives new ones from the new mode of life he has embraced, the new government he obeys, and the new rank he holds. He becomes an American by being received in the broad lap of our great alma mater.

Here individuals of all nations are melted into a new race of men, whose labors and posterity will one day cause great changes in the world. Americans are the western pilgrims who are carrying along with them that great mass of arts, sciences, vigor, and industry which began long since in the east; they will finish the great circle. The Americans were once scattered all over Europe; here they are incorporated into one of the finest systems of population which has ever appeared, and which will hereafter become distinct by the power of the different climates they inhabit. The American ought, therefore, to love this country much better than that wherein either he or his forefathers were born. Here the rewards of his industry follow with equal steps the progress of his labor; his labor is founded on the basis of nature, self-interest. Can it want a stronger allurement? Wives and children, who before in vain demanded of him a morsel of bread, now, fat and frolicsome, gladly help their father to clear those fields whence exuberant crops are to arise to feed and to clothe them all, without any part being claimed, either by a despotic prince, a rich abbot, or a mighty lord. Here, religion demands but little of him; a small voluntary salary to the minister, and gratitude to God. Can he refuse these?

The American is a new man, who acts upon new principles; he must, therefore, entertain new ideas, and form new opinions. From involuntary idleness, servile dependence, penury, and useless labor, he has passed to toils of a very different nature, rewarded by ample subsistence. This is an American.

---

descendant (dih SEN dunt) a person who is the offspring of a certain ancestor, family, group, etc.
prejudices (PREJ uh disses) judgments or opinions formed before the facts are known
posterity (pos TERR i tee) descendants; succeeding generations
abbot (AB ut) a man who is head of a monastery

Review the Selection

UNDERSTAND THE SELECTION

Recall

1. Where were the colonists from?

2. What will Americans' labors bring?

3. In America, what quickly follows labor?

Infer

4. What is one European prejudice Americans did not share?

5. Which nations affected our arts and sciences?

6. What was the advantage of being gathered together in one country?

7. Why would the American love this new country so much?

Apply

8. If you lived in the 18th century, which arts and sciences would you have valued most?

9. Predict what would have happened to people with the "American spirit" if they had stayed in Europe.

10. Which new ideas would have appealed to you if you had lived at that time?

Respond to Literature
What values do you think Crévecoeur's American possessed?

THINK ABOUT POINT OF VIEW

Point of view is the position writers take in relation to their subject matter. Because their subject matter is often factual, or theoretical, essay writers frequently choose the third person. Some topics, however, lend themselves to the use of the first or second person.

1. Is Crèvecoeur's point of view first, second, or third person?

2. The author never states that he is an American. Would the reader be more or less likely to accept Crèvecoeur's opinions as fact if the essay began, "I am an American . . ."? Explain your answer.

3. Do you think Crèvecoeur is accurate in his opinions about Americans and Europeans? Explain your answer.

4. At one point in the essay, the author makes a statement about living conditions in Europe. What is Crèvecoeur's opinion of life in Europe?

5. Select one of the author's opinions. Explain why you think it is true or not true today.

READING FOCUS
Compare and Contrast You have explored your own ideas about what it means to be an American and read about Crèvecoeur's ideas. Now write a paragraph in which you compare and contrast your views with those of Crèvecoeur.

DEVELOP YOUR VOCABULARY

Etymology is the study of word origins. Every word has a history. This includes the names of the town, city, and state in which you live. Place names may reflect the ancestry of the original settlers. Dutch colonists named one of their settlements New Amsterdam after the capital of their native country, the Netherlands. When the English drove them out, the name was changed to New York. York is a city in England. This is why there are so many place names in America that include the word "new." How many can you think of?

Use a dictionary or encyclopedia to find the origin of the following place names. List each on a sheet of paper. Write your answer in an original sentence beside the name.

1. New Hampshire   **3.** Newark
2. Maine   **4.** Boston

Places may also be named for people, events, geographical features, or other characteristics. Using local sources (if necessary), find the origin of the name of your town or city and the state in which you live.

Learn About

FOLKLORE

People who have no written tradition pass their beliefs on from generation to generation as **folklore**. The materials passed on consist of myths, stories, riddles, proverbs, superstitions, ballads, songs, and customs. Among the stories told are legends and tall tales.

A **legend** is a story of the past. It often tells of an extraordinary happening. The people who tell the legend believe it. The main character may be heroic, with superhuman powers and excellent character. Legends often try to explain some mystery of human life.

A **tall tale** is a form of humor popular in early American history. It is usually set in the narrator's lifetime. For its humor, it relies on exaggeration. Its plot is deliberately outrageous and unbelievable.

As you read the next two selections, ask yourself:

1. Which selection is a legend?
2. Which selection is a tall tale?

READING FOCUS

Recognize Main Idea and Supporting Details The main idea of a story is the most important point—the statement or concept that the writer or storyteller wants you to remember. The writer provides details—descriptions, reasons, and examples—that support that main idea.

As you read "Sunrise in His Pocket" and "Godasiyo, the Woman Chief," think about the main idea of each. How can you summarize each in one sentence? What are some details that support the main idea?

WRITING CONNECTION

Look up the word *hero* in a dictionary. Choose a popular athlete or entertainer. Describe this person in heroic terms. Write your description so that it has the characteristics of either a tall tale or a legend.

Sunrise in His Pocket

by Davy Crockett

I'm that same Davy Crockett that is fresh from the backwoods. I'm half horse, half alligator—and part snapping turtle, too. I can wade the Mississippi River and leap over the Ohio River. I can ride upon a streak of lightning. Thorns wouldn't dare to scratch me. I can whip my weight in wildcats—and if anyone pleases—I'll wrestle a panther, or hug a bear too close for comfort. Here is what I did on the day the sun froze.

One January morning, it was so cold the trees were too stiff to shake. The very daybreak froze solid just as it was trying to dawn. The tinder-box I used to light my fire wouldn't spark. It would no more catch fire than a raft sunk to the bottom of the sea.

Well, I decided the only way I was going to get some fire was to make it myself. I brought my knuckles together like two thunderclouds, but the sparks froze before I could collect them. So out I walked whistling "Fire in the Mountains!" as I went along in double quick time. Well, after I had walked about twenty miles I came to Daybreak Hill and discovered what was the matter.

The earth had actually frozen fast on her axis. She couldn't turn round. The sun had gotten jammed between cakes of ice under the wheels. The sun had been shining and working to get loose until he froze in his cold sweat.

---

tinderbox (TIN dur BAHKS) formerly, a metal box for holding flint for starting a fire

"C-r-e-a-t-i-o-n!" thought I. "This is the toughest form of sus-pension. It mustn't be endured. Something must be done or human creation is done for!"

It was so cold that my teeth and tongue were all collapsed together as tight as an oyster. But I took a fresh bear from my back. (I had picked it up along the road.) I beat the animal against the ice until the hot oil began to pour out of it on all sides. I then held the bear over the earth's axis. I squeezed the hot bear oil until I'd thawed the earth loose. Then, I poured about a ton of the hot bear oil over the sun's face.

I gave the earth's cogwheel one kick backward until I got the sun loose. I whistled, "Push along; keep moving!" In about fifteen seconds the earth gave a grunt and began to move.

The sun walked back up into the sky. It saluted me with such gratitude that it made me sneeze. Then I shouldered my bear and saluted back. As I walked home, I introduced people to the fresh daylight with a piece of sunrise in my pocket.

---

suspension (suh SPEN shun) temporary stoppage
cogwheel (KAHG hweel) a wheel with a rim notched into teeth, which
    mesh with those of another wheel to transmit or receive motion

GODASIYO, the Woman Chief

a Seneca legend retold by Dee Brown

At the beginning of time when America was new, a woman chief named Godasiyo ruled over an Indian village beside a large river in the East. In those days all the tribes spoke one language and lived in harmony and peace. Because Godasiyo was a wise and progressive chief, many people came from faraway places to live in her village, and they had no difficulty understanding one another.

At last the village grew so large that half the people lived on the north side of the river and half on the south side. They spent much time canoeing back and forth to visit, attend dances, and exchange gifts of venison, hides, furs, and dried fruits and berries. The tribal council house was on the south side, which made it necessary for those who lived on the north bank to make frequent canoe trips to consult with their chief. Some complained about this, and to make it easier for everybody to cross the rapid stream, Godasiyo ordered a bridge to be built of saplings and tree limbs carefully fastened together. This bridge brought the tribe close together again and the people praised Godasiyo for her wisdom.

Not long after this, a white dog appeared in the village, and Godasiyo claimed it for her own. Everywhere the chief went the dog followed her, and the people on the north side of the river became jealous of the animal. They spread stories that the dog was possessed by an evil spirit that would bring harm to the tribe. One day a delegation from the north bank crossed the bridge to the council house and demanded that Godasiyo kill the white dog. When she refused to do so, the delegates returned to their side of the river, and that night they destroyed the bridge.

From that time on, people on the north bank and those on the south bank began to distrust each other. The tribe divided into two factions, one renouncing Godasiyo as their chief, the other supporting her. Bad feelings between them grew so deep that Godasiyo foresaw that the next step would surely lead to fighting and war. Hoping to avoid bloodshed, she called all members of the tribe who supported her to a meeting in the council house.

"Our people," she said, "are divided by more than a river. No longer is there goodwill and contentment among us. Not wishing to see brother fight against brother, I propose that those who recognize me as their chief follow me westward up the great river to build a new village."

Almost everyone who attended the council meeting agreed to follow Godasiyo westward. In preparation for the migration, they built many canoes of birch bark. Two young men who had been friendly rivals in canoe races volunteered to construct a special watercraft for their chief. With strong poles they fastened two large canoes together and then built a platform which extended over the canoes and the space between them. Upon this platform was a seat for Godasiyo and places to store her clothing, extra leggings, belts, robes, moccasins, mantles, caps, awls, needles, and adornments.

At last everything was ready. Godasiyo took her seat on the platform with the white dog beside her, and the two young men who had built the craft began paddling the double canoes beneath. Behind them the chief's followers and defenders launched their own canoes, which contained all their belongings. This flotilla of canoes covered the shining waters as far as anyone could see up and down the river.

After they had paddled a long distance, they came to a fork in the river. Godasiyo ordered the two young canoeists to stop in the middle of the river until the others caught up with them. In a few minutes the flotilla was divided, half of the canoes on her left, the others on her right.

The chief and the people on each side of her began to discuss the advantages and disadvantages of the two forks in the river. Some wanted to go one way, some preferred the other way. The arguments grew heated with anger. Godasiyo said that she would

---

flotilla (floh TIL uh) a fleet of boats or small ships

take whichever fork her people chose, but they could agree on neither. Finally those on the right turned the prows of their canoes up the right channel, while those on the left began paddling up the left channel. And so the tribe began to separate.

When this movement started, the two young men paddling the two canoes carrying Godasiyo's float disagreed as to which fork they should take, and they fell into a violent quarrel. The canoeist on the right thrust his paddle into the water and started toward the right, and at the same time the one on the left swung his canoe toward the left. Suddenly, Godasiyo's platform slipped off its supports and collapsed into the river, carrying her with it.

Hearing the loud splash, the people on both sides turned their canoes around and tried to rescue their beloved chief. But she and the white dog, the platform, and all her belongings had sunk to the bottom, and the people could see nothing but fish swimming in the clear waters.

Dismayed by this tragic happening, the people of the two divisions began to try to talk to each other, but even though they shouted words back and forth, those on the right could not understand the people on the left, and those on the left could not understand the people on the right. When Godasiyo drowned in the great river, her people's language had become changed. This was how it was that the Indians were divided into many tribes spreading across America, each of them speaking a different language.

Dee Brown (1908–)

Dee Brown has spent a lifetime writing about the American West. His popular histories are authentic, and provide a great deal of wisdom regarding human nature.

In the area of nonfiction, he is well known for his book *Bury My Heart at Wounded Knee*. In the book, Brown uses the words of such famous Native Americans as Crazy Horse and Sitting Bull to tell the history of Native Americans between 1860 and 1890. Brown has been one of the few writers to treat westward expansion from the viewpoint of its victims—the Native American tribes.

In his most popular fictional work, *Creek Mary's Blood*, Brown tells the story of five generations of Native Americans. He wrote this story after he found an item about Creek Mary in an old book. She stormed Savannah, Georgia, with a group of male warriors to drive out the British during the Revolutionary War.

Among Brown's other works is a book about trail-driving days and the woman's role in the Old West. His first book, written in 1941, was about Davy Crockett.

Brown was born in a lumber camp in Louisiana. He grew up in Arkansas, where he first became interested in Native American history and the West.

He went to college in Arkansas and later did graduate work at George Washington University in Washington, D.C. Upon graduation, he went to work for the Department of Agriculture as a librarian. In 1948, he became a librarian at the University of Illinois. Being at the university allowed him to do extensive research on his favorite subject—the American West. Because of Brown's many years of careful research and sensitive writing, people are better able to understand the devastating effect westward expansion had on Native Americans.

Review the Selection

Recall

1. In "Sunrise in His Pocket," what did Crockett use to thaw the earth?

2. How many languages did all the tribes speak during Godasiyo's rule?

3. Why did the tribe on the north bank want Godasiyo to kill the white dog?

Infer

4. Why did Godasiyo refuse to kill the white dog?

5. Why did Godasiyo want to move her supporters?

6. What did the legend of Godasiyo attempt to explain?

7. How did Crockett portray his character in "Sunrise in His Pocket"?

Apply

8. Predict what would happen if the sun actually did freeze.

9. Imagine Davy Crockett telling his story to a live audience. How do you think the audience would react?

10. Predict what would have happened if Godasiyo had killed the white dog.

Respond to Literature

How do heroes in tall tales reflect the spirit of their time?

THINK ABOUT FOLKLORE

Folk stories tell about many wonderful characters—talking animals, tricksters, magical beasts, supernatural helpers, ogres, numskulls, and heroes. The legend and the tall tale both tell of heroic persons. All the tales have one thing in common; they come from an oral tradition.

1. Is "Sunrise in His Pocket" a legend or a tall tale? What characteristics in the story tell you which it is?

2. Is "Godasiyo, the Woman Chief" a legend or a tall tale? What characteristics in the story tell you which it is?

3. Compare the heroic qualities of Crockett and Godasiyo.

4. The legend writer is trying to teach a history lesson. How would the use of exaggeration interfere with the writer's purpose?

5. If exaggeration were eliminated from Crockett's story, would it become believable? Why or why not?

READING FOCUS

Recognize Main Idea and Supporting Details Summarize the main idea of each story in one sentence. Then provide at least three details from each story that support the main idea.

DEVELOP YOUR VOCABULARY

There are many ways of using language for humorous effect. In "Sunrise in His Pocket," Davy Crockett used exaggeration as his main tool for humor. The use of exaggeration for literary effect is called **hyperbole**. Some everyday examples of hyperbole, not necessarily humorous, are "as old as the hills" or "my feet are killing me." Neither of these expressions is meant literally, but the pictures they bring to mind are vivid. Think about what people really mean when they use these expressions.

Writers who use hyperbole for humorous effect must make it clear that they do not expect the reader to believe the exaggerations. If they do not make it clear, the statements would be taken seriously and the humor would be lost.

Look through "Sunrise in His Pocket" and choose three examples of hyperbole. List each of your choices and explain what each would mean if taken literally. Then tell why the example succeeds in being funny.

Writers in a Growing Nation

There's a better day a'coming,
Will you go along with me?
There's a better day a'coming,
Go sound the jubilee!
   —Pre-Civil War Spiritual

Allegory of Freedom, c. 1863, Anonymous. The Granger Collection

Learn About

AUTOBIOGRAPHY

An **autobiography** is the true story of a person's life told by that person. Since autobiography consists of facts about a person's life, it is nonfiction.

A person's life is a story—a true story, of course. Thus, it is told in **narrative** form. That is, it tells about events as they happened, usually in chronological order. Autobiographies are usually long; most make up a whole book. Besides the facts of a person's life, the author usually writes of his or her thoughts, ideas, and inner struggles.

The point of view in an autobiography is the first person. It is the natural point of view of someone telling a personal story.

As you read this selection, ask yourself:

1. What part of his life was Douglass writing about?
2. How would his story have sounded if he had used the third-person point of view? In what way might it have been more effective? In what way might it have been less effective?

READING FOCUS

Make Inferences An inference is an understanding based on ideas or things already known. In an autobiography, you can make inferences by thinking about the significance, or importance, of events in the author's life that the author has decided to include. You may also make inferences about the author's character and values. As you read, make inferences based on the actions of the people and the events described in the autobiography.

WRITING CONNECTION

Make a list of some events or ideas that you would include in your autobiography. What point of view would you use? Would you write in chronological order?

from

My Bondage and My Freedom

by Frederick Douglass

I lived in the family of Master Hugh, at Baltimore, seven years, during which time—as the almanac makers say of the weather—my condition was variable. The most interesting feature of my history here, was my learning to read and write, under somewhat marked disadvantages. In attaining this knowledge, I was compelled to resort to indirections by no means congenial to my nature, and which were really humiliating to me. My mistress—who . . . had begun to teach me—was suddenly checked in her benevolent design, by the strong advice of her husband. In faithful compliance with this advice, the good lady had not only ceased to instruct me, herself, but had set her face as a flint against my learning to read by any means. It is due, however, to my mistress to say, that she did not adopt this course in all its stringency at the first. She either thought it unnecessary, or she lacked the depravity indispensable to shutting me up in mental darkness. It was, at least, necessary for her to have some training, and some hardening, in the exercise of the slaveholder's prerogative, to make her equal to forgetting my human nature and character, and to treating me as a thing destitute of a moral or an intellectual nature. Mrs. Auld—my mistress—was, as I have said, a most kind and tender-hearted woman; and, in the humanity of her heart, and the simplicity of her mind, she set out, when I first went to live with her, to treat me as she supposed one human being ought to treat another.

It is easy to see, that, in entering upon the duties of a slaveholder, some little experience is needed. Nature has done almost nothing to prepare men and women to be either slaves or slaveholders. Nothing but rigid training, long persisted in, can perfect the character of the one or the other. One cannot easily forget to love

---

variable (VAIR ee ih bul) likely to change
humiliating (hyoo MIL ee ayt ing) lowering of pride or dignity

View of Baltimore, Maryland, 1839. The Granger Collection

freedom; and it is as hard to cease to respect that natural love in our fellow creatures. On entering upon the career of a slaveholding mistress, Mrs. Auld was singularly deficient; nature, which fits nobody for such an office, had done less for her than any lady I had known. It was no easy matter to induce her to think and to feel that the curly-headed boy, who stood by her side, and even leaned on her lap; who was loved by little Tommy [her son], and who loved little Tommy in turn; sustained to her only the relation of a chattel. I was more than that, and she felt me to be more than that. I could talk and sing; I could laugh and weep; I could reason and remember; I could love and hate. I was human, and she, dear lady, knew and felt me to be so. How could she, then, treat me as a brute, without a mighty struggle with all the noble powers of her own soul. That struggle came, and the will and power of the husband was victorious. Her noble soul was overthrown; but, he that overthrew it did not, himself, escape the consequences. He, not less than the other parties, was injured in his domestic peace by the fall.

When I went into their family, it was the abode of happiness and contentment.

---

chattel (CHAT ul) a movable article of personal property; owned property

The mistress of the house was a model of affection and tenderness. Her fervent piety and watchful uprightness made it impossible to see her without thinking and feeling—"that woman is a Christian." There was no sorrow nor suffering for which she had not a tear, and there was no innocent joy for which she did not a smile. She had bread for the hungry, clothes for the naked, and comfort for every mourner that came within her reach. Slavery soon proved its ability to divest her of these excellent qualities, and her home of its early happiness. Conscience cannot stand much violence. Once thoroughly broken down, who is he that can repair the damage? It may be broken toward the slave, on Sunday, and toward the master on Monday. It cannot endure such shocks. It must stand entire, or it does not stand at all. If my condition waxed bad, that of the family waxed not better. The first step, in the wrong direction, was the violence done to nature and to conscience, in arresting the benevolence that would have enlightened my young mind. In ceasing to instruct me, she must begin to justify herself to herself; and, once consenting to take sides in such a debate, she was riveted to her position. One needs very little knowledge of moral philosophy, to see where my mistress now landed. She finally became even more violent in her opposition to my learning to read, than was her husband himself. She was not satisfied with simply doing as well as her husband had commanded her, but seemed resolved to better his instruction. Nothing appeared to make my poor mistress—after her turning toward the downward path—more angry, than seeing me, seated in some nook or corner, quietly reading a book or a newspaper. I have had her rush at me, with the utmost fury, and snatch from my hand such newspaper or book, with something of the wrath and consternation which a traitor might be supposed to feel on being discovered in a plot by some dangerous spy.

Mrs. Auld was an apt woman, and the advice of her husband, and her own experience, soon demonstrated, to her entire satisfaction, that education and slavery are incompatible with each other. When this conviction was thoroughly established, I was most narrowly watched in all my movements. If I remained in a separate room from the family for any considerable length of time, I was sure to be suspected of having a book, and was at once called upon to give an account of myself. All this, however, was entirely too late. The first, and never to be retraced, step had been taken. In teaching me the alphabet, in the days of her simplicity and kindness, my mistress had given me the "inch," and now, no ordinary precaution could prevent me from taking the "ell."

Seized with a determination to learn to read, at any cost, I hit upon many expedients to accomplish the desired end. The plea which I mainly adopted, and the one

---

enlightened (en LYT und) to have given the light of knowledge to
moral philosophy (MAWR ul fuh LOS uh fee) ethics; standards of conduct and
    moral judgment
incompatible (in kum PAT uh bul) not in agreement

by which I was most successful, was that of using my young white playmates, with whom I met in the streets as teachers. I used to carry, almost constantly, a copy of Webster's spelling book in my pocket; and, when sent of errands, or when play time was allowed me, I would step, with my young friends, aside, and take a lesson in spelling. I generally paid my tuition fee to the boys, with bread, which I also carried in my pocket. For a single biscuit, any of my hungry little comrades would give me a lesson more valuable to me than bread. Not every one, however, demanded this consideration, for there were those who took pleasure in teaching me, whenever I had a chance to be taught by them. I am strongly tempted to give the names of two or three of those little boys, as a slight testimonial of the gratitude and affection I bear them, but prudence forbids; not that it would injure me, but it might, possibly, embarrass them; for it is almost an unpardonable offense to do any thing, directly or indirectly, to promote a slave's freedom, in a slave state. It is enough to say, of my warm-hearted little play fellows, that they lived on Philpot street, very near Durgin & Bailey's shipyard.

Although slavery was a delicate subject, and very cautiously talked about among grown up people in Maryland, I frequently talked about it—and that very freely—with the white boys. I would, sometimes, say to them, while seated on a curb stone or a cellar door, "I wish I could be free, as you will be when you get to be men." "You will be free, you know, as soon as you are twenty-one, and can go where you like, but I am a slave for life. Have I not as good a right to be free as you have?" Words like these, I observed, always troubled them; and I had no small satisfaction in wringing from the boys, occasionally, that fresh and bitter condemnation of slavery, that springs from nature, unseared and unperverted. Of all consciences let me have those to deal with which have not been bewildered by the cares of life. I do not remember ever to have met with a boy, while I was in slavery, who defended the slave system; but I have often had boys to console me, with the hope that something would yet occur, by which I might be made free. Over and over again, they have told me, that "they believed I had as good a right to be free as they had;" and that "they did not believe God ever made any one to be a slave." The reader will easily see, that such little conversations with my play fellows, had no tendency to weaken my love of liberty, nor to render me contented with my condition as a slave.

When I was about thirteen years old, and had succeeded in learning to read, every increase of knowledge, especially respecting the free states, added something to the almost intolerable burden of the thought—I am a slave for life. To my bondage I saw no end. It was a terrible reality, and I shall never be able to tell how sadly that thought chafed my young spirit. Fortunately, or unfortunately,

---

prudence (PROOD uns) the quality of being cautious or discreet in conduct
curb stone (KURB stohn) stone or concrete edging of a sidewalk
intolerable (in TOL ur uh bul) unbearable

A House Slave and His Mistress at Baltimore, 1861.
The Granger Collection

about this time in my life, I had made enough money to buy what was then a very popular school book, viz: the *Columbian Orator*. I bought this addition to my library, of Mr. Knight, on Thames street, Fell's Point, Baltimore, and paid him fifty cents for it. I was first led to buy this book, by hearing some little boys say they were going to learn some little pieces out of it for the Exhibition. This volume was, indeed, a rich treasure, and every opportunity afforded me, for a time, was spent in diligently perusing it. Among much other interesting matter, that which I had perused and reperused with unflagging satisfaction, was a short dialogue between a master and his slave. . . . And thereafter the whole argument, for and against slavery, was brought out. . . .

This, however, was not all the fanaticism which I found in this *Columbian Orator*. I met there one of Sheridan's mighty speeches, on the subject of Catholic Emancipation, Lord Chatham's speech on the American war, and speeches by the great William Pitt and by Fox. These were all choice documents to me, and I read them, over and over again, with an interest that was ever increasing, because it was ever gaining in intelligence; for the more I read them, the better I understood them. The reading of these speeches added much to my limited stock of language, and enabled me to give tongue to many interesting thoughts, which had frequently flashed through my soul, and died away for want of utterance. . . . If I ever wavered under the consideration, that the Almighty, in some way, ordained slavery, and willed my enslavement for his own glory, I wavered no longer. I had now penetrated the secret of all slavery and oppression, and had ascertained their true foundation to be in the pride, the power and the avarice of man.

The dialogue and the speeches were all redolent of the principles of liberty, and poured floods of light on the nature and character of slavery. . . . As I read, behold! the very discontent so graphically predicted by Master Hugh, had already come upon me. I was no longer the light-hearted, gleesome boy, full of mirth and play, as when I landed first at Baltimore. Knowledge had come; light had penetrated the moral dungeon where I dwelt; and, behold! there lay the bloody whip, for my back, and here was the iron chain; and my good, kind master, he was the author of my situation. The revelation haunted me, stung me, and made me gloomy and miserable. As I writhed under the sting and torment of this knowledge, I almost envied my fellow slaves their stupid contentment.

This knowledge opened my eyes to the horrible pit, and revealed the teeth of the frightful dragon that was ready to pounce upon me, but it opened no way for my escape. I have often wished myself a beast, or a bird—anything, rather than a slave. I was wretched and gloomy, beyond my ability to describe. I was too thoughtful to be happy. It was this everlasting thinking which distressed and tormented me; and yet there was no getting rid of the subject of my thoughts. All nature was redolent of it. Once awakened by the silver trump of knowledge, my spirit was roused to eternal wakefulness. Liberty! the inestimable birthright of every man, had, for me, converted every object into an asserter of this great right. It was heard in every sound, and beheld in every object. It was ever present, to torment me with a sense of my wretched condition. The more beautiful and charming were the smiles of nature, the more horrible and desolate was my condition. I saw nothing without seeing it, and I heard nothing without hearing it. I do not exaggerate, when I say, that it looked from every star, smiled in every calm, breathed in every wind, and moved in every storm.

I have no doubt that my state of mind had something to do with the change in the treatment adopted, by my once kind mistress toward me. I can easily believe, that my leaden, downcast, and discontented look, was very offensive to her. Poor lady! She did not know my trouble, and I dared not tell her. Could I have freely made her acquainted with the real state of my mind, and given her the reasons therefor, it might have been well for both of us. Her abuse of me fell upon me like the blows of the false prophet upon his ass; she did not know that an angel stood in the way; and—such is the relation of master and slave I could not tell her. Nature had made us friends; slavery made us enemies. My interests were in a direction opposite to hers, and we both had our private thoughts and plans. She aimed to keep me ignorant; and I resolved to know, although knowledge only increased my discontent. My feelings were not the result of any marked cruelty in the treatment I received; they sprung from the consideration of my being a slave at all. It was *slavery*—not its mere *incidents*—that I hated. I had been cheated. I saw through the attempt to keep me in ignorance; I saw that slaveholders would have gladly made me believe that they were merely acting under the authority of

---

birthright (BURTH ryt) the rights that a person has because he/she was born in a certain family, nation, etc.
downcast (DOUN kast) sad
incidents (IN suh dents) things that happen as the result of other things (here referring to the abuses of slavery)

God, in making a slave of me, and in making slaves of others; and I treated them as robbers and deceivers. The feeding and clothing me well, could not atone for taking my liberty from me. The smiles of my mistress could not remove the deep sorrow that dwelt in my young bosom. Indeed, these, in time, came only to deepen my sorrow. She had changed; and the reader will see that I had changed, too. We were both victims to the same overshadowing evil—she, as mistress, I, as slave. I will not censure her harshly; she cannot censure me, for she knows I speak but the truth, and have acted in my opposition to slavery, just as she herself would have acted, in a reverse of circumstances.

---

overshadowing (oh vur SHAD oh ing) hanging or looming over
censure (SEN shur) blame

Review the Selection

Recall

1. Who began teaching Douglass?

2. Where was Douglass enslaved as a young child?

3. In what book did Douglass find writings about the principles of freedom?

Infer

4. Why did Douglass say that Mrs. Auld was ill-prepared to be a slaveholder?

5. Why did Douglass never meet a boy who approved of the slave system?

6. Why was Master Hugh so opposed to Douglass's education?

7. Why were Douglass and Mrs. Auld both victims of slavery?

Apply

8. Why did Mrs. Auld teach Douglass to read?

9. In what way did Master Hugh pay for his victory over his wife's natural kindness?

10. If Douglass had not learned to read, predict what might have happened.

Respond to Literature

What does the popularity of Douglass's writings reveal about the changing attitude toward slavery at the time?

THINK ABOUT AUTOBIOGRAPHY

An **autobiography** is the history of a person's life, written by him- or herself. It is a narrative. A well-written autobiography tells of the inner struggles of the author, interprets the events in light of history, and draws thoughtful conclusions about life in general.

1. Why is an autobiography written in narrative form?

2. Do you think Douglass's characterization of Mrs. Auld was accurate? Why or why not?

3. Douglass could not read Mrs. Auld's mind. On what could he judge what she might be thinking?

4. Do you agree that first-person point of view is appropriate for an autobiography? Why or why not?

5. Why do you think learning to read was so important to Douglass?

READING FOCUS

Make Inferences As you read the excerpt from *My Bondage and My Freedom*, you were asked to make inferences about different aspects of the narrative. What inference did you make about how Douglass felt about Mrs. Auld? Tell which details from the autobiography helped you to make this inference.

DEVELOP YOUR VOCABULARY

Nouns can be classified in various ways. One useful distinction is between concrete and abstract nouns. **Concrete nouns** name things that exist in the physical world. The things they name can be felt, seen, heard, smelled, or tasted. Examples are *wind, mountain, horn, perfume, soup*. **Abstract nouns** name ideas, qualities, or characteristics that do not exist physically and cannot be recognized by the senses. Examples are *liberty, beauty, kindness*.

Frederick Douglass used many abstract nouns in his autobiography. List the following words from the Douglass selection. Beside each word write whether it is *concrete* or *abstract*.

1. slaveholder
2. humanity
3. freedom
4. conscience
5. newspaper
6. playmate
7. prudence
8. schoolbook
9. slavery
10. joy

Learn About

Sojourner Truth, 1864. The Granger Collection

READING FOCUS

Understand Persuasive Techniques
Writers sometimes try to persuade readers to agree with their opinions by appealing to the readers' emotions. Persuasive techniques, such as appealing to the readers' emotions, can be very effective. Think about the emotions the author is appealing to as you read.

PERSUASION

Have you ever tried to persuade your parents that you need new, more expensive tennis shoes? Have you ever tried to convince a teacher that you deserve a higher grade? Did you use supporting statements or arguments to back up your appeal? Then you have used a form of discourse called **persuasion**.

The purpose of persuasion is to convince readers or listeners of the truth or falsity of a proposition. A **proposition** is a statement of what is supported or upheld. In your persuasive appeals, the propositions would have been something like: "I need new shoes" or "I should get a better grade." Then you would have given some arguments that your statements were true.

As you read this selection, ask yourself:

1. What proposition is Sojourner Truth trying to uphold?
2. Why do you think she repeats the question in the title so often? What is the purpose of repetition?

WRITING CONNECTION

Assume that you are running for the office of class president. Write a paragraph showing that you are the best person for the job. Include facts to support your propositions.

AIN'T I A WOMAN?

by Sojourner Truth

Well, children, where there is so much racket there must be something out of kilter. I think that 'twixt the Negroes of the South and the women at the North, all talking about rights, the white men will be in a fix pretty soon. But what's all this here talking about?

That man over there says that women need to be helped into carriages, and lifted over ditches, and to have the best place everywhere. Nobody ever helps me into carriages, or over mud-puddles, or gives me any best place! And ain't I a woman? Look at me! Look at my arm! I have ploughed and planted, and gathered into barns, and no man could head me! And ain't I a woman? I could work as much and eat as much as a man—when I could get it—and bear the lash as well! And ain't I a woman? I have borne thirteen children, and seen most all sold off to slavery, and when I cried out with my mother's grief, none but Jesus heard me! And ain't I a woman?

Then they talk about this thing in the head; what's this they call it? ("Intellect," whispered someone near.) That's it, honey. What's that got to do with women's rights or Negroes' rights? If my cup won't hold but a pint, and yours holds a quart, wouldn't you be mean not to let me have my little half-measure full?

Then that little man in black there, he says women can't have as much rights as men, 'cause Christ wasn't a woman! Where did your Christ come from? Where did your Christ come from? From God and a woman! Man had nothing to do with Him.

If the first woman God ever made was strong enough to turn the world upside down all alone, these women together ought to be able to turn it back, and get it right side up again! And now they is asking to do it, the men better let them.

Obliged to you for hearing me, and now old Sojourner ain't got nothing more to say.

---

kilter (KIL tur) good condition; proper order
ploughed (PLOUD) plowed; made furrows in the soil
lash (LASH) whip

Review the Selection

UNDERSTAND THE SELECTION

Recall

1. How many children did Sojourner Truth have?

2. What happened to her children?

3. Who does Truth believe can straighten out the world?

Infer

4. Who is Sojourner Truth?

5. What do you think Truth really means when she asks, "Ain't I a woman?"

6. What group of women does Truth represent in expressing her feelings?

7. Why does she believe she should have as many rights as men?

Apply

8. Assume a loved one is sold into slavery. How would you react?

9. Suppose you live in the nineteenth century. You hear Truth give her speech. How does the audience react?

10. Do you think Truth presented a persuasive argument? Explain.

Respond to Literature

In what way does this selection illustrate the sentiments toward African Americans and women during the nineteenth century?

THINK ABOUT PERSUASION

Like Patrick Henry's and George Washington's speeches in Unit 1, Sojourner Truth's "Ain't I a Woman?" was originally an oration. An **oration** is a speech that is meant to inspire listeners to take some action. The orator appeals to the listener's intelligence but also to the listener's emotions.

1. What does Sojourner Truth accomplish by the constant repetition of her title question?

2. A rhetorical question is asked for its effect on the audience; it does not require an answer. Find at least one rhetorical question, other than the title question, in Truth's speech.

3. Does Truth's use of *ain't* and other colloquial words and phrases add to or detract from the effect of her speech? Explain your answer.

4. Which argument do you think is Truth's most effective one? Why?

5. Which aspect of Truth's speech made the stronger impression on you—her reasons or her emotional appeal? Explain your answer.

READING FOCUS

Understand Persuasive Techniques Sojourner Truth made several powerful points to appeal to the audience's emotions. Choose the point you found most compelling and explain why it made an impact on you.

DEVELOP YOUR VOCABULARY

Many words have more than one meaning. When you read these words, it is always important to understand which meaning the author intends. For example, the word *racket* can have several different meanings. In this selection, *racket* means loud, confused talk. What other meanings can it have? If a word appears to be familiar, but the meaning does not make sense in a sentence, look in a dictionary for another meaning that does make sense. By paying close attention to context clues, you will be able to figure out the correct meaning.

Following are common words that have more than one meaning. Read the list, then think of two meanings for each word. Check your meanings in a dictionary. Then, write an original sentence for each meaning of each word. Be sure that your sentences make it clear which of its meanings the word is carrying.

1. racket
2. ball
3. board
4. foot
5. band
6. ring
7. fork
8. address
9. kind
10. strike

Learn About

The Legend of Sleepy Hollow, Anonymous.
Corbis Bettmann

READING FOCUS

Identify Hyperbole Hyperbole is an exaggerated statement often used to suggest that something is greater than it really is. An example is: "better than Mom's apple pie." Hyperbole is often found in figures of speech that compare two things, such as "my love burns brighter than the stars above."

As you read, look for instances where the author is comparing two things. Then decide if it is an exaggeration, or hyperbole. Ask yourself: Does the exaggeration make the situation humorous? Does it heighten the suspense about what will happen next?

PLOT

Plot is the series of events that make up the story line of a literary work. Conflict and climax are two main elements of plot.

Conflict is a clash between two opposing forces. The clash provides the dramatic action. The opposing forces may be two people—the protagonist, or main character, and an antagonist, or rival character. Sometimes the opposing forces are the main character and nature, or the main character and different impulses in his or her own mind.

The main character's attempts to resolve the conflict advance the plot toward the climax. The **climax** is the decisive turning point in the action. It is the moment when the character begins to resolve the conflict. The climax is followed by the **dénouement**, the final resolution, or outcome.

For the next selection, ask yourself:
1. Who is the protagonist?
2. Who is the antagonist?

WRITING CONNECTION

Summarize the plot of a movie you have seen recently. Name the protagonist, and explain the conflict and its resolution.

from

THE LEGEND OF
Sleepy Hollow

by Washington Irving
FOUND AMONG THE PAPERS
OF THE LATE DIEDRICH KNICKERBOCKER

In the bosom of one of those spacious coves which indent the eastern shore of the Hudson, at that broad expansion of the river denominated by the ancient Dutch navigators the Tappan Zee, and where they always prudently shortened sail and implored the protection of St. Nicholas when they crossed, there lies a small market-town or rural port, which by some is called Greensburgh, but which is more generally and properly known by the name of Tarry Town. This name was given, we are told, in former days, by the good housewives of the adjacent country, from the inveterate propensity of their husbands to linger about the village tavern on market days. Be that as it may, I do not vouch for the fact, but merely advert to it, for the sake of being precise and authentic. Not far from this village, perhaps about two miles, there is a little valley, or rather lap of land among high hills, which is one of the quietest places in the whole world. A small brook glides through it, with just murmur enough to lull one to repose; and the occasional whistle of a quail, or tapping of a woodpecker, is almost the only sound that ever breaks in upon the uniform tranquillity.

I recollect that, when a stripling, my first exploit in squirrel-shooting was in a grove of tall walnut-trees that shade one side of the valley. I had wandered into it at noon time, when all nature is peculiarly quiet, and was startled by the roar of my own gun, as it broke the Sabbath stillness around, and was prolonged and reverberated by the angry echoes. If ever I should wish for a retreat, whither I might steal from the world and its distractions, and dream quietly away the remnant of a troubled live, I know of none more promising than this little valley.

[The narrator explains that this area is called Sleepy Hollow because of its "listless repose." The people of the area are "given to all kinds of marvellous beliefs," including one in a ghost called "the Headless Horseman of Sleepy Hollow."]

In this by-place of nature, there abode, in a remote period of American history, that is to say, some thirty years since, a worthy wight of the name of Ichabod Crane; who sojourned, or, as he expressed it, "tarried," in Sleepy Hollow, for the purpose of instructing the children of the vicinity. He was a native of Connecticut; a State which supplies the Union with pioneers for the mind as well for the forest, and sends forth yearly its legions of frontier woodsmen and country schoolmasters. The cognomen of Crane was not inapplicable to his person. He was tall, but exceedingly lank, with narrow shoulders, long arms and legs, hands that dangled a mile out of his sleeves, feet that might have served for shovels, and his whole frame most loosely hung together. His head was small, and flat at top, with huge ears, large green glassy eyes, and a long snipe nose so that it looked like a weathercock, perched upon his spindle neck, to tell which way the wind blew. To see him striding along the profile of a hill on a windy day, with his clothes bagging and fluttering about him, one might have mistaken him for the genius of famine descending upon the earth, or some scarecrow eloped from a cornfield.

His school-house was a low building of one large room, rudely constructed of logs; the windows partly glazed, and partly patched with leaves of old copy-books. It was most ingeniously secured at vacant hours, by a withe twisted in the handle of the door, and stakes set against the window shutter so that, though a thief might get in with perfect ease, he would find some embarrassment in getting out; and idea most probably borrowed by the architect, Yost Van Houten, from the mystery of an eel-pot. The school-house stood in a rather lonely but pleasant situation, just at the foot of a woody hill, with a brook running close by, and a formidable birch tree growing at one end of it. From hence the low murmur of his pupils' voices, conning over their lessons, might be heard in a drowsy summer's day, like the hum of a bee-hive; interrupted now and then by the authoritative voice of the master, in the tone of menace or command; or, peradventure, by the appalling sound of the birch, as he urged some tardy loiterer along the flowery path of knowledge. Truth to say, he was a conscientious man, and ever bore in mind the golden maxim, "Spare the rod and spoil the child."—Ichabod Crane's scholars certainly were not spoiled.

[As was the custom, Ichabod Crane boarded a week at a time with farmers whose children he taught. He did light chores around the farms and tended the youngest children "rendering himself both useful and agreeable." To add to his income, he gave singing lessons, though his own voice was a piercing, nasal quaver.]

The schoolmaster is generally a man of some importance in the female circle of a

---

wight (WHYT) human being
cognomen (kog NOH men) name
withe (WITH) flexible branch or twig
peradventure (PURR ad VEN chur) archaic word for *perhaps*

rural neighborhood; being considered a kind of idle gentlemanlike personage, of vastly superior taste and accomplishment to the rough country swains, and, indeed, inferior in learning only to the parson. His appearance, therefore, is apt to occasion some little stir at the tea-table of a farmhouse, and the addition of a supernumerary dish of cakes or sweetmeats, or, peradventure, the parade of a silver tea-pot. Our man of letters, therefore, was peculiarly happy in the smiles of all the country damsels. How he would figure among them in the church-yard, between services on Sundays! gathering grapes for them from the wild vines that overrun the surrounding trees; reciting for their amusement all the epitaphs on the tombstones; or sauntering, with a whole bevy of them, along the banks of the adjacent mill-pond; while the more bashful country bumpkins hung sheepishly back, envying his superior elegance and address.

From his half-itinerant life, also, he was a kind of travelling gazette, carrying the whole budget of local gossip from house to house, so that his appearance was always greeted with satisfaction. He was, moreover, esteemed by the women as a man of great erudition, for he had read several books quite through, and was a perfect master of Cotton Mather's[1] "History of New England Witchcraft," in which, by the way, he most firmly and potently believed.

He was, in fact, an odd mixture of small shrewdness and simple credulity. His appetite for the marvellous, and his powers of digesting it, were equally extraordinary; and both had been increased by his residence in this spell-bound region. No tale was too gross or monstrous for his capacious swallow.

[Ichabod, in addition to reading "old Mather's direful tales," liked to listen to the farm wives' "marvellous tales of ghosts and goblins, and haunted houses, and particularly of the headless horseman." He paid for these pleasures by imagining "terrors" on his "subsequent walk homewards." But these fears ended in daylight, and Ichabod had a pleasant life until he met "a being that causes more perplexity to mortal man than ghosts, goblins, and the whole race of witches put together, and that was—a woman."]

Among the musical disciples who assembled, one evening in each week, to receive his instructions in psalmody, was Katrina Van Tassel, the daughter and only child of a substantial Dutch farmer. She was a blooming lass of fresh eighteen; plump as a partridge; ripe and melting and rosy cheeked as one of her father's peaches, and universally famed, not merely for her beauty, but her vast expectations. She was withal a little of a coquette, as might be perceived even in her dress, which was a mixture of ancient and modern fashions, as most suited to set

---

supernumerary (SOO per NOO mer AIRY) extra
[1]**Cotton Mather** Puritan clergyman who wrote two works about witchcraft: *Memorable Providences, Relating to Witchcraft and Possessions* and *The Wonders of the Invisible World*
credulity (kreh DOO lih tee) willingness to believe readily without proof; gullibility
coquette (co KETT) flirt

from The Legend of Sleepy Hollow ■ 83

off her charms. She wore the ornaments of pure yellow gold, which her great-great-grandmother had brought over from Saardam; the tempting stomacher of the olden time; and withal a provokingly short petticoat, to display the prettiest foot and ankle in the country round.

Ichabod Crane had a soft and foolish heart towards the sex; and it is not to be wondered at, that so tempting a morsel soon found favor in his eyes; more especially after he had visited her in her paternal mansion. Old Baltus van Tassel was a perfect picture of a thriving, contented, liberal-hearted farmer. He seldom, it is true, sent either his eyes or his thoughts beyond the boundaries of his own farm; but within those every thing was snug, happy, and well-conditioned. He was satisfied with his wealth, but not proud of it; and piqued himself upon the hearty abundance, rather than the style in which he lived.

[The narrator gives a detailed description of the Van Tassel farm.]

The pedagogue's mouth watered, as he looked upon this sumptuous promise of luxurious winter fare. In his devouring mind's eye, he pictured to himself every roasting-pig running about with a pudding in his belly, and an apple in his mouth; the pigeons were snugly put to bed in a comfortable pie, and tucked in with a coverlet of crust; the geese were swimming in their own gravy; and the ducks pairing cosily in dishes, like snug married couples, with a decent competency on onion sauce. In the porkers he saw carved out the future sleek side of bacon, and juicy relishing ham; not a turkey but he beheld daintily trussed up, with its gizzard under its wing, and, peradventure, a necklace of savory sausages; and even bright chanticleer himself lay sprawling on his back, in a side dish, with uplifted claws, as if craving that quarter which his chivalrous spirit disdained to ask while living.

As the enraptured Ichabod fancied all this, and as he rolled his great green eyes over the fat meadow-lands, the rich fields of wheat, of rye, of buckwheat, and Indian corn, and the orchards burthened with ruddy fruit, which surrounded the warm tenement of Van Tassel, his heart yearned after the damsel who was to inherit these domains, and his imagination expanded with the idea, how they might be readily turned into cash, and the money invested in immense tracts of wild land, and shingle palaces in the wilderness. Nay, his busy fancy already realized his hopes, and presented to him the blooming Katrina, with a whole family of children, mounted on top of a wagon loaded with household trumpery, with pots and kettles dangling beneath;

---

stomacher (STUM uhk ur) a decorated garment worn over the stomach and chest
piqued (PEEKED) archaic meaning: *prided himself*
pedagogue (PED ah gog) teacher
chanticleer (SHAHN tih cleer) rooster
quarter (KWAR tur) mercy or indulgence
burthened (BURR thend) archaic word for *burdened*
tenement (TEN uh ment) archaic meaning: *residence* or *habitation*

and he beheld himself bestriding a pacing mare, with a colt at her heels, setting out for Kentucky, Tennessee, or the Lord knows where.

[*Once Ichabod sees inside the house, which is described in detail, "his only study was how to gain the affections of the peerless daughter of Van Tassel". However, he has rivals in Katrina's "numerous rustic admirer's."*]

Among the most formidable [competitors] was a burly, roaring, roistering blade, of the name of Abraham, or, according to the Dutch abbreviation, Brom Van Brunt, the hero of the country round, which rang with his feats of strength and hardihood. He was broad-shouldered and double-jointed, with short curly black hair, and a bluff, but not unpleasant countenance, having a mingled air of fun and arrogance. From his Herculean frame and great powers of limb, he had received the nickname of Brom Bones, by which he was universally known. He was famed for great knowledge and skill in horsemanship, being as dexterous on horseback as a Tartar.[2] He was foremost at all races and cock-fights; and, with the ascendancy which bodily strength acquires in rustic life, was the umpire in all disputes, setting his hat on one side, and giving his decisions with an air and tone admitting of no gainsay or appeal. He was always ready for either a fight or a frolic; but had more mischief than ill-will in his composition; and, with all his overbearing roughness, there was a strong dash of waggish good humor at bottom.

[*Brom Bones and his companions dash around to every "feud or merriment" in the countryside. When any "madcap prank or rustic brawl occurred, the neighbors good-naturedly "always shook their heads, and warranted Brom Bones was at the bottom of it." Brom courted Katrina, causing other suitors to stay away from her because they did not want to "cross a lion in his amours."*]

Such was the formidable rival with whom Ichabod Crane had to contend, and, considering all things, a stouter man than he would have shrunk from the competition, and a wiser man would have despaired. He had, however, a happy mixture of pliability and perseverance in his nature; he was in form and spirit like a supple-jack[3]—yielding, but tough; though he bent, he never broke; and though he bowed beneath the slightest pressure, yet, the moment it was away—jerk! he was as erect, and carried his head high as ever.

To have taken the field openly against his rival would have been madness; for he was not a man to be thwarted in his amours, any more than that stormy lover, Achilles.[4] Ichabod, therefore, made his advances in a quiet and gently-insinuating manner. Under cover of his character of

---

roistering (ROY stir ing) swaggering, unrestrained
blade (BLAYD) dashing, jaunty, young man
[2]**Tartar** fierce Mongolian warrior of the 13th century
gainsay (GAYN say) denying or opposing
[3]**supple-jack** a strong woody vine
[4]**Achilles** hero of Homer's *Iliad* who became enraged when Agamemnon stole his love, Briseis

singing-master, he made frequent visits at the farmhouse.

[*Ichabod "would carry on his suit with the daughter" while her parents were busy around the farm. Katrina's interest in Brom Bones seemed to decline "from the moment Ichabod Crane made his advances" and a feud arose between the two suitors. Brom would have preferred "open warfare" but Ichabod avoided giving him any opportunity for a fight, so Brom began playing practical jokes on Ichabod. This situation continues until one day Ichabod receives an invitation to a "merry-making" at the Van Tassel farm. He dismisses school early.*]

The gallant Ichabod bow spent at least an extra half hour at his toilet, brushing and furbishing up his best, and indeed only suit of rusty black, and arranging his looks by a bit of broken looking-glass, that hung up in the school-house. That he might make his appearance before his mistress in the true style of a cavalier, he borrowed a horse from the farmer with whom he was domiciliated, a choleric old Dutchman, of the name of Hans van Ripper, and, thus gallantly mounted, issued forth, like a knight-errant in quest of adventures. But it is meet I should, in the true spirit of romantic story, give some account of the looks and equipment of my hero and his steed. The animal he bestrode was a broken-down plough-horse, that had outlived almost every thing but his viciousness. He was gaunt and shagged, with a ewe neck and a head like a hammer; his rusty mane and tail were tangled and knotted with burrs; one ye had lost its pupil, and was glaring and spectral; but the other had the

gleam of a genuine devil in it. Still he must have had fire and mettle in his day, if we may judge from the name he bore of Gunpowder. He had, in fact, been a favorite steed of his masters, the choleric Van Ripper, who was a furious rider, and had infused, very probably, some of his own spirit into the animal; for old and broken-down as he looked, there was more of the lurking devil in him than in any young filly in the country.

Ichabod was a suitable figure for such a steed. He rode with short stirrups, which brought his knees nearly up to the pommel of the saddle; his sharp elbows stuck out like grasshoppers'; he carried his whip perpendicularly in his hand, like a sceptre, and as his horse jogged on, the motion of his arms was not unlike the flapping of a pair of wings. A small wool hat rested on the top of his nose, for so his scanty strip of forehead might be called; and the skirts of his black coat fluttered out almost to the horse's tail. Such was the appearance of Ichabod and his steed, as they shambled out of the gate of Hans Van Riper, and it was altogether such an apparitions as seldom to be met with in broad daylight.

[*The narrator now describes the "fine autumnal day" and the abundance of the fields ready for harvest. As he rides to the party, Ichabod daydreams of the riches he will gain when he marries Katrina. When he arrives at the Van Tassel "castle," he finds it "thronged" with guests wearing their best, "homespun" clothes.*]

Brom Bones, however, was the hero of the scene, having come to the gathering on his favorite steed, Daredevil, a creature like himself, full of mettle and mischief, and which no one but himself could manage. He was, in fact, noted for preferring vicious animals, given to all kinds of tricks, which kept the rider in constant risk of his neck, for he held a tractable well-broken horse as unworthy of a lad of spirit.

[There is a brief description of "the ample charms of a genuine Dutch country tea-table" because the narrator is "too eager to get on with" the story. Ichabod "did ample justice to every dainty," while he thought about how all the "luxury and splendor" might be his. Baltus Van Tassel, an affable host, encourages his guests to eat, and then has a fiddler play so guests can dance.]

Ichabod prided himself upon his dancing as much as upon his vocal powers. Not a limb, not a fibre about him was idle' and to have seen his loosely hung frame in full motion, and clattering about the room, you would have thought Saint Vitus[5] himself, that blessed patron of the dance, was figuring before you in person....how could the flogger of urchins be otherwise than animated and joyous? The lady of his heart was his partner in the dance, and smiling graciously in reply to all his amorous oglings; while Brom Bones, sorely smitten with love and jealousy, sat brooding by himself in one corner.

When the dance was at an end, Ichabod was attracted to a knot of the sager folks, who, with old Van Tassel, sat smoking at one end of the piazza, gossiping over former times, and drawing out long stories about the war.

Ichabod Crane and Katrina Van Tassel, George Henry Boughton. New York Historical Society, New York

[Several guests exaggerate their experiences during the Revolutionary War.]

But all these were nothing to the tales of ghosts and apparitions that succeeded. The neighborhood is rich in legendary treasures of the kind. Local tales and superstitions thrive best in these sheltered long-settled retreats; but are trampled under foot by the shifting throng that forms the population of most of our country places. Besides, there is no encouragement for ghosts in most of our villages, for they have scarcely had time to finish their first nap, and turn themselves in their graves, before their surviving friends have travelled away from the neighborhood; so that when they turn out at night to walk their rounds, they have no acquaintance left to call upon. This is perhaps the reason why we so seldom

---

[5]**Saint Vitus** patron saint of people suffering from chorea, a nervous disease that causes involuntary jerking called "St. Vitus's Dance"

hear of ghosts except in our long-established Dutch communities.

The immediate cause, however, of the prevalence of supernatural stories in these parts, was doubtless owing to the vicinity of Sleepy Hollow. There was a contagion in the very air that blew from that haunted region; it breathed forth an atmosphere of dreams and fancies infecting all the land. Several of the Sleepy Hollow people were present at Van Tassel's and, as usual, were doling out their wild and wonderful legends. Many dismal tales were told about funeral trains, and mourning cries and wailings heard and seen about the great tree where the unfortunate Major Andre[6] was taken, and which stood in the neighborhood. Some mention was made also of the woman in white, that haunted the ark glen at Raven Rock, and was often heard to shriek on winter nights before a storm, having perished there in the snow. The chief part of the stories, however, turned upon the favorite spectre of Sleepy Hollow, the headless horseman, who had been heard several times of late, patrolling the country; and, it was said, tethered his horse nightly among the graves in the churchyard.

The sequestered situation of this church seems always to have made it a favorite haunt of troubled spirits. It stands on a knoll, surrounded by locust-trees and lofty elms, from among which its decent whitewashed walls shine modestly forth, like Christian purity beaming through the shades of retirement. A gentle slope descends from it to a silver sheet of water, bordered by high trees, between which, peeps may be caught at the blue hills of the Hudson. To look upon its grass-grown yard, where the sunbeams seem to sleep so quietly, one would think that there at least the dead might rest in peace. On one side of the church extends a wide woody dell, along which raves a large brook among broken rocks and trunks of fallen trees. Over a deep black part of the stream, not far from the church, was formerly thrown a wooden bridge; the road that led to it, and the bridge itself, were thickly shaded by overhanging trees, which cast a gloom about it, even in the daytime; but occasioned a fearful darkness at night. This was one of the favorite haunts of the headless horseman; and the place where he was most frequently encountered. The tale was told of old Brouwer, a most heretical disbeliever in ghosts, how he met the horseman returning from his foray into Sleepy Hollow, and was obliged to get up behind him; how they galloped over bush and brake, over hill and swamp, until they reached the bridge; when the horseman suddenly turned into a skeleton, threw old Brouwer into the brook, and sprang away over the tree-tops with a clap of thunder.

This story was immediately matched by a thrice marvellous adventure of Brom

---

[6]**Major Andre** John Andre was a British spy hanged during the Revolutionary War.
sequestered (suh QUEST erd) secluded; sheltered; withdrawn

Bones, who made light of the galloping Hessian[7] as an arrant jockey. He affirmed that, on returning one night from the neighboring village of Sing Sing, he had been overtaken by this midnight trooper; that he had offered to race with him for a bowl of punch, and should have won it too, for Daredevil beat the goblin horse all hollow, but just as they came to the church bridge, the Hessian bolted, and vanished in a flash of fire.

All these tales, told in that drowsy undertone with which men talk in the dark, the countenances of the listeners only now and then receiving a casual gleam from the glare of a pipe, sank deep in the mind of Ichabod. He repaid them in kind with large extracts from his invaluable author, Cotton Mather, and added many marvellous events that had taken place in his native State of Connecticut, and fearful sights which he had seen in his nightly walks about Sleepy Hollow.

The revel now gradually broke up. The old farmers gathered together their families in their wagons, and were heard for some time rattling along the hollow roads, and over the distant hills. Some of the damsels mounted on pillions behind their favorite swains, and their light-hearted laughter, mingling with the clatter of hoofs, echoed along the silent woodlands, sounding fainter and fainter until they gradually died away—and the late scene of noise and frolic was all silent and deserted. Ichabod only lingered behind according to the custom of country lovers, to have a tete-a-tete with the heiress, fully convinced that he was now on the high road to success. What passed at this interview I will not pretend to say, for in fact I do not know. Something, however, I fear me, must have gone wrong, for he certainly sallied forth, after no very great interval, with an air quite desolate and chip-fallen.—Oh these women! these women! Could that girl have been playing off any of her coquettish tricks?—Was her encouragement of the poor pedagogue all a mere sham to secure her conquest of his rival?—Heaven only knows, not I!—Let it suffice to say, Ichabod stole forth with the air of one who had been sacking a hen-roost, rather than a fair lady's heart. Without looking to the right or left to notice the scene of rural wealth, on which he had so often gloated, he went straight to the stable, and with several hearty cuffs and kicks, roused his steed most uncourteously from the comfortable quarters in which he was soundly sleeping, dreaming of mountains of corn and oats, and whole valleys of timothy and clover.

It was the very witching time of night that Ichabod, heavy-hearted and crest-fallen, pursued his travel homewards, along the sides of the lofty hills which rise above Tarry Town, and which he had traversed so cheerily in the afternoon. The hour was as dismal as himself. Far below him, the

---

[7]**Hessian** German mercenary hired by the British to fight during the American Revolution
arrant (AIR int) bare-faced; out-and-out
jockey (JOCK ee) cheater
pillions (PILL yons) cushions for a passenger behind the saddle
swains (SWAYNS) suitors; boyfriends
tête-a-tête (TET ah TET) private conversation

Tappan Zee spread its dusky and indistinct waste of waters, with here and there the tall mast of a sloop, riding quietly at anchor under the land. In the dead hush of midnight, he could even hear the barking of the watch dog from the opposite shore of the Hudson; but it was so vague and faint as only to give an idea of his distance from this faithful companion of a man. Now and then, too, the long-drawn crowing of a cock, accidentally wakened, would sound far, far off, from some farmhouse away among the hills— but it was like a dreaming sound in his ear. No signs of life occurred near him, but occasionally the melancholy chirp of a cricket, or perhaps the guttural twang of a bull-frog, from a neighboring marsh, as if sleeping uncomfortably, and turning suddenly in his bed.

All the stories of ghosts and goblins that he had heard in the afternoon, now came crowding upon his recollection. The night grew darker and darker, the stars seemed to sink deeper in the sky, and driving clouds occasionally hid them from his sight. He had never felt so lonely and dismal. He was, moreover, approaching the very place where many of the scenes of the ghost stories had been laid. In the centre of the road stood an enormous tulip-tree, which towered like a giant above all the other trees of the neighborhood, and formed a kind of landmark. Its limbs were gnarled, and fantastic, large enough to form trunks for ordinary trees, twisting down almost to the earth, and rising again into the air. It was connected with the tragical story of the unfortunate Andre who had been taken prisoner hard by; and was universally known by the name of Major Andre's tree. The common people regarded it with a mixture of respect and superstition, partly out of sympathy for the fate of its ill-starred namesake, and partly from the tales of strange sights and doleful lamentations told concerning it.

As Ichabod approached this fearful tree, he began to whistle: he thought his whistle was answered—it was but a blast sweeping sharply through the dry branches. As he approached a little nearer, he thought he saw something white, hanging in the midst of the tree—he paused and ceased whistling; but on looking more narrowly, perceived that it was a place where the tree had been scathed by lightning, and the white wood laid bare. Suddenly he heard a grown— his teeth chattered and his knees smote against the saddle: it was but the rubbing of one huge bough upon another, as they were swayed about by the breeze. He passed the tree in safety, but new perils lay before him.

About two hundred yards from the tree a small brook crossed the road, and ran into a marshy and thickly-wooded glen, known by the name of Wiley's swamp. A few rough logs, laid side by side, served for a bridge over this stream. On that side of the road where the brook entered the wood, a group of oaks and chestnuts, matted thick with wild grapevines, threw a cavernous gloom over it. To pass this bridge was the severest trial. It was at this identical spot that the unfortunate Andre was captured, and under the covert of those chestnuts and

Mahantango Valley Farm c. 1860. Anonymous. The Granger Collection

vines were the sturdy yeomen concealed who surprised him. This has ever since been considered a haunted stream, and fearful are the feelings of the schoolboy who has to pass it alone after dark.

As he approached the stream his heart began to thump; he summoned up, however, all his resolution, gave his horse half a score of kicks in the ribs, and attempted to dash briskly across the bridge; but instead of starting forward, the perverse old animal made a lateral movement, and ran broadside against the fence. Ichabod, whose fears increased with the delay, jerked the reins on the other side, and kicked lustily with the contrary foot: it was all in vain; his steed started, it is true, but it was only to plunge to the opposite side of the road into a thicket of brambles and alder bushes. The schoolmaster now bestowed the whip and heel upon the starveling ribs of old Gunpowder, who

dashed forward, snuffling and snorting, but came to a stand just by the bridge with a suddenness that had nearly sent his rider sprawling over his head. Just at this moment a plashy tramp by the side of the bridge caught the sensitive ear of Ichabod. In the dark shadow of the grove, on the margin of the brook, he beheld something huge, misshapen, black and towering. It stirred not, but seemed gathered up in the gloom, like some gigantic monster ready to spring upon the traveller.

The hair of the affrighted pedagogue rose upon his head with terror. What was to be done? To turn and fly was now too late; and besides, what chance was there of escaping ghost or goblin, if such it was, which could ride upon the wings of the wind? Summoning up, therefore, a show of courage, he demanded in stammering accents—"Who are you?" He received no reply. He repeated his demand in a still

---

tramp (TRAMP) sound of a heavy footstep

more agitated voice. Still there was no answer. Once more he cudgelled the sides of the inflexible Gunpowder, and, shutting his eyes, broke forth with involuntary fervor into a psalm tune. Just then the shadowy object of alarm put itself in motion, and, with a scramble and a bound, stood at once in the middle of the road. Though the night was dark and dismal, yet the form of the unknown might now in some degree be ascertained. He appeared to be a horseman of large dimensions, and mounted on a black horse of powerful frame. He made no offer of molestation or sociability, but kept aloof on one side of the road, jogging along on the blind side of old Gunpowder, who had now got over his fright and waywardness.

Ichabod, who had no relish for this strange midnight companion, and bethought himself of the adventure of Brom Bones with the Galloping Hessian, now quickened his steed, in hopes of leaving him behind. The stranger, however, quickened his horse to an equal pace. Ichabod pulled up, and fell into a walk, thinking to lag behind—the other did the same. His heart began to sink within him; he endeavored to resume his psalm tune, but his parched tongue clove to the roof of his mouth, and he could not utter a stave. There was something in the moody and dogged silence of this pertinacious companion that was mysterious and appalling. It was soon fearfully accounted for. On mounting a rising ground, which brought the figure of his fellow-traveller in relief against the sky, gigantic in height, and muffled in a cloak, Ichabod was horror-struck, on perceiving that he was headless!— but his horror was still more increased, on observing that the head, which should have rested on his shoulders, was carried before him on the pommel of the saddle: his terror rose to desperation; he rained a shower of kicks and blows upon Gunpowder, hoping by a sudden movement, to give his companion the slip—but the spectre started full jump with him. Away then they dashed, through thick and thin; stones flying, and sparks flashing at every bound. Ichabod's flimsy garments fluttered in the air, as he stretched his long lank body away over his horse's head, in the eagerness of his flight.

They had now reached the road which turns off to Sleepy Hollow; but Gunpowder, who seemed possessed with a demon, instead of keeping up it, made an opposite turn, and plunged headlong down hill to the left. This road leads through a sandy hollow, shaded by trees for about a quarter of a mile, where it crossed the bridge famous in the goblin story, and just beyond swells the green knoll on which stands the whitewashed church.

As yet the panic of the steed had given his unskillful rider an apparent advantage in the chase; but just as he had got half way through the hollow, the girths of the saddle gave way, and he felt it slipping from under him. He seized it by the pommel, and endeavored to hold it firm, but in vain; and had just time to save himself by clasping old Gunpowder round the neck, when the saddle fell to the earth and he heard it trampled under foot by his pursuer. For a moment the terror of Hans Ban Ripper's wrath passed across his mind—

for it was his Sunday saddle; but this was no time for petty fears; the goblin was hard on his haunches; and (unskillful rider that he was!) he had much ado to maintain his seat; sometimes slipping on one side, sometimes on another, and sometimes jolted on the high ridge of his horse's back-bone, with a violence that he verily feared would cleave him asunder.

An opening in the trees now cheered him with the hopes that the church bridge was at hand. The wavering reflection of a silver star in the bosom of the brook told him that he was not mistaken. He saw the walls of the church dimly glaring under the trees beyond. He recollected the place where Brom Bones's ghostly competitor had disappeared. "If I can but reach that bridge," thought Ichabod, "I am safe." Just then he heard the black steed panting and blowing close behind him; he even fancied that he felt his hot breath. Another convulsive kick in the ribs, and old Gunpowder sprang upon the bridge; he thundered over the resounding planks; he gained the opposite side; and now Ichabod cast a look behind to see if his pursuer should vanish, according to rule, in a flash of fire and brimstone. Just then he saw the goblin rising in his stirrups, and in the very act of hurling his head at him. Ichabod endeavored to dodge the horrible missile, but too late. It encountered his cranium with a tremendous crash—he was tumbled headlong into the dust, and Gunpowder, the black steed, and the goblin rider passed by like a whirlwind.

The next morning the old horse was found without his saddle, and with the bridle under his feet, soberly cropping the grass at his master's gate. Ichabod did not make his appearance at breakfast—dinner-hour came, but no Ichabod. The boys assembled at the school-house, and strolled idly about the banks of the brook, but no schoolmaster. Hans Van Ripper now began to feel some uneasiness about the fate of poor Ichabod, and his saddle. And inquiry was set on foot, and after diligent investigations they came upon his traces. In one part of the road leading to the church was found the saddle trampled in the dirt; the tracks of horses' hoofs deeply dented in the road, and evidently at furious speed, were traced to the bridge, beyond which, on the bank of a broad part of the brook, where the water ran deep and black, was found the hat of the unfortunate Ichabod, and close beside it was a shattered pumpkin.

The brook was searched, but the body of the schoolmaster was not to be discovered. Hans Van Ripper, as executor of his estate, examined the bundle which contained all his worldly effects. They consisted of two shirts and a half; two stocks for the neck; a pair or two of worsted stockings; and old pair of corduroy small-clothes; a rusty razor; a book of psalm tunes, full of dog's ears; and a broken pitchpipe. As to the books and furniture of the school-house, they belonged to the community, excepting Cotton Mather's "History of Witchcraft," a New England almanac, and a book of dreams and fortune-telling; in which last was sheet of foolscap much scribbled and blotted in

---

small-clothes (SMALL CLOTHZ) knee breeches

several fruitless attempts to make a copy of verses in honor of the heiress of Van Tassel. These magic books and the poetic scrawl were forthwith consigned to the flames by Hans Van Ripper; who from that time forward determined to send his children no more to school, observing, that he never know any good come of this same reading and writing. Whatever money the schoolmaster possessed, and he had received his quarter's pay but a day or two before, he must have had about his person at the time of his disappearance.

The mysterious event caused much speculation at the church on the following Sunday. Knots of gazers and gossips were collected in the church-yard, at the bridge, and at the spot where the hat and pumpkin had been found. The stories of Brouwer, of Bones, and a whole budget of others, were called to mind; and when they had diligently considered them all, and compared them with the symptoms of the present case they shook their heads, and came to the conclusion that Ichabod had been carried off by the galloping Hessian. As he was a bachelor, and in nobody's debt, nobody troubled his head any more about him. The school was removed to a different quarter of the hollow, and another pedagogue reigned in his stead.

It is true, an old farmer, who had been down to New York on a visit several years after, and from whom this account of the ghostly adventure was received, brought home the intelligence that Ichabod Crane was still alive; that he had left the neighborhood, partly through fear of the goblin and Hans van Ripper and partly in mortification at having suddenly dismissed by the heiress; that he had changed his quarters to a distant part of the country; had kept school and studied law at the same time, had been admitted to the bar, turned politician, electioneered, written for the newspapers, and finally had been made a justice of the Ten Pound Court.[8] Brom Bones too, who shortly after his rival's disappearance conducted the blooming Katrina in triumph to the altar, was observed to look exceedingly knowing whenever the story of Ichabod was related, and always burst into a hearty laugh at the mention of the pumpkin; which led to some suspect that he knew more about the matter than he chose to tell.

The old country wives, however, who are the best judges of these matters, maintain to this day that Ichabod was spirited away by supernatural means and it is a favorite story often told about the neighborhood round the winter evening fire. The bridge became more than ever an object of superstitious awe, and that may be the reason why the road has been altered of late years, so as to approach the church by the border of the mill-pond. The school-house being deserted, soon fell to decay, and was reported to be haunted by the ghost of the unfortunate pedagogue' and the plough-boy, loitering homeward of a still summer evening, has often fancied his voice at a distance, chanting a melancholy psalm tune among the tranquil solitudes of Sleepy Hollow.

---

mortification (MORE tih fih KAY shun) embarrassment; humiliation
[8]**"Ten Pound Court"** court that tried cases involving no more than 10

Washington Irving (1783–1859)

Washington Irving has often been called America's first great writer, a title he well deserves. Even people who have not read "Rip Van Winkle" seem to know about the character of the same name, the man who slept for twenty years. Other characters are just as famous. Irving's headless horseman, some say, still rides about Sleepy Hollow on gloomy, gray days. And what would New York City be without the Knicks, or the name "Knickerbocker"? The first Knickerbocker was one "Diedrich Knickerbocker," a name Irving invented for the author of his make-believe *History of New York*.

There is a stereotyped character known as "the typical American author" whose life goes like this. The author is born poor, struggles through early hardships, risks all to be a writer, and finally achieves success. Only the last of these is true for Irving. He was born into a comfortable business family. Instead of going to college, he traveled through Europe. At first his writing was just a hobby, and he always took a relaxed approach to his work. He defined the "happy age" of life as the time when a person can be idle and not feel guilty about it. A very social man, Irving could appreciate a well-set table and a good cigar.

Yet Irving did achieve great success. His easy, effortless style transformed all that it touched. He was equally good at humor (*Knickerbocker's History*) and horror ("The Adventure of the German Student"). In addition to many short stories, he wrote travel books, histories, and biographies. He even wrote a hit play. If Mark Twain was "the Lincoln of our literature," Irving was definitely the Washington. What is unusual about the way Washington Irving got his start as a writer?

Review the Selection

Recall

1. Who was Ichabod Crane?

2. Who was the daughter of the wealthiest Dutch farmer?

3. What two items did the villagers find on the bank near the water?

Infer

4. Who was pretending to be the headless horseman? Why?

5. What answer did Katrina give Ichabod the night of the party? Explain.

6. Did Brom Van Brunt really see the headless horseman? Explain.

7. How do you think the school children reacted to Ichabod's disappearance?

Apply

8. What qualities does Ichabod seem to think are most important in a wife?

9. What admirable qualities do you see in either Brom or Ichabod? Explain.

10. Suppose that Ichabod and Katrina did marry. Describe their conversations.

Respond to Literature

Each character in this story has a story of his or her own to tell. Choose a character and explain what happens to him or her after this play ends.

THINK ABOUT PLOT

In designing the plot of a work, an author will try to keep the audience's curiosity alive and build suspense. In a carefully worked-out plot, each event serves as the cause of the next event. Cause-and-effect relationships are especially important in dramas, which have only a short time to set up the action and advance the plot.

1. What is the central conflict in "The Legend of Sleepy Hollow"? What questions come to mind at the beginning of the story?

2. Which character is the protagonist? Which character is the antagonist? How do they relate to one another?

3. At what point does the climax come?

4. What clues do you find to show that Ichabod believes the headless horseman really exists?

READING FOCUS

Identify Hyperbole Choose two instances where the author used hyperbole. Write the phrases. How did Irving's use of hyperbole make the story more interesting to you?

DEVELOP YOUR VOCABULARY

Some words imitate the natural sounds they represent. For example, when you read "clanging bells," the word "clanging" imitates the sound of a bell. The formulation of words in this way is **onomatopoeia** (AHN-uh-MAT-uh-PEE-uh). Onomatopoeia can be a particularly useful tool to communicate the setting to the readers through sounds. In this selection, you have seen onomatopoeia used for this purpose.

Following are phrases that were used in this selection. Choose the word in each phrase that illustrates onomatopoeia. Then, use each word to write an original sentence.

1. clap of thunder
2. drowsy undertone
3. clatter of hoofs
4. crowing of a cock
5. chirp of cricket
6. twang of a bull-frog

Learn About

NARRATION

Narration, as you have learned, is one of the four forms of discourse. One of its purposes is to describe an event or a series of events.

Ordinarily, narration is an end in itself. Its main purpose is to interest and entertain. This is the case for short stories and novels. However, narration can also be used for other purposes. Sometimes narration is used to explain; that is, its intent is **expository**. It may also be used to present a plea for a change in attitude or to support a particular action. In this case, its purpose is **persuasive**.

The narrative itself, therefore, becomes a means to an end. Like a fable or parable in fiction, a factual narrative can also serve to illustrate a point—to teach a lesson or to seek a change in the attitudes of readers or listeners.

As you read this selection, ask yourself:

1. What is the intent of Chief Joseph's speech?
2. Is his aim well supported by his narrative?

WRITING CONNECTION

Write a narrative paragraph about an injustice that you know about that was done to an individual or a group.

READING FOCUS

Understand Sequence of Events The sequence, or order, of events can be very important to understanding a selection. Often, an event only makes sense if you know what preceded it. As you read "No More Forever," think about the sequence of events and how they are related.

from an article in **North American Review,** *April, 1879 entitled*

"An Indian's Views of Indian Affairs"

by Chief Joseph
(In-mut-too-yah-lat-lat)

My friends, I have been asked to show you my heart. I am glad to have a chance to do so. I want the white people to understand my people. Some of you think an Indian is like a wild animal. This is a great mistake. I will tell you all about our people, and then you can judge whether an Indian is a man or not. I believe much trouble and blood would be saved if we opened our hearts more. I will tell you in my way how the Indian sees things. The white man has more words to tell you how they look to him, but it does not require many words to speak the truth. What I have to say will come from my heart, and I will speak with a straight tongue. Ah-cum-kin-i-ma-me-hut (the Great Spirit) is looking at me, and will hear me.

My name is In-mut-too-yah-lat-lat (Thunder Traveling over the Mountains). I am chief of the Wal-lam-wat-kin band of Chute-pa-lu, or Nez Percés (nose-pierced Indians). I was born in eastern Oregon, thirty-eight winters ago. My father was

chief before me. When a young man, he was called Joseph by Mr. Spaulding, a missionary. He died a few years ago. There was no stain on his hands of the blood of a white man. He left a good name on the earth. He advised me well for my people.

Our fathers gave us many laws, which they had learned from their fathers. These laws were good. They told us to treat all men as they treated us; that we should never be the first to break a bargain; that it was a disgrace to tell a lie; that we should speak only the truth; that it was a shame for one man to take from another his wife, or his property without paying for it. We were taught to believe that the Great Spirit sees and hears everything, and that he never forgets; that hereafter he will give every man a spirit-home according to his deserts: if he has been a good man, he will have a good home; if he has been a bad man, he will have a bad home. This I believe, and all my people believe the same.

---

deserts (dih ZURTS) reward or punishment; what is deserved

We did not know there were other people besides the Indian until about one hundred winters ago, when some men with white faces came to our country. . . . These men were Frenchmen, and they called our people Nez Percés, because they wore rings in their noses for ornaments. Although very few of our people wear them now, we are still called by the same name. . . .

The first white men of your people who came to our country were named Lewis and Clark. . . . They talked straight, and our people gave them a great feast, as a proof that their hearts were friendly. These men were very kind. They made presents to our chiefs and our people made presents to them. We had a great many horses, of which we gave them what they needed, and they gave us guns and tobacco in return. All the Nez Percés made friends with Lewis and Clark, and agreed to let them pass through their country, and never to make war on white men. This promise the Nez Percés have never broken. . . .

It has always been the pride of the Nez Percés that they were the friends of the white men. When my father was a young man there came to our country a white man (Rev. Mr. Spaulding) who talked spirit law. He won the affections of our people because he spoke good things to them. At first he did not say anything about white men wanting to settle on our lands. Nothing was said about that until about twenty winters ago, when a number of white people came into our country and built houses and made farms. At first our people made no complaint. They thought there was room enough for all to live in peace, and they were learning many things from the white men that seemed to be good. But we soon found that the white men were growing rich very fast, and were greedy to possess everything the Indian had. My father was the first to see through the schemes of the white men, and he warned his tribe to be careful about trading with them. He had suspicion of men who seemed so anxious to make money. I was a boy then, but I remember well my father's caution. He had sharper eyes than the rest of our people.

Next there came a white officer (Governor Stevens), who invited all the Nez Percés to a treaty council. After the council was opened he made known his heart. He said there were a great many white people in the country, and many more would come; that he wanted the land marked out so that the Indians and white men could be separated. If they were to live in peace it was necessary, he said, that the Indians should have a country set apart for them, and in that country they must stay. My father, who represented his band, refused to have anything to do with the council, because he wished to be a free man. He claimed that no man owned any part of the earth, and a man could not sell what he did not own.

. . . Governor Stevens urged my father to sign his treaty, but he refused. "I will not sign your paper," he said. "You go where you please, so do I; you are not a child, I am no child; I can think for myself. No man can think for me. I have no other home than this. I will not give it up to any man. My people would have no home. Take away your paper. I will not touch it with my hand."

My father left the council. Some of the chiefs of the other bands of the Nez Percés signed the treaty, and then Governor Stevens gave them presents of blankets. My father cautioned his people to take no presents, for after a while, he said, they will claim that you have accepted pay for your country. Since that time four bands of the Nez Percés have received annuities from the United States. My father was invited to many councils, and they tried hard to make him sign the treaty, but he was firm as the rock, and would not sign away his home. His refusal caused a difference among the Nez Percés.

Eight years later (1863) was the next treaty council. A chief called Lawyer, because he was a great talker, took the lead in this council, and sold nearly all the Nez Percés country. My father was not there. He said to me: "When you go into council with the white man, always remember your country. Do not give it away. The white man will cheat you out of your home." I have taken no pay from the United States. I have never sold our land. In this treaty Lawyer acted without authority from our band. He had no right to sell the Wallowa . . . country. That had always belonged to my father's own people, and the other bands had never disputed our right to it. No other Indians ever claimed Wallowa. . . .

The United States claimed they had bought all the Nez Percés country outside of Lapwai Reservation, from Lawyer and other chiefs, but we continued to live on this land in peace until eight years ago, when white men began to come. . . . We warned them against this great wrong, but they would not leave our land, and some bad blood was raised. . . .

The United States Government again asked for a treaty council. My father had become blind and feeble. He could no longer speak for his people. It was then that I took my father's place as chief. In this council I made my first speech to white men. I said to the agent who held the council: "I did not want to come to this council, but I came hoping that we could save blood. The white man has no right to come here and take our country. We have never accepted any presents from the Government. Neither Lawyer nor any other chief had authority to sell this land. It has always belonged to my people. It came unclouded to them from our fathers, and we will defend this land as long as a drop of Indian blood warms the hearts of our men."

The agent said he had orders, from the Great White Chief at Washington, for us to go upon the Lapwai Reservation, and that if we obeyed he would help us in many ways. "You must move to the agency," he said. I answered him: "I will not. I do not need your help; we have plenty, and we are contented and happy if the white man will let us alone. The reservation is too small for so many people with all their stock. You can keep your presents; we can go to your towns and pay for all we need; we have plenty of horses and cattle to sell, and we won't have any help from you; we are free now; we can go where we please. . . ." The agent went away, and we had peace for a little while.

---

annuities (uh NOO uh teez) regular payments
stock (STOK) farm animals

Soon after this my father sent for me. I saw he was dying. I took his hand in mine. He said: "My son, my body is returning to my mother earth, and my spirit is going very soon to see the Great Spirit Chief. When I am gone, think of your country. You are the chief of these people. They look to you to guide them. Always remember that your father never sold his country. You must stop your ears whenever you are asked to sign a treaty selling your home. A few years more, and white men will be all around you. They have their eyes on this land. My son, never forget my dying words. This country holds your father's body. Never sell the bones of your father and your mother." I pressed my father's hand and told him I would protect his grave with my life. My father smiled and passed away to the spirit-land.

I buried him in that beautiful valley of winding waters. I love that land more than all the rest of the world. A man who would not love his father's grave is worse than a wild animal. For a short time we lived quietly. But this could not last. White men had found gold in the mountains around the land of winding water. They stole a great many horses from us, and we could not get them back because we were Indians. The white men told lies for each other. They drove off a great many of our cattle. Some white men branded our young cattle so they could claim them. We had no friend who would plead our cause before the law councils. It seemed to me that some of the white men in Wallowa were doing these things on purpose to get up a war. They knew that we were not strong enough to fight them. I labored hard to avoid trouble and bloodshed. . . . When the white men were few and we were strong we could have killed them all off, but the Nez Percés wished to live at peace.

If we have not done so, we have not been to blame. I believe that the old treaty has never been correctly reported. If we ever owned the land we own it still, for we never sold it. In the treaty councils the commissioners have claimed that our country had been sold to the Government. Suppose a white man should come to me and say, "Joseph, I like your horses, and I want to buy them." I say to him, "No, my horses suit me, I will not sell them." Then he goes to my neighbor, and says to him: "Joseph has some good horses. I want to buy them, but he refuses to sell." My neighbor answers, "Pay me the money, and I will sell you Joseph's horses." The white man returns to me, and says, "Joseph, I have bought your horses, and you must let me have them." If we sold our lands to the Government, this is the way they were bought.

On account of the treaty made by the other bands of the Nez Percés, the white men claimed my lands. We were troubled greatly by white men crowding over the line. Some of these were good men, and we lived on peaceful terms with them, but they were not all good.

Nearly every year the agent came over from Lapwai and ordered us on to the reservation. We always replied that we were satisfied to live in Wallowa. We were careful to refuse the presents or annuities which he offered.

Through all the years since the white men came to Wallowa we have been threatened and taunted by them and the treaty Nez Percés. They have given us no rest. We have had a few good friends among white men, and they have always advised my people to bear these taunts without fighting. Our young men were quick-tempered, and I have had great trouble in keeping them from doing rash things. . .

Year after year we have been threatened, but no war was made upon my people until General Howard came to our country two years ago and told us that he was the white war-chief of all that country. He said: "I have a great many soldiers at my back. I am going to bring them up here, and then I will talk to you again. . . . The country belongs to the Government, and I intend to make you go upon the reservation." . . .

The next spring . . . General Howard sent out runners and called all the Indians in to a grand council. I was in that council. . . . I said to General Howard: "I am ready to talk today. I have been in a great many councils, but I am no wiser. We are all sprung from a woman, although we are unlike in many things. We cannot be made over again. You are as you were made, and as you were made you can remain. We are just as we were made by the Great Spirit, and you cannot change us; then why should children of one mother and one father quarrel? Why should one try to cheat the other? I do not believe that the Great Spirit Chief gave one kind of men the right to tell another kind of men what they must do."

General Howard replied: "You deny my authority, do you? You want to dictate to me, do you?"

Then one of my chiefs, Too-hool-hool-suit, rose in the council and said to General Howard: "The Great Spirit Chief made the world as it is, and as he wanted it, and he made a part of it for us to live upon. I do not see where you get authority to say that we shall not live where he placed us."

General Howard lost his temper and said: "Shut up! I don't want to hear any more of such talk. The law says you shall go upon the reservation to live, . . . but you persist in disobeying the law. . . ."

Too-hool-hool-suit answered: "Who are you, that you ask us to talk, and then tell me I shan't talk? Are you the Great Spirit? Did you make the world? Did you make the sun? Did you make the rivers to run for us to drink? Did you make the grass to grow? Did you make all these things, that you talk to us as though we were boys? If you did, then you have the right to talk as you do."

General Howard replied, "You are an impudent fellow, and I will put you in the guard-house," and then ordered a soldier to arrest him. Too-hool-hool-suit made no resistance. . . .

My men whispered among themselves whether they should let this thing be done. I counseled them to submit. I knew if we resisted that all the white men present, including General Howard, would be killed in a moment, and we would be blamed. If I had said nothing, General Howard would never have given

---

rash (RASH) reckless; foolhardy
impudent (IM pyoo dunt) rude; insulting

"An Indian's Views of Indian Affairs" ■ 103

another unjust order against my men. I saw the danger, and, while they dragged Too-hool-hool-suit to prison, I arose and said: "I am going to talk now. I don't care whether you arrest me or not." I turned to my people and said: "The arrest of Too-hool-hool-suit was wrong, but we will not resent the insult. We were invited to this council to express our hearts, and we have done so." Too-hool-hool-suit was prisoner for five days before he was released. The council broke up for that day. . . .

In the council, next day, General Howard informed me, in a haughty spirit, that he would give my people thirty days to go back home, collect all their stock, and move on to the reservation, saying, "If you are not here in that time, I shall consider that you want to fight, and will send my soldiers to drive you on."

I said: "War can be avoided, and it ought to be avoided. I want no war. My people have always been the friends of the white man. Why are you in such a hurry? I cannot get ready to move in thirty days. Our stock is scattered, and Snake River is very high. Let us wait until fall, then the river will be low. We want time to hunt up our stock and gather supplies for winter." General Howard replied, "If you let the time run over one day, the soldiers will be there to drive you on to the reservation, and all your cattle and horses outside of the reservation at that time will fall into the hands of the white men."

I knew I had never sold my country, and that I had no land in Lapwai; but I did not want bloodshed. I did not want my people killed. I did not want anybody killed. . . . I said in my heart that, rather than have war, I would give up my country. I would give up my father's grave. I would give up everything rather than have the blood of white men upon the hands of my people. General Howard refused to allow me more than thirty days to move my people and their stock. I am sure that he began to prepare for war at once.

When I returned to Wallowa I found my people very much excited upon discovering that the soldiers were already in the Wallowa Valley. We held a council, and decided to move immediately, to avoid bloodshed. Too-hool-hool-suit, who felt outraged by his imprisonment, talked for war. . . . It required a strong heart to stand up against such talk, but I urged my people to be quiet, and not to begin a war.

We gathered all the stock we could find, and made an attempt to move. We left many of our horses and cattle in Wallowa, and we lost several hundred in crossing the river. All of my people succeeded in getting across in safety. Many of the Nez Percés came together in Rocky Canyon to hold a grand council. I went with all my people. This council lasted ten days. There was a great deal of war-talk, and a great deal of excitement. There was one young brave present whose father had been killed by a white man five years before. This man's blood was bad against white men, and he left the council calling for revenge.

Again I counseled peace, and I thought the danger was past. We had not

---

outraged (OUT rayjd) insulted; made very angry

complied with General Howard's order because we could not, but we intended to do so as soon as possible. I was leaving the council to kill beef for my family, when news came that the young man whose father had been killed had gone out with several other hot-blooded young braves and killed four white men. He rode up to the council and shouted: "Why do you sit here like women? The war has begun already." I was deeply grieved. . . .

I heard then that Too-hool-hool-suit . . . had succeeded in organizing a war-party. I knew that their acts would involve all my people. I saw that the war could not then be prevented. The time had passed. I counseled peace from the beginning. I knew that we were too weak to fight the United States. We had many grievances, but I knew that war would bring more. . . .

I know that my young men did a great wrong, but I ask, who was first to blame? They had been insulted a thousand times; their fathers and brothers had been killed; their mothers and wives had been disgraced; they had been driven to madness by whisky sold to them by white men; they had been told by General Howard that all their horses and cattle which they had been unable to drive out of Wallowa were to fall into the hands of white men; and, added to all this, they were homeless and desperate.

I would have given my own life if I could have undone the killing of white men by my people. I blame my young men and I blame the white men. I blame General Howard for not giving my people time to get their stock away from Wallowa. I do not acknowledge that he had the right to order me to leave Wallowa at any time. I deny that either my father or myself ever sold that land. It is still our land. It may never again be our home, but my father sleeps there, and I love it as I love my mother. I left there, hoping to avoid bloodshed.

If General Howard had given me plenty of time to gather up my stock, and treated Too-hool-hool-suit as a man should be treated, there would have been no war. My friends among white men have blamed me for the war. I am not to blame. When my young men began the killing, my heart was hurt. Although I did not justify them, I remembered all the insults I had endured, and my blood was on fire. Still I would have taken my people to the buffalo country without fighting, if possible. I could see no other way to avoid a war.

We moved over to White Bird Creek, sixteen miles away, and there encamped, intending to collect our stock before leaving; but the soldiers attacked us, and the first battle was fought. We numbered in that battle 60 men, and the soldiers 100. The fight lasted but a few minutes, when the soldiers retreated before us for 12 miles. They lost 33 killed, and had seven wounded. When an Indian fights, he only shoots to kill; but soldiers shoot at random. None of the soldiers were scalped. We do not believe in scalping, nor in killing wounded men. Soldiers do not kill many Indians unless they are wounded and left upon the battlefield. Then they kill Indians.

Seven days after the first battle, General Howard arrived in the Nez Percés country, bringing 700 more soldiers. It was

Trail of Tears, Robert Lindneux. Corbis Bettmann

now war in earnest. We crossed over Salmon River, hoping General Howard would follow. We were not disappointed. He did follow us, and we got back between him and his supplies, and cut him off for three days. . . .

Five days later he attacked us with 350 soldiers and settlers. We had 250 warriors. The fight lasted 27 hours. We lost four killed and several wounded. General Howard's loss was 29 men killed and 60 wounded.

The following day the soldiers charged upon us, and we retreated with our families and stock a few miles, leaving 80 lodges to fall into General Howard's hands. Finding that we were outnumbered, we retreated to Bitter Root Valley.

Here another body of soldiers came upon us and demanded our surrender. We refused. They said, "You cannot get by us." We answered, "We are going by you without fighting if you will let us, but we are going by you anyhow." We then made a treaty with these soldiers. We agreed not to molest anyone, and they agreed that we might pass through the Bitter Root country in peace. We bought provisions and traded stock with white men there. We understood that there was to be no more war. We intended to go peaceably to the buffalo country, and leave the question of returning to our country to be settled afterward.

With this understanding we traveled on for four days, and, thinking that the trouble was all over, we stopped and prepared tent-poles to take with us. We started again, and at the end of two days we saw three white men passing our

molest (muh LEST) bother; annoy

camp. Thinking that peace had been made, we did not molest them. We could have killed or taken them prisoners, but we did not suspect them of being spies, which they were.

That night the soldiers surrounded our camp. About daybreak one of my men went out to look after his horses. The soldiers saw him and shot him down like a coyote. I have since learned that these soldiers were not those we had left behind. They had come upon us from another direction. The new white war-chief's name was Gibbon. He charged upon us while some of my people were still asleep. We had a hard fight. Some of my men crept around and attacked the soldiers from the rear. In this battle we lost nearly all our lodges, but we finally drove General Gibbon back.

. . . In the fight with General Gibbon we lost 50 women and children and 30 fighting men. We remained long enough to bury our dead. The Nez Percés never make war on women and children; we could have killed a great many women and children while the war lasted, but we would feel ashamed to do so cowardly an act.

We never scalp our enemies, but when General Howard came up and joined General Gibbon, their Indian scouts dug up our dead and scalped them. I have been told that General Howard did not order this great shame to be done.

We retreated as rapidly as we could toward the buffalo country. After six days General Howard came close to us, and we went out and attacked him, and captured nearly all his horses and mules (about 250 head). We then marched on to the Yellowstone Basin. . . .

Nine days' march brought us to the mouth of Clark's Fork of the Yellowstone. We did not know what had become of General Howard, but we supposed that he had sent for more horses and mules. He did not come up, but another new war-chief (General Sturgis) attacked us. We held him in check while we moved all our women and children and stock out of danger, leaving a few men to cover our retreat. Several days passed, and we heard nothing of General Howard, or Gibbon, or Sturgis. We had repulsed each in turn, and began to feel secure, when another army, under General Miles, struck us. This was the fourth army, each of which outnumbered our fighting force, that we had encountered within sixty days.

We had no knowledge of General Miles's army until a short time before he made a charge upon us, cutting our camp in two, and capturing nearly all of our horses. About seventy men, myself among them, were cut off. My little daughter, twelve years of age, was with me. I gave her a rope, and told her to catch a horse and join the others who were cut off from the camp. I have not seen her since, but I have learned that she is alive and well.

I thought of my wife and children, who were now surrounded by soldiers, and I resolved to go to them or die. With a prayer in my mouth to the Great Spirit

---

repulsed (rih PULST) drove back; repelled
resolved (rih ZOLVD) determined; decided

Chief who rules above, I dashed unarmed through the line of soldiers. It seemed to me that there were guns on every side, before and behind me. My clothes were cut to pieces and my horse was wounded, but I was not hurt. As I reached the door of my lodge, my wife handed me my rifle, saying: "Here's your gun. Fight!"

The soldiers kept up a continuous fire. . . . We fought at close range, not more than twenty steps apart, and drove the soldiers back upon their main line, leaving their dead in our hands. We secured their arms and ammunition. We lost, the first day and night, 18 men and three women. General Miles lost 26 killed and 40 wounded. The following day General Miles sent a messenger into my camp under protection of a white flag. I sent my friend Yellow Bull to meet him.

Yellow Bull understood the messenger to say that General Miles wished me to consider the situation; that he did not want to kill my people unnecessarily. Yellow Bull understood this to be a demand for me to surrender and save blood. . . . I sent him back with my answer, that I had not made up my mind, but would think about it and send word soon. . . . I walked on to General Miles's tent. He met me and we shook hands. He said, "Come, let us sit down by the fire and talk this matter over." I remained with him all night; next morning Yellow Bull came over to see if I was alive, and why I did not return.

General Miles would not let me leave the tent to see my friend alone. Yellow Bull said to me: "They have got you in their power, and I am afraid they will never let you go again. I have an officer in our camp, and I will hold him until they let you go free." I said: "I do not know what they mean to do with me, but if they kill me you must not kill the officer. It will do no good to avenge my death by killing him." Yellow Bull returned to my camp. I did not make any agreement that day with General Miles. The battle was renewed while I was with him. I was very anxious about my people. I knew that we were near Sitting Bull's camp in King George's land, and I thought maybe the Nez Percés who had escaped would return with assistance. No great damage was done to either party during the night.

On the following morning I returned to my camp by agreement, meeting the officer who had been held a prisoner in my camp at the flag of truce. My people were divided about surrendering. We could have escaped from Bear Paw Mountain if we had left our wounded, old women, and children behind. We were unwilling to do this. We had never heard of a wounded Indian recovering while in the hands of white men. . . .

I could not bear to see my wounded men and women suffer any longer; we had lost enough already. General Miles had promised that we might return to our own country with what stock we had left. I thought we could start again. I believed General Miles, or I never would have surrendered. I have heard that he has been censured for making the promise to return us to Lapwai. He could not have made any other terms with me at that time. I would have held him in check until my friends came to my assistance, and then neither of the generals nor their soldiers would have ever left Bear Paw

Mountain alive. On the fifth day I went to General Miles and gave up my gun, and said, "From where the sun now stands I will fight no more." My people needed rest; we wanted peace.

I was told we could go with General Miles to Tongue River and stay there until spring, when we would be sent back to our country. Finally it was decided that we were to be taken to Tongue River. We had nothing to say about it. After our arrival at Tongue River, General Miles received orders to take us to Bismarck. The reason given was, that subsistence would be cheaper there. General Miles was opposed to this order. He said: "You must not blame me. I have endeavored to keep my word, but the chief who is over me has given the order, and I must obey it or resign. That would do you no good. Some other officer would carry out the order."

I believe General Miles would have kept his word if he could have done so. I do not blame him for what we have suffered since the surrender. I do not know who is to blame. . . .

[*Chief Joseph tells of illness and deaths among the tribe as well as the loss of their horses, saddles, and lodges as his pople are moved from Bismark, North Dakota to Fort Leavenworth and then Baxter Springs in Kansas and finally to Indian Territory in Oklahoma.*]

We have had a great many visitors who have talked many ways. Some of the chiefs (General Fish and Colonel Stickney) from Washington came to see us, and selected land for us to live upon. We have not moved to that land, for it is not a good place to live.

The Commissioner Chief (E. A. Hayt) came to see us. I told him, as I told everyone, that I expected General Miles's word would be carried out. He said it could not be done; that white men now lived in my country and all the land was taken up; that, if I returned to Wallowa, I could not live in peace; that law-papers were out against my young men who began the war, and that the Government could not protect my people. This talk fell like a heavy stone upon my heart. I saw that I could not gain anything by talking to him. Other law chiefs (Congressional Committee) came to see me and said they would help me to get a healthy country. I did not know who to believe. The white people have too many chiefs. They do not understand each other. They do not all talk alike. . . .

Then the Inspector Chief (General McNiel) came to my camp and we had a long talk. He said I ought to have a home in the mountain country north, and that he would write a letter to the Great Chief at Washington. Again the hope of seeing the mountains of Idaho and Oregon grew up in my heart.

At last I was granted permission to come to Washington and bring my friend Yellow Bull and our interpreter with me. I am glad we came. I have shaken hands with a great many friends, but there are some things I want to know which no one seems able to explain. I cannot understand how the Government sends a man out to fight us, as it did General Miles, and then breaks his word. Such a Government has something wrong about it. I cannot understand why so many chiefs are allowed to talk so many different ways, and promise so many different things. I have seen the Great Father Chief (the President), the next Great Chief (Secretary of the Interior), the Commissioner Chief (Hayt), the Law Chief (General Butler), and many other law chiefs (Congressmen), and they all say they are my friends, and that I shall have justice, but while their mouths all talk right I do not understand why nothing is done for my people. I have heard talk and talk, but nothing is done.

Good words do not last long unless they amount to something. . . . It makes my heart sick when I remember all the good words and all the broken promises. . . . If the white man wants to live in peace with the Indian he can live in peace. There need be no trouble. Treat all men alike. Give them all the same law. Give them all an even chance to live and grow. All men were made by the same Great Spirit Chief. They are all brothers. The earth is the mother of all people, and all people should have equal rights upon it. You might as well expect the rivers to run backward as that any man who was born a free man should be contented when penned up and denied liberty to go where he pleases. . . . I have asked some of the great white chiefs where they get their authority to say to the Indian that he shall stay in one place, while he sees white men going where they please. They cannot tell me.

I only ask of the Government to be treated as all other men are treated. If I cannot go to my own home, let me have a home in some country where my people will not die so fast. I would like to go to Bitter Root Valley. There my people would be healthy; where they are now they are dying. Three have died since I left my camp to come to Washington.

When I think of our condition my heart is heavy. I see men of my race treated as outlaws and driven from country to country, or shot down like animals. I know that my race must change. We cannot hold our own with the white men as we are. We only ask an even chance to live as other men live. We ask to be recognized as men. We ask that the same law shall work alike on all men. If the Indian breaks the law, punish him by the law. If the white man breaks the law, punish him also. Let me be a free man—free to travel, free to stop, free to work, free to trade where I choose, free to choose my own teachers, free to follow the religion of my fathers, free to think and talk and act for myself—and I will obey every law, or submit to the penalty.

Whenever the white man treats the Indian as they treat each other, then we will have no more wars. We shall all be alike, brothers of one father and one mother, with one sky above us and one country around us, and one government for all. Then the Great Spirit Chief who rules above will smile upon this land, and send rain to wash out the bloody spots made by brother's hands from the face of the earth. For this time the Indian race are waiting and praying. I hope that no more groans of wounded men and women will ever go to the ear of the Great Spirit Chief above, and that all people may be one people.

In-mut-too-yah-lat-lat has spoken for his people.

AUTHOR BIOGRAPHY
Chief Joseph (1840–1904)

By the end of the 1870s, nearly all Native Americans in the United States had been forced onto reservations. The famous Sitting Bull had escaped to Canada. The Apache chief Geronimo was in Mexico. Then quite suddenly, in 1877, another great leader—called "Chief Joseph" by the white settlers—gained wide attention.

According to newspaper stories, Chief Joseph was the leader of the "unruly" Nez Percé (NEZ PURS) "troublemakers" in the northwestern United States. The papers claimed that rather than move onto a reservation, Joseph and his people decided to take on the U.S. Army. Recreating over a 1300-mile path through four western states, he fought off attack after attack, in each of which his force was greatly outnumbered. Moreover, all this was done while protecting hundreds of women and children and thousands of horses and cattle. Chief Joseph was not stopped until he was about 40 miles from his goal—Canada and freedom.

Once the Nez Percé War was over, however, quite a different story came out. Chief Joseph's people were not rebels but in the right: they had twice been guaranteed their homeland in the Wallowa Valley of Oregon (in 1855 and 1873). Moreover, Joseph was only one of several Nez Percé chiefs, and because he had always been a man of peace, he had lost much of his influence when the war started. In fact, during the months of the long march, Joseph's job had been to protect the women, children, and elderly, not to engage in combat. Only after the war did he emerge as *the* leader.

His hopes were never fully realized. Not until 1885 was he permitted to return to the Northwest, and then to a reservation in Washington, not to his Oregon homeland. He died on September 21, 1904.

Review the Selection

UNDERSTAND THE SELECTION

Recall

1. To which tribe did Chief Joseph belong?

2. Where did Chief Joseph surrender?

3. Who were the first American white men that the Nez Percé ever saw?

Infer

4. Why did Chief Joseph say the government was being unfair?

5. What does Chief Joseph mean by "talking with a straight tongue"?

6. Why did the government not keep its agreement with Chief Joseph?

7. Why did Chief Joseph stop fighting?

Apply

8. If you were an Indian in Chief Joseph's band, would you have favored surrender?

9. What would have happened if Chief Joseph's band continued fighting?

10. Do you think Chief Joseph's father would have been proud of his son?

Respond to Literature
Was the treatment the Native Americans received a good example of the beliefs on which the United States was founded?

THINK ABOUT NARRATION

In nonfiction, narration is concerned with personal and historical events. The intention of the narrative, however, may be **expository** (to explain) or **persuasive** (to persuade). In such writing, the narrative serves as a long example to support the point that the author wishes to make.

1. Was Chief Joseph's intention in relating the history of the Nez Percé band expository or persuasive?

2. Does Chief Joseph make a thesis statement in his speech? If so, what is it?

3. Tell where the introduction, body, and conclusion of Chief Joseph's speech occur.

4. How did Chief Joseph establish with the reader or listener that he was honest and that he spoke truthfully?

5. What is the lesson that Chief Joseph's narrative best illustrates?

READING FOCUS
Understand the Sequence of Events List three key events in this selection. Explain the order in which they occur and how they are related to one another.

DEVELOP YOUR VOCABULARY

Words sometimes have several meanings. If you are not sure of the meaning of a word, context clues may help. Look at the words surrounding the unfamiliar word; they may give you a hint of its meaning. Chief Joseph explains, "I am chief of a *band* of Nez Percé." The word *chief* suggests that *band* means "a group."

Read each item below. Use the context to try to figure out the meaning of each italicized word. Check your meaning in a dictionary to see that it is correct. Write an original sentence using each word.

1. The *reservation* is too small for so many people with all their stock.

2. No, my horses *suit* me, I will not sell them.

3. . . . I have had great trouble in keeping them from doing *rash* things.

4. We are all *sprung* from a woman. . . .

5. We held him in *check*, while we moved our women and children. . . .

Learn About

METER

You have learned that all poetry has **rhythm**. It is the natural sense of movement that occurs when successive syllables are stressed or not stressed. It comes from the natural rise and fall of language.

Poets often build into their poems a strong pattern of stressed and unstressed syllables. The rhythmic pattern is so pronounced that the reader may tap a pencil to its beat. Such a pattern is called **meter**. The difference between natural rhythm and meter is that in natural rhythm, the accented syllables are random; in metrical lines of poetry, the accents come at regular intervals. Meter carries a reader along toward a planned conclusion.

The music of poetry can be enhanced by other means, too. The repetition of words and phrases and the use of rhyme add to the flow of sound.

As you read this selection, ask yourself:

1. What kind of meter can I detect in this poem?
2. Does the poet use repetition and rhyme for musical effects?

READING FOCUS

Identify Cause and Effect A cause-and-effect relationship is one in which one event (the cause) is responsible for another event (the effect). An author connects thoughts and actions by showing a cause-and-effect relationship. This helps the reader better understand the reasons why things happen. As you read this poem, note the effects, or what happens. As you reread the poem, look for the causes of each effect you noted.

WRITING CONNECTION

Write down four lines of lyrics from a favorite song. Can you detect a metrical pattern? Write a paragraph about it.

Annabel Lee

by Edgar Allan Poe

It was many and many a year ago,
    In a kingdom by the sea,
That a maiden there lived whom you may know
    By the name of Annabel Lee;
5   And this maiden she lived with no other thought
    Than to love and be loved by me.

I was a child and *she* was a child,
    In this kingdom by the sea,
But we loved with a love that was more than love—
10   I and my Annabel Lee;
With a love that the wingèd seraphs of heaven
    Coveted her and me.

And this was the reason that, long ago,
    In this kingdom by the sea,
15 A wind blew out of a cloud, chilling
    My beautiful Annabel Lee;
So that her high-born kinsmen came
    And bore her away from me,
To shut her up in a sepulcher
20   In this kingdom by the sea.

The angels, not half so happy in heaven,
    Went envying her and me—
Yes!—that was the reason (as all men know,
    In this kingdom by the sea)
25 That the wind came out of the cloud by night,
    Chilling and killing my Annabel Lee.

---

seraph (SER uf) kind of heavenly being; winged angel
covet (KUV it) desire what belongs to another
high-born (HY bawrn) of noble birth
sepulcher (SEP ul kur) tomb; burial place

But our love it was stronger by far than the love
    Of those who were older than we—
    Of many far wiser than we—
30   And neither the angels in heaven above
      Nor the demons down under the sea,
Can ever dissever my soul from the soul
    Of the beautiful Annabel Lee,

For the moon never beams, without bringing me dreams
35   Of the beautiful Annabel Lee;
And the stars never rise, but I feel the bright eyes
    Of the beautiful Annabel Lee;
And so, all the night-tide, I lie down by the side
Of my darling—my darling—my life and my bride,
40   In the sepulcher there by the sea,
    In her tomb by the sounding sea.

---

dissever (dih SEV ur) separate
night-tide (NYT tyd) nighttime

Edgar Allan Poe (1809–1849)

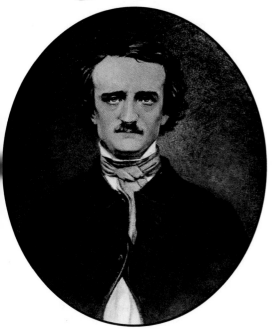

For some authors, writing is a carefully studied skill. For others, writing is a refined art. But for a very few, writing seems the outpouring of genius that cannot be contained. Edgar Allan Poe was such an author. His life proves that true talent is a powerful force indeed.

Born in 1809, Edgar Poe never knew his father, an actor who left his family and simply disappeared. Death claimed Poe's mother, an actress, when the boy was two. But luckily, the child was taken in by John Allan, a wealthy tobacco dealer. In 1815 the Allans went to England on business, and for five years Edgar went to a private school there.

Poe's luck, however, was not to continue. He quarreled violently with John Allan. He was forced to leave the University of Virginia because of gambling debts. He joined the army for a time and then drifted here and there, unable to settle down. He got a number of jobs as an editor but lost them because of excessive drinking.

In midlife Poe was taken in by an aunt, Maria Clemm. She gave him the comfort he needed, and he began to write—and sell!—the fantastic stories that made him famous. He married Mrs. Clemm's daughter, Virginia, a girl of 13.

Troubles continued to follow the struggling author. He could not hold a job for long. His stories and poems brought in some money, but never enough for a comfortable life. He, Virginia, and Mrs. Clemm drifted into poverty. Virginia died in 1847. Two years later Poe himself was found near death in Baltimore, Maryland. He died four days later. In your opinion, what were the two worst misfortunes in Poe's unhappy life?

Review the Selection

UNDERSTAND THE SELECTION

Recall

1. Where did Annabel Lee live?

2. Where did her kinsmen bury her?

3. What killed Anabell Lee?

Infer

4. What may have been the real cause of Annabel Lee's death?

5. What made Annabel Lee's death so difficult for the author?

6. Why was it necessary for her kinsmen to take her away to be buried?

7. Do you think the narrator accepted her death after a short period of time?

Apply

8. Suppose that Annabel Lee could speak from the grave. What might she say to the narrator?

9. Assume that you are one of the residents of this kingdom. Would you visit the narrator? Why or why not?

10. Do you think Annabel Lee's family opposed this marriage? Why?

Respond to Literature

Most of the literature of this period had an American setting. What about this selection is typical of the period?

THINK ABOUT METER

Meter refers to a pattern of stressed and unstressed syllables in poetry. It is distinguished from rhythm by its use of regularly recurring accented and unaccented syllables. Each patterned group of syllables has a name. For example, one unstressed syllable followed by one stressed syllable (as in con-TROL) is called an **iamb**. Similarly, two unstressed syllables followed by a stressed syllable (as in con-tra-DICT) is called an **anapest**.

1. Which meter is the basic one in "Annabel Lee"—an iamb or an anapest? Why do you say so?

2. The first two lines of the poem have been likened to the opening of a fairy tale. Do you agree? Why or why not?

3. In line 15, the meter is broken temporarily by the word *chilling*. Why do you think Poe did this?

4. What other "musical" effects did Poe use in the poem?

5. What words and phrases did Poe often repeat in the poem?

READING FOCUS

Identify Cause and Effect "Annabel Lee" describes the death of someone the speaker loved deeply. What two things does the speaker say caused Annabel Lee's death?

DEVELOP YOUR VOCABULARY

An **antonym** is a word that has a meaning opposite or nearly opposite to that of another word. For example, in this selection, Poe refers to "the angels . . . in heaven" and "the demons down under the sea." *Angels* and *demons* are antonyms, or words that are opposite in meaning to each other.

Following are words used in this selection. Read the words, review the meaning of each word whose meaning is not clear to you. Some of the words are not in common use today. Check the poem to help you figure out the meanings of these words.

Select an antonym for each word. Check a dictionary for the meaning of each antonym you have selected. Double check to be sure it has a meaning opposite to that of the original word. Then, use each antonym to write an original sentence. Be sure that your sentences include context clues to the words' meanings.

1. love	**5.** chilling
2. beautiful	**6.** wise
3. highborn	**7.** dissever
4. shut	**8.** bright

Learn About

SUSPENSE

Suspense is the growing excitement that a reader or listener feels while waiting for the climax or resolution of the events in a work of fiction. There are two kinds of suspense. In one kind, the author leaves the outcome in doubt until the very end so that the audience will wonder *who*, *what*, or *how*. In the other kind, the author lets the audience know about the outcome before the end. The big suspense is then focused on *when*.

Authors have ways of building suspense. They can create an atmosphere that contributes to it and they can **foreshadow** events, that is, they can give tantalizing hints of what may happen in the plot.

Suspense plays a part in all fiction—short stories, novels, and plays. In some works, however, it is the main ingredient.

As you read this selection, ask yourself:

1. Which of the two kinds of suspense does Poe use in this story?
2. What details besides the plot contribute to the suspense?

READING FOCUS

Identify Signal Words Authors use the relationships between events to string together a story in a believable way. They often use signal words to suggest a cause-and-effect relationship or time order. As you read "The Tell-Tale Heart," look for words that signal cause and effect, such as *because*, *so*, and *since*. Also look for words that signal a time order, such as *first*, *next*, *last*, *finally*, and *soon*.

WRITING CONNECTION

In a paragraph, describe a movie thriller you have seen recently. Explain how the suspense was achieved.

THE TELL-TALE HEART

by Edgar Allan Poe

True!—nervous—very, very dreadfully nervous I have been and am. But why *will* you say that I am mad? The disease had sharpened my senses—not destroyed—not dulled them. Above all was the sense of hearing acute. I heard all things in the heaven and in the earth. I heard many things in hell. How, then, am I mad? Hearken! And observe how healthily—how calmly I can tell you the whole story.

It is impossible to say how first the idea entered my brain; but once conceived, it haunted me day and night. Object was there none. Passion was there none. I loved the old man. He had never wronged me. He had never given me insult. For his gold I had no desire. I think it was his eye! Yes, it was this! One of his eyes resembled that of a vulture—a pale blue eye, with a film over it. Whenever it fell upon me, my blood ran cold; so by degrees—very gradually—I made up my mind to take the life of the old man, and thus rid myself of the eye forever.

Now this is the point. You fancy me mad. Madmen know nothing. But you should have seen me. You should have seen how wisely I proceeded—with what caution—with what foresight—with what dissimulation I went to work! I was never kinder to the old man than during the whole week before I killed him. And every night, about midnight, I turned the latch of his door and opened it—oh so gently! And then, when I had made an opening sufficient for my head, I put in a dark lantern, all closed, closed so that no light shone out, and then I thrust in my head. Oh you would have laughed to see how cunningly I thrust it in! I moved it slowly—very, very slowly, so that I might not disturb the old man's sleep. It took me an hour to place my whole head in the opening so far that I could see him as he

---

acute (uh KYOOT) sharp, sensitive
conceived (kun SEEVD) thought of; imagined
cunningly (KUN ing lee) slyly

lay upon his bed. Ha!—would a madman have been so wise as this? And then, when my head was well into the room, I undid the lantern cautiously—oh, so cautiously—cautiously (for the hinges creaked) I undid it just so much that a single thin ray fell upon the vulture eye. And this I did for seven long nights—every night just at midnight—but I found the eye was always closed; and so it was impossible to do the work; for it was not the old man who vexed me, but his Evil Eye. And every morning, when the day broke, I went boldly into the chamber, and spoke courageously to him calling him by name in a hearty tone, and inquiring how he had passed the night. So you see he would have been a very profound old man, indeed, to suspect that every night, just at twelve, I looked in upon him while he slept.

Upon the eighth night I was more than usually cautious in opening the door. A watch's minute hand moves more quickly than did mine. Never before that night had I *felt* the extent of my own powers—of my sagacity. I could scarcely contain my feelings of triumph. To think that there I was, opening the door, little by little, and he not even to dream of my secret deeds or thoughts! I fairly chuckled at the idea—and perhaps he heard me; for he moved on the bed suddenly, as if he startled. Now you may think that I drew back—but no. His room was black as

pitch with the thick darkness (for the shutters were close fastened through fear of robbers) and so I knew that he could not see the opening of the door, and I kept it on steadily, steadily.

I had my head in, and was about to open the lantern, when my thumb slipped upon the tin fastening, and the old man sprang up in the bed, crying out—"Who's there?"

I kept quite still and said nothing. For a whole hour I did not move a muscle, and in the meantime I did not hear him lie down. He was still sitting up in the bed listening, hearkening to the deathwatches in the wall.

Presently, I heard a slight groan, and I knew it was the groan of mortal terror. It was not a groan of pain or of grief—oh, no!—It was the low stifled sound that arises from the bottom of the soul when overcharged with awe. I knew the sound well. Many a night, just at midnight, when all the world slept, it has welled up from my own bosom, deepening, with its dreadful echo, the terrors that distracted me. I say I knew it well. I knew what the old man felt, and pitied him—although I chuckled at heart. I knew that he had been lying awake ever since the first slight noise, when he had turned in the bed. His fears had been ever since growing upon him. He had been trying to fancy them causeless, but could not. He had been saying to himself—"It is nothing but the wind in the

---

vexed (VEKST) disturbed; annoyed; irritated
profound (pruh FOUND) wise; intellectually deep
pitch (PICH) a black, sticky substance formed from distilling of tar
mortal (MAWR tul) fatal; causing death
stifled (STY fuld) muffled, smothered

chimney," "it is only a mouse crossing the floor," or "it is merely a cricket which has made a single chirp." Yes he had been trying to comfort himself with all these suppositions; but he had found all in vain. *All in vain;* because Death, in approaching him, had stalked with his black shadow before him, and enveloped the victim. And it was the mournful influence of the unperceived shadow that caused him to feel—although he neither saw nor heard—to feel the presence of my head within the room.

When I had waited a very long time, very patiently, without hearing him lie down, I resolved to open a little, a very, very little crevice in the lantern. So I opened it—you cannot imagine how stealthily, stealthily—until at length, a single dim ray, like the thread of a spider, shot from out the crevice and fell upon the vulture eye.

It was open—wide, wide open. I grew furious as I gazed upon it. I saw it with perfect distinctness—all a dull blue, with a hideous veil over it that chilled the very marrow in my bones; but I could see nothing else of the old man's face or person;

---

vain (VAYN) without success; useless
hideous (HID ee us) very ugly or frightening

for I had directed the ray as if by instinct, exactly upon the damned spot.

And now have I not told you that what you mistake for madness is but overacuteness of the senses? Now, I say, there came to my ears a low, dull, quick sound, much such a sound as a watch makes when enveloped in cotton. I knew *that* sound well too. It was the beating of the old man's heart. It increased my fury as the beating of a drum stimulates the soldier into courage.

But even yet I refrained and kept still. I scarcely breathed. I held the lantern motionless. I tried how steadily I could keep the ray upon the eye. Meantime the hellish tattoo of the heart increased. It grew quicker and quicker, and louder and louder every instant. The old man's terror *must* have been extreme! It grew louder, I say, louder every moment!—do you mark me well? I have told you that I am nervous; so I am. And now at the dead hour of the night amid the dreadful silence of that old house, so strange a noise as this excited me to uncontrollable terror. Yet, for some minutes longer, I refrained and stood still. But the beating grew louder, louder! I thought the heart must burst. And now a new anxiety seized me—the sound would be heard by a neighbor! The old man's hour had come! With a loud yell, I threw open the lantern and leaped into the room. He shrieked once—once only. In an instant I dragged him to the floor, and pulled the heavy bed over him. I then smiled gaily to find the deed so far done. But for many minutes, the heart beat on with a muffled sound. This, however, did not vex me; it would not be heard through the wall. At length it ceased. The old man was dead. I removed the bed and examined the corpse. Yes he was stone, stone dead. I placed my hand upon the heart and held it there many minutes. There was not pulsation. He was stone dead. His eye would trouble me no more.

If you still think me mad, you will think so no longer when I describe the wise precautions I took for the concealment of the body. The night waned, and I worked hastily, but in silence. First of all, I dismembered the corpse. I cut off the head and the arms and the legs.

I then took up three planks from the flooring of the chamber, and deposited all between the scantlings. I then replaced the boards so cleverly, so cunningly, that no human eye—not even *his*—could have detected anything wrong. There was nothing to wash out—no stain of any kind, no blood-spot whatever. I had been too wary for that. A tub had caught all— ha! ha!

When I had made an end of these labors, it was four o'clock—still dark as midnight. As the bell sounded the hour, there came a knocking at the street door. I went down to open it with a light heart— for what had I *now* to fear? There entered three men, who introduced themselves with perfect suavity, as officers of the police. A shriek had been heard by a neighbor during the night; suspicion of foul play had been aroused; information

---

enveloped (en VEL upd) wrapped up
anxiety (ang ZY uh tee) worry

had been lodged at the police office. And they (the officers) had been deputed to search the premises.

I smiled—for *what* had I to fear? I made the gentleman welcome. The shriek, I said, was my own in a dream. The old man, I added was absent in the country. I took my visitors all over the house. I told them to search—search *well*. I led them, at length, to *his* chamber. I showed them his treasures, secure, undisturbed. In the enthusiasm of my confidence, I brought chairs into the room, desired them *here* to rest from their fatigues, while I myself, in the wild audacity of my perfect triumph, placed my own seat upon the very spot beneath which reposed the corpse of the victim.

The officers were satisfied. My *manner* had convinced them. I was singularly at ease. They sat while I answered cheerily, they chatted of familiar things. But ere long, I felt myself getting pale and wished them gone. My head ached, and I fancied a ringing in my ears; but still they sat, and still chatted. The ringing became more distinct—it continued and became ever more distinct. I talked more freely to get rid of the feeling; but it continued and gained definitiveness—until, at length, I found that the noise was *not* within my ears.

No doubt I grew *very* pale; but I talked more fluently, and with a heightened voice. Yet the sound increased—and what could I do? It was *a low, dull, quick sound—much such a sound as a watch makes when enveloped in cotton.* I gasped for breath—and yet the officers heard it not. I talked more quickly—more vehemently; but the noise steadily increased. I arose and argued about trifles, in a high key and with violent gesticulations. But the noise steadily increased. Why *would* they not be gone? I paced the floor to and fro with heavy strides, as if excited to fury by the observations of the men—but the noise steadily increased. Oh God! What could I do? I foamed—I raved—I swore! I swung the chair upon which I had been sitting, and grated it upon the boards, but the noise arose all over and continually increased. It grew louder—and louder—*louder!* And still the men chatted pleasantly, and smiled. Was it possible they heard it not? Almighty God! No, no! They heard!—they suspected—they *knew!* They were making a mockery of my horror!—this I thought, and this I think. But anything was better than this agony! Anything was more tolerable than this derision! I could bear those hypocritical smiles no longer! I felt that I must scream or die!—and now—again! —hark! — louder! louder! *louder!*—

"Villains!" I shrieked. "Dissemble no more. I admit the deed! Tear up the planks!—here, here!—it is the beating of his hideous heart!"

---

audacity (aw DAS uh tee) boldness; daring
fluently (FLOO unt lee) easily (of talking)
trifles (TRY fulz) unimportant things
mockery (MOK uh ree) person or thing made fun of
hypocritical (hip uh KRIT ih kul) false; not sincere

Review the Selection

Recall

1. At what hour every night did the narrator enter the old man's room?

2. What vexed the narrator?

3. Why did the policemen come?

Infer

4. Why do you think the narrator acted more kindly toward the old man for a week prior to the murder?

5. Who might the old man have been?

6. What do you think might have caused the glaze on the old man's eye that the narrator thought was evil?

7. Why did the policemen stay after the narrator answered their questions?

Apply

8. How does the expression "You protest too much," apply to the narrator's comments about his sanity?

9. What questions might the police ask the narrator?

10. Assume you are the old man. You sense something sinister. Who do you think has entered the room? Why?

Respond to Literature

Is Poe's suspenseful tale typical of the literature of this period? Explain.

To achieve suspense in a story, an author may foreshadow events, create atmospheric details, add events that heighten the tension the reader feels, and use character traits that make the reader feel strongly, one way or another, about a character.

1. Who is the narrator of the story?

2. How does Poe make it clear from the outset that the narrator is insane?

3. There are two kinds of suspense, one that leaves the outcome in doubt until the end of the story and one in which the outcome is known but not when it will happen. Which type does Poe use in this story?

4. What are some details that Poe uses to build suspense in the story?

5. Why did the narrator think he heard the old man's heart beating under the floor?

READING FOCUS

Identify Signal Words As you read this selection, you identified cause-and-effect relationships and the sequence of events by using signal words. Choose a series of events from the story. Write the signal words you identified. Tell why you think these words make the relationships among these events clear.

DEVELOP YOUR VOCABULARY

You will find it difficult to understand and appreciate any literary work if you do not understand the vocabulary used by the author. Sometimes you may be able to figure out the meaning of a word from **context clues**—from the words that surround the unfamiliar word. However, it is always wise to check the meaning of the unfamiliar word in a dictionary as well. At times, unfamiliar words will be defined within or following a selection. This is true in this text. Be sure to check these definitions as you read.

Review the meanings of the following words from "The Tell-Tale Heart." When you are sure you understand the words, write an original sentence for each one that shows you understand the meaning.

1. vexed   **6.** fluently
2. pitch   **7.** mockery
3. enveloped   **8.** hypocritical
4. audacity   **9.** stifled
5. acute   **10.** mortal

Focus ON FICTION

*F*iction has several recognizable elements. Knowing them will help you to understand fictional works better. The most basic elements are setting, characters, plot, theme, and point of view.

Setting   Setting is the physical place, the time, and the general background against which the action or events in a story take place. The physical place might be the great outdoors or a single room. It might be a city street or a country estate. The time might include the time of day, a particular season, or a period in history. The general background often includes a specific kind of weather or the general climate of a region.

The action of a novel, play, or short story may be set in more than one place. One part of the work may take place in one setting; another part in another setting.

Sometimes a setting can be a major force affecting events of the story. A blizzard, for example, may change the plans the characters had for going on a journey. The setting may also help the reader to understand a character better. A character who lives on a houseboat, for example, is likely to be accustomed to water and self-reliance.

Characters   Characters are the inhabitants of the fictional world the author creates. Characters have physical features and personalities. The author may use physical features to shed light on a character's personality. Usually, the characters are human. Occasionally, an animal may be given a personality. Then, that animal becomes a character.

The author creates personality through the character's thoughts, words, and deeds. A character's personality may also be revealed through the opinions and attitudes expressed by other people in the story. Some characters are well-rounded and believable. A **well-rounded** character has strengths and weaknesses, as real people do. Minor characters are often **flat**, not round. They have one-dimensional personalities and may even be stereotypes.

Plot   Plot is the series of events in a literary work. Conflict provides the dramatic action that advances the plot. Conflict arises when two characters important to the story struggle against one another. The main character is called the **protagonist**. His or her rival is called the **antagonist**. Conflict may also arise when one character struggles within his or her own mind about something. This kind of struggle is called **internal conflict**.

The **climax** is the decisive turning point in the action of the story. The dramatic tension, caused by the conflict, reaches its highest point at the climax. At that moment, the conflict begins to be resolved. The tension is released, and the **dénouement**, or conclusion, follows.

Theme   Theme is the central or dominating idea of a literary work. In nonfiction, the theme is often stated directly. Theme is rarely stated in fiction. Instead, the author uses the other elements of fiction, such as plot, character, and setting, to communicate an idea or concept to the reader.

Point of View   Point of view is the position from which the story is told. A fictional story may be told from the first-person or the third-person point of view.

In **first-person** point of view, the narrator is a participant in the action. He or she has a limited view of the action, and can tell the reader only what he or she sees, hears, and knows.

In **third-person** point of view, the narrator is an observer who stands outside the action. A third-person narrator might be able to see, hear, and know everything that happens to all the characters or a third-person narrator's point of view might be limited to the information experienced by just one character.

When the narrator can tell the innermost feelings and thoughts of only one character, the point of view is called **third-person limited**. When the third person narrator is all-knowing, the point of view is called **omniscient**. An omniscient narrator can tell the reader what the characters are thinking.

from

The Prairie

by James Fenimore Cooper

In the following excerpt, Natty Bumppo is close to death. He is visited by Duncan Uncas Middleton, an army officer whose life Bumppo had saved a year earlier, and by Middleton's scouting party. Bumppo has been living with the tribe of Hard-Heart, a young Pawnee chief, whom Bumppo had adopted as a son. As Bumppo's death approaches, the Pawnee chief and the army officer both share a deep sadness.

When they entered the town, its inhabitants were seen collected in an open space, where they were arranged with the customary deference to age and rank. The whole formed a large circle, in the center of which were perhaps a dozen of the principal chiefs. Hard-Heart waved his hand as he approached, and, as the mass of bodies opened, he rode through, followed by his companions. Here they dismounted; and as the beasts were led apart, the strangers found themselves environed by a thousands grave, composed, but solicitous faces.

Middleton gazed about him in growing concern, for no cry, no song, no shout welcomed him among a people from whom he had so lately parted with regret. His uneasiness, not to say apprehensions, was shared by all his followers. Determination and stern resolution began to assume the place of anxiety in every eye, as each man silently felt for his arms, and assured himself that his several weapons were in a state for service. But there was no answering

---

grave (GRAYV) serious
apprehensions (ap ree HEN shunz) fears, dreads

symptom of hostility on the part of their hosts. Hard-Heart beckoned for Middleton and Paul to follow, leading the way toward the cluster of forms that occupied the center of the circle. Here the visitors found a solution of all the movements which had given them so much reason for apprehension.

The trapper was placed on a rude seat, which had been made, with studied care, to support his frame in an upright and easy attitude. The first glance of the eye told his former friends that the old man was at length called upon to pay the last tribute of nature. His eye was glazed, and apparently as devoid of sight as of expression. His features were a little more sunken and strongly marked than formerly; but there all change, so far as exterior was concerned, might be said to have ceased. His approaching end was not to be ascribed to any positive disease, but had been a gradual and mild decay of the physical powers. Life, it is true, still lingered in his system; but it was as if at times entirely ready to depart, and then it would appear to reanimate the sinking form, reluctant to give up the possession of a tenement that had never been corrupted by vice, or undermined by disease. It would have been no violent fancy to have imagined that the spirit fluttered about the placid lips of the old woodsman, reluctant to depart from a shell that had so long given it an honest and an honorable shelter.

His body was placed so as to let the light of the setting sun fall full upon the solemn features. His head was bare, the long, thin locks of gray fluttering lightly in the evening breeze. His rifle lay upon his knee, and the other accoutrements of the chase were placed at his side, within reach of his hand. Between his feet lay the figure of a hound, with its head crouching to the earth as if it slumbered; and so perfectly easy and natural was its position, that a second glance was necessary to tell Middleton he saw only the skin of Hector, stuffed by Indian tenderness and ingenuity in a manner to represent the living animal.... Le Balafré [the Pawnee chief] was seated nigh the dying trapper, with every mark about his person that the hour of his own departure was not far distant. The rest of those immediately in the center were aged men, who had apparently drawn near, in order to observe the manner in which a just and fearless warrior would depart on the greatest of his journeys.

The author gives details of the setting.

The author describes the character's physical appearance.

The conflict is revealed—Bumppo vs. death.

The character of Bumppo is slowly revealed.

---

placid (PLAS id) quiet
ingenuity (in juh NOO uh tee) cleverness; originality

The author sets limits on the conflict.

The old man was reaping the rewards of a life remarkable for temperance and activity in a tranquil and placid death. His vigor in a manner endured to the very last. Decay, when it did occur, was rapid, but free from pain. He had hunted with the tribe in the spring, and even throughout most of the summer, when his limbs suddenly refused to perform their customary offices. A sympathizing weakness took possession of all his faculties; and the Pawnees believed that they were going to lose, in this unexpected manner, a sage and counsellor whom they had begun both to love and respect. But as we have already said, the immortal occupant seemed unwilling to desert its tenement. The lamp of life flickered without becoming extinguished. On the morning of the day on which Middleton arrived, there was a general reviving of the pow-

Omniscient point of view continues.

ers of the whole man. His tongue was again heard in wholesome maxims, and his eye from time to time recognized the person of his friends. It merely proved to be a brief and final . . . [exchange] with the world on the part of one who had already been considered, as to mental communion, to have taken his leave of it forever.

When he had placed his guests in front of the dying man, Hard-Heart, after a pause that proceeded as much from sorrow as decorum, leaned a little forward and demanded–

Bumppo and the Pawnee speak to each other with respect.

"Does my father hear the words of his son?"

"Speak," returned the trapper, in tones that issued from his chest, but which were rendered awfully distinct by the stillness that reigned in the place. "I am about to depart from the village of the Loups, and shortly shall be beyond the reach of your voice."

"Let the wise chief have no cares for his journey," continued Hard-Heart, with an earnest solicitude that led him to forget, for the moment, that others were waiting to address his adopted parent; "a hundred Loups shall clear his path from briers."

The author hints at theme through dialogue.

"Pawnee, I die as I have lived, a Christian man," resumed the trapper, with a force of voice that had the same startling effect on his hearers as is produced by the trumpet, when its blast rises suddenly and freely on the air after its obstructed sounds have been heard struggling in the distance; "as I came into life so will I leave it. Horses and arms are not needed to stand in the presence of the Great Spirit of my people. . . . And according to my gifts will he judge my deeds."

---

temperance (TEM pur uns) self-restraint in conduct, appetite, etc.

Sunset over the Marshes, Martin Johnson Heade. Corbis Bettmann

"My father will tell my young men how many Mingoes he has struck, and what acts of valor and justice he has done, that they may know how to imitate him."

"A boastful tongue is not heard in the heaven of a white man!" solemnly returned the old man. "What I have done He has seen. His eyes are always open. That which has been well done will He remember; wherein I have been wrong will He not forget to chastise, though He will do the same in mercy. No, my son; a paleface may not sing his own praises, and hope to have them acceptable before his God!"

A little disappointed, the young partisan stepped modestly back, making way for the recent comers to approach. Middleton took one of the meager hands of the trapper, and struggling to command his voice, he succeeded in announcing his presence. The old man listened like one whose thoughts were dwelling on a very different subject, but when the other had succeeded in making him understand that he was present, an expression of joyful recognition passed over his faded features–

"I hope you have not so soon forgotten those whom you so materially served!" Middleton concluded. "It would pain me to think my hold on your memory was so light."

---

chastise (chas TYZ) punish

"Little that I have ever seen is forgotten," returned the trapper; "I am at the close of many weary days, but there is not one among them all that I could wish to overlook. I remember you with the whole of your company; ay, and your gran'ther that went before you. I am glad that you have come back upon these plains, for I had need of one who speaks the English, since little faith can be put in the traders of these regions. Will you do a favor to an old and dying man?"

"Name it," said Middleton; "it shall be done."

"It is a far journey to send such trifles," resumed the old man, who spoke as short intervals, as strength and breath permitted; "a far and weary journey is the same; but kindnesses and friendships are things not to be forgotten. There is a settlement among the Otsego hills——"

"I know the place," interrupted Middleton, observing that he spoke with increasing difficulty; "proceed to tell me what you would have done."

"Take this rifle, and pouch, and horn, and send them to the person whose name is graven on the plates of the stock–a trader cut the letters with his knife,–for it is long that I have intended to send him such a token of my love!"

"It shall be so. Is there more that you could wish?"

"Little else have I to bestow. My traps I give to my Indian son; for honestly and kindly has he kept his faith. Let him stand before me."

Middleton explained to the chief what the trapper had said, and relinquished his own place to the other.

"Pawnee," continued the old man, always changing his language to suit the person he addressed, and not unfrequently according to the ideas he expressed, "it is a custom of my people for the father to leave his blessing with the son before he shuts his eyes forever. This blessing I give to you; take it, for the prayers of a Christian man will never make the path of a just warrior to the blessed prairies either longer or more tangled. May the God of a white man look on your deeds with friendly eyes, and may you

never commit an act that shall cause Him to darken His face. I know not whether we shall ever meet again. There are many traditions concerning the place of Good Spirits. It is not for one like me, old and experienced though I am, to set up my opinions against a nation's. You believed in the blessed prairies, and I have faith in the sayings of my fathers. If both are true, our parting will be final; but if should prove that same meaning is hid under different words, we shall yet stand together, Pawnee, before the face of your Wahcondah, who will then be no other than my God. There is much to be said in favor of both religions, for each seems suited to its own people, and no doubt it was so intended. I fear I have not altogether followed the gifts of my color, inasmuch as I find it a little painful to give up forever the use of the rifle, and the comforts of the chase. But then the fault has been my own, seeing that it could not have been His. Ay, Hector," he continued, leaning forward a little, and feeling for the ears of the hound, "our parting has come at last, dog, and it will be a long hunt. You have been an honest, and a bold, and a faithful hound. Pawnee, you cannot slay the pup on my grave, for where a Christian dog falls, there he lies forever; but you can be kind to him after I am gone, for the love you bear his master."

"The words of my father are in my ears," returned the young partisan, making a grave and respectful gesture of assent.

"Do you hear what the chief has promised, dog?" demanded the trapper, making an effort to notice the insensible effigy of his hound. Receiving no answering look, nor hearing any friendly whine, the old man felt his mouth and endeavored to force his hand between the cold lips. The truth then flashed upon him, although he was far from perceiving the whole extent of the deception. Falling back in his seat, he hung his head like one who felt a severe and unexpected shock. Profiting by this momentary forgetfulness, two young Indians removed the skin with the same delicacy of feeling that had induced them to attempt the pious fraud.

The author takes pains to show the Indians' sensitivity and respect for Bumppo.

"The dog is dead!" muttered the trapper, after a pause of many minutes; "a hound has his time as well as a man; and well has he filled his days! Captain," he added, making an effort to wave his hand for Middleton, "I am glad you have come; for though kind and well meaning according to the gifts of their color, these Indians are not the men to lay the head of a white man in his grave. I have been thinking, too, of this god at my feet; it will not do to set forth the opinion that a Christian can expect to meet his hound again; still there can be little harm in placing what is left of so faithful a servant nigh the bones of his master."

The stuffed dog is used as a symbol for the mortality of all creatures.

"It shall be as you desire."

"I'm glad you think of me in this matter. In order, then, to save labor lay the pup at my feet, or, for that matter, put him side by side. A hunter need never be ashamed to be found in company with his dog!"

"I charge myself with your wish."

The old man made a long and apparently a musing pause. At times he raised his eyes wistfully as if he would again address Middleton, but some innate feeling appeared always to suppress his words. The other, who observed his hesitation, inquired in a way most likely to encourage him to proceed, whether there was aught else that he could wish to have done.

The author gives more clues to Bumppo's character.

"I am without kith or kin in the wide world!" the trapper answered; "when I am gone, there will an end of my . . . [blood line]. We have never been chiefs; but honest and useful in our way, I hope it cannot be denied, we have always proved ourselves. My father lies buried near the sea, and the bones of his son will whiten on the prairies——"

"Name the spot, and your remains shall be placed by the side of your father," interrupted Middleton.

"Not so, not so, Captain. Let me sleep where I have lived, beyond the din of the settlements! Still, I see no need why the grave of an honest man should be hid, like a redskin in his ambushment. I paid a man in the settlements to make and put a graven stone at the head of my father's resting place. It was of the value of twelve beaver skins, and cunningly and curiously was it carved! Then it told all comers that the body of such a Christian lay beneath; and it spoke of his manner of life, of his years, and of his honesty....

"And such a stone you would have at your grave?"

"I! no, no, I have no son but Hard-Heart, and it is little that an Indian knows of white fashions and usages. Besides, I am his debtor already, seeing it is so little I have done since I have lived in his tribe. The rifle might bring the value of such a thing–but then I know it will give the boy pleasure to hang the piece in his hall, for many is the deer and the bird that he has seen it destroy. No, no, the gun must be sent to him whose name is graven on the lock!"

"But there is one who would gladly prove his affection in the way you wish; he who owes you not only his own deliverance from so many dangers, but who inherits a heavy debt of gratitude

---

kith (KITH) archaic word for friends
kin (KIN) relatives

Chief Tustennuggee, 19th century. Corbis Bettmann

from his ancestors. The stone shall be put at the head of your grave."

The old man extended his emaciated hand and gave the other a squeeze of thanks.

"I thought you might be willing to do it, but I was backward in asking the favor," he said, "seeing that you are not of my kin. Put

---

emaciated (ih MAY see ayt id) abnormally lean

no boastful words on the same, but just the name, the age, and the time of the death, with something from the Holy Book; no more, no more. My name will then not be altogether lost on 'arth; I need no more."

The plot is advanced through a change in Bumppo's condition.

Middleton intimated his assent, and then followed a pause that was only broken by distant and broken sentences from the dying man. He appeared now to have closed his accounts with the world, and to await merely for the final summons to quit it. Middleton and Hard-Heart placed themselves on the opposite sides of his seat, and watched with melancholy solicitude the variations of his countenance. For two hours there was no very sensible alterations. The expression of his faded and time-worn features was that of a calm and dignified repose. From time to time he spoke, uttering some brief sentence in the way of advice, or asking some simple questions concerning those in whose fortunes he still took a friendly interest. During the whole of that solemn and anxious period each individual of the tribe kept his place in the most self-restrained patience. When the old man spoke, all bent their heads to listen; and when his words were uttered, they seemed to ponder on their wisdom and usefulness.

As the flame drew nigher to the socket, his voice was hushed, and there were moments when his attendants doubted whether he still belonged to the living. Middleton, who watched each wavering expression of his weather-beaten visage with the interest of a keen observer of human nature, softened by the tenderness of personal regard, fancied he could read the workings of the old

Notice that the narrator, using the editorial "we," demonstrates his omniscience.

man's soul in the strong lineaments of his countenance. Perhaps what the enlightened soldier took for the delusion of mistaken opinion did actually occur, for who has returned from that unknown world to explain by what forms and in what manner he was introduced into its awful precincts? Without pretending to explain what must ever be a mystery to the quick, we shall simply relate facts as they occurred.

The author hints at theme through setting and symbol. What does the sunset stand for?

The trapper had remained nearly motionless for an hour. His eyes alone had occasionally opened and shut. When opened, his gaze seemed fastened on the clouds which hung around the western horizon, reflecting the bright colors and giving form and loveliness to the glorious tints of an American sunset. The hour–the calm beauty of the season–the occasion, all conspired to fill the spectators with solemn awe. Suddenly, while musing on the remarkable position in which he was placed, Middleton felt the hand which he held grasp his own with incredible power, and the old man, supported on either side by his friends, rose upright to his feet. For a moment he looked about him, as if to invite all in presence to listen (the lingering remnant of human frailty), and then, with a fine military elevation of the head, and with a voice that might be heard in every part of that numerous assembly, he pronounced the word–

"Here!"

The climax has arrived.

A movement so entirely unexpected, and the air of grandeur and humility which were so remarkably united in the mien of the trapper, together with the clear and uncommon force of his utterance, produced a short period of confusion in the faculties of all present. When Middleton and Hard-Heart, each of whom had involuntarily extended a hand to support the form of the old man, turned to him again, they found that the subject of their interest was removed forever beyond the necessity of their care. They mournfully placed the body in its seat, and Le Balafré arose to announce the termination of the scene to the tribe. The voice of the old Indian seemed a sort of echo from that invisible world to which the meek spirit of the trapper had just departed.

The dénouement begins.

"A valiant, a just, and a wise warrior has gone on the path which will lead him to the blessed grounds of his people!" he said. "When the voice of the Wahcondah called him, he was ready to answer. Go, my children; remember the just chief of the pale-faces, and clear your own tracks from briers!"

Bumppo's character is revealed through the opinion of another.

The grave was made beneath the shade of some noble oaks. It has been carefully watched to the present hour by the Pawnees of the Loup, and is often shown to the traveler and the trader as a spot where a just white man sleeps. In due time the stone was placed at its head, with the simple inscription which the trapper had himself requested. The only liberty taken by Middleton was to add–*"May no wanton hand ever disturb his remains!"*

---

utterance (UT ur uns) expressing by voice
wanton (WAHN tun) mischievous, unruly

Review the Selection

UNDERSTAND THE SELECTION

Recall

1. Who was Bumppo's adopted son?

2. What was the name of Bumppo's dog?

3. Where was Bumppo's father buried?

Infer

4. Why did the Indians respect Bumppo?

5. Why did Bumppo want a tombstone?

6. Why was Middleton afraid when he first rode in to camp?

7. Why does the author say the reward for Bumppo's temperance was a peaceful death?

Apply

8. Suppose that you are the person whose name had been engraved on Bumppo's rifle. How would you have reacted when Middleton delivered it?

9. Suppose Hard-Heart died. Does he leave the world with as much grace as Bumppo did?

10. Suppose that you are one of the Indians present when Bumppo spoke of past events. What did he talk about?

Respond to Literature

What does Bumppo's life and death on the prairie symbolize?

THINK ABOUT FICTION

Fiction is primarily narrative writing that comes from the imagination of an author. Unlike nonfiction narrative, it is not based on history or fact. Stories, told in novels, short stories, and plays, make up the category of fictional narrative. Through fiction, the reader experiences sadness, joy, humor, and other emotions common to human life and watches the resolution of lifelike conflicts and struggles.

1. Who is the protagonist in the excerpt you read? Who is the antagonist? Are they in conflict? Explain.

2. Does the setting of the excerpt contribute to your understanding of Bumppo's character?

3. What element of plot follows the climax?

4. What is an omniscient narrator able to do that narrators using other points of view cannot? Is this an advantage? Explain.

5. What do you think the theme of the excerpt is?

DEVELOP YOUR VOCABULARY

Root words are English words that have no letters or syllables added to them. **Suffixes** are word parts that can be added to base words to change their part of speech. For example, *-ful* is a commonly used suffix. Add it to *care* or *pain*, both nouns, and you have formed *careful* or *painful*, both adjectives. Here are some other suffixes and what they do:

Noun-forming suffixes: *-ance, -ion, -ity, -ment, -ness, -or, -ship*
Adjective-forming suffixes: *-able, -ful, -less*
Adverb-forming suffixes: *-ly, -ward*

Write the following words from *The Prairie*. Circle each suffix and write whether the word is a noun, an adjective, or an adverb.

1. visitor
2. comfortable
3. settlement
4. boastful
5. politely
6. kindness
7. friendship
8. modestly
9. fearless
10. outwardly
11. utterance
12. sensitively

Learn About

READING FOCUS

Draw Conclusions Sometimes you must think beyond the words on the page to get a full meaning of the author's intent. Readers draw conclusions by using prior knowledge to arrive at a decision or judgment. As you read "To a Waterfowl," draw conclusions about what the author might think of his own life, as well as how he views birds.

THE LYRIC

A **lyric** is a short poem usually expressing intense personal feeling. A lyric is like a still photograph as opposed to a movie. The lyric does not have a plot that is advanced through a series of events. Instead, it captures a moment in time and focuses on it very closely.

The lyric poet attempts to create a specific emotional response in the reader. The poet achieves this effect through the details, impressions, and insights that a heightened awareness makes him or her capable of expressing. The result is a vivid word picture of an experience to which the poet may give new meaning for the reader.

As you read "To a Waterfowl," ask yourself:

1. What lesson or new meaning does the author find in the migration of the bird?
2. In what way does this poem illustrate the poet's heightened awareness?

WRITING CONNECTION

Select a common experience in nature, for example, leaves falling from a tree in autumn or a deer running across a green meadow. In a prose paragraph, use details, impressions, or insights to give this experience a new meaning.

TO A WATERFOWL

by William Cullen Bryant

Whither, midst falling dew,
While glow the heavens with the last steps of day,
Far, through their rosy depths, dost thou pursue
    Thy solitary way?

5   Vainly the fowler's eye
Might mark thy distant flight to do thee wrong,
As, darkly seen against the crimson sky,
    Thy figure floats along.

       Seek'st thou the plashy brink
10   Of weedy lake, or marge of river wide,
Or where the rocking billows rise and sink
    On the chafed ocean-side?

There is a Power whose care
Teaches thy way along that pathless coast—
15   The desert and illimitable air—
    Lone wandering, but not lost.

---

whither (HW*ITH* ur) to what place, point, etc.
fowler (FOUL ur) hunter of wildfowl
plashy (PLASH ee) marshy; wet
marge (MAHRJ) edge or border
chafed (CHAYFT) to have been worn away; eroded
illimitable (ih LIM ih tuh bul) endless

All day thy wings have fanned,
At that far height, the cold, thin atmosphere,
Yet stoop not, weary, to the welcome land,
20   Though the dark night is near.

    And soon that toil shall end;
Soon shalt thou find a summer home, and rest,
And scream among thy fellows; reeds shall bend,
      Soon, o'er thy sheltered nest.

25   Thou'rt gone, thy abyss of heaven
Hath swallowed up thy form; yet, on my heart
Deeply has sunk the lesson thou hast given,
      And shall not soon depart.

    He who, from zone to zone,
30   Guides through the boundless sky thy certain flight,
In the long way that I must tread alone,
      Will lead my steps aright.

---

abyss (uh BIS) a thing too big for measurement

Review the Selection

UNDERSTAND THE SELECTION

Recall

1. What color was the sky? How does the bird show up against it?

2. Was the bird alone or was it part of a flock?

3. What will the bird soon find?

Infer

4. At what time of day did Bryant observe the bird?

5. Why could a hunter not harm the bird?

6. Where was the bird headed?

7. What type of bird was this?

Apply

8. What lesson did Bryant learn from observing the bird?

9. Predict what might have happened if Bryant had found an injured water-fowl. Explain why.

10. Suppose that Bryant was a hunter. Do you think he would have seen the bird any differently? Compare and contrast the two viewpoints.

Respond to Literature

What characteristics do Bumppo and the speaker of this poem share?

THINK ABOUT LYRIC

A **lyric** is a poem that usually expresses intense personal feeling. The poet tries to create a specific emotional response in the reader. Through this response, the poet hopes the reader will share his or her intense feeling for the experience.

1. Why do you think the poet describes a "solitary" bird rather than a flock?

2. The bird is flying too high to be shot by hunters. How did you react when you read that? Why?

3. What is meant by "There is a Power whose care/Teaches thy way along that pathless coast"?

4. In stanza 8, do you think the poet's "long way" refers to his journey home or his life? Why?

5. The English poet William Wordsworth said that "poetry . . . takes its origin from emotion recollected in tranquility." How does this describe the way Bryant wrote "To a Waterfowl"? Why?

READING FOCUS

Draw Conclusions Tell about one conclusion that you drew about the deeper meaning of the poem. What details in the poem led you to this conclusion?

DEVELOP YOUR VOCABULARY

A poet must carefully select words to fit the meter of a poem as well as to express his or her thoughts and feelings. The **meter** is the pattern of stressed and unstressed syllables in each line of the poem.

Poets sometimes shorten words to keep the meter. They may make a contraction of a word or words not commonly used as contractions. A contraction is a shortened form of one or two words. Letters are removed. An apostrophe takes the place of the missing letter or letters. For example, 'twas is a contraction of *it was*; *o'er* is the poetic contraction of *over*.

Following is a list of several contractions poets sometimes use. Study each contraction. Write the word or words you think the contraction represents. Check in a dictionary to be sure you are correct. (Not all the contractions will be found there, however.) Then use each contraction in an original sentence.

1. e'en
2. 'twill
3. shall't
4. 'tween
5. e'er
6. 'twixt

Learn About

DIALOGUE

The written conversation of two or more people is called **dialogue**. Although it is used most often in fiction, dialogue is also used in nonfiction.

The writer of an autobiographical narrative may use dialogue to help give an easy, natural flow to the work. The people who were a part of the author's life are allowed to speak in their own words as the author remembers them. Their dialogue advances the narrative and shows events as they were.

Conversational give-and-take helps to define the personality and develop the character of each speaker. Using the direct words of people makes the writing seem more realistic.

As you read this selection, ask yourself:

1. How is dialogue used in Alcott's autobiographical narrative?
2. Does the dialogue help to make the people she worked with seem more real?

WRITING CONNECTION

Think of a conversation you recently had with a friend. Try to recall exact words. Write your conversation as accurately as you can, using each person's words in quotation marks.

READING FOCUS

Make Inferences Authors often do not explain the thoughts, feelings, and personalities of the characters in a story. Instead, the reader infers, or guesses, what the characters are like based on their words.

As you read this text, make inferences about each of these characters: the narrator, Teddy, John, and the doctor. Think about how the dialogue reveals aspects of them.

from Hospital Sketches

(Chapter IV "A Night")

by Louisa May Alcott

Being fond of the night side of nature, I was soon promoted to the post of night nurse. . . . I usually found my boys in the jolliest state of mind their condition allowed; for it was a know fact that Nurse Periwinkle objected to blue devils, and entertained a belief that he who laughed most was surest of recovery. . . .

More flattering than the most gracefully turned compliment, more grateful than the most admiring glance, was the sight of those rows of faces, all strange to me a little while ago, now lighting up, with smiles of welcome, as I came among them, enjoying that moment heartily, with a womanly pride in their regard, a motherly affection for them all. The evenings were spent in reading aloud, writing letters, waiting on and amusing the men, going the rounds with Dr. P., as he made his second daily survey, dressing my dozen wounds afresh, giving last doses, and making them cozy for the long hours to come, till the nine o'clock bell rang, the gas was turned down, the day nurses went off duty, the night watch came on, and my nocturnal adventure began.

My ward was now divided into three rooms; and, under favor of the matron, I had managed to sort out the patients in such a way that I had what I called, "my duty room," my "pleasure room," and my "pathetic room," and worked for each in a different way. One, I visited, armed with a dressing tray, full of rollers, plasters, and pins; another, with books, flowers, games, and gossip; a third, with teapots, lullabies, consolation, and sometimes, a shroud. . . .

The night whose events I have a fancy to record, opened with a little comedy, and closed with a great tragedy; for a virtuous and useful life untimely ended is always tragical to those who see not as God sees. My headquarters were beside the bed of a New Jersey boy, crazed by the horrors of that dreadful Saturday. A slight wound on the knee brought him there; but his mind had suffered more than his body; some string of that delicate machine was over strained, and, for days, he had been reliving in imagination, the scenes he could not forget, till his distress broke out in incoherent ravings, pitiful to hear. As I sat by him, endeavoring to soothe his poor distracted brain by the constant touch of wet hands over his hot forehead, he lay cheering his comrades on, hurrying them back, then counting them as they fell around him, often clutching my arm, to drag me from the vicinity of a bursting shell, or covering up his head to screen himself from a shower of shot; his face brilliant with fever; his eyes restless; his head never still; every muscle strained and rigid; while an incessant stream of defiant shouts, whispered warnings, and broken laments, poured from his lips with that forceful bewilderment which makes such wanderings so hard to overhear.

It was past eleven, and my patient was slowly wearying himself into fitful intervals of quietude, when, in one of these pauses, a curious sound arrested my attention. Looking over my shoulder, I saw a one-legged phantom hopping nimbly down the room; and, going to meet it, recognized a certain Pennsylvania gentleman, whose wound-fever had taken a turn for the worse, and, depriving him of the few wits a drunken campaign had informed me, touching the military cap which formed a striking contrast to the severe simplicity of the rest of his decidedly undress uniform. When sane, the least movement produced a roar of pain or a volley of oaths; but the departure of reason seemed to have wrought an agreeable change, both in the man and his manners; for, balancing himself on one leg, like a meditative stork, he plunged into an animated discussion of the war, the President, lager beer, and Enfield rifles, regardless of any suggestions of mine as to the propriety of returning to bed, lest he be court-martialed for desertion.

Any thing more supremely ridiculous can hardly be imagined than this figure, scantily draped in white, its one foot covered with a big blue sock, a dingy cap set rakingly askew on its shaven head, and placid satisfaction beaming in its broad red face, as it flourished a mug in one hand, an old boot in the other, calling them canteen and knapsack, while it skipped and fluttered in the most unearthly fashion. What to do with the creature I didn't know; Dan [the watchman] was absent, and if I went to find him, the perambulator might festoon himself out of the window, set his toga on fire, or do some of his neighbors a mischief. . . . I was about to slam the door in his face, and run for help, when a second and saner phantom, "all in white," came to the rescue, in the likeness of a big Prussian, who spoke no English, but divined the crisis, and put an end to it, by bundling the lively monoped into his bed, like a baby. . . . Rather exhausted by his excursion, the member from Pennsylvania subsided; and, after an irrepressible laugh together, my Prussian ally and myself were returning to our places, when the echo of a sob caused us to glance along the beds. It came from one in the corner—such a little bed!—and such a tearful little face looked up at us, as we stopped beside it! The twelve years old drummer boy was not singing now, but sobbing, with a manly effort all the while to stifle the distressful sounds that would break out.

"What is it, Teddy?" I asked, as he rubbed the tears away, and checked himself in the middle of a great sob to answer plaintively:

"I've got a chill, ma'am, but I aint cryin' for that, 'cause I'm used to it. I dreamed Kit was here, and when I waked up he wasn't, and I couldn't help it, then."

The boy came in with the rest, and the man who was taken dead from the ambulance was the Kit he mourned. Well he might; for, when the wounded were brought from Fredericksburg, the child lay in one of the camps thereabout, and this good friend, though sorely hurt himself, would not leave him to the exposure and neglect of such a time and place; but, wrapping him in his own blanket, carried him in his arms to the transport, tended him during the passage, and only yielded up his charge when Death met him at the door of the hospital which promised care and comfort for the boy. For ten days, Teddy had shivered or burned with fever and ague, pining the while for Kit, and refusing to be comforted, because he had not been able to thank him for the generous protection, which, perhaps, had cost the giver's life. The vivid dream had wrung the childish heart with a fresh pang, and when I tried the solace fitted for his years, the remorseful fear that haunted him found vent in a fresh burst of tears, and he looked at the wasted hands I was endeavoring to warm:

"Oh! if I'd only been as thin when Kit carried me as I am now, maybe he wouldn't have died; but I was heavy, he was hurt worser than we knew, and so it killed him; and I didn't see him, to say good bye."

This thought had troubled him in secret; and my assurances that his friends would probably have died at all events,

hardly assuaged the bitterness of his regretful grief.

At this juncture, the delirious man began to shout; the one-legged rose up in his bed, as if preparing for another dart, Teddy bewailed himself more piteously than before; and if ever a woman was at her wit's end, that distracted female was Nurse Periwinkle, during the space of two or three minutes, as she vibrated between the three beds, like an agitated pendulum. Like a most opportune reinforcement, Dan, the bandy, appeared, and devoted himself to the lively party, leaving me free to return to my post; for the Prussian, with a nod and a smile, took the lad away to his own bed, and lulled him to sleep with a soothing murmur, like a mammoth humble bee. I liked that in Fritz, and if he ever wondered afterward at the dainties which sometimes found their way into his rations, or the extra comforts of his bed, he might have found a solution of the mystery in sundry persons' knowledge of the fatherly action of that night.

Hardly was I settled again, when

the . . . [attendant of the "pathetic room"] delivered a message I had expected, yet dreaded to receive:

"John is going, ma'am, and wants to see you, if you can come."

"The moment this boy is asleep; tell him so, and let me know if I am in danger of being too late."

My Ganymede departed, and while I quieted poor Shaw, I thought of John. He came in a day or two after the others; and, one evening, when I entered my "pathetic room," I found a lately emptied bed occupied by a large, fair man, with a fine face, and the serenest eyes I ever met. One of the earlier comers had often spoken of a friend, who had remained behind, that those apparently worse wounded than himself might reach a shelter first. . . .

I had some curiosity to behold this piece of excellence, and when he came, watched him for a night or two, before I made friends with him; for, to tell the truth, I was a little afraid of the stately looking man, whose bed had to be lengthened to accommodate his commanding stature; who seldom spoke, uttered no complaint, asked no sympathy, but tranquilly observed what went on about him; and, as he lay high upon his pillows, no picture of dying stateman or warrior was ever fuller of real dignity than this Virginia blacksmith. A most attractive face he had, framed in brown hair and beard, comely featured and full of vigor, as yet unsubdued by pain; thoughtful and often beautifully mild while watching the afflictions of others, as if entirely forgetful of his own. . . .

The next night, as I went my rounds with Dr. P., I happened to ask which man in the room probably suffered most; and, to my great surprise, he glanced at John:

"Every breath he draws is like a stab; for the ball pierced the left lung, broke a rib, and did no end of damage here and there; so the poor lad can find neither forgetfulness nor ease, because he must lie on his wounded back or suffocate. It will be a hard struggle, and a long one, for he possesses great vitality; but even his temperate life can't save him; I wish it could."

"You don't mean he must die, Doctor?"

"Bless you there's not the slightest hope for him; and you'd better tell him so before long; women have a way of doing such things comfortably, so I leave it to you. He won't last more than a day or two, at furthest."

I could have sat down on the spot and cried heartily, if I had not learned the wisdom of bottling up one's tears for leisure moments. Such an end seemed very hard for such a man, when half a dozen worn out, worthless bodies round him, were gathering up the remnants of wasted lives, to linger on for years perhaps, burdens to others, daily reproaches to themselves. The army needed men like John, earest, brave, and faithful; fighting for liberty and justice with both heart and hand, true soldiers of the Lord. I could not give him up so soon, or think with any patience of so excellent a nature robbed of its fulfillment, and blundered into eternity by the rashness of stupidity of those at whose hands so many lives may be required. It was an easy think for Dr. P. to

---

Ganymede (GAN uh MEED) a beautiful young boy in Greek mythology

say: "Tell him he must die," but a cruelly hard thing to do, and by no means as "comfortable" as he politely suggested. I had not the heart to do it then, and privately indulged the hope that some change for the better might take place, in spite of gloomy prophesies; so, rendering my task unnecessary. A few minutes later, as I came in again, with fresh rollers, I saw John sitting erect, with no one to support him, while the surgeon dressed his back. I had never hitherto seen it done; for, having simpler wounds to attend to, and knowing the fidelity of both strength and experience were needed in his case. I had forgotten that the strong man might long for the gentle tendance of a woman's hands, the sympathetic magnetism of a woman's presence, as well as the feebler souls about him. The Doctor's words caused me to reproach myself with neglect, not of any real duty perhaps, but of those little cares and kindnesses that solace homesick spirits, and make the heavy hours pass easier. John looked lonely and forsaken just then, as he sat with bent head, hands folded on his knee, and no outward sign of suffering, till, looking nearer, I saw great tears roll down and drop upon the floor. It was a new sight there; for, though I had seen many suffer, some swore, some groaned, most endured silently, but none wept. Yet it did not seem weak, only very touching, and straightway my fear vanished, my heart opened wide and took him in, as, gathering the bent head in my arms, as freely as if he had been a little child, I said, "Let me help you bear it, John."

Never, on any human countenance, have I seen so swift and beautiful a look of gratitude, surprise and comfort, as that which answered me more eloquently than the whispered

"Thank you, ma'am, this is right good! this is what I wanted!"

"Then why not ask for it before?"

"I didn't like to be a trouble; you seemed so busy, and I could manage to get on alone."

"You shall not want it any more, John."

Nor did he; for now I understood the wistful look that sometimes followed me, as I went out, after a brief pause beside his bed, or merely a passing nod, while busied with those who seemed to need me more than he, because more urgent in their demands; now I knew that to him, as to so many, I was the poor substitute for mother, wife, or sister, and in his eyes no stranger, but a friend who hitherto had seemed neglectful; for, in his modesty, he had never guessed the truth. This was changed now; and, through the tedious operation of probing, bathing, and dressing his wounds, he leaned against me, holding my hand fast, and, if pain wrung further tears from him, no one saw them fall but me. . . . Although the manliest man among my forty, he said, "Yes, ma'am," like a little boy; received suggestions for his comfort with the quick smile that brightened his whole face; and now and then, as I stood tidying the table by his bed, I felt him softly touch my gown, as if to assure himself that I was there. Anything more natural and frank I never saw, and found this brave John as bashful as brave, yet full of excellencies and fine aspirations, which, having no power to express themselves in words, seemed to have bloomed into his character and made him what he was.

After that night, an hour of each evening that remained to him was devoted to his ease or pleasure. He could not talk much, for breath was precious, and he spoke in whispers; but from occasional conversations, I gleaned scraps of private history which only added to the affection and respect I felt for him. Once he asked me to write a letter, and as I settled pen and paper, I said, with an irrepressible glimmer of feminine curiosity, "Shall it be addressed to wife, or mother, John?"

"Neither, ma'am; I've got no wife, and will write to mother when I get better. . . ."

"Do you ever regret that you came, when you lie here suffering so much?"

"Never, ma'am; I haven't helped a great deal, but I've shown I was willing to give my life, and perhaps I've got to; but I don't blame anybody, and if it was to do over again, I'd do it. I'm a little sorry I wasn't wounded in front; it looks cowardly to be hit in the back, but I obeyed orders, and it don't matter in the end, I know."

Poor John! it did not matter now, except that a shot in the front might have spared the long agony in store for him. He seemed to read the thought that troubled me, as he spoke so hopefully when there was no hope, for he suddenly added:

"This is my first battle; do they think it's going to be my last?"

"I'm afraid they do, John."

It was the hardest question I had ever been called upon to answer; doubly hard with those clear eyes fixed on mine, forcing a truthful answer by their own truth. He seemed a little startled at first, pon-dered over the fateful fact a moment, then shook his head, with a glance at the broad chest and muscular limbs stretched out before him:

"I'm not afraid, but it's difficult to believe all at once. I'm so strong it don't seem possible for such a little wound to kill me."

"Shall I write to your mother, now?" I asked, thinking that these sudden tidings might change all plans and purposes; but they did not. . . .

"No, ma'am; to Laurie [my brother] just the same; he'll break it to her best, and I'll add a line to her myself when you get done."

So I wrote that which he dictated. . . . He added a few lines, with steady hand, and, as I sealed it, said, with a patient sort of sigh, "I hope the answer will come in time for me to see it." . . .

These things had happened two days before; now John was dying, and the letter had not come. I had been summoned to many death beds in my life, but to none that made my heart ache as it did then. . . . As I went in, John stretched out both hands:

"I knew you'd come! I guess I'm moving on, ma'am."

He was; and so rapidly that, even while he spoke, over his face I saw the grey veil falling that no human hand can lift. I sat down by him, wiped the drops from his forehead, stirred the air about him with the slow wave of a fan, and waited to help him die. He stood in the sore need of help and I could do so little; for as the doctor had foretold, the strong body rebelled against death, and fought every inch of the way, forcing him to draw each breath with a spasm. . . . For hours he suffered, . . . yet through it all, his eyes never lost their perfect serenity, and the man's soul seemed to sit therein, undaunted by the ills that vexed his flesh. . . .

I thought him nearly gone, and had just laid down the fan, believing its help to be no longer needed, when suddenly he rose up in his bed, and cried out with a bitter cry that broke the silence, sharply startling every one with its agonized appeal:

"For God's sake, give me air!"

It was the only cry pain or death had wrung from him, the only boon he had asked; and none of us could grant it, for all the airs that blew were useless now. Dan flung up the window. The first red streak of dawn was warming the grey east, a herald of the coming sun; John saw it, and with the love of light which lingers in us to the end, seemed to read in it a sign of hope of help, for, over his whole face there broke that mysterious expression, brighter than any smile, which often comes to eyes that look their last. . . . He never spoke again, but to the end held my hand close, so close that when he was asleep at last, I could not but be glad that, through its touch, the presence of human sympathy, perhaps, had lightened that hard hour.

When they had made him ready for the grave, John lay in state for half an hour, a thing which seldom happened in that busy place; but a universal sentiment of reverence and affection seemed to fill the hearts of all who had known or heard of him; and when the rumor of his death went through the house, always astir, many came to see him, and I felt a tender sort of pride in my lost patient; for he looked a most heroic figure, lying there stately and still as the statue of some young knight asleep upon his tomb. . . . As we stood looking at him, the ward master handed me a letter, saying it had been forgotten the night before. It was John's letter, come just an hour too late to gladden the eyes that had longed and looked for it so eagerly! Yet he had it; for, after I had cut some brown locks for his mother, and taken off the ring to send her, telling how well the talisman had done its work, I kissed this good son for her sake, and laid the letter in his hand, still folded as when I drew my own away, feeling that its place was there, and making myself happy with the thought, that even in his solitary place the "Government Lot," he would not be without some token of the love which makes life beautiful and outlives death. Then I left him, glad to have known so genuine a man, and carrying with me an enduring memory of the brave Virginia blacksmith, as he lay serenely waiting for the dawn of that long day which knows no night.

Review the Selection

UNDERSTAND THE SELECTION

Recall

1. What is the setting of this selection?

2. How old is the youngest patient?

3. What patient does Alcott most admire?

Infer

4. Why did Teddy dream about Kit?

5. Why did John think his wound was not serious?

6. Why did Alcott have difficulty answering when John asked if he had been in his last battle?

7. Why did Alcott admire John so much?

Apply

8. Suppose you have to explain to John that he will die. How would you feel?

9. Suppose you were John's brother. How would you tell your mother about his death?

10. Is the suffering the same in every war?

Respond to Literature

Realism in literature is the attempt to picture things as they really are. How does this selection illustrate that trend?

THINK ABOUT DIALOGUE

Dialogue is the words of real people or fictional characters. Thus, it is a conversation between two or more people. In drama, it can be the main way that the plot is developed. In nonfiction, it allows participants in a narrative to speak for themselves.

1. How does the use of dialogue in "A Night" make the people seem real?

2. Cite one example of how a speaker revealed his or her personality in dialogue.

3. Do you think Alcott understates or exaggerates the horrors of life in a wartime hospital? Explain.

4. Where is the main focus in "A Night" —on Alcott or on the men in the hospital? Explain your answer.

5. Most of the activity Alcott discusses happened in one night. Why do you think she chose to write about such a short period of time?

READING FOCUS

Make Inferences As you read, you made inferences about the characters' personalities from the dialogue. What can you infer about the doctor's personality from his description of John's condition? Why do you think the author did not just report what the doctor said?

DEVELOP YOUR VOCABULARY

Sometimes a specialized vocabulary develops around a place or occupation. New words or new meanings for existing words become part of this specialized vocabulary, which is often called *jargon*. For example, if you hear the words *classroom*, *teacher*, or *schoolbus*, you immediately think of school. If you hear the words *backstage*, *cast*, or *script*, you immediately think of the theater. Can you think of other words related to the school or theater setting?

A hospital was the setting for this selection. Consequently, words commonly associated with the vocabulary of a hospital have been used. Following are words found in this selection. Review each word carefully. Look the words up in a dictionary, if necessary. Then write an original paragraph using each word at least once.

1. ambulance
2. hospital
3. medicine
4. bandage
5. rounds
6. nurse
7. doctor
8. wound

Schofield -
'22

New England Speaks

We looked upon a world unknown,
On nothing we could call our own.
Around the glistening wonder bent
The blue walls of the firmament,
No cloud above, no earth below,—
A universe of sky and snow!
                    —John Greenleaf Whittier

Morning Light, Walter Elmer Schofield. Giraudon/Art Resource

Learn About

RHYME

Poets use various techniques to convey their ideas and feelings. One of the devices a poet uses is repetition of sounds to create rhyme. In poetry, **rhyme** is a regular repetition of sounds.

There are two ways in which a poet can use rhyme in a poem. The kind of rhyme most frequently used is **end rhyme**. End rhymes occur when words at the end of lines rhyme with each other. *Splash* and *crash* rhyme in these lines:

Tiny waves just splash
While giant waves do crash
Upon the silent shore.

However, some writers use internal rhymes; that is, words that rhyme within a single line. In this line, *Squirrels leaping and creeping on waving branches*, the words *leaping* and *creeping* are an example of internal rhyme.

As you read the following poems, ask yourself:

1. Would the flow of the poems change if Longfellow had not used rhyme?
2. How did Longfellow's use of rhyme contribute to the pace of the poem?

READING FOCUS

Understand Figures of Speech A simile is a comparison of two things using *like* or *as*. For example, "the pencil was red" might be written as "the pencil was as red as a licorice stick." A metaphor also compares but without the use of the words *like* or *as*. As you read "Paul Revere's Ride," look for these types of figures of speech. Think about how these figures of speech help create the mood, or feeling, of the poem.

WRITING CONNECTION

Make a list of six pairs of rhyming words. Then use one pair of words to write an end rhyme.

from
Paul Revere's Ride

by Henry Wadsworth Longfellow

Listen, my children, and you shall hear
Of the midnight ride of Paul Revere,
On the eighteenth of April, in Seventy-five;
Hardly a man is now alive
5   Who remembers that famous day and year.[1]

He said to his friend, "If the British march
By land or sea from the town to-night,
Hang a lantern aloft in the belfry arch
Of the North Church tower as a signal light,—
10   One, if by land, and two, if by sea;
And I on the opposite shore will be,
Ready to ride and spread the alarm
Through every Middlesex village and farm,
For the country folk to be up and to arm."

15   Then he said, "Good night!" and with muffled oar
Silently rowed to the Charlestown shore,
Just as the moon rose over the bay,
Where swinging wide at her moorings lay
The Somerset, British man-of-war;
20   A phantom ship, with each mast and spar
Across the moon like a prison bar,
And a huge black hulk, that was magnified
By its own reflection in the tide.

---

belfry (BEL free) bell tower
moorings (MUUR ingz) ropes to fasten a ship
man-of-war (man uv WAWR) warship
spar (SPAHR) pole attached to mast
hulk (HULK) old ship
[1]**famous day and year:** Longfellow's poem was written about 80 years after the
  events described.

Meanwhile, his friend, through alley and street,
25 Wanders and watches with eager ears,
Till in the silence around him he hears
The muster of men at the barrack door,
The sound of arms, and the tramp of feet,
And the measured tread of the grenadiers,
30 Marching down to their boats on the shore. . . .

On the opposite shore walked Paul Revere.
Now he patted his horse's side,
Now gazed at the landscape far and near,
Then, impetuous, stamped the earth,
35 And turned and tightened his saddle-girth;
But mostly he watched with eager search
The belfry-tower of the Old North Church,
As it rose above the graves on the hill,
Lonely and spectral and sombre and still.
40 And lo! as he looks, on the belfry's height
A glimmer, and then a gleam of light!
He springs to the saddle, the bridle he turns,
But lingers and gazes, till full on his sight
A second lamp in the belfry burns!

45 A hurry of hoofs in a village street,
A shape in the moonlight, a bulk in the dark,
And beneath, from the pebbles, in passing, a spark
Struck out by a steed flying fearless and fleet:
That was all! And yet, through the gloom and the light,
50 The fate of a nation was riding that night;
And the spark struck out by that steed, in his flight,
Kindled the land into flame with its heat. . .

It was twelve by the village clock,
When he crossed the bridge into Medford town. . . .

---

muster (MUS tur) roll call
grenadier (gren uh DIR) foot soldier
impetuous (im PECH oo us) eager; violent
girth (GURTH) strap that holds saddle on horse
spectral (SPEK trul) ghostlike
sombre (SOM bur) usually spelled somber; dark and gloomy
bulk (BULK) object; shape
fleet (FLEET) very fast

Paul Revere's Ride from Boston to Lexington, 19th century. The Granger Collection

55   It was one by the village clock,
      When he galloped into Lexington. . . .

      It was two by the village clock,
      When he came to the bridge in Concord town.
      He heard the bleating of the flock,
60   And the twitter of birds among the trees,
      And felt the breath of the morning breeze
      Blowing over the meadows brown.
      And one was safe and asleep in his bed
      Who at the bridge would be first to fall,

---

bleating (BLEET ing) cry of sheep

65   Who that day would be lying dead,
      Pierced by a British musket-ball.

      You know the rest. In the books you have read,
      How the British Regulars[2] fired and fled,—
      How the farmers gave them ball for ball,
70   From behind each fence and farm-yard wall,
      Chasing the red-coats down the lane,
      Then crossing the fields to emerge again
      Under the trees at the turn of the road,
      And only pausing to fire and load.

75   So through the night rode Paul Revere;
      And so through the night went his cry of alarm
      To every Middlesex village and farm, —
      A cry of defiance and not of fear,
      A voice in the darkness, a knock at the door,
80   And a word that shall echo forevermore!
      For, borne on the night-wind of the Past,
      Through all our history, to the last,
      In the hour of darkness and peril and need,
      The people will waken and listen to hear
85   The hurrying hoof-beats of that steed,
      And the midnight message of Paul Revere.

---

[2]**British Regulars:** These were regular army troops.

Twilight on the Shawangunk, 1865, T. Worthington Whittredge. The Granger Collection

from

THE DAY IS DONE

by Henry Wadsworth Longfellow

The day is done, and the darkness
Falls from the wings of Night,
As a feather is wafted downward
From an eagle in his flight.

5   I see the lights of the village
Gleam through the rain and the mist,
And a feeling of sadness comes o'er me
That my soul cannot resist:

A feeling of sadness and longing,
10   That is not akin to pain,
And resembles sorrow only
As the mist resembles the rain.

---

wafted (WAHFT id) blown along smoothly
akin (uh KIN) related

Come, read to me some poem,
Some simple and heartfelt lay,
15   That shall soothe this restless feeling,
And banish the thoughts of day.

. . . .

Such songs have power to quiet
The restless pulse of care,
And come like the benediction
20   That follows after prayer.

Then read from the treasured volume
The poem of thy choice,
And lend to the rhyme of the poet
The beauty of thy voice.

25   And the night shall be filled with music,
And the cares, that infest the day,
Shall fold their tents, like the Arabs,
And as silently steal away.

---

heartfelt (HAHRT felt) sincere; meaningful
lay (LAY) short song or story poem
benediction (ben uh DIK shun) blessing
infest (in FEST) trouble; disturb

Henry Wadsworth Longfellow (1807–1882)

At the time of his death, and for years after, Henry Wadsworth Longfellow had no rival as America's best-loved poet. His poetry often appeared in magazines. His books were in constant demand. Schoolchildren read dozens of his poems and often had to memorize several.

Longfellow's popularity is easy to understand. He saw beauty everywhere—in an old ship against the moon in Boston Harbor, in the forests, in the fields. He was interested in the common life of the common people. He usually wrote rather simple, melodious poems that nearly everyone could understand. But most of all, he calmed the nerves of the nation. In an age when life was often hard, Longfellow told his American readers to work hard and to accept whatever fate had to offer.

Longfellow's life was mostly a comfortable one. He grew up in Maine, graduated from college at an early age, and went to Europe for further study. Afterwards, he kept two careers going at the same time—first as a poet, and second as a professor of foreign languages. He lived to see his poetry translated into 24 languages. But as he told his readers, "Into each life some rain must fall." In 1861, his wife burned to death when her dress accidentally caught fire. Longfellow's own struggle out of sorrow is reflected in some of his poems.

In his own day, what features of Longfellow's poetry do you think most appealed to his readers?

Review the Selection

UNDERSTAND THE SELECTION

Recall

1. When did Paul Revere make his ride?

2. Upon whom did he depend for information about the British troops?

3. What did the speaker in "The Day Is Done" like at the end of the day?

Infer

4. Paraphrase what Longfellow wrote about in "The Day Is Done."

5. Describe how you think the *Somerset* looked to Paul Revere as he rowed by.

6. Why do you think Longfellow wrote that "the fate of a nation was riding that night"?

7. Why do you think Longfellow wrote a poem about this night?

Apply

8. Predict what might have happened if the British had come by land.

9. What might Revere have thought while waiting for the signal?

10. Predict what you think happened to the speaker in "The Day Is Done" after hearing the poem.

Respond to Literature

How does "Paul Revere's Ride" reflect the feelings of Americans in the 1800s?

THINK ABOUT RHYME

Rhyme contributed greatly to the movement and pace of the two poems you have just read. Some words that rhyme have soft sounds that can make a poem seem to move slowly. Other words have crisp sounds that produce a steady pace. In "Paul Revere's Ride," the rhymes contribute to the feeling of urgency that Longfellow has written into the poem. How will the British advance? Will it be by land or sea? Will Paul Revere warn the colonists in time?

1. What kind of rhymes did Longfellow use in "Paul Revere's Ride"?

2. What was the pace of "Paul Revere's Ride"?

3. How did the pace of "The Day Is Done" differ from that of "Paul Revere's Ride"?

4. Which of the rhyming words in the second stanza of "Paul Revere's Ride" move the poem along at a steady pace?

5. Why do these words help move the poem along at a steady pace?

READING FOCUS

Understand Figures of Speech As you read "Paul Revere's Ride" and "The Day Is Done," you were asked to look for figures of speech. Choose your favorite simile or metaphor and explain how the comparison helped to create the mood of the poem.

DEVELOP YOUR VOCABULARY

Review the meanings of the vocabulary words from this selection. Context can often help you figure out the meaning of an unfamiliar word. Read this sentence: The captain gave his *heartfelt* thanks to the crew, and his warm sincerity touched them all. By the author's use of the words *warm sincerity* and *touched* you are better able to understand what *heartfelt* meant.

Read the following sentences. Use context clues to help you figure out the meaning of each italicized word. Underline the words that help you.

1. The *moorings* of the boat were not fastened tightly, and the ropes loosened.

2. The *spar* snapped in the rough winds, toppling the pole into the sea.

3. The leaves *wafted* gently through the air, moving slowly to the ground.

4. He watched the *belfry* closely, knowing at any moment he would hear the signal from the tower.

5. The *tempestuous* sea threw the boat violently in all directions.

6. The *grenadiers* moved slowly along on foot, not knowing that enemy soldiers were close behind.

Learn About

ESSAYS

Essays are nonfictional compositions. They are usually short and can be either formal or informal in style.

Formal essays are serious, very organized writings intended to inform or persuade. **Informal essays**, on the other hand, usually have a less serious purpose. They are not so rigorously organized and exhibit a more conversational style. These essays are usually meant to describe a personal experience.

There are many other classifications of essays. Sometimes essays are classified as narrative, descriptive, reflective, or editorial. These categories correspond roughly to the four types of writing: narrative, descriptive, expository, and persuasive.

As you read the following selections, ask yourself:

1. What purpose did each author have in writing the essay?
2. How would you classify each essay?

READING FOCUS

Identify Supporting Details Essays are an opportunity for authors to present their own opinions on a subject. They develop their ideas through the use of details, facts, and examples. As you read the selections from *Walden* and *Nature*, look for ways in which the authors support their opinions. Jot down each opinion and how it is supported by details.

WRITING CONNECTION

Think of a prized possession that you own. Write a paragraph explaining your personal view or feeling about the object.

from

WALDEN

by Henry David Thoreau

[2. Where I Lived, and What I Lived for]

At a certain season of our life we are accustomed to consider every spot as the possible site of a house. I have thus surveyed the country on every side within a dozen miles of where I live. In imagination I have bought all the farms in succession, for all were to be bought, and I knew their price. I walked over each farmer's premises, tasted his wild apples, discoursed on husbandry with him, took his farm at his price, at any price, mortgaging it to him in my mind; even put a higher price on it—took everything but a deed of it—took his word for his deed, for I dearly love to talk—cultivated it, and him too to some extent, I trust, and withdrew when I had enjoyed it long enough, leaving him to carry it on. This experience entitled me to be regarded as a sort of real-estate broker by my friends. Wherever I sat, there I might live, and the landscape radiated from me accordingly. What is a house but a *sedes*, a seat?—better if a country seat. I discovered many a site for a house not likely to be soon improved, which some might have thought too far from the village, but to my eyes the village was too far from it. Well, there I might live, I said; and there I did live, for an hour, a summer and a winter life; saw how I could let the years run off, buffet the winter through, and see the spring come in. The future inhabitants of this region, wherever they may place their houses, may be sure that they have been anticipated. An afternoon sufficed to lay out the land into orchard, wood-lot, and pasture, and to decide what fine oaks or pines should be left to stand before the door, and whence each blasted tree could be seen to the best advantage; and then I let it lie, fallow, perchance, for a man is rich in proportion to the number of things which he can afford to let alone.

My imagination carried me so far that I even had the refusal of several farms—the refusal was all I wanted—but I never got my fingers burned by actual possession. The nearest that I came to actual possession was when I bought the Hollowell place, and had begun to sort my seeds, and collected materials with which to make a wheelbarrow to carry it on or off with; but before the owner gave

---

husbandry (HUHZ buhn dree) farming; agriculture
cultivated (CUL tuh vay tid) prepared and cared for land on which to grow crops; nurtured, as a friendship
fallow (FAL oh) land that is plowed, but not seeded
perchance (pur CHANS) perhaps

me a deed of it, his wife—every man has such a wife—changed her mind and wished to keep it, and he offered me ten dollars to release him. Now, to speak the truth, I had but ten cents in the world, and it surpassed my arithmetic to tell, if I was that man who had ten cents, or who had a farm, or ten dollars, or all together. However, I let him keep the ten dollars and the farm too, for I had carried it far enough; or rather, to be generous, I sold him the farm for just what I gave for it, and, as he was not a rich man, made him a present of ten dollars, and still had my ten cents, and seeds, and materials for a wheelbarrow left. I found thus that I had been a rich man without any damage to my poverty. But I retained the landscape, and I have since annually carried off what it yielded without a wheelbarrow. With respect to landscapes,

"I am monarch of all I *survey,*
My right there is none to dispute."

I have frequently seen a poet withdraw, having enjoyed the most valuable part of a farm, while the crusty farmer supposed that he had got a few wild apples only. Why, the owner does not know it for many years when a poet has put his farm in rhyme, the most admirable kind of invisible fence, has fairly impounded it, milked it, skimmed it, and got all the cream, and left the farmer only the skimmed milk.

The real attractions of the Hollowell farm, to me, were: its complete retirement, being, about two miles from the village, half a mile from the nearest neighbor, and separated from the highway by a broad

---

crusty (KRUS tee) curt; rude

field; its bounding on the river, which the owner said protected it by its fogs from frosts in the spring, though that was nothing to me; the gray color and ruinous state of the house and barn, and the dilapidated fences, which put such an interval between me and the last occupant; the hollow and lichen-covered apple trees, gnawed by rabbits, showing what kind of neighbors I should have; but above all, the recollection I had of it from my earliest voyages up the river, when the house was concealed behind a dense grove of red maples, through which I heard the house-dog bark. I was in haste to buy it, before the proprietor finished getting out some rocks, cutting down the hollow apple trees, and grubbing up some young birches which had sprung up in the pasture, or, in short, had made any more of his improvements. To enjoy these advantages I was ready to carry it on; like Atlas,[1] to take the world on my shoulders—I never heard what compensation he received for that—and do all those things which had no other motive or excuse but that I might pay for it and be unmolested in my possession of it; for I knew all the while that it would yield the most abundant crop of the kind I wanted, if I could only afford to let it alone. But it turned out as I have said.

All that I could say, then, with respect to farming on a large scale—I have always cultivated a garden—was, that I had had my seeds ready. Many think that seeds improve with age. I have no doubt that time discriminates between the good and the bad; and when at last I shall plant, I shall be less likely to be disappointed. But I would say to my fellows, once for all, As long as possible live free and uncommitted. It makes but little difference whether you are committed to a farm or the county jail.

Old Cato,[2] whose "De Re Rustica" is my "Cultivator," says—and the only translation I have seen makes sheer nonsense of the passage—"When you think of getting a farm turn it thus in your mind, not to buy greedily; nor spare your pains to look at it, and do not think it enough to go round it once. The oftener you go there the more it will please you, if it is good." I think I shall not buy greedily, but go round and round it as long as I live, and be buried in it first, that it may please me the more at last. . . .

When first I took up my abode in the woods, that is, began to spend my nights as well as days there, which, by accident, was on Independence Day, or the Fourth of July, 1845, my house was not finished for winter, but was merely a defence against the rain, without plastering or chimney, the walls being of rough, weather-stained boards, with wide chinks, which made it cool at night. The upright white hewn studs and freshly planed door and window casings gave it a clean and airy look, especially in the morning, when its timbers were saturated with dew, so that I fancied that by noon some sweet gum would exude from them. To

---

[1]**Atlas:** from Greek mythology, a Titan who supported the heavens on his shoulders
[2]**Old Cato:** Roman statesman (234–149 B.C.)
abode (uh BOHD) home; residence

Wisconsin Farm Scene, Paul Seifert. The Granger Collection

my imagination it retained throughout the day more or less of this auroral character, reminding me of a certain house on a mountain which I had visited a year before. This was an airy and unplastered cabin, fit to entertain a travelling god, and where a goddess might trail her garments. The winds which passed over my dwelling were such as sweep over the ridges of mountains, bearing the broken strains, or celestial parts only, of terrestrial music. The morning wind forever blows, the poem of creation is uninterrupted; but few are the ears that hear it. Olympus[3] is but the outside of the earth everywhere. . . .

I went to the woods because I wished to live deliberately, to front only the essential facts of life, and see if I could not learn what it had to teach, and not, when I came to die, discover that I had not lived. I did not wish to live what was not life, living is so dear; nor did I wish to practise resignation, unless it was quite necessary. I wanted to live deep and suck out all the marrow of life, to live so sturdily and Spartan-like as to put to rout all that was not life, to cut a broad swath and shave close, to drive life into a corner, and reduce it to its lowest terms, and, if it proved to be mean, why then to get the whole and genuine meanness of it, and publish its meanness to the world; or if it were sublime, to know it by experience,

---

[3]**Olympus:** in Greek mythology, the home of the gods
Spartan-like (SPAHR tuhn-lyk) brave and frugal

and be able to give a true account of it in my next excursion. For most men, it appears to me, are in a strange uncertainty about it, whether it is of the devil or of God. . . .

Still we live meanly, like ants; though the fable tells us that we were long ago changed into men; . . . it is error upon error, and clout upon clout, and our best virtue has for its occasion a superfluous and evitable wretchedness. Our life is frittered away by detail. An honest man has hardly need to count more than his ten fingers, or in extreme cases he may add his ten toes, and lump the rest. Simplicity, simplicity, simplicity! I say, let your affairs be as two or three, and not a hundred or a thousand; instead of a million count half a dozen, and keep your accounts on your thumb-nail. In the midst of this chopping sea of civilized life, such are the clouds and storms and quicksands and thousand-and-one items to be allowed for, that a man has to live, if he would not founder and go to the bottom and not make his port at all, by dead reckoning, and he must be a great calculator indeed who succeeds. Simplify, simplify. Instead of three meals a day, if it be necessary eat but one; instead of a hundred dishes, five; and reduce other things in proportion. . . .

The nation itself, with all its so-called internal improvements, which, by the way are all external and superficial, is just such an unwieldy and overgrown establishment, cluttered with furniture and tripped up by its own traps, ruined by luxury and heedless expense, by want of calculation and a worthy aim, as the million households in the land; and the only cure for it, as for them, is in a rigid economy, a stern and more than Spartan simplicity of life and elevation of purpose. It lives too fast. Men think that it is essential that the *Nation* have commerce, and export ice, and talk through a telegraph, and ride thirty miles an hour, without a doubt, whether *they* do or not; but whether we should live like baboons or like men, is a little uncertain. If we do not get out sleepers, and forge rails, and devote days and nights to the work, but go to tinkering upon our *lives* to improve *them*, who will build railroads? And if railroads are not built, how shall we get to heaven in season? But if we stay at home and mind our business, who will want railroads? We do not ride on the railroad; it rides upon us. . . .

---

superfluous (suu PUR floo us) beyond what is required
evitable (EH vuh tuh bul) avoidable
dead reckoning (DED REK un ing) navigating without the assistance of stars
sleepers (SLEE purz) railroad ties

[18. Conclusion]

. . . I left the woods for as good a reason as I went there. Perhaps it seemed to me that I had several more lives to live, and could not spare any more time for that one. It is remarkable how easily and insensibly we fall into a particular route, and make a beaten track for ourselves. I had not lived there a week before my feet wore a path from my door to the pond-side; and though it is five or six years since I trod it, it is still quite distinct. It is true, I fear, that others may have fallen into it, and so helped to keep it open. The surface of the earth is soft and impressible by the feet of men; and so with the paths which the mind travels. How worn and dusty, then, must be the highways of the world, how deep the ruts of tradition and conformity! I did not wish to take a cabin passage, but rather to go before the mast and on the deck of the world, for there I could best see the moonlight amid the mountains. I do not wish to go below now.

I learned this, at least, by my experiment: that if one advances confidently in the direction of his dreams, and endeavors to live the life which he has imagined, he will meet with a success unexpected in common hours. He will put some things behind, will pass an invisible boundary; new, universal, and more liberal laws will begin to establish themselves around and within him; or the old laws be expanded, and interpreted in his favor in a more liberal sense, and he will live with the license of a higher order of beings. In proportion as he simplifies his life, the laws of the universe will appear less complex, and solitude will not be solitude, nor poverty poverty, nor weakness weakness. If you have built castles in the air, your work need not be lost; that is where they should be. Now put the foundations under them. . . .

Why should we be in such desperate haste to succeed and in such desperate enterprises? If a man does not keep pace with his companions, perhaps it is because he hears a different drummer. Let him step to the music which he hears, however measured or far away. It is not important that he should mature as soon as an apple tree or an oak. Shall he turn his spring into summer? If the condition of things which we were made for is not yet, what were any reality which we can substitute? We will not be shipwrecked on a vain reality. Shall we with pains erect a heaven of blue glass over ourselves, though when it is done we shall be sure to gaze still at the true ethereal heaven far above, as if the former were not? . . .

However mean your life is, meet it and live it; do not shun it and call it hard names. It is not so bad as you are. It looks poorest when you are richest. The fault-finder will find faults even in paradise. Love your life, poor as it is. You may perhaps have some pleasant, thrilling, glorious hours, even in a poorhouse. The setting sun is reflected from the windows of the almshouse as brightly as from the rich man's abode; the snow melts before its door as early in the spring. I do not see but a quiet mind may live as contentedly there, and have as cheering thoughts, as in

---

conformity (kun FAWR muh tee) behavior that is in agreement with current rules

a palace. The town's poor seem to me often to live the most independent lives of any. Maybe they are simply great enough to receive without misgiving. Most think that they are above being supported by the town; but it oftener happens that they are not above supporting themselves by dishonest means, which should be more disreputable. Cultivate poverty like a garden herb, like sage. Do not trouble yourself much to get new things, whether clothes or friends. Turn the old; return to them. Things do not change; we change. Sell your clothes and keep your thoughts. God will see that you do not want society. If I were confined to a corner of a garret all my days, like a spider, the world would be just as large to me while I had my thoughts about me. The philosopher said: "From an army of three divisions one can take away its general, and put it in disorder; from the man the most abject and vulgar one cannot take away his thought." Do not seek so anxiously to be developed, to subject yourself to many influences to be played on; it is all dissipation. Humility like darkness reveals the heavenly lights. The shadows of poverty and meanness gather around us, "and lo! creation widens to our view."[4] We are often reminded that if there were bestowed on us the wealth of Croesus,[5] our aims must still be the same, and our means essentially the same. Moreover, if you are restricted in your range by poverty, if you cannot buy books and newspapers, for instance, you are but confined to the most

A Catskill Waterfall, Homer D. Martin.
Corbis Bettmann

significant and vital experiences; you are compelled to deal with the material which yields the most sugar and the most starch. It is life near the bone where it is sweetest. You are defended from being a

---

[4] **and lo! creation widens to our view:** from the sonnet "To Night" by British poet Joseph Blanco White
[5] **Croesus:** the king of Lydia (516 B.C.) thought to be the wealthiest person of his time

trifler. No man loses ever on a lower level by magnanimity on a higher. Superfluous wealth can buy superfluities only. Money is not required to buy one necessary of the soul. . . .

The life in us is like the water in the river. It may rise this year higher than man has ever known it, and flood the parched uplands; even this may be the eventful year, which will drown out all our muskrats. It was not always dry land where we dwell. I see far inland the banks which the stream anciently washed, before science began to record its freshets. Every one has heard the story which has gone the rounds of New England, of a strong and beautiful bug which came out of the dry leaf of an old table of apple-tree wood, which had stood in a farmer's kitchen for sixty years, first in Connecticut, and afterward in Massachusetts—from an egg deposited in the living tree many years earlier still, as appeared by counting the annual layers beyond it; which was heard gnawing out for several weeks, hatched perchance by the heat of an urn.

Who does not feel his faith in a resurrection and immortality strengthened by hearing of this? Who knows what beautiful and winged life, whose egg has been buried for ages under many concentric layers of woodenness in the dead dry life of society, deposited at first in the alburnum of the green and living tree, which has been gradually converted into the semblance of its well-seasoned tomb—heard perchance gnawing out now for years by the astonished family of man, as they sat round the festive board—may unexpectedly come forth from amidst society's most trivial and handselled furniture, to enjoy its perfect summer life at last!

I do not say that John or Jonathan[6] will realize all this; but such is the character of that morrow which mere lapse of time can never make to dawn. The light which puts out our eyes is darkness to us. Only that day dawns to which we are awake. There is more day to dawn. The sun is but a morning star.

---

alburnum (al BURN um) sapwood
[6]**John or Jonathan** *John Bull* was a nickname for the average British citizen and *Brother Jonathan* referred to the average American.

from
Nature

by Ralph Waldo Emerson

Nature is a setting that fits equally well a comic or a mourning piece. In good health, the air is a cordial of incredible virtue. Crossing a bare common, in snow puddles, at twilight, under a clouded sky, without having in my thoughts any occurrence of special good fortune, I have enjoyed a perfect exhilaration. I am glad to the brink of fear. In the woods too, a man casts off his years, as the snake his slough, and at what period soever of life, is always a child. In the woods, is perpetual youth. Within these plantations of God, a decorum and sanctity reign, a perennial festival is dressed, and the guest sees not how he should tire of them in a thousand years. In the woods, we return to reason and faith. There I feel that nothing can befall me in life,—no disgrace, no calamity, (leaving me my eyes,) which nature cannot repair. Standing on the bare ground,—my head bathed by the blithe air, and uplifted into infinite space,—all mean egotism vanishes. I become a transparent eye-ball; I am nothing; I see all; the currents of the Universal Being circulate through me; I am part or particle of God.

The name of the nearest friend sounds then foreign and accidental: to be brothers, to be acquaintances,—master or servant, is then a trifle and a disturbance. I am the lover of uncontained and immortal beauty. In the wilderness, I find something more dear and connate than in streets or villages. In the tranquil landscape, and especially in the distant line of the horizon, man beholds somewhat as beautiful as his own nature.

The greatest delight which the fields and woods minister, is the suggestion of an occult relation between man and the vegetable. I am not alone and unacknowledged. They nod to me, and I to them. The waving of the boughs in the storm, is new to me and old. It takes me by surprise, and yet is not unknown. Its effect is like that of a higher thought or a better emotion coming over me, when I deemed I was thinking justly or doing right.

Yet it is certain that the power to produce this delight, does not reside in nature, but in man, or in a harmony of both. It is necessary to use these pleasures

---

cordial (CORD juhl) stimulating drink
slough (SLUF) shed skin
connate (CON ate) allied; existing together
occult (ah CULT) mysterious

Pool in the Woods, George Inness. Corbis Bettmann

with great temperance. For, nature is not always tricked in holiday attire, but the same scene which yesterday breathed perfume and glittered as for the frolic of the nymphs, is overspread with melancholy today. Nature always wears the colors of the spirit. To a man laboring under calamity, the heat of his own fire hath sadness in it. Then, there is a kind of contempt of the landscape felt by him who has just lost by death a dear friend. The sky is less grand as it shuts down over less worth in the population.

---

tricked (TRIKT) dressed
nymphs (NIMFS) mythological spirits or fairies of the woods

Review the Selection

UNDERSTAND THE SELECTION

Recall

1. List two of Thoreau's examples that suggest that people live too fast.

2. When did Thoreau start living in the woods?

3. Where did Emerson find beauty?

Infer

4. Why did Thoreau live in the woods?

5. Why did Thoreau believe people should follow their dreams?

6. Briefly paraphrase how Emerson felt when he was in the woods.

7. How did nature help Emerson and Thoreau explore their feelings?

Apply

8. If you lived in the woods, would you spend a lot of time observing nature?

9. Predict what you think might happen if Thoreau had continued to live in the woods.

10. Select a line from one of the essays that you believe is a good and wise thought and tell why.

Respond to Literature

List several ways in which Thoreau's and Emerson's writings reflect the feelings of the time in which they wrote.

THINK ABOUT ESSAYS

Although the Thoreau essay is an excerpt from a full-sized book, his prose and purpose follow essay style. Emerson is perhaps better known for his essays than his poetry. A very wide variety of topics and types are included in the genre of essay—so many, in fact, that critics find it difficult to categorize them all.

1. How would you classify the Thoreau excerpt—as narrative, descriptive, reflective (expository), or editorial (persuasive)? Explain.

2. Which of Thoreau's ideas did you find most thought-provoking? Why?

3. A parable is a short simple story used to point out a moral lesson. What parable did Thoreau use in his essay? What did it teach?

4. How would you classify the Emerson excerpt—as narrative, descriptive, reflective, or editorial? Explain.

5. Are the essays you have read formal or informal in style? Explain.

READING FOCUS

Identify Supporting Details Writers can make readers agree with them more readily if they provide strong support for their opinions. Thoreau and Emerson state many opinions in their essays. Choose an opinion from one of their essays and list several supporting details provided.

DEVELOP YOUR VOCABULARY

An *allusion* is a reference in speech or writing to an event, person, place, or thing that presumably is familiar to the listener or reader. Thoreau makes several allusions in his essay—to the mythological giant Atlas, to the Roman statesman Cato, and to the extremely rich king of ancient Lydia, Croesus, to name three of them.

There are a large number of English words that allude to people and places. They are called **eponymous** words. They are words derived from the name of a real or mythical person. For example, *saxophone* comes from the name of its inventor, Adolphe Sax. *Panic*, the word for a sudden, unreasoning fear, comes from the mythical god Pan, who had a reputation for frightening travelers in woodland areas.

Look up the following words in a dictionary that has word histories. Identify the meaning and place or person each word comes from.

1. cardigan   **4.** quixotic
2. sandwich   **5.** watt
3. marathon   **6.** cereal

Learn About

THEME

The **theme** of a piece of literature is the message that the writer wants to convey to the reader. There are several reasons why it is important to understand the theme. First, theme helps you to understand how the writer feels about something. For example, it may be the writer's view of life. Second, theme underscores the relationship between character, events, and the outcome of the story. Finally, theme adds an extra dimension of interest to the story.

Sometimes, writers directly state the theme. However, if they do not, think about what the characters do and what happens to the characters as you read.

As you read "David Swan," ask yourself:

1. Is Hawthorne's message stated directly or indirectly?
2. What is Hawthorne's message to the reader?

WRITING CONNECTION

Suppose that you are a writer. Think of a message you would like to convey to readers. Then think about a character who might be able to carry your message to the readers. Write a brief paragraph describing the character.

Reading Focus

Draw Conclusions When a character in a story does something, the reader can draw a conclusion about why the character acted in such a way. As you read "David Swan," think about the characters' motivation, or why they act as they do. Ask yourself: What motivates their actions? What do their actions tell about their personalities?

184 ■ Unit 3

David Swan

by *Nathaniel Hawthorne*

We can be but partially acquainted even with the events which actually influence our course through life, and our final destiny. There are innumerable other events, if such they may be called, which come close upon us, yet pass away without actual results, or even betraying their near approach by the reflection of any light or shadow across our minds. Could we know all the vicissitudes of our fortunes, life would be too full of hope and fear, exultation or disappointment, to afford us a single hour of true serenity. This idea may be illustrated by a page from the secret history of David Swan.

We have nothing to do with David, until we find him, at the age of twenty, on the high road from his native place to the city of Boston, where his uncle, a small dealer in the grocery line, was to take him behind the counter. Be it enough to say, that he was a native of New Hampshire, born of respectable parents, and had received an ordinary school education, with a classic finish by a year at Gilmanton academy. After journeying on foot, from sunrise till nearly noon of a summer's day, his weariness and the increasing heat determined him to sit down in the first convenient shade, and await the coming up of the stage-coach. As if planted on purpose for him, there soon appeared a little tuft of maples, with a delightful recess in the midst, and such a fresh, bubbling spring, that it seemed never to have sparkled for any wayfarer but David Swan. Virgin or not, he kissed it with his thirsty lips, and then flung himself along the brink, pillowing his head upon some shirts and a pair of pantaloons, tied up in a striped cotton handkerchief. The sunbeams could not reach him; the dust did not yet rise from

---

vicissitudes (vuh SIS uh toodz) ups and downs; changes
serenity (suh REN ih tee) peacefulness
tuft (TUFT) small bunch

the road, after the heavy rain of yesterday; and his grassy lair suited the young man better than a bed of down. The spring murmured drowsily beside him; the branches waved dreamily across the blue sky overhead; and a deep sleep, perchance hiding dreams within its depth, fell upon David Swan. But we are to relate events which he did not dream of.

While he lay sound asleep in the shade, other people were wide awake, and passed to and fro, afoot, on horseback, and in all sorts of vehicles, along the sunny road by his bed-chamber. Some looked neither to the right hand nor to the left, and know not that he was there; some merely glanced that way, without admitting the slumberer among their busy thoughts; some laughed to see how soundly he slept; and several, whose hearts were brimming full of scorn, ejected their venomous superfluity on David Swan.

A middle-aged widow, when nobody else was near, thrust her head a little way into the recess, and vowed that the young fellow looked charming in his sleep. A temperance lecturer saw him, and wrought poor David into the texture of his evening's discourse, as an awful instance of dead drunkenness by the roadside. But censure, praise, merriment, scorn, or indifference, were all one, or rather all nothing to David Swan.

He had slept only a few moments, when a brown carriage, drawn by a handsome pair of horses, bowled easily along, and was brought to a stand-still nearly in front of David's resting-place. A linch-pin had fallen out, and permitted one of the wheels to slide off. The damage was slight, and occasioned merely a momentary alarm to an elderly merchant and his wife, who were returning to Boston in the carriage. While the coachman and a servant were replacing the wheel, the lady and gentleman sheltered themselves beneath the maple trees, and there espied the bubbling fountain, and David Swan asleep beside it. Impressed with the awe which the humblest sleeper usually sheds around him, the merchant trod as lightly as the gout would allow; and his spouse took good heed not to rustle her silk gown, lest David should start up, all of a sudden.

---

venomous (VEN uh mus) poisonous; spiteful
superfluity (SOO pur FLOO ih tee) excess feelings
temperance (TEM pur uns) belief that no one should drink alcohol
indifference (in DIF ur uns) lack of interest
spouse (SPOUS) husband or wife

"How soundly he sleeps!" whispered the old gentleman. "From what a depth he draws that easy breath! Such sleep as that, brought on without an opiate, would be worth more to me than half my income; for it would suppose health, and an untroubled mind."

"And youth, besides," said the lady. "Healthy and quiet age does not sleep thus. Our slumber is no more like his, than our wakefulness."

The longer they looked, the more did this elderly couple feel interested in the unknown youth, to whom the way-side and the maple shade were a secret chamber, with the rich gloom of damask curtains brooding over him. Perceiving that a stray sunbeam glimmered down upon his face, the lady contrived to twist a branch aside, so as to intercept it. And having done this little act of kindness, she began to feel like a mother to him.

"Providence seems to have laid him here," whispered she to her husband, "and to have brought us hitter to find him, after our disappointment in our cousin's son. Methinks I can see a likeness to our departed Henry. Shall we waken him?"

"To what purpose?" said the merchant, hesitating. "We know nothing of the youth's character."

"That open countenance!" replied his wife, in the same hushed voice, yet earnestly. "This innocent sleep!"

While these whispers were passing, the sleeper's heart did not throb, nor his breath become agitated, nor his features betray the least token of interest. Yet Fortune was bending over him, just ready to let fall a burthen of gold. The old merchant had lost his only son, and had no heir to his wealth, except a distant relative, with whose conduct he was dissatisfied. In such cases, people sometimes do stranger things than to act the magician, and awaken a young man to splendor, who fell asleep in poverty.

"Shall we not waken him?" repeated the lady, persuasively.

"The coach is ready, sir," said the servant, behind.

The old couple started, reddened, and hurried away, mutually wondering, that they should ever have dreamed of doing anything so very ridiculous. The merchant threw himself back in the carriage, and occupied his mind with the plan of a magnificent

---

contrived (kun TRYVD) planned; devised
departed (dih PAHRT id) dead
countenance (COUNT in ens) face

asylum for unfortunate men of business. Meanwhile, David Swan enjoyed his nap.

The carriage could not have gone above a mile or two, when a pretty young girl came along, with a tripping pace, which showed precisely how her little heart was dancing in her bosom. Perhaps it was this merry kind of motion that caused–is there any harm in saying it?–her garter to slip its knot. Conscious that the silken girth, if silk it were, was relaxing its hold, she turned aside into the shelter of the maple trees, and there found a young man asleep by the spring! Blushing, as red as any rose, that she should have intruded into a gentleman's bed-chamber, and for such a purpose too, she was about to make her escape on tiptoe. But there was a peril near the sleeper. A monster of a bee had been wandering overhead–buzz, buzz, buzz–now among the leaves, now flashing through the strips of sunshine, and now lost in the dark shade, till finally he appeared to be settling on the eyelid of David Swan. The sting of a bee is sometimes deadly. As freehearted as she was innocent, the girl attacked the intruder with her handkerchief, brushing him soundly, and drove him from beneath the maple shade. How sweet a picture! This good deed accomplished, with quickened breath, and a deeper blush, she stole a glance at the youthful stranger, for whom she had been battling with a dragon in the air.

"He is handsome!" thought she, and blushed redder yet.

How could it be that no dream of bliss grew so strong within him, that, shattered by its very strength, it should part asunder, and allow him to perceive the girl among its phantoms? Why, at least, did no smile of welcome brighten upon his face? She was come, the maid whose soul, according to the old and beautiful idea, had been severed from his own, and whom, in all his vague but passionate desires, he yearned to meet. Her, only, could he love with a perfect love–him, only, could she receive into the depths of her heart–and now her image was faintly blushing in the fountain by his side; should it pass away, its happy lustre would never gleam upon his life again.

"How sound he sleeps!" murmured the girl.

She departed, but did not trip along the road so lightly as when she came.

---

asylum (uh SY lum) shelter
bliss (BLIS) happiness; joy

Now, this girl's father was a thriving country merchant in the neighborhood, and happened, at that identical time, to be looking out for just such a young man as David Swan. Had David formed a way-side acquaintance with the daughter, he would have become the father's clerk, and all else in natural succession. So here, again, had good fortune–the best of fortunes–stolen so near, that her garments brushed against him; and he knew nothing of the matter.

The girl was hardly out of sight, when two men turned aside beneath the maple shade. Both had dark faces, set off by cloth caps, which were drawn aslant over their brows. Their dresses were shabby, yet had a certain smartness. These were a couple of rascals, who got their living by whatever the devil sent them, and now, in the interim of other business, had staked the joint profits of their next piece of villany on a game of cards, which was to have been decided here under the trees. But, finding David asleep by the spring, one of the rogues whispered to his fellow,

"Hist!–Do you see that bundle under his head?"

The other villain nodded, winked, and leered.

"I'll bet you a horn of brandy," said the first, "that the chap has either a pocket-book, or a snug little hoard of small change, stowed away amongst his shirts. And if not there, we shall find it in his pantaloons' pocket."

"But how if he wakes?" said the other.

His companion thrust aside his waistcoat, pointed to the handle of a dirk, and nodded.

"So be it!" muttered the second villain.

They approached the unconscious David, and, while one pointed the dagger towards his heart, the other began to search the bundle beneath his head. Their two faces, grim, wrinkled, and ghastly with guilt and fear, bent over their victim, looking horrible enough to be mistaken for fiends, should he suddenly awake. Nay, had the villains glanced aside into the spring, even they would hardly have known themselves, as reflected there. But David Swan had never worn a more tranquil aspect, even when asleep on his mother's breast.

"I must take away the bundle," whispered one.

"If he stirs, I'll strike," muttered the other.

But, at this moment, a dog, scenting along the ground, came in beneath the maple trees, and gazed alternately at each of these

---

tranquil (TRANG kwul) peaceful; at rest

wicked men, and then at the quiet sleeper. He then lapped out of the fountain.

"Pshaw!" said one villain. "We can do nothing now. The dog's master must be close behind."

"Let's take a drink, and be off," said the other.

The man with the dagger thrust back the weapon into his bosom, and drew forth a pocket pistol, but not of the kind which kills by a single discharge. It was a flask of liquor, with a block tin tumbler screwed upon the mouth. Each drank a comfortable dram, and left the spot, with so many jests, and such laughter at their unaccomplished wickedness, that they might be said to have gone on their way rejoicing. In a few hours, they had forgotten the whole affair, nor once imagined that the recording angel had written down the crime of murder against their souls, in letters as durable as eternity. As for David Swan, he still slept quietly, neither conscious of the shadow of death when it hung over him, nor of the glow of renewed life, when that shadow was withdrawn.

He slept, but no longer so quietly as at first. An hour's repose had snatched from his elastic frame the weariness with which many hours of toil had burthened it. Now, he stirred–now, moved his lips, without a sound–now, talked, in an inward tone, to the noonday spectres of his dream. But a noise of wheels came rattling louder and louder along the road, until it dashed through the dispersing mist of David's slumber–and there was the stage-coach. He started up, with all his ideas about him.

"Halloo, driver!–Take a passenger?" shouted he.

"Room on top," answered the driver.

Up mounted David, and bowled away merrily towards Boston, without so much as a parting glance at the fountain of dreamlike vicissitude. He knew not that a phantom of wealth had thrown a golden hue upon its waters–nor that one of love had sighed softly to their murmur–nor that one of death had threatened to crimson them with his blood–all in the brief hour since he lay down to sleep. Sleeping or waking, we hear not the airy footsteps of the strange things that almost happen. Does it not argue a superintending Providence, that, while viewless and unexpected events thrust themselves continually athwart our path, there should still be regularity enough, in mortal life, to render foresight even partially available?

---

repose (rih POHZ) rest

AUTHOR BIOGRAPHY
Nathaniel Hawthorne (1804–1864)

The life of the American writer Nathaniel Hawthorne is living proof that "practice makes perfect." Upon graduation from Bowdoin College in 1825, he made up his mind to be a writer. This was a courageous decision, for at the time the number of Americans who earned a living writing fiction could be counted on the fingers of one hand. Hawthorne knew what his decision would mean—practice, practice, and more practice. He returned to his mother's house in Salem, Massachusetts to write. A year passed and he was still at it. Another year went by, and then more years. After five years of effort, he had sold only one of his stories. Still more time passed. Hawthorne just wouldn't give up. Finally, after "twelve dark years" as he later called them, he published his first book, *Twice-Told Tales*.

But Hawthorne's practice paid off in perfection. Today he's recognized as one of the giants in American literature. Behind his polished sentences, the reader senses a kind, thoughtful man. Hawthorne wrote about the people of his time, of course, but first of all he wrote about ideas. What really makes a person a "criminal"? Is any person completely "good"? Which are more important to the individual, the dreams of youth or the rewards of age? Questions such as these will never die, and neither will the best of Hawthorne's stories.

What did the mature Hawthorne mean when he said there had been "twelve dark years" in his life?

Review the Selection

Recall

1. Where is David Swan going?

2. List three major events that occur.

3. How is this story like a fantasy?

Infer

4. How do the people who pass feel about David Swan?

5. Interpret "But centure, praise, merriment, scorn, or indifference, were all one, or rather all nothing to David Swan."

6. Why doesn't the elderly merchant want to wake up David Swan?

7. Why are the girl's footsteps not so lively when she leaves?

Apply

8. Predict what might have happened if Swan had awakened.

9. Which event might Swan choose to wake up for? Why?

10. Explain this quote as it applies to the story: "Could we know all the vicissitudes of our fortunes, life would be too full of hope and fear, exultation or disappointment, to afford us a single hour of true serenity."

Respond to Literature

How does the theme of this story illustrate the writing style of the 1800s?

THINK ABOUT THEME

By understanding the theme, you can have a greater appreciation for stories you read. It also helps you to develop a clearer understanding of what a writer thinks and feels. Hawthorne introduces his own story, in which he gives the reader a clear picture of what the theme is. Then he explains that the story will illustrate this idea. In effect, he is saying to the reader: This is what I believe and now I am going to give you examples that support my idea.

1. What is the theme of "David Swan"?

2. By what means did Nathaniel Hawthorne illustrate the theme of his story?

3. What larger picture did the three events represent?

4. Did Hawthorne directly state his theme? If so, where?

5. How did the events help you understand the theme?

READING FOCUS

Draw Conclusions As you read "David Swan" you drew conclusions about each character. Choose two characters and describe the conclusions you drew about each one. On which of their actions did you base your conclusions?

DEVELOP YOUR VOCABULARY

A **synonym** is a word whose meaning is similar to, or the same as, another word. For example, *indifference* means "lack of interest." Words that have similar meanings are *disinterest*, *apathy*, and *unconcern*. Knowing synonyms for many words can make your writing more interesting.

Read the sentences below. Choose a word from the list that is a synonym for each italicized word.

melodious   venomous
peril   thriving
tuft

1. The small *clump* of flowers caught his eye when he sat down by the pond.

2. Jeremy's *hostile* words hurt Kira.

3. Her antique business was *prospering* despite the business slump.

4. Because it was so cold on the mountain, the climbers were at great *risk*.

5. The parakeet imitated the *tuneful* music.

Learn About

SYMBOLISM

A **symbol** is something that represents, or stands for, something else. You will recognize some symbols from ordinary life: the scales of justice, the dove of peace, the donkey and elephant of the Democratic and Republican parties, the Stars and Stripes for the United States of America, the "V for Victory" sign. The meaning of all of these symbols is commonly agreed upon, but it is not always simple. The image behind a symbol may be a blend of many ideas and attitudes.

In literature, authors may not depend upon commonly agreed-upon symbols. Instead, they may devise their own from the context or substance of what they write about. The reader must make the connection between the literal image and the idea or the quality it stands for.

As you read these poems, ask yourself:
1. What symbol or symbols does Whitman use in each poem?
2. Why did he choose that symbol?

WRITING CONNECTION

There are many symbols associated with the United States. Think of two such symbols and describe what they mean to you and why you associate them with this country.

READING FOCUS

Compare and Contrast You compare things by looking at what they have in common, and you contrast them by looking at their differences. Three poems by the same person may have many things in common, but their differences can surprise you and teach you something about the poet. As you read the poems of Walt Whitman, think about their similarities and differences. How do you know that they were all written by the same person? What qualities tell you this?

I HEAR AMERICA SINGING

by Walt Whitman

I hear America singing, the varied carols I hear,
Those of mechanics, each one singing his as it
    should be blithe and strong,
The carpenter singing his as he measures his
    plank or beam,
The mason singing his as he makes ready for
    work, or leaves off work,
5   The boatman singing what belongs to him in his
    boat, the deck-hand singing on the
    steamboat deck,
The shoemaker singing as he sits on his bench,
    the hatter singing as he stands,
The wood-cutter's song, the plowboy's on his way
    in the morning, or at noon intermission or at
    sundown,
The delicious singing of the mother, or of the
    young wife at work, or of the girl sewing or
    washing,
Each singing what belongs to him or her and to
    none else,
10   The day what belongs to the day—at night the
    party of young fellows, robust, friendly,
Singing with open mouths their strong melodious
    songs.

---

blithe (BLY*TH*) happy; cheerful
mason (MAY sun) stone worker
hatter (HAT ur) hat maker
robust (roh BUST) strong; healthy

The League Long Breakers Thundering on the Reef, William Trost Richards.
The Brooklyn Museum

O CAPTAIN! MY CAPTAIN!

by Walt Whitman

O Captain! my Captain! our fearful trip is done,
The ship has weather'd every rack, the prize we
    sought is won,
The port is near, the bells I hear, the people
    all exulting,
While follow eyes the steady keel, the vessel grim
    and daring;
5   But O heart! heart! heart!
       O the bleeding drops of red,
          Where on the deck my Captain lies,
             Fallen cold and dead.

---

weather (WETH ur) last through; endure
rack (RAK) hardship; torture
exulting (ig ZULT ing) rejoicing; showing joy
keel (KEEL) "backbone" of a ship

O Captain! my Captain! rise up and hear the
     bells;
10   Rise up—for you the flag is flung—for you the
          bugle trills,
     For you bouquets and ribbon'd wreaths—for you
          the shores a-crowding
     For you they call, the swaying mass, their eager
          faces turning;
     Here Captain! dear father!
          This arm beneath your head!
15   It is some dream that on the deck,
                    You've fallen cold and dead.

     My Captain does not answer, his lips are pale and
          still,
     My father does not feel my arm, he has no pulse
          nor will,
     The ship is anchor'd safe and sound, its voyage
          closed and done,
20   From fearful trip the victor ship comes in with
               object won;
          Exult O shores, and ring O bells!
               But I with mournful tread,
                    Walk the deck my Captain lies,
                         Fallen cold and dead.

---

trill (TRIL) play music with a quivering sound
will (WIL) wishes; desires
object (OB jekt) purpose; goal
tread (TRED) step; walk

WHEN I HEARD THE LEARN'D ASTRONOMER

by Walt Whitman

When I heard the learn'd astronomer,
When the proofs, the figures, were ranged in
    columns before me,
When I was shown the charts and diagrams, to
    add, divide, and measure them,
When I sitting heard the astronomer where he
    lectured with much applause in the lecture-
    room,
How soon unaccountable I became tired and sick,
Till rising and gliding out I wandered off by
    myself,
In the mystical moist night-air, and from time to
    time,
Looked up in perfect silence at the stars.

---

ranged (RAYNJD) set forth; arranged
unaccountable (un uh KOWN tuh bul) for no apparent reason
mystical (MIS tih kul) mysterious; having a hidden meaning

Walt Whitman (1819–1892)

"Wake up, America!" Walt Whitman's poetry seems to shout. "Wake up and look around. Wake up and listen. Wake up to a new life in a world that is wonder-full."

If any American deserves the title "People's Poet," it is Walt Whitman. He thought of himself as the poet of democracy. Everything inspired Whitman. Everything had meaning for him. His aim was to tell Americans about themselves in a way that would make them, too, feel fully alive.

Whitman was born into a farm family on Long Island, near New York City. At the age of eleven, he dropped out of school and went to work for a lawyer. In the years that followed, he worked as a carpenter, teacher, and newspaper writer and editor. These different trades and his travels around the United States gave him firsthand knowledge of the people he was later to celebrate in his poetry.

In 1850 Whitman suddenly quit a job as an editor and went back to live with his mother and father. Once a well-known figure in newspaper and political circles, he simply dropped out of sight. Then followed the five "dark years" in his life. Apparently he worked now and then as a carpenter, but most of the time he must have written poetry. In 1855 the "dark years" came to an end. In that year he gave the world *Leaves of Grass*, which, with its original poetic style, became perhaps the most important single collection of poems by an American poet. *Leaves of Grass* marks a turning point in American poetry, for it touches on all aspects of life, including subjects not previously found in verse. In 1856 an expanded edition appeared, after which Whitman continued to work on the volume, adding and dropping poems throughout most of his life.

Whitman was over 40 when the Civil War began, but he insisted on doing his part. He spent the war years nursing and comforting injured soldiers. By the end of the war, many wounded soldiers had met the big friendly man who usually dressed in a shabby wide-brimmed hat and an open shirt and jacket. The war service, however, affected Whitman's own health. In 1873, he suffered a stroke which made him an invalid for the last years of his life.

Why is Walt Whitman suited to the title "People's Poet"?

Review the Selection

UNDERSTAND THE SELECTION

Recall

1. Name four occupations Whitman mentions in "I Hear America Singing."

2. What is wrong with the Captain in "O Captain! My Captain!"?

3. What is "When I Heard the Learn'd Astronomer" about?

Infer

4. Identify a common element among the occupations mentioned in "I Hear America Singing."

5. In "O Captain! My Captain!," whom does the Captain symbolize?

6. What does the ship symbolize?

7. Describe the speaker in "When I Heard the Learn'd Astronomer."

Apply

8. In "I Hear America Singing," what does Whitman really hear?

9. Was "O Captain! My Captain!" written to sadden or cheer people?

10. What did the speaker learn from the "learn'd astronomer"? Explain.

Respond to Literature

Many changes in American life took place during this period. Identify a change implied in any of the poems.

THINK ABOUT SYMBOLISM

A **symbol** is something that represents, or stands for, something else. It does not always stand for an actual object, organization, or other concrete thing, however. It can also represent something intangible, such as an emotion or an idea.

1. In "I Hear America Singing," what do you think the various trades symbolize? Why do the tradespeople sing?

2. In "O Captain! My Captain!" Whitman uses the image of the ship symbolically. What does the ship symbolize?

3. What "fearful trip" has the Captain, who was Abraham Lincoln, been through?

4. In the same poem, what would you say was the "prize" that was sought and won?

5. What did the actual stars in "When I Heard the Learn'd Astronomer" symbolize and why was their meaning so important?

READING FOCUS

Compare and Contrast As you read the poetry of Walt Whitman, you probably noticed that the poems are similar in some ways but different in others. In what ways are the poems alike? What are some important differences?

DEVELOP YOUR VOCABULARY

English has been enriched by borrowing words from other languages such as Latin and Greek. Latin words entered English at several times in history. In ancient times, settlers from Roman-occupied areas brought Latin words with them wherever they traveled. Later, Roman missionaries brought words as well as religion to Britain. In the eleventh century, the French conquered England. Both Latin and Greek words entered English through French. The last great period of borrowing from Latin and Greek came in the sixteenth century. Interest in classical learning flourished, and English writers used many Latin and Greek words in their writing.

The following words all came from Latin or Greek. Look up each word in a dictionary that gives word histories and write whether the word is of Latin or Greek origin.

1. astronomer
2. port
3. mechanic
4. mystical
5. star
6. lecture

Focus ON POETRY

What is a poem, and what does a poem do? Poetry is writing in which imaginative, colorful language is used to paint a picture in the reader's mind. It can tell a story, express feelings and thoughts, or describe things.

You can tell a poem the minute you see it; its structure is different from prose. Thoughts and feelings are captured in a more concise way. The poems you have read in this unit are made up of stanzas. **Stanzas** are divisions in poems that are made up of two or more lines. The poets have chosen their words carefully to create rhythm and rhyme, two elements that convey thoughts and feelings and move the poem along at a steady pace.

There are a number of elements besides rhythm and rhyme that poets use to help them write poetry. These elements work together to make a poem come alive in the reader's mind. Let's look at some of these elements so that you can learn how to understand and enjoy poetry better.

Figurative Language Figurative language, such as simile, metaphor, personification, and hyperbole, is another device poets use to convey their feelings and thoughts. Figurative language paints a picture in the reader's mind that is different from that conveyed by the literal, or dictionary meaning, of individual words. It helps the reader think of something in a different way.

A **simile** compares two unlike objects using the words *like* or *as*. *She sang like a bird* is an example. A **metaphor** compares two unlike things, without using extra words to show that a comparison is being made. An example of a metaphor is: *The young dancer is a butterfly.* **Personification** gives human qualities to nonhuman objects. *The laughing brook* is an example of person-ification. **Hyperbole** is an exaggerated statement, such as: *That cat is as big as an elephant!* Uses of these different kinds of figurative language help to make poems more interesting and to describe things in a different way. Simile and metaphor make a connection between two unlike things that the reader might never have thought about before. On the other hand, personification and hyperbole can be used in a humorous way or for exaggeration.

Character/Speaker The voice or narrator of a poem is not necessarily the real voice of the poet. Often, poets put on a mask. They create a voice, separate from their own, to express their thoughts. The poet can write in the voice of a child, a father, a nation, or even the world.

Connotation and Denotation A reader should look closely at how poets use words. Often, writers use words that have two kinds of meanings. The connotation of a word suggests its emotional meaning—the feeling the word suggests to the reader. The denotation of a word is the actual meaning of a word as given in a dictionary. In the poem "I'm nobody" Dickinson wrote:

> How dreary to be somebody!
> How public, like a frog
> To tell your name the livelong day
> To an admiring bog!

Bog has an emotional meaning here. Dickinson did not use it to mean *swamp*, which is its dictionary meaning. She used it connotatively to imply a group of nameless, faceless people.

Sound Devices Poets also use sound devices, such as onomatopoeia and alliteration. **Onomatopoeia** is the use of words that sound like their meaning. *Splash* is an example. **Alliteration** is the repetition of initial consonant sounds in a line of poetry. *Some keep the Sabbath in surplice* is an example of alliteration. Poets use different elements because they want to share their thoughts in ways that will appeal to the imagination.

THE FIRST SNOW-FALL

by James Russell Lowell

FOCUS ON POETRY
STUDY HINTS

Notice how Lowell
uses end rhymes
to link thoughts.

Think about the
connotation of the
words *ermine* and
pearl. What feelings
do they suggest
to you?

The poet uses
onomatopoeia.
Which word is it?

Lowell uses a simile
here. What is it?

The snow had begun in the gloaming,
    And busily all the night
Had been heaping field and highway
    With a silence deep and white.

5 Every pine and fir and hemlock
    Wore ermine too dear for an earl,
And the poorest twig on the elm-tree
    Was ridged inch deep with pearl.

From sheds new-roofed with Carrara
10   Came Chanticleer's muffled crow,
The stiff rails softened to swan's-down,
    And still fluttered down the snow.

I stood and watched by the window
    The noiseless work of the sky,
15 And the sudden flurries of snow-birds,
    Like brown leaves whirling by.

---

gloaming (GLOHM ing) twilight
ermine (UR min) the fur of a weasel, which turns to white in the winter
Carrara (kuh RAHR uh) fine, white marble
chanticleer (CHAN tih klir) a rooster

I thought of a mound in sweet Auburn[1]
    Where a little headstone stood;
How the flakes were folding it gently,
20   As did robins the babes in the wood.

Create a picture in your mind of what these words are saying.

Up spoke our own little Mabel,
    Saying, "Father, who makes it snow?"
And I told of the good All-father
    Who cares for us here below.

Here, you find out who the speaker is. Who is it?

25 Again I looked at the snow-fall,
    And thought of the leaden sky
That arched o'er our first great sorrow,
    When that mound was heaped so high.

Here, the speaker shares his feelings of grief.

I remembered the gradual patience
30   That fell from that cloud like snow,
Flake by flake, healing and hiding
    The scar that renewed our woe.

What simile does Lowell use here?

And again to the child I whispered,
    "The snow that husheth all,
35 Darling, the merciful Father
    Alone can make it fall!"

Think about the connotation of the words in this stanza.

Then, with eyes that saw not, I kissed her;
    And she, kissing back, could not know
That *my* kiss was given to her sister,
    Folded close under deepening snow.

Finally the speaker reveals for whom he grieves and how much he misses her.

---

leaden (LED un) dull, dark gray
[1]**Mt. Auburn:** a cemetery in Cambridge, Massachusetts

Review the Selection

UNDERSTAND THE SELECTION

Recall

1. When had the snow begun to fall?

2. What is the speaker watching?

3. What are the speaker's feelings, and what caused them?

Infer

4. Describe in your own words how the landscape looks outside the window.

5. How do you know the speaker has tried to hide his grief?

6. Explain in your own words what the speaker is saying in this poem.

7. Discuss why Mabel could not know what her father was thinking.

Apply

8. Select three words from the poem that describe the speaker's voice.

9. Suppose that you are the speaker in this poem. You are looking out the window at the snow. How does the snow make you feel?

10. Select the stanza from the poem that tells the reader the speaker may be recovering from his great sorrow.

Respond to Literature

How does Lowell use nature to share his feelings with the reader?

THINK ABOUT POETRY

Various elements of poetry work together to make a poem stimulating and interesting to read. Poets work hard to choose colorful words that will express their thoughts, feelings, and ideas in an imaginative way.

In the first stanza of "The First Snow Fall," you learn the snow began at twilight. Then, through a choice of such words as *busily*, *heaping*, and *silence*, a picture begins to emerge of how the snow must have looked. Lowell's choice of words creates a quiet, rhythmic feeling, similar to a gentle snowfall.

1. Whose voice does Lowell create in this poem?

2. Which kind of figurative language does Lowell use?

3. What is being compared in the simile "And the sudden flurries of snow-birds, Like brown leaves whirling by"?

4. What is the connotation of the word "husheth" in the line "The snow that husheth all, . . ."?

5. Name the sound device that Lowell uses and give two examples of it.

DEVELOP YOUR VOCABULARY

Homophones are words that sound the same when you say them but have different meanings and spellings. For example, the words *throne* and *thrown* are homophones.

Read the following sentences. Think of a homophone for each italicized word. Then use it in an original sentence.

1. The *beech* tree my grandfather planted last year has grown a lot.

2. Samantha read her report *aloud* to the other students.

3. Christopher put a lot of hot spices in the *chili* he made last night.

4. The *herd* of wolves moved quickly through the storm to nearby caves.

5. Rosa and Luke *rowed* across Rainbow Lake to a small island where they had a picnic.

6. The best time to look for shells is when the *tide* has gone out.

7. The *weight* of the package made me think it held the books I ordered.

8. How long does Becky have to *beat* the egg whites?

Learn About

CONFLICT

Plot, as you know, consists of a conflict, an attempt to resolve the conflict, a climax (or turning point in the events), and the dénouement, the final resolution, or outcome, of the events.

The essential element in any plot, however, is the conflict. A plot cannot exist without it. The conflict is what sets off the interplay of forces that make up the events that occur.

The conflict may be of several kinds. It may be between the main character and the forces of nature, another person, or social forces, or even between opposing sides of the character's own personality.

In weaving the events of a plot, an author must arrange incidents so that they seem to grow inevitably out of the conflict. Each incident must be the cause of the next one, down to the very end.

As you read the excerpts from *Moby-Dick*, ask yourself:

1. What is the main conflict in the story?
2. Where is the turning point in the events?

READING FOCUS

Visualize One of the things that makes a story exciting is the picture that you build in your mind from the details the author provides. When an author uses imagery—words that describe the sights, tastes, smells, sounds, and feelings—in a story, you can use your mind's eye to visualize more clearly what is happening. As you read this excerpt from *Moby-Dick*, use the imagery to visualize the events.

from
MOBY-DICK

by Herman Melville

[Chapter 36, The Quarter-Deck]

[When the crew signed aboard the Pequod, *the voyage was to be nothing more than a business venture. However, early in the voyage, Ahab makes clear to the crew that his purpose is to seek revenge against Moby-Dick.]*

It was not a great while after the affair of the pipe, that one morning shortly after breakfast, Ahab, as was his wont, ascended the cabin-gangway to the deck. There most sea-captains usually walk at that hour, as country gentlemen, after the same meal, take a few turns in the garden.

Soon his steady, ivory stride was heard, as to and fro he paced his old rounds, upon planks so familiar to his tread, that they were all over dented, like geological stones, with the peculiar mark of his walk. Did you fixedly gaze, too, upon that ribbed and dented brow; there also, you would see still stranger footprints–the footprints of his one unsleeping, ever-pacing thought.

But on the occasion in question, those dents looked deeper, even as his nervous step that morning left a deeper mark. And, so full of his thought was Ahab, that at every uniform turn that he made, now at the main-mast and now at the binnacle, you could almost see that thought turn in him as he turned, and pace in him as he paced; so completely possessing him, indeed, that it all but seemed the inward mould of every outer movement.

"D'ye mark him, Flask?" whispered Stubb; "the chick that's in him pecks the shell. T'will soon be out."

The hours wore on–Ahab now shut up within his cabin; anon, pacing the deck, with the same intense bigotry of purpose in his aspect.

It drew near the close of day. Suddenly he came to a halt by the bulwarks, and inserting his bone leg into the auger-hole there, and with one hand grasping a shroud, he ordered Starbuck to send everybody aft.

"Sir!" said the mate, astonished at an order seldom or never given on shipboard except in some extraordinary case.

wont (WANT) habit
binnacle (BIN uh kuhl) wooden case holding the ship's compass
bigotry of purpose (BIG uh tree) singlemindedness
bulwarks (BUL works) wall around the main deck
shroud (SHROWD) group of ropes
aft (AFT) to the rear of the boat

"Send everybody aft," repeated Ahab. "Mastheads, there! come down!"

When the entire ship's company were assembled, and with curious and not wholly unapprehensive faces, were eyeing him, for he looked not unlike the weather horizon when a storm is coming up, Ahab, after rapidly glancing over the bulwarks, and then darting his eyes among the crew, started from his standpoint; and as though not a soul were nigh him resumed his heavy turns upon the deck. With bent head and half-slouched hat he continued to pace, unmindful of the wondering whispering among the men; till Stubb cautiously whispered to Flask, that Ahab must have summoned them there for the purpose of witnessing a pedestrian feat. But this did not last long.

Vehemently pausing, he cried: "What do ye do when ye see a whale, men?"

"Sing out for him!" was the impulsive rejoinder from a score of clubbed voices.

"Good!" cried Ahab, with a wild approval in his tones; observing the hearty animation into which his unexpected question had so magnetically thrown them.

"And what do ye next, men?"

"Lower away, and after him!"

"And what tune is it ye pull to, men?"

"A dead whale or a stove boat!"

More and more strangely and fiercely glad and approving, grew the countenance of the old man at every shout; while the mariners began to gaze curiously at each other, as if marvelling how it was that they themselves became so excited at

The Whale Fishery "Laying On," 1852, Nathaniel Currier. The Granger Collection

such seemingly purposeless questions.

But, they were all eagerness again, as Ahab, now half-revolving in his pivot-hole, with one hand reaching high up a shroud, and tightly, almost convulsively grasping it, addressed them thus:

"All ye mastheaders have before now heard me give orders about a White Whale. Look ye! d'ye see this Spanish ounce of gold?"–holding up a broad bright coin to the sun–"it is a sixteen dollar piece, men. D'ye see it? Mr. Starbuck, hand me yon top-maul."

While the mate was getting the hammer, Ahab, without speaking, was slowly rubbing the gold piece against the skirts of his jacket, as if to heighten its lustre, and without using any words was meanwhile lowly humming to himself, producing a sound so strangely muffled and inarticulate that it seemed the mechanical humming of the wheels of his vitality in him.

Receiving the top-maul from Starbuck, he advanced towards the mainmast with the hammer uplifted in one hand, exhibiting the gold with the other, and with a high raised voice exclaiming: "Whosoever of ye raises me a white-headed whale with a wrinkled brow and a crooked jaw; whosoever of ye raises me that white-headed whale, with three holes punctured in his starboard fluke–look ye, whosoever of ye raises me that same white whale, he shall have this gold ounce, my boys!"

"Huzza! huzza!" cried the seamen, as with swinging tarpaulins they hailed the act of nailing the gold to the mast.

"It's a white whale, I say," resumed Ahab, as he threw down the top-maul, "a white whale. Skin your eyes for him, men; look sharp for white water; if ye see but a bubble, sing out."

All this while Tashtego, Daggoo, and Queequeg had looked on with even more intense interest and surprise than the rest, and at the mention of the wrinkled brow and crooked jaw they had started as if each was separately touched by some specific recollection.

"Captain Ahab," said Tashtego, "that white whale must be the same that some call Moby Dick."

"Moby Dick?" shouted Ahab. "Do ye know the white whale then, Tash?"

"Does he fan-tail a little curious, sir, before he goes down?" said the Gay-Header[1] deliberately.

"And has he a curious spout, too," said Daggoo, "very bushy, even for a parmacetty, and mighty quick, Captain Ahab?"

"And he have one, two, tree–oh! good many iron in him hide, too, Captain," cried Queequeg disjointedly, "all twisketee betwisk, like him–him–" faltering hard for a word, and screwing his hand round and round as though uncorking a bottle–"like him–him–"

"Corkscrew!" cried Ahab, "aye, Queequeg, the harpoons lie all twisted and wrenched in him; aye, Daggoo, his spout

---

tarpaulins (TAR pul inz) sailors' hats made of canvas waterproofed with tar or wax
fan-tail (FAN tayl) spread the tail like a fan
[1]**Gay-Header:** Gay Head is a town on Martha's Vineyard, another island off the coast of Massachusetts that had a large whaling community.
parmacetty (parm uh SEH tee) dialect for spermaceti, meaning a sperm whale

is a big one, like a whole shock of wheat, and white as a pile of our Nantucket[2] wool after the great annual sheep-shearing; aye, Tashtego, and he fan-tails like a split jib in a squall. Death and devils! men, it is Moby Dick ye have seen–Moby Dick–Moby Dick!"

"Captain Ahab," said Starbuck, who, with Stubb and Flask, had thus far been eyeing his superior with increasing surprise, but at last seemed struck with a thought which somewhat explained all the wonder. "Captain Ahab, I have heard of Moby Dick–but it was not Moby Dick that took off thy leg?"

"Who told thee that?" cried Ahab; then pausing, "Aye, Starbuck; aye, my hearties all round; it was Moby Dick that dismasted me; Moby Dick that brought me to this dead stump I stand on now. Aye, aye," he shouted with a terrific, loud, animal sob, like that of a heart-stricken moose; "Aye, aye! it was that accursed white whale that razed me; made a poor pegging lubber of me for ever and a day!" Then tossing both arms, with measureless imprecations he shouted out: "Aye, aye! and I'll chase him round Good Hope, and round the Horn,[3] and round the Norway maelstrom,[4] and round perdition's flames before I give him up. And this is what ye have shipped for, men! to chase that white whale on both sides of land, and over all sides of earth, till he spouts black blood and rolls fin out. What say ye, men, will ye splice hands on it, now? I think ye do look brave."

"Aye, aye!" shouted the harpooneers and seamen, running closer to the excited old man: "A sharp eye for the White Whale; a sharp lance for Moby Dick!"

"God bless ye," he seemed to half sob and half shout. "God bless ye, men. Steward! go draw the great measure of grog. But what's this long face about, Mr. Starbuck; wilt thou not chase the white whale? art not game for Moby Dick?"

"I am game for his crooked jaw, and for the jaws of Death too, Captain Ahab, if it fairly comes in the way of the business we follow; but I came here to hunt whales, not my commander's vengeance. How many barrels will thy vengeance yield thee even if thou gettest it, Captain Ahab? it will not fetch thee much in our Nantucket market."

"Nantucket market! Hoot! But come closer, Starbuck; thou requirest a little lower layer. If money's to be the measurer, man, and the accountants have computed their great counting-house the globe, by girdling it with guineas, one to every three parts of an inch; then, let me tell thee, that my vengeance will fetch a great premium here!"

"He smites his chest," whispered Stubb, "what's that for? methinks it rings most vast, but hollow."

"Vengeance on a dumb brute!" cried Starbuck, "that simply smote thee from blindest instinct! Madness! To be enraged with a dumb thing, Captain Ahab, seems blasphemous."

---

[2]**Nantucket:** an island, off the coast of Massachusetts, that was a huge whaling community
[3]**Good Hope** and **the Horn:** two of the most dangerous sea passages in the world
[4]**Norway maelstrom** dangerous whirlpool off the coast of Norway
perdition's (pur DIH shunz) Hell's

Whalers Capturing a Sperm Whale, 1847. The Granger Collection

"Hark ye yet again,–the little lower layer. All visible objects, man, are but as pasteboard masks. But in each event–in the living act, the undoubted deed–there, some unknown but still reasoning thing puts forth the mouldings of its features from behind the unreasoning mask. If man will strike, strike through the mask! How can the prisoner reach outside except by thrusting through the wall? To me, the white whale is that wall, shoved near to me. Sometimes I think there's naught beyond. But 'tis enough. He tasks me; he heaps me; I see in him outrageous strength, with an inscrutable malice sinewing it. That inscrutable thing is chiefly what I hate; and be the white whale agent, or be the white whale principal, I will wreak that hate upon him. Talk not to me of blasphemy, man; I'd strike the sun if it insulted me. For could the sun do that, then could I do the other; since there is ever a sort of fair play herein, jealousy presiding over all creations. But not my master, man, is even that fair play. Who's over me? Truth hath

---

inscrutable (in SCROO tuh bul) mysterious; unexplainable
malice (MAL is) desire to inflict harm out of meanness; malevolence
sinewing (SIN yoo ing) joining, like a tendon joins muscle to bone

no confines. Take off thine eye! more intolerable than fiends' glarings is a doltish stare! So, so; thou reddenest and palest; my heat has melted thee to anger-glow. But look ye, Starbuck, what is said in heat, that thing unsays itself. There are men from whom warm words are small indignity. I meant not to incense thee. Let it go. Look! see yonder Turkish cheeks of spotted tawn—living, breathing pictures painted by the sun. The Pagan leopards–the unrecking and unworshipping things, that live; and seek, and give no reasons for the torrid life they feel! The crew, man, the crew! Are they not one and all with Ahab, in this matter of the whale? See Stubb! he laughs! See yonder Chilian! he snorts to think of it. Stand up amid the general hurricane, thy one tost sapling cannot, Starbuck! And what is it? Reckon it. 'Tis but to help strike a fin; no wondrous feat for Starbuck. What is it more? From this one poor hunt, then, the best lance out of all Nantucket, surely he will not hang back, when every foremast-hand has clutched a whetstone? Ah! constrainings seize thee; I see! the billow lifts thee! Speak, but speak! - Aye, aye! thy silence, then, that voices thee. (Aside) something shot from my dilated nostrils, he has inhaled it in his lungs. Starbuck now is mine; cannot oppose me now, without rebellion.

"God keep me!–keep us all!" murmured Starbuck, lowly.

But in his joy at the enchanted, tacit acquiescence of the mate, Ahab did not hear his foreboding invocation; nor yet the low laugh from the hold; nor yet the presaging vibrations of the winds in the cordage; nor yet the hollow flap of the sails against the masts, as for a moment their hearts sank in. For again Starbuck's downcast eyes lighted up with the stubbornness of life; the subterranean laugh died away; the winds blew on; the sails filled out; the ship heaved and rolled as before. Ah, ye admonitions and warnings! why stay ye not when ye come? But rather are ye predictions than warnings, ye shadows! Yet not so much predictions from without, as verifications of the foregoing things within. For with little external to constrain us, the innermost necessities in our being, these still drive us on.

"The measure! the measure!" cried Ahab.

Receiving the brimming pewter, and turning to the harpooneers, he ordered them to produce their weapons. Then ranging them before him near the capstan, with their harpoons in their hands, while his three mates stood at his side with their lances, and the rest of the ship's company formed a circle round the group; he stood for an instant searchingly eyeing every man of his crew. But those wild eyes met his, as the bloodshot eyes of the prairie wolves meet the eye of their leader, ere he rushes on at their head in the trail of the bison; but, alas! only to fall into the hidden

---

whetstone (HWET stohn) a stone used for sharpening tools
tacit (TASS it) unspoken; understood
acquiescence (ak we ESS cents) agreement; submission
presaging (pree SAYG ing) foreboding; warning
capstan (CAP stuhn) cylinder on which ropes are wound

snare of the Indian.

"Drink and pass!" he cried, handing the heavy charged flagon to the nearest seaman. "The crew alone now drink. Round with it, round! Short draughts–long swallows, men; 'tis hot as Satan's hoof. So, so; it goes round excellently. It spiralizes in ye; forks out at the serpent-snapping eye. well done; almost drained. That way it went, this way it comes. Hand it me–here's a hollow! Men, ye seem the years; so brimming life is gulped and gone. Steward, refill!

"Attend now, my braves. I have mustered ye all round this capstan; and ye mates, flank me with your lances; and ye harpooneers, stand there with your irons; and ye, stout mariners, ring me in, that I may in some sort revive a noble custom of my fisherman fathers before me. . . .

"Advance, ye mates! Cross your lances full before me. Well done! Let me touch the axis." So saying, with extended arm, he grasped the three level, radiating lances at their crossed centre; while so doing, suddenly and nervously twitched them; meanwhile, glancing intently from Starbuck to Stubb; from Stubb to Flask. It seemed as though, by some nameless, interior volition, he would fain have shocked into them the same fiery emotion accumulated within the Leyden jar[5] of his own magnetic life. The three mates quailed before his strong, sustained, and mystic aspect. Stubb and Flask looked sideways from him; the honest eye of Starbuck fell downright.

"In vain!" cried Ahab; "but, maybe, 'tis well. For did ye three but once take the full-forced shock, then mine own electric thing, that had perhaps expired from out me. Perchance, too, it would have dropped ye dead. Perchance ye need it not. Down lances! And now, ye mates, I do appoint ye three cup-bearers to my three pagan kinsmen there–yon three most honorable gentlemen and noblemen, my valiant harpooneers. Disdain the task? What, when the great Pope washes the feet of beggars, using his tiara for ewer? Oh, my sweet cardinals! your own condescension, that shall bend ye to it. I do not order ye; ye will it. Cut your seizings and draw the poles, ye harpooneers!"

Silently obeying the order, the three harpooneers now stood with the detached iron part of their harpoons, some three feet long, held, barbs up, before him.

"Stab me not with that keen steel! Cant them; cant them over! know ye not the goblet end? Turn up the socket! So, so; now, ye cup-bearers, advance. The irons! take them; hold them while I fill! Forthwith, slowly going from one officer to the other, he brimmed the harpoon sockets with the fiery waters from the pewter.

"Now, three to three, ye stand. Commend the murderous chalices! Bestow them, ye who are now made parties to this indissoluble league. Ha! Starbuck! but the deed is done! Yon ratifying sun now waits to sit upon it. Drink, ye har-

---

[5]**Leyden jar** device for storing an electric charge
tiara (tee AHR uh) crown
ewer (YOO er) pitcher
condescension (con duh SEN shun) snobbish behavior

pooneers! drink and swear, ye men that man the deathful whaleboat's bow–Death to Moby Dick! God hunt us all, if we do not hunt Moby Dick to his death!" The long, barbed steel goblets were lifted; and to cries and maledictions against the white whale, the spirits were simultaneously quaffed down with a hiss. Starbuck paled, and turned, and shivered. Once more, and finally, the replenished pewter went the rounds among the frantic crew; when, waving his free hand to them, they all dispersed; and Ahab retired within his cabin.

[Chapter 135, The Chase—Third Day]

[After Moby-Dick has been sighted in the Pacific Ocean, the Pequod's boats follow the whale for two days. One of the boats has been sunk, and Ahab's ivory leg has been broken off. However, as the next day dawns, the chase continues.]

The morning of the third day dawned fair and fresh, and once more the solitary night-man at the fore-mast-head was relieved by crowds of the daylight look-outs, who dotted every mast and almost every spar.

"D'ye see him?" cried Ahab; but the whale was not yet in sight.

"In his infallible wake, though; but follow that wake, that's all. Helm there; steady, as thou goest, and hast been going. What a lovely day again; . . . these same Trades that so directly blow my good ship on; these Trades, or something like them–something so unchangeable,

and full as strong, blow my keeled soul along! To it! Aloft there! What d'ye see?"

"Nothing, Sir."

"Nothing! and noon at hand! The doubloon goes a-begging! See the sun! Aye, aye, it must be so. I've oversailed him. How, got the start? Aye, he's chasing me now; not I, him–that's bad; I might have known it, too. Fool! the lines–the harpoons he's towing. Aye, aye, I have run him by last night. About! about! Come down, all of ye, but the regular look outs! Man the braces!"

Steering as she had done, the wind had been somewhat on the Pequod's quarter, so that now being pointed in the reverse direction, the braced ship sailed hard upon the breeze as she rechurned the cream in her own white wake.

"Against the wind he now steers for the open jaw," murmured Starbuck to himself, as he coiled the new-hauled main brace upon the rail. "God keep us, but already my bones feel damp within me, and from the inside wet my flesh. I misdoubt me that I disobey my God in obeying him!"

"Stand by to sway me up!" cried Ahab, advancing to the hempen basket. "We should meet him soon."

"Aye, aye, Sir," and straightway Starbuck did Ahab's bidding, and once more Ahab swung on high.

A whole hour now passed; gold-beaten out to ages. Time itself now held long breaths with keen suspense. But at last, some three points off the weather bow, Ahab descried the spout again, and

---

indissoluble (in duh SAHL u bul) incapable of coming apart; permanent
maledictions (mal uh DIK shunz) curses

instantly from the three mastheads three shrieks went up as if the tongues of fire had voiced it.

"Forehead to forehead I meet thee, this third time, Moby Dick! On deck there!–brace sharper up; crowd her into the wind's eye. He's too far off to lower yet, Mr. Starbuck. The sails shake! Stand over that helmsman with a top-maul! So, so; he travels fast, and I must down. But let me have one more good round look aloft here at the sea; there's time for that. An old, old sight, and yet somehow so young; aye, and not changed a wink since I first saw it, a boy, from the sand-hills of Nantucket! The same!–the same!–the same to Noah as to me. There's a soft shower to leeward. Such lovely leewardings! They must lead somewhere–to something else than common land, more palmy than the palms. Leeward! the white whale goes that way; look to windward, then; the better if the bitterer quarter. But good bye, good bye, old mast-head! What's this?–green? aye, tiny mosses in these warped cracks. No such green weather stains on Ahab's head! There's the difference now between man's old age and matter's. But aye, old mast, we both grow old together; sound in our hulls, though, are we not, my ship? Aye, minus a leg, that's all. By heaven this dead wood has the better of my live flesh every way. I can't compare with it; and I've known some ships made of dead trees outlast the lives of men made of the most vital stuff of vital fathers. What's that he said? he should still go before me, my pilot; and yet to be seen again? But where? Will I have eyes at the bottom of the sea, supposing I descend those endless stairs? and all night I've been sailing from him, wherever he did sink to. . . . Good bye, masthead–keep a good eye upon the whale, the while I'm gone. We'll talk tomorrow, nay, tonight, when the white whale lies down there, tied by head and tail."

He gave the word; and still gazing round him, was steadily lowered through the cloven blue air to the deck.

In due time the boats were lowered, but as standing in his shallop's stern, Ahab just hovered upon the point of the descent, he waved to the mate,–who held one of the tackle-ropes on deck–and bade him pause.

"Starbuck!"

"Sir?"

"For the third time my soul's ship starts upon this voyage, Starbuck."

"Aye, Sir, thou wilt have it so."

"Some ships sail from their ports, and ever afterwards are missing, Starbuck!"

"Truth, Sir: saddest truth."

"Some men die at ebb tide; some at low water; some at the full of the flood;–and I feel now like a billow that's all one crested comb, Starbuck. I am old;–shake hands with me, man."

Their hands met; their eyes fastened; Starbuck's tears the glue.

"Oh, my captain, my captain!–noble heart–go not–go not!–see, it's a brave man that weeps; how great the agony of the persuasion then!"

"Lower away!"–cried Ahab, tossing

---

leeward (LEE word) the direction toward which the wind blows downwind
windward (WIND word) the direction from which the wind blows; a position of advantage

the mate's arm from him. "Stand by the crew!"

In an instant the boat was pulling round close under the stern.

"The sharks! the sharks!" cried a voice from the low cabin-window there; "O master, my master, come back!"

But Ahab heard nothing; for his own voice was high-lifted then; and the boat leaped on. . . .

"Heart of wrought steel!" murmured Starbuck gazing over the side, and following with his eyes the receding boat–"canst thou yet ring boldly to that sight?–lowering thy keel among ravening sharks, and followed by them, open-mouthed to the chase; and this the critical third day?—For when three days flow together in one continuous intense pursuit; be sure the first is the morning, the second the noon, and the third the evening and the end of that thing - be that end what it may. Oh! my God! what is this that shoots through me, and leaves me so deadly calm, yet expectant,–fixed at the top of a shudder! Future things swim before me, as in empty outlines and skeletons; all the past is somehow grown dim. . . ."

The boats had not gone very far, when by a signal from the mastheads–a downward pointed arm, Ahab knew that the whale had sounded; but intending to be near him at the next rising, he held on his way a little sideways from the vessel; the becharmed crew maintaining the profoundest silence, as the head-beat waves hammered and hammered against the opposing bow.

"Drive, drive in your nails, oh ye waves! to their uttermost heads, drive them in! ye but strike a thing without a lid; and no coffin and no hearse can be mine–and hemp only can kill me! Ha! ha!"

Suddenly the waters around them slowly swelled in broad circles; then quickly upheaved, as if sideways sliding from a submerged berg of ice, swiftly rising to the surface. A low rumbling sound was heard; a subterraneous hum; and then all held their breaths; as bedraggled with trailing ropes, and harpoons, and lances, a vast form shot lengthwise, but obliquely from the sea. Shrouded in a thin drooping veil of mist, it hovered for a moment in the rainbowed air; and then fell swamping back into the deep. Crushed thirty feet upwards, the waters flashed for an instant like heaps of fountains, then brokenly sank in a shower of flakes, leaving the circling surface creamed like new milk round the marble trunk of the whale.

"Give way!" cried Ahab to the oarsmen, and the boats darted forward to the attack; but maddened by yesterday's fresh irons that corroded in him, Moby Dick seemed combinedly possessed by all the angels that fell from heaven. The wide tiers of welded tendons overspreading his broad white forehead, beneath the transparent skin, looked knitted together; as head on, he came churning his tail among the boats; and once more flailed them apart; spilling out the irons and lances from the two mates' boats, and dashing in one side of the upper part of their bows, but leaving Ahab's almost without a scar.

---

sounded (SOWND ed) dove deeply downward (by a whale or fish)

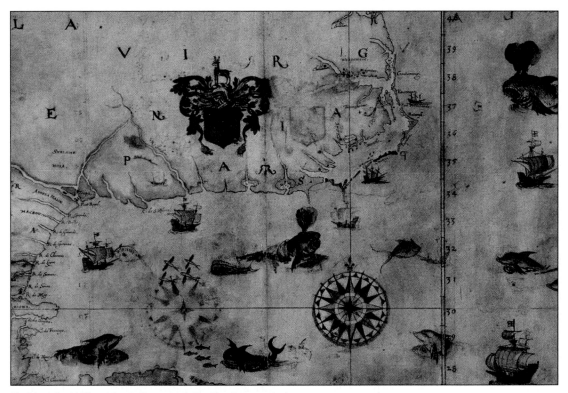

Florida, John White. John R. Freeman & Co./The Fotomas Index

While Daggoo and Queequeg were stopping the strained planks; and as the whale swimming out from them, turned, and showed one entire flank as he shot by them again; at that moment a quick cry went up. Lashed round and round to the fish's back; pinioned in the turns upon turns in which, during the past night, the whale had reeled the involutions of the lines around him, the half torn body of the Parsee[6] was seen; his sable raiment frayed to shreds; his distended eyes turned full upon old Ahab.

The harpoon dropped from his hand.

"Befooled, befooled!"–drawing in a long lean breath–"Aye, Parsee! I see thee again.–Aye, and thou goest before; and this, this then is the hearse that thou didst promise. But I hold thee to the last letter of thy word. Where is the second hearse? Away, mates, to the ship! those boats are useless now; repair them if ye can in time, and return to me; if not, Ahab is enough to die–Down, men! the first thing that but offers to jump from this boat I stand in, that thing I harpoon. Ye are not other men, but my arms and my legs; and so obey me.–Where's the whale? gone down again?"

But he looked too nigh the boat; for as

---

[6]**The Parsee** the leader of a crew of Parsee or Zoroastrian sailors that Ahab had secretly hired to man his personal whaleboat

if bent upon escaping with the corpse he bore, and as if the particular place of the last encounter had been but a stage in his leeward voyage, Moby Dick was now again steadily swimming forward; and had almost passed the ship,–which thus far had been sailing in the contrary direction to him, though for the present her headway had been stopped. He seemed swimming with his utmost velocity, and now only intent upon pursuing his own straight path in the sea.

"Oh! Ahab," cried Starbuck, "not too late is it, even now, the third day, to desist. See! Moby Dick seeks thee not. It is thou, thou, that madly seekest him!"

Setting sail to the rising wind, the lonely boat was swiftly impelled to leeward, by both oars and canvas. And at last when Ahab was sliding by the vessel, so near as plainly to distinguish Starbuck's face as he leaned over the rail, he hailed him to turn the vessel about, and follow him, not too swiftly, at a judicious interval. Glancing upwards, he saw Tashtego, Queequeg, and Daggoo, eagerly mounting to the three mastheads; while the oarsmen were rocking in the two staved boats which had but just been hoisted to the side, and were busily at work in repairing them. One after the other, through the portholes, as he sped, he also caught flying glimpses of Stubb and Flask, busying themselves on deck among bundles of new irons and lances. As he saw all this; as he heard the hammers in the broken boats; far other hammers seemed driving a nail into his heart. But he rallied. And now marking that the vane or flag was gone from the main masthead, he shouted to Tashtego, who had just gained that perch, to descend again for another flag, and a hammer and nails, and so nail it to the mast.

Whether fagged by the three days' running chase, and the resistance to his swimming in the knotted hamper he bore; or whether it was some latent deceitfulness and malice in him: whichever was true, the White Whale's way now began to abate, as it seemed, from the boat so rapidly nearing him once more; though indeed the whale's last start had not been so long a one as before. And still as Ahab glided over the waves the unpitying sharks accompanied him; and so pertinaciously stuck to the boat; and so continually bit at the plying oars, that the blades became jagged and crunched, and left small splinters in the sea, at almost every dip.

"Heed them not! those teeth but give new rowlocks to your oars. Pull on! 'tis the better rest, the shark's jaw than the yielding water."

"But at every bite, Sir, the thin blades grow smaller and smaller!"

"They will last long enough! pull on!– But who can tell"–he muttered–"whether these sharks swim to feast on the whale or on Ahab?–But pull on! Aye, all alive, now–we near him. The helm! take the helm; let me pass,"–and so saying, two of the oarsmen helped him forward to the bows of the still flying boat.

At length as the craft was cast to one side, and ran ranging along with the White Whale's flank, he seemed strangely

---

pertinaciously (pur tuh NAY shus ly) persistently; stubbornly oblivious of its advance–as the whale sometimes will–and Ahab was fairly within the smoky mountain mist, which, thrown off from the whale's spout, curled round his great, Monadnock[7] hump; he was even thus close to him; when, with body arched back, and both arms lengthwise high-lifted to the poise,[8] he darted his fierce iron, and his far fiercer curse into the hated whale. As both steel and curse sank to the socket, as if sucked into a morass, Moby Dick sideways writhed; spasmodically rolled his nigh flank against the bow, and, without staving a hole in it, so suddenly canted the boat over, that had it not been for the elevated part of the gunwale to which he then clung, Ahab would once more have been tossed into the sea.

As it was, three of the oarsmen–who foreknew not the precise instant of the dart, and were therefore unprepared for its effects—these were flung out; but so fell, that, in an instant two of them clutched the gunwale again, and rising to its level on a combing wave, hurled themselves bodily inboard again; the third man helplessly dropping astern, but still afloat and swimming.

Almost simultaneously, with a mighty volition of ungraduated, instantaneous swiftness, the White Whale darted through the weltering sea. But when Ahab cried out to the steersman to take new turns with the line, and hold it so; and commanded the crew to turn round on their seats, and tow the boat up to the mark; the moment the treacherous line felt that double strain and tug, it snapped in the empty air!

"What breaks in me? Some sinew cracks!–'tis whole again; oars! oars! Burst in upon him!"

Hearing the tremendous rush of the sea-crashing boat, the whale wheeled round to present his blank forehead at bay; but in that evolution, catching sight of the nearing black hull of the ship; seemingly seeing in it the source of all his persecutions; bethinking it–it may be–a larger and nobler foe; of a sudden, he bore down upon its advancing prow, smiting his jaws amid fiery showers of foam.

Ahab staggered; his hand smote his forehead. "I grow blind; hands! stretch out before me that I may yet grope my way. Is't night?"

"The whale! The ship!" cried the cringing oarsmen.

"Oars! oars Slope downwards to thy depths, O sea, that ere it be for ever too late, Ahab may slide this last, last time upon his mark; I see: the ship! the ship! Dash on, my men! Will ye not save my ship?"

But as the oarsmen violently forced their boat through the sledge-hammering seas, the before whale-smitten bow-ends of two planks burst through, and in an instant almost, the temporarily disabled boat lay nearly level with the waves; its half-wading, splashing crew, trying hard to stop the gap and bale out the pouring water.

Meantime, for that one beholding

---

[7]**Monadonock** mountain in New Hampshire, hence, mountainous
[8]**to the poise** to a state of balance; equipoise
volition (voh LIH shun) will, determination

instant, Tashtego's mast-head hammer remained suspended in his hand; and the red flag, half-wrapping him as with a plaid, then streamed itself straight out from him, as his own forward-flowing heart; while Starbuck and Stubb, standing upon the bowsprit beneath, caught sight of the down-coming monster just as soon as he. . . .

From the ship's bows, nearly all the seamen now hung inactive; hammers, bits of plank, lances, and harpoons, mechanically retained in their hands, just as they had darted from their various employments; all their enchanted eyes intent upon the whale, which from side to side strangely vibrating his predestinating head, sent a broad band of overspreading semicircular foam before him as he rushed. Retribution, swift vengeance, eternal malice were in his whole aspect, and spite of all that mortal man could do, the solid white buttress of his forehead smote the ship's starboard bow, till men and timbers reeled. Some fell flat upon their faces. Like dislodged trucks, the heads of the harpooneers aloft shook on their bull-like necks. Through the breach, they heard the waters pour, as mountain torrents down a flume.

"The ship! The hearse!–the second hearse!" cried Ahab from the boat; "its wood could only be American!"

Diving beneath the settling ship, the whale ran quivering along its keel; but turning under water, swiftly shot to the surface again, far off the other bow, but within a few yards of Ahab's boat, where,

for a time, he lay quiescent.

"I turn my body from the sun. What ho, Tashtego! Let me hear thy hammer. Oh! ye three unsurrendered spires of mine; thou uncracked keel; and only god-bullied hull; thou firm deck, and haughty helm, and Pole-pointed prow,–death-glorious ship! must ye then perish, and without me? Am I cut off from the last fond pride of meanest ship-wrecked captains? Oh, lonely death on lonely life! Oh, now I feel my topmost greatness lies in my topmost grief. Ho, ho! from all your furthest bounds, pour ye now in, ye bold billows of my whole foregone life, and top this one piled comber of my death! Towards thee I roll, thou all-destroying but unconquering whale; to the last I grapple with thee; from hell's heart I stab at thee; for hate's sake I spit my last breath at thee. Sink all coffins and all hearses to one common pool! and since neither can be mine, let me then tow to pieces, while still chasing thee, though tied to thee, thou damned whale! Thus, I give up the spear!"

The harpoon was darted; the stricken whale flew forward; with igniting velocity the line ran through the groove;–ran foul. Ahab stooped to clear it; he did clear it; but the flying turn caught him round the neck, and voicelessly, . . . he was shot out of the boat, ere the crew knew he was gone. Next instant, the heavy eye-splice in the rope's final end flew out of the stark-empty tub, knocked down an oarsman, and smiting the sea, disappeared in its depths.

---

keel (KEEL) a piece of wood that runs along the centerline from front of the boat to the back
quiescent (kwee ES ent) quiet; motionless

For an instant, the tranced boat's crew stood still; then turned. "The ship? Great God, where is the ship?" Soon they through dim, bewildering mediums saw her sidelong fading phantom, as in the gaseous Fata Morgana[7]; only the uppermost masts out of water; while fixed by infatuation, or fidelity, or fate, to their once lofty perches, the pagan harpooneers still maintained their sinking lookouts on the sea. And now, concentric circles seized the lone boat itself, and all its crew, and each floating oar, and every lance-pole, and spinning, animate and inanimate, all round and round in one vortex, carried the smallest chip of the *Pequod* out of sight. . . .

Now small fowls flew screaming over the yet yawning gulf; a sullen white surf beat against its steep sides; then all collapsed, and the great shroud of the sea rolled on as it rolled five thousand years ago.

---

[7]**Fata Morgana** a mirage often seen by sailors near the Straits of Messina separating Sicily from Italy; it consists of multiple images resembling castles
shroud (SHROWD) something that hides or protects

Review the Selection

UNDERSTAND THE SELECTION

Recall

1. Why did Ahab seek revenge?

2. What did Ahab offer the men if they killed Moby-Dick?

3. Where did Ahab say he would go to search for Moby-Dick?

Infer

4. Why did Starbuck protest Ahab's intention to kill Moby-Dick?

5. Give a brief description of Ahab telling what kind of man he was.

6. What might the fight between Ahab and Moby-Dick really represent?

7. Read the last paragraph of *Moby-Dick* again. Then use your own words to tell what Melville meant.

Apply

8. How might Ahab have felt upon first seeing Moby-Dick?

9. Suppose that you are Moby-Dick. Describe your feelings about human beings.

10. Select an important event from *Moby-Dick* and tell why it made the story more interesting.

Respond to Literature

Explain how Emerson's influence on Melville is reflected in *Moby-Dick*.

THINK ABOUT CONFLICT

One type of conflict in literature is the struggle that results from the interaction between characters representing opposite forces in a plot. The main character is called the **protagonist**; the rival character is called the **antagonist**. The protagonist and the antagonist struggle against each other. Each should be motivated to resolve the conflict. If the characters lack purpose or other motivation, the plot will seem amateurish to the reader or listener. If the characters are well-motivated, the plot will be more satisfying.

1. Who is the protagonist in the excerpts? Who is the antagonist? Describe the main conflict between them.

2. At what point does the climax, or the turning point, of the story come?

3. In the madness of the pursuit, one character was the voice of reason. Whose voice was that?

4. Why did Ahab not heed the warnings of the voice of reason? What was driving him?

5. What was the resolution of the story?

READING FOCUS

Visualize As you read this excerpt from *Moby-Dick*, you were able to visualize certain scenes from the story. What scene in this story remains most vivid to you? Give some examples of the imagery that helped you visualize this scene.

DEVELOP YOUR VOCABULARY

An **antonym** is a word that has a meaning opposite, or almost opposite, to that of another word. For example, *enormous* means "huge" or "very big." Words that mean the opposite are *tiny* and *little*.

Read the sentences below. Choose a word from the list that is an antonym for each italicized word. Then write a sentence using the word.

malice	effortless
vague	vengeance
ominous	calm

1. The weather was *favorable* for an afternoon sail.

2. No *mercy* was shown to the defendant when his sentence was given.

3. Your *kindness* during this difficult time is greatly appreciated.

4. Lucy gave a *specific* description of the house so they wouldn't miss it.

5. The first day of rehearsal is always *chaotic*!

6. The sailors' work was *arduous*; it lasted from morning until night.

Learn About

IMAGERY

People learn about the world through their senses—sight, hearing, smell, taste, and touch. The poet is especially sensitive to sense impressions. To express an experience of a place, for example, the poet will depend greatly on sense impressions. These, added to thought and emotion, bring the scene alive for the reader.

Sense impression translated into words is called **imagery**. The poet will generally choose specific words rather than general ones to make the strongest statement. A *white-petaled daisy*, for example, is more specific than a *flower*. The more specific the poet is, the more vivid the imagery in the poem will be. The poet looks for fresh ways of expressing sense impressions, of course.

As you read the poem, ask yourself:

1. What sense impression did Whittier express in the poem?
2. Which sense did he call upon most for his imagery?

READING FOCUS

Understand Contrast To contrast is to look at differences. Seeing how one situation differs from another often provides important information. As you read "Song of Slaves in the Desert," think about how the lives of the people who have been captured will differ in quality from their lives in Africa. Look for places in the poem that contrast these two ways of life.

WRITING CONNECTION

Write *sight, sound, smell, taste, touch* on a piece of paper. Under each heading, write several phrases that create an image for that word. For example, *sound*: crashing, pounding waves.

Song of Slaves in the Desert

by John Greenleaf Whittier

Where are we going? where are we going,
Where are we going, Rubee?
Lord of peoples, lord of lands,
Look across these shining sands,
5   Through the furnace of the noon,
Through the white light of the moon.
Strong the Ghiblee wind is blowing,
Strange and large the world is growing!
Speak and tell us where we are going,
10   Where are we going, Rubee?

Bornou land was rich and good,
Wells of water, fields of food,
Dourra fields, and bloom of bean,
And the palm-tree cool and green:
15   Bornou land we see no longer,
Here we thirst and here we hunger,
Here the Moor-man smites in anger:
     Where are we going, Rubee?

When we went from Bornou land,
20   We were like the leaves and sand,
We were many, we are few;
Life has one, and death has two:
Whitened bones our path are showing,
Thou All-seeing, thou All-knowing!

Ghiblee (GIB lee) night wind that makes an eerie sound
Bornou land (BAWR noo) reference to homeland in Africa
Dourra (DUUR uh) (usually spelled durra) a kind of grain grown in Northern Africa
smites (SMYTS) inflicts a heavy blow; kills by striking
Moor (MUUR) a Muslim from northwest Africa, here referring specifically to slave traders

25   Hear us, tell us, where are we going,
        Where are we going, Rubee?

    Moons of marches from our eyes
    Bornou land behind us lies;
    Stranger round us day by day
30   Bends the desert circle gray;
    Wild the waves of sand are flowing,
    Hot the winds above them blowing,—
    Lord of all things! where are we going?
        Where are we going, Rubee?

35   We are weak, but Thou art strong;
    Short our lives, but Thine is long;
    We are blind, but Thou hast eyes;
    We are fools, but Thou art wise!
    Thou, our morrow's pathway knowing
40   Through the strange world round us growing,
    Hear us, tell us where are we going,
        Where are we going, Rubee?

African Slave Trade, The Granger Collection

Review the Selection

UNDERSTAND THE SELECTION

Recall

1. About whom is this poem written?

2. Where did the Africans live?

3. Identify the speaker of the poem.

Infer

4. Explain the line, "Where are we going, . . . ?"

5. In your own words describe what "Bornou land" was like.

6. Interpret this line: "Here the Moor-man smites in anger."

7. Which line did Whittier use to describe the passage of time?

Apply

8. Which line best describes what the song of the slaves was?

9. Suppose that you could answer the speaker in this poem. How would you respond?

10. The speaker states several times that the world is getting larger and growing. What does he or she mean by these words?

Respond to Literature

How does the "Song of Slaves in the Desert" reflect the views of writers of the 1800s?

THINK ABOUT IMAGERY

Imagery is the translation into words of sense impressions gained through sight, hearing, smell, taste, and touch, or feeling. No poem can be judged by its imagery alone, but imagery can vastly enhance the impact of the poem on the reader.

1. What senses does Whittier call on to tell how hot the march across the desert was?

2. What specific images do the African people in this poem have of their native Bornou land?

3. What specific images do they have of their desert environment?

4. What does Whittier mean when he says the Africans "were like the leaves and sand"? Why does he use the past tense?

5. The captured people repeatedly ask "Where are we going, Rubee?" To whom do you think the name *Rubee* refers? Explain your answer.

READING FOCUS

Understand Contrast What contrast does the poem make between the people's fate in an unknown land and their lives in Africa? Provide lines from the poem that illustrate the contrast.

---

230 ■ **Unit 3**

DEVELOP YOUR VOCABULARY

Images that use specific words are more vivid than those that use general words. Specific words, however, can differ in their meaning. The most specific words in a language are those that refer to one-of-a-kind people, animals, places, or things: Bruce Springsteen, Lassie, Mount St. Helens, the *Mona Lisa*. It is not always necessary to be quite so specific as these, however. Somewhat more general terms would be *singer*, *dog*, *volcano*, and *painting*. Least specific of all would be *man*, *animal*, *mountain*, and *artwork*.

Rearrange these lists in order from most specific to most general.

1. shoe, footwear, cross-trainers, sneaker

2. publication, *Time*, periodical, magazine

3. male, Michael J. Fox, actor, TV star

4. literature, poetry, poem, "Song of Slaves in the Desert"

5. drum, percussion instrument, musical instrument, snare drum

A Nation Expresses Itself

Dark hills at evening in the west,
Where sunset hovers like a sound
Of golden horns that sang to rest
Old bones of warriors under ground.
    —Edwin Arlington Robinson

A Rest on the Ride, Albert Bierstadt. Three Lions/Superstock

Learn About

SOUNDS IN POETRY

Rhythm, meter, and rhyme all add musical effects to poetry, but they are not the only devices available to poets. The use of certain letters of the alphabet affects the sound of poetry. Some letters have a soft "liquid" sound: *l, m, n,* and *r.* Other letters have a more "explosive" sound: *b, d, g, k, p,* and *t.* Poets can manipulate the use of these sounds to create soothing or exciting lines.

Repetition is part of all music, and it plays a part in the music of poetry too. For example, the repetition of initial consonant sounds, as in "They *s*at in *s*olemn *s*ilence," is called **alliteration.** The repetition of vowel sounds, as in "*I* can f*i*nd the t*i*me," is called **assonance.** The repetition of final consonant sounds, as in "fir*st* and la*st*," is called **consonance.**

As you read the following poems, ask yourself:

1. Which sound devices did Dickinson use in her poems?
2. What effect do the devices have on the poems?

WRITING CONNECTION

Write a sentence using "liquid" letters and another using "explosive" letters. Explain the effect of each sentence on you.

READING FOCUS

Make Inferences An inference is a conclusion drawn from facts or evidence. You can use your own insights and knowledge of human behavior and the world around you in order to make inferences.

Reading poetry often requires the reader to infer meaning, or to think beyond the words on the page. As you read each poem, use your own knowledge and details in the poem to make inferences about the poem's meaning.

In the Garden, Irving Ramsay Wiles. Christie's Images

I'm nobody

by Emily Dickinson

I'm nobody! Who are you?
Are you nobody, too?
Then there's a pair of us—don't tell!
They'd banish us, you know.

How dreary to be somebody!
How public, like a frog
To tell your name the livelong day
To an admiring bog!

---

dreary (DRIR ee) dull; tiresome
bog (BOG) swamp; wet ground

A word is dead

by Emily Dickinson

A word is dead
When it is said,
Some say.
I say it just
Begins to live
That day.

I never saw a moor

by Emily Dickinson

I never saw a moor,
I never saw the sea;
Yet know I how the heather looks,
And what a wave must be.

I never spoke with God,
Nor visited in heaven;
Yet certain am I of the spot
As if the chart were given.

moor (MUUR) open wasteland
heather (HETH ur) low evergreen plant that often grows on moors

The sky is low

by Emily Dickinson

The sky is low, the clouds are mean,
A travelling flake of snow
Across a barn or through a rut
Debates if it will go.

A narrow wind complains all day
How some one treated him;
Nature, like us, is sometimes caught
Without her diadem.

Home at Montclair, George Inness. The Granger Collection

---

rut (RUT) a track made by a wheeled vehicle
diadem (DY uh dem) crown (more like halo here)

Some keep the Sabbath

by Emily Dickinson

Some keep the Sabbath going to church;
I keep it staying at home,
With a bobolink for a chorister,   ] *Rhyme*
And an orchard for a dome.

5   Some keep the Sabbath in surplice;   – *alliteration*
I just wear my wings,
And instead of tolling the bell for church,
Our little sexton sings.

God preaches,—a noted clergyman,—
10   And the sermon is never long;
So instead of getting to heaven at last,] *assonance*
I'm going all along!

bobolink (BOB uh lingk) kind of song bird
chorister (KAWR ih stur) singer in a choir
surplice (SUR plis) loose-fitting garment worn by members of the clergy and choirs
sexton (SEKS tun) church caretaker who rings the bells

Letter to Thomas Wentworth Higginson

by Emily Dickinson

Letter to Mr. T. W. Higginson
April 15, 1862

Mr. Higginson,

Are you too deeply occupied to say if my verse is alive?

The Mind is so near itself—it cannot see, distinctly—and I have none to ask. Should you think it breathed—and had you the leisure to tell me, I should feel quick gratitude—

If I make the mistake—that you dared to tell me— would give me sincerer honor toward you—

I enclosed my name—asking you. If you please— Sir- to tell me what is true? That you will not betray me—it is needless to ask—since honor is its own pawn—

Emily Dickinson (1830–1886)

"If I read a book," wrote Emily Dickinson, "and it makes my whole body so cold no fire can ever warm me, I know that is poetry. If I feel . . . as if the top of my head were taken off, I know that is poetry. These are the only ways I know it. Is there any other way?"

". . . *as if the top of my head were taken off. . .* "! Those are strong words, but Emily Dickinson knew what she was talking about. Today Emily Dickinson is considered one of the greatest American poets—if not *the* greatest.

Her story is a strange one. Nearly all her life was passed in a large house in Amherst, Massachusetts. As a girl she was active and fun-loving. She had a year of college. Then, in her early 20s, something happened that changed her life. It was probably a disappointing romance, but that may not be the whole story. At any rate, she started spending more and more time alone. She read a lot. She helped with family chores. She watched the wonders of nature in a private yard and garden. She stopped going to church. By and by her parents died, and her world grew smaller still. What happened outside this private world—even the Civil War—held little interest for her. She dressed in white. She left chores outside the house to her unmarried sister, Vinnie. She refused to meet strangers. During the last ten years of her life she never went out.

Emily Dickinson died at the age of 55. Her relatives knew that poetry had been one of her interests. But she had written poetry mainly to please herself. During her lifetime, only seven of her poems had been published. Her family and a few friends had seen some others, but no one had dreamed of the surprise that came following her death. Her sister Vinnie entered her room to find drawers full of poems, trunks full of poems! In all, 1,775 were found! Most of them were arranged by year. In 1862, for instance, she had written 366 poems!

In a way, Emily Dickinson's world was small. But in another way, the world that she created was huge. Her mind stretched far, far out, beyond death—even beyond the world as we know it. Our world is richer for it.

In your opinion, what might have happened to make an active young woman slowly withdraw from society?

Review the Selection

UNDERSTAND THE SELECTION

Recall

1. Where does the speaker keep the Sabbath?

2. With whom does the speaker keep the Sabbath?

3. Who is the sexton in "Some keep the Sabbath" and what does it do?

Infer

4. Explain why you think the speaker in "I'm nobody" likes being nobody.

5. In "A word is dead," why does a word come alive when it is spoken?

6. Why did Dickinson write to Higginson?

7. In your opinion, what is the theme of "The sky is low"?

Apply

8. Select your favorite Dickinson poem. Explain why it is your favorite.

9. Suppose you are a poet. Name two things you have never seen or experienced about which you might write.

10. Why might Dickinson choose to use a frog as an example of somebody?

Respond to Literature

How does Dickinson's poetry reflect the transcendentalist views of writing?

THINK ABOUT SOUNDS IN POETRY

Poetry has musical qualities that prose does not have. Repetition of initial consonant letters (**alliteration**), of vowel sounds (**assonance**), and of final consonant sounds (**consonance**) help the poet to create musical effects. The use of liquid and explosive letters of the alphabet can also add to the music of poetry.

1. Which musical device is used in the first two lines of "I'm nobody"? Cite the words that produce this device.

2. Which musical device is used in the first line of "A word is dead"? Cite the words that produce this device.

3. The use of one particular letter, especially at the beginning of words, is repeated in "Some keep the Sabbath." What letter is it, and what is the name of the device it represents?

4. Does "I never saw a moor" have more liquid or more explosive sounds in the first stanza? In the second stanza?

5. Which is more important in musical devices, spelling or sound? Why?

READING FOCUS

Make Inferences Choose one of Emily Dickinson's poems that you read in this selection. What inferences can you make about the poem's meaning based on your own experiences? What inferences can you make based on words or images in the poem?

Figurative language is the use of imagery, symbols, or other devices to create meaning beyond the dictionary meanings of the words used. For example, in the line "A narrow wind complains all day," Dickinson wrote words that do not mean exactly what they say. The wind makes a lot of noise all day; the word *complains* is used figuratively. In the line "I never saw the sea," however, Dickinson uses words with their exact dictionary meanings. The language is **literal**.

Read the sentences below. For each, indicate whether the figurative or literal meaning of the italicized word is used.

1. "How *dreary* to be somebody!"

2. "I never saw a *moor*, . . ."

3. "Nature, like us, is sometimes caught Without her *diadem*."

4. "Bell-shaped *heather* flowers were in bloom."

5. "And instead of tolling the bell for church, Our little *sexton* sings."

6. "They'd *banish* us, you know."

Learn About

CHARACTER

A character is a person in a narrative. In fiction, characters are made-up people. They may be patterned after real persons, or they may be figments of the author's imagination.

Authors determine when and how much to tell readers about the characters. They may give a great deal of detail about a character right away, or they may let the reader determine what the character is like through his or her words and actions as the story progresses. They may give a detailed physical description of a character, or they may let the reader create his or her own mental image. A character's personality traits, value system, or frame of mind may be well-defined from the beginning of the story or may be left to the reader to figure out as the plot unfolds.

As you read "The Gift of the Magi," ask yourself:

1. What do the characters look like?
2. What type of people are they?

WRITING CONNECTION

If you were to write a short, fictional story, describe two characters that you would include. Give details of their physical appearance and personality.

READING FOCUS

Understand Imagery Imagery is language that appeals to your senses. Writers use imagery to try to make readers see sights, hear sounds, feel textures, smell scents, and taste flavors. Writers use only words to make you sense these things. As you read "The Gift of the Magi," look for images that make the settings and characters come alive for you. Note places in the text that make you see, hear, feel, smell, or taste something specific.

THE GIFT OF THE MAGI

by O. Henry

One dollar and eighty-seven cents. That was all. And sixty cents of it was in pennies. Pennies saved one and two at a time by bulldozing the grocer and the vegetable man and the butcher until one's cheeks burned with the silent imputation of parsimony that such close dealing implied. Three times Della counted it. One dollar and eighty-seven cents. And the next day would be Christmas.

There was clearly nothing to do but flop down on the shabby little couch and howl. So Della did it. Which instigates the moral reflection that life is made up of sobs, sniffles, and smiles, with sniffles predominating.

While the mistress of the home is gradually subsiding from the first stage to the second, take a look at the home. A furnished flat at $8 per week. It did not exactly beggar description, but it certainly had that word on the lookout for the mendicancy squad.

In the vestibule below was a letter-box into which no letter would go, and an electric button from which no mortal finger could coax a ring. Also appertaining thereunto was a card bearing the name "Mr. James Dillingham Young."

The "Dillingham" had been flung to the breeze during a former period of prosperity when its possessor was being paid $30 per week. Now, when the income was shrunk to $20, though, they were thinking seriously of contracting to a modest and unassuming D. But whenever Mr. James

---

Magi (MAY jy) the three wise men who, according to the biblical story, made the journey to Bethlehem to present gifts to the Christ child
bulldozing (BUL dohz ing) bullying; threatening
imputation (IM pyoo TAY shun) a charge or attribution of guilt or fault; blame
parsimony (PAR suh MOHN ee) stinginess
instigates (IN stuh gaytz) brings about; stirs up
mendicancy (MEN dih CAN cee) beggary; poverty
appertaining (ap pur TAYN ing) belonging; fixed

Dillingham Young came home and reached his flat above he was called "Jim" and greatly hugged by Mrs. James Dillingham Young, already introduced to you as Della. Which is all very good.

Della finished her cry and attended to her cheeks with the powder rag. She stood by the window and looked out dully at a gray cat walking a gray fence in a gray backyard. Tomorrow would be Christmas Day, and she had only $1.87 with which to buy Jim a present. She had been saving every penny she could for months, with this result. Twenty dollars a week doesn't go far. Expenses had been greater than she had calculated. They always are. Only $1.87 to buy a present for Jim. Her Jim. Many a happy hour she had spent planning for something nice for him. Something fine and rare and sterling—something just a little bit near to being worthy of the honor of being owned by Jim.

There was a pier-glass between the windows of the room. Perhaps you have seen a pier-glass in an $8 flat. A very thin and very agile person may, by observing his reflection in a rapid sequence of longitudinal strips, obtain a fairly accurate conception of his looks. Della, being slender, had mastered the art.

Suddenly she whirled from the window and stood before the glass. Her eyes were shining brilliantly, but her face had lost its color within twenty seconds. Rapidly she pulled down her hair and let it fall to its full length.

Now, there were two possessions of the James Dillingham Youngs in which they both took a mighty pride. One was Jim's gold watch that had been his father's and his grandfather's. The other was Della's hair. Had the Queen of Sheba[1] lived in the flat across the airshaft, Della would have let her hair hang out the window some day to dry just to depreciate Her Majesty's jewels and gifts. Had King Solomon been the janitor, with all his treasures piled up in the basement, Jim would have pulled out his watch every time he passed, just to see him pluck at his beard from envy.

So now Della's beautiful hair fell about her rippling and shining like a cascade of brown waters. It reached below her knee and made itself almost a garment for her. And then she did it up again nervously and quickly. Once she faltered for a minute and stood still while a tear or two splashed on the worn red carpet.

On went her old brown jacket; on went her old brown hat. With a whirl of skirts and with the brilliant sparkle still in her eyes, she fluttered out the door and down the stairs to the street.

Where she stopped the sign read: "Mne. Sofronie. Hair Goods of All Kinds." One flight up Della ran, and

---

pier-glass (PEER GLAS) mirror
agile (AJ ul) nimble; well-coordinated
depreciate (duh PREE she ayt) devalue
cascade (kas KAYD) waterfall
[1]**Queen of Sheba:** According to the Bible, the Queen of Sheba traveled from ancient Ethiopia to Israel to visit King Solomon. Amazed by the King's wisdom, she gave him much gold and other valuable gifts. (I Kings 10:1–13.)

collected herself, panting. Madame, large, too white, chilly, hardly looked the "Sofronie."

"Will you buy my hair?" asked Della.

"I buy hair," said Madame. "Take yer hat off and let's have a sight at the looks of it."

Down rippled the brown cascade.

"Twenty dollars," said Madame, lifting the mass with a practised hand.

"Give it to me quick," said Della.

Oh, and the next two hours tripped by on rosy wings. Forget the hashed metaphor. She was ransacking the stores for Jim's present.

She found it at last. It surely had been made for Jim and no one else. There was no other like it in any of the stores, and she had turned all of them inside out. It was a platinum fob chain simple and chaste in design, properly proclaiming its value by substance alone and not by meretricious ornamentation—as all good things should do. It was even worthy of The Watch. As soon as she saw it she knew that it must be Jim's. It was like him. Quietness and value--the description applied to both. Twenty-one dollars they took from her for it, and she hurried home with the 87 cents. With that chain on his watch Jim might be properly anxious about the time in any company. Grand as the watch was, he sometimes looked at it on the sly on account of the old leather strap that he used in place of a chain.

When Della reached home her intoxication gave way a little to prudence and reason. She got out her curling irons and lighted the gas and went to work repairing the ravages made by generosity added to love. Which is always a tremendous task, dear friends—a mammoth task.

Within forty minutes her head was covered with tiny, close-lying curls that made her look wonderfully like a truant schoolboy. She looked at her reflection in the mirror long, carefully, and critically.

"If Jim doesn't kill me," she said to herself, "before he takes a second look at me, he'll say I look like a Coney Island chorus girl.[2] But what could I do—oh! what could I do with a dollar and eighty-seven cents?"

At 7 o'clock the coffee was made and the frying-pan was on the back of the stove hot and ready to cook the chops.

Jim was never late. Della doubled the fob chain in her hand and sat on the corner of the table near the door that he always entered. Then she heard his step on the stair away down on the first flight, and she turned white for just a moment. She had a habit for saying little silent prayers about the simplest everyday things, and now she whispered: "Please God, make him think I am still pretty."

The door opened and Jim stepped in and closed it. He looked thin and very serious. Poor fellow, he was only twenty-two—and to be burdened with a family!

---

tripped (TRIPD) ran gracefully and lightly
hashed (HASHT) jumbled; all mixed up
ransacking (RAN sak ing) searching furiously
intoxication (in tox ih KAY shun) great excitement
[2]**Coney Island chorus girl:** A night-club dancer at Coney Island, once a busy amusement center on the edge of New York City.

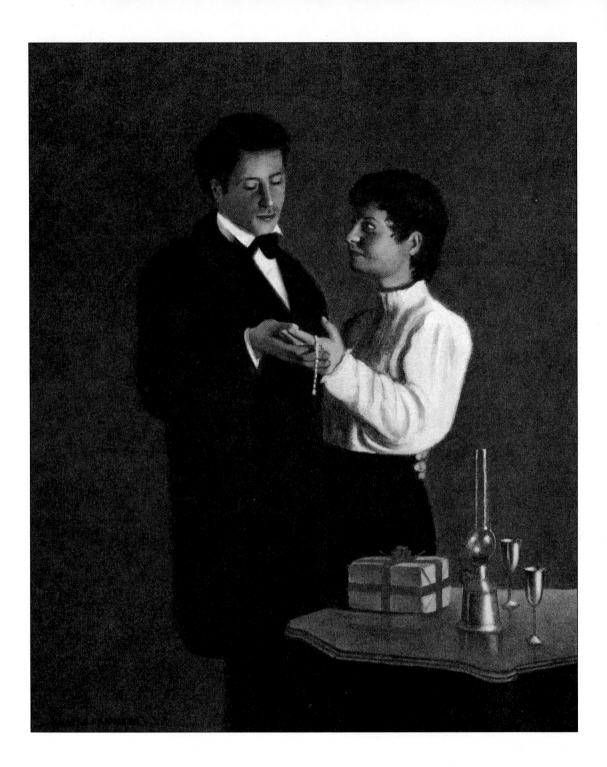

He needed a new overcoat and he was without gloves.

Jim stopped inside the door, as immovable as a setter at the scent of quail. His eyes were fixed upon Della, and there was an expression in them that she could not read, and it terrified her. It was not anger, nor surprise, nor disapproval, nor horror, nor any of the sentiments that she had been prepared for. He simply stared at her fixedly with that peculiar expression on his face.

Della wriggled off the table and went for him.

"Jim, darling," she cried, "don't look at me that way. I had my hair cut off and sold because I couldn't have lived through Christmas without giving you a present. It'll grow out again—you won't mind, will you? I just had to do it. My hair grows awfully fast. Say `Merry Christmas!' Jim, and let's be happy. You don't know what a nice—what a beautiful, nice gift I've got for you."

"You've cut off your hair?" asked Jim, laboriously, as if he had not arrived at that patent fact yet even after the hardest mental labor.

"Cut it off and sold it," said Della. "Don't you like me just as well, anyhow? I'm me without my hair, ain't I?"

Jim looked about the room curiously.

"You say your hair is gone?" he said, with an air almost of idiocy.

"You needn't look for it," said Della. "It's sold, I tell you—sold and gone, too. It's Christmas Eve, boy. Be good to me, for it went for you. Maybe the hairs of my head were numbered," she went on with sudden serious sweetness, "but nobody could ever count my love for you. Shall I put the chops on, Jim?"

Out of his trance Jim seemed quickly to wake. He enfolded his Della. For ten seconds let us regard with discreet scrutiny some inconsequential object in the other direction. Eight dollars a week or a million a year—what is the difference? A mathematician or a wit would give you the wrong answer. The magi brought valuable gifts, but that was not among them. This dark assertion will be illuminated later on.

Jim drew a package from his overcoat pocket and threw it upon the table.

"Don't make any mistake, Dell," he said, "about me. I don't think there's anything in the way of a haircut or a shave or a shampoo that could make me like my girl any less. But if you'll unwrap that package you may see why you had me going a while at first."

White fingers and nimble tore at the string and paper. And then an ecstatic scream of joy; and then, alas! a quick feminine change to hysterical tears and wails, necessitating the immediate employment of all the comforting powers of the lord of the flat.

For there lay The Combs—the set of combs, side and back, that Della had worshipped long in a Broadway window.

---

laboriously (luh BAWR ee us lee) with much labor and care
discreet (dih SKREET) wisely careful
inconsequential (in con suh KWEN shul) unimportant; trivial
illuminated (ih LOO muh nayt id) made clear

Beautiful combs, pure tortoise shell, with jewelled rims—just the shade to wear in the beautiful vanished hair. They were expensive combs, she knew, and her heart had simply craved and yearned over them without the least hope of possession. And now, they were hers, but the tresses that should have adorned the coveted adornments were gone.

But she hugged them to her bosom, and at length she was able to look up with dim eyes and a smile and say: "My hair grows so fast, Jim!"

And then Della leaped up like a little singed cat and cried, "Oh, oh!"

Jim had not yet seen his beautiful present. She held it out to him eagerly upon her open palm. The dull precious metal seemed to flash with a reflection of her bright and ardent spirit.

"Isn't it a dandy, Jim? I hunted all over town to find it. You'll have to look at the time a hundred times a day now. Give me your watch. I want to see how it looks on it."

Instead of obeying, Jim tumbled down on the couch and put his hands under the back of his head and smiled.

"Dell," said he, "let's put our Christmas presents away and keep 'em a while. They're too nice to use just at present. I sold the watch to get the money to buy your combs. And now suppose you put the chops on."

The magi, as you know, were wise men—wonderfully wise men—who brought gifts to the Babe in the manger. They invented the art of giving Christmas presents. Being wise, their gifts were no doubt wise ones, possibly bearing the privilege of exchange in case of duplication. And here I have lamely related to you the uneventful chronicle of two foolish children in a flat who most unwisely sacrificed for each other the greatest treasures of their house. But in a last word to the wise of these days let it be said that of all who give gifts these two were the wisest. Of all who give and receive gifts, such as they are wisest. Everywhere they are wisest. They are the magi.

---

ardent (AHR dunt) very eager; passionate

O. Henry (1862–1910)

William Sydney Porter, or "O. Henry," was born in Greensboro, North Carolina. As a young man, he worked in Texas on a ranch, in a bank, and on a newspaper. Charged with stealing money from the bank, he fled to Central America. But news of his wife's illness brought him back, and he faced the bank robbery charges.

He practiced writing short stories while in prison. After his release, he moved to New York City and wrote a story a week for popular magazines. He made a lot of money but died before he was 50.

Today O. Henry is remembered as the master of the surprise ending. Among his best-known stories are "The Last Leaf," "The Furnished Room," and "The Gift of the Magi."

Review the Selection

UNDERSTAND THE SELECTION

Recall

1. How much money does Della have at the beginning of the story?

2. How much does she receive for selling her hair?

3. What gift does she buy for her husband?

Infer

4. Why does Jim use his middle name on his card?

5. How does Della feel while shopping for Jim's present?

6. Why does she buy the particular present that she does?

7. Why are these two "the wisest"?

Apply

8. How do you think Della feels about her poverty? Why do you think so?

9. What adjectives would you use to describe Della's feeling toward Jim?

10. Is your mental picture of one character clearer than the other? If so, explain why.

Respond to Literature

How do you think "The Gift of the Magi" reflects the material values of the early 1900s?

THINK ABOUT CHARACTER

Authors sometimes discuss the characteristics and traits of a character directly. In addition, they often give indirect clues from which the reader can surmise or guess other traits of the individual. Readers can watch for things the characters say, descriptions of what they think, and their actions.

1. How does O. Henry define Jim and Della's characters?

2. What indirect clues about their personalities can you find in the story?

3. Do you think that one character appreciates his or her Christmas present more than the other? Why?

4. What is your mental picture of Madame Sofronie?

5. What would you say the future holds for Della and Jim's marriage?

READING FOCUS

Understand Imagery As you read "The Gift of the Magi," you looked for imagery in the story. What are some images that helped the story come alive for you? To which of your five senses did these images appeal?

An **idiom** is an expression that has a meaning that is often different from the literal meaning of the words that form it. *With a high hand*, for example, has nothing to do with the position of a hand; it means "in a dictatorial manner."

Idioms are listed in your dictionary after the definitions of the entry word that is the main word in the phrase. Look up the italicized idioms in these quotations from "The Gift of the Magi." Then write an original sentence, using the idiom as it is used here.

1. ". . . life is *made up* of three stages, sobs, sniffles, and smiles."

2. "And then she *did* it *up* again . . ."

3. ". . . *at length* she was able to look up with . . . a smile."

Focus ON Fiction

*F*iction is any literary work that portrays imaginary characters and events. The basis of all fiction is the imagination of the author. Fiction is meant primarily to be entertaining. It may also be used for such purposes as teaching, influencing, or inspiring.

A work of fiction can take many forms. Chief among these are novels, short stories, plays, and poems. Several literary elements are associated with these various forms of fiction: setting, character, plot, theme, tone, imagery, and symbolism.

Setting The setting of a story is the time and place in which it happens. The time may be the hour of the day, the season, the year, or a period in history. The place may include the general geographical location and environment as well as weather, scenery, terrain, sounds, and smells. It can also include specific places and objects such as buildings, furniture, clothing, windows, and animals. The clearer and more well-defined the setting, the more real and believable the story becomes.

Character A character is a person in a story. There is often a great deal to find out about characters, particularly main characters. For example, values and frame of mind are two features to look for. Characters can be **flat**, one-dimensional stereotypes. These are usually secondary figures. Main characters should be **round**—individuals with personalities you get to know.

Plot The plot consists of the events that happen in a story. It serves as a framework that establishes a relationship between episodes. Plot brings order by showing a few selected characters and incidents and uniting them into a whole. It organizes a story into a beginning, a middle, and an ending.

Sometimes, an author will give clues about what is going to happen in the plot. This is known as **foreshadowing**. Incidents build, through **rising action**, to a **climax**, or turning point. This may happen at the end of the story, or the climax may be followed by **falling action** and the **resolution** of the conflict.

The plot always centers on a **conflict**. This meeting of opposing forces may be internal (within the character) or external (between characters or between a character and some other force, such as nature). In the case of conflict between two characters, the main character is the **protagonist**; the other is the **antagonist**.

Theme   The theme is the meaning or message of a story. It is some central idea about life that the author is attempting to communicate. The theme may be stated clearly at any point in the story, or the author might leave it for the reader to determine.

Tone   Tone is the author's attitude toward either the subject matter or the reader. It may take many forms—serious or humorous, formal or informal, or direct or symbolic.

Imagery and Figurative Language   Imagery refers to the collection of images in a work of literature. Images are sensory in nature, meaning that they are designed to appeal to one of the five senses. Figures of speech, or figurative language, include simile and metaphor. **Similes** state a direct comparison between two unlike objects. They are introduced with *like* or *as*. For example, *The house was like an empty cavern.* **Metaphors** suggest a comparison, giving one object the qualities of another. For example, *The house was an empty cavern.*

Symbolism   Symbolism is the use of one thing to represent another. Usually, the symbol is concrete and stands for some abstract idea, feeling, or quality.

The following is an annotated version of "The Revolt of Mother." **Annotated** means that notes have been added at various points in the story. The purpose of these annotations is to help you see and understand the function and interrelationships of literary elements in a work of fiction.

As you read, ask yourself:
1. How closely connected are the elements of character and plot? Is the concept of conflict involved with both of these?
2. What is the theme? What clues are given about the theme?

Homestead of Ellsworth Ball, detail, Sallie Cover. Private Collection

THE REVOLT OF MOTHER

by Mary E. Wilkins Freeman

"Father!"

"What is it?"

"What are them men diggin' over there in the field for?"

There was a sudden dropping and enlarging of the lower part of the old man's face, as if some heavy weight had settled therein; he shut his mouth tight, and went on harnessing the great bay mare. He hustled the collar on to her neck with a jerk.

"Father!"

The old man slapped the saddle upon the mare's back.

"Look here, Father, I want to know what them men are diggin' over in the field for, an' I'm goin' to know."

"I wish you'd go into the house, Mother, an' 'tend to your own affairs," the old man said then. He ran his words together, and his speech was almost as inarticulate as a growl.

But the woman understood; it was her most native tongue. "I ain't goin' into the house till you tell me what them men are doin' over there in the field," said she.

Then she stood waiting. She was a small woman, short and straight-waisted like a child in her brown cotton gown. Her forehead was mild and benevolent between the smooth curves of gray hair; there were meek downward lines about her nose and mouth; but her eyes, fixed upon the old man, looked as if the meekness had been the result of her own will, never of the will of another.

They were in the barn, standing before the wide open doors. The spring air, full of the smell of growing grass and unseen blossoms, came in their faces. The deep yard in front was littered with farm wagons and piles of wood; on the edges, close to the fence and the house, the grass was a vivid green, and there were some dandelions.

The old man glanced doggedly at his wife as he tightened the last buckles on the harness. She looked as immovable to him as one of the rocks in his pasture-land, bound to the earth with generations of blackberry vines. He slapped the reins over the horse, and started forth from the barn.

"*Father!*" said she.

The old man pulled up. "What is it?"

"I want to know what them men are diggin' over there in that field for."

"They're diggin' a cellar, I s'pose, if you've got to know."

"A cellar for what?"

"A barn."

"A barn? You ain't goin' to build a barn over there where we was goin' to have a house, Father?"

The old man said not another word. He hurried the horse into the farm wagon, and clattered out of the yard, jouncing as sturdily on his seat as a boy.

The woman stood a moment looking after him, then she went out of the barn across a corner of the yard to the house. The house, standing at right angles with the great barn and a long reach of sheds and out-buildings, was infinitesimal compared with them. It was scarcely as commodious for people as the little boxes under the barn eaves were for doves.

A pretty girl's face, pink and delicate as a flower, was looking out of one of the house windows. She was watching three men who were digging over in the field which bounded the yard near the road line. She turned quietly when the woman entered.

"What are they diggin' for, Mother?" said she. "Did he tell you?"

"They're diggin' for—a cellar for a new barn."

"Oh, Mother, he ain't goin' to build another barn?"

---

doggedly (DAWG id lee) persistently; stubbornly
infinitesimal (in fin ih TES uh mul) too small to be measured
commodious (kuh MOH dee us) spacious; roomy

"That's what he says."

A boy stood before the kitchen glass combing his hair. He combed slowly and painstakingly, arranging his brown hair in a smooth hillock over his forehead. He did not seem to pay any attention to the conversation.

"Sammy, did you know Father was goin' to build a new barn?" asked the girl.

The boy combed assiduously.

"Sammy!"

He turned, and showed a face like his father's under his smooth crest of hair. "Yes, I s'pose I did," he said, reluctantly.

"How long have you known it?" asked his mother.

"'Bout three months, I guess."

"Why didn't you tell of it?"

"Didn't think 'twould do no good."

"I don't see what Father wants another barn for," said the girl, in her sweet, slow voice. She turned again to the window, and stared out at the digging men in the field. Her tender, sweet face was full of a gentle distress. Her forehead was as bald and innocent as a baby's, with the light hair strained back from it in a row of curl-papers. She was quite large, but her soft curves did not look as if they covered muscles.

Her mother looked sternly at the boy. "Is he goin' to buy more cows?" said she.

How does the plot begin to develop?

The boy did not reply; he was tying his shoes.

"Sammy, I want you to tell me if he's goin' to buy more cows."

"I s'pose he is."

"How many?"

"Four, I guess."

His mother said nothing more. She went into the pantry, and there was a clatter of dishes. The boy got his cap from a nail behind the door, took an old arithmetic from the shelf, and started for school. He was lightly built, but clumsy. He went out of the yard with a curious spring in the hips, that made his loose home-made jacket tilt up in the rear.

The girl went to the sink, and began to wash the dishes that were piled up there. Her mother came promptly out of the pantry,

---

hillock (HIL uk) a small hill; mound

and shoved her aside. "You wipe 'em," said she; "I'll wash. There's a good many this mornin'."

The mother plunged her hands vigorously into the water, the girl wiped the plates slowly and dreamily. "Mother," said she, "don't you think it's too bad Father's goin' to build that new barn, much as we need a decent house to live in?"

This shows the author's attitude toward the two main characters.

Her mother scrubbed a dish fiercely. "You ain't found out yet we're women-folks, Nanny Penn," said she. "You ain't seen enough of men-folks yet to. One of these days you'll find it out, an' then you'll know that we know only what men-folks think we do, so far as any use of it goes, an' how we'd ought to reckon men-folks in with Providence, an' not complain of what they do any more than we do of the weather."

"I don't care; I don't believe George is anything like that, anyhow," said Nanny. Her delicate face flushed pink, her lips pouted softly, as if she were going to cry.

"You wait an' see. I guess George Eastman ain't no better than other men. You hadn't ought to judge Father, though. He can't help it, 'cause he don't look at things jest the way we do. An' we've been pretty comfortable here, after all. The roof don't leak—ain't never but once—that's one thing. Father's kept it shingled right up."

"I do wish we had a parlor."

"I guess it won't hurt George Eastman any to come to see you in a nice clean kitchen. I guess a good many girls don't have as good a place as this. Nobody's ever heard me complain."

"I ain't complained either, Mother."

"Well, I don't think you'd better, a good father an' a good home as you've got. S'pose your father made you go out an' work for your livin'? Lots of girls have to that ain't no stronger an' better able to than you be."

Can you find any theme clues here?

Sarah Penn washed the frying-pan with a conclusive air. She scrubbed the outside of it as faithfully as the inside. She was a masterly keeper of her box of a house. Her one living-room never seemed to have in it any of the dust which the friction of life with inanimate matter produces. She swept, and there seemed to be no dirt to go before the broom; she cleaned, and one could see no difference. She was like an artist so perfect that he has

---

inanimate (in AN uh mit) not living or moving

apparently no art. Today she got out a mixing bowl and a board, and rolled some pies, and there was no more flour upon her than upon her daughter who was doing finer work. Nanny was to be married in the fall, and she was sewing on some white cambric and embroidery. She sewed industriously while her mother cooked, her soft milk-white hands and wrists showed whiter than her delicate work.

"We must have the stove moved out in the shed before long," said Mrs. Penn. "Talk about not havin' things, it's been a real blessin' to be able to put a stove up in that shed in hot weather. Father did one good thing when he fixed that stove-pipe out there."

The literary elements of setting and character are interwoven here.

Sarah Penn's face as she rolled her pies had that expression of meek vigor which might have characterized one of the New Testament saints. She was making mince-pies. Her husband, Adoniram Penn, liked them better than any other kind. She baked twice a week. Adoniram often liked a piece of pie between meals. She hurried this morning. It had been later than usual when she began, and she wanted to have a pie baked for dinner. However deep a resentment she might be forced to hold against her husband, she would never fail in sedulous attention to his wants.

Nobility of character manifests itself at loop-holes when it is not provided with large doors. Sarah Penn's showed itself today in flaky dishes of pastry. So she made the pies faithfully, while across the table she could see, when she glanced up from her work, the sight that rankled in her patient and steadfast soul—the digging of the cellar of the new barn in the place where Adoniram forty years ago had promised her their new house should stand.

What is the author's attitude toward Sarah?

The pies were done for dinner. Adoniram and Sammy were home a few minutes after twelve o'clock. The dinner was eaten with serious haste. There was never much conversation at the table in the Penn family. Adoniram asked a blessing, and they ate promptly, then rose up and went about their work.

Sammy went back to school, taking soft sly lopes out of the yard like a rabbit. He wanted a game of marbles before school, and feared his father would give him some chores to do. Adoniram hastened to the door and called after him, but he was out of sight.

---

cambric (KAM brik) very fine, thin linen or cotton
sedulous (SEJ uh lus) hard-working; diligent; persistent

The Revolt of Mother ■ 261

"I don't see what you let him go for, Mother," said he. "I wanted him to help me unload that wood."

Adoniram went to work out in the yard unloading wood from the wagon. Sarah put away the dinner dishes, while Nanny took down her curl-papers and changed her dress. She was going down to the store to buy some more embroidery and thread.

When Nanny was gone, Mrs. Penn went to the door. "Father!" she called.

"Well, what is it?"

"I want to see you jest a minute, Father."

"I can't leave this wood nohow. I've got to git it unloaded an' go for a load of gravel afore two o'clock. Sammy had ought to helped me. You hadn't ought to let him go to school so early."

"I want to see you jest a minute."

"I tell ye I can't, nohow, Mother."

Imagery is used to describe Sarah's movements.

"Father, you come here." Sarah Penn stood in the door like a queen; she held her head as if it bore a crown; there was that patience which makes authority royal in her voice. Adoniram went.

Mrs. Penn led the way into the kitchen, and pointed to a chair. "Sit down, Father," said she; "I've got somethin' I want to say to you."

He sat down heavily; his face was quite stolid, but he looked at her with restive eyes. "Well, what is it, mother?"

"I want to know what you're buildin' that new barn for, Father?"

"I ain't got nothin' to say about it."

"It can't be you think you need another barn?"

"I tell ye I ain't got nothin' to say about it, Mother; an' I ain't goin' to say nothin'."

"Be you goin' to buy more cows?"

Adoniram did not reply; he shut his mouth tight.

"I know you be, as well as I want to. Now, Father, look here"— Sarah Penn had not sat down; she stood before her husband in the humble fashion of a Scripture woman—"I'm goin' to talk real plain to you; I never have sence I married you, but I'm goin' to now. I ain't never complained, an' I ain't goin' to complain now, but I'm goin' to talk plain. You see this room here, Father; you look at it well. You see there ain't no carpet on the floor, an' you see the paper is all dirty, an' droppin' off the walls. We ain't had no new paper on it for ten year, an' then I put it on myself, an' it didn't cost but ninepence a roll. You see this room, Father; it's all the one I've had to work in an' eat in an' sit in sence we was married. There ain't another woman in the whole town whose husband ain't got half the means you have but what's got better. It's all the room Nanny's got to have her company in; an' there ain't one of her mates but what's got better, an' their fathers not so able as hers is. It's all the room she'll have to be married in. What would you have thought, Father, if we had had our weddin' in a room no better than this? I was married in my mother's parlor, with a carpet on the floor, an' stuffed furniture, an' a mahogany card-table. An' this is all the room my daughter will have to be married in. Look here, Father!"

Sarah Penn went across the room as though it were a tragic stage. She flung open a door and disclosed a tiny bedroom, only large enough for a bed and bureau, with a path between. "There, Father," said she—"there's all the room I've had to sleep in forty

---

stolid (STOL id) expressing little emotion
restive (RES tiv) impatient; uneasy; stubborn

year. All my children were born there—the two that died, an' the two that's livin'. I was sick with a fever there."

She stepped to another door and opened it. It led into the small, ill-lighted pantry. "Here," said she, "is all the buttery I've got—every place I've got for my dishes, to set away my victuals in, an' to keep my milk-pans in. Father, I've been takin' care of the milk of six cows in this place, an' now you're goin' to build a new barn, an' keep more cows, an' give me more to do in it."

She threw open another door. A narrow crooked flight of stairs wound upward from it. "There, Father," said she, "I want you to look at the stairs that go up to them two unfinished chambers that are all the places our son an' daughter have had to sleep in all their lives. There ain't a prettier girl in town nor a more ladylike one than Nanny, an' that's the place she has to sleep in. It ain't so good as your horse's stall; it ain't so warm an' tight."

Setting, character, and plot all come together here. This illustrates the interrelationship among these elements.

Sarah Penn went back and stood before her husband. "Now, Father," said she, "I want to know if you think you're doin' right an' accordin' to what you profess. Here, when we was married, forty year ago, you promised me faithful that we should have a new house built in that lot over in the field before the year was out. You said you had money enough, an' you wouldn't ask me to live in no such place as this. It is forty year now, an' you've been makin' more money, an' I've been savin' of it for you ever since, an' you ain't built no house yet. You've built sheds an' cow-houses an' one new barn, an' now you're goin' to build another. Father, I want to know if you think it's right. You're lodgin' your dumb beasts better than you are your own flesh an' blood. I want to know if you think it's right."

"I ain't got nothin' to say."

"You can't say nothin' without ownin' it ain't right, Father. An' there's another thing—I ain't complained; I've got along forty year, an' I s'pose I should forty more, if it wa'n't for that—if we don't have another house. Nanny she can't live with us after she's married. She'll have to go somewheres else to live away from us, an' it don't seem as if I could have it so, noways, Father. She wa'n't ever strong. She's got considerable color, but there wa'n't never any backbone to her. I've always took the heft of everything off

---

pantry (PAN tree) a small room or closet off the kitchen, where cooking ingredients and utensils, china, etc., are kept

her, an' she ain't fit to keep house an' do everything herself. She'll be all worn out inside of a year. Think of her doin' all the washin' an' ironin' an' bakin' with them soft white hands an' arms, an' sweepin'! I can't have it so, noways, Father."

Mrs. Penn's face was burning; her mild eyes gleamed. She had pleaded her little cause like a Webster; she had ranged from severity to pathos; but her opponent employed that obstinate silence which makes eloquence futile with mocking echoes. Adoniram arose clumsily.

"Father, ain't you got nothin' to say?" said Mrs. Penn.

"I've got to go off after that load of gravel. I can't stan' here talkin' all day."

"Father, won't you think it over, an' have a house built there instead of a barn?"

"I ain't got nothin' to say."

Adoniram shuffled out. Mrs. Penn went into her bedroom. When she came out, her eyes were red. She had a roll of unbleached cotton cloth. She spread it out on the kitchen table, and began cutting out some shirts for her husband. The men over in the field had a team to help them this afternoon; she could hear their halloos. She had a scanty pattern for the shirts; she had to plan and piece the sleeves.

Nanny came home with her embroidery, and sat down with her needlework. She had taken down her curl-papers, and there was a soft roll of fair hair like an aureole over her forehead; her face was as delicately fine and clear as porcelain. Suddenly she looked up, and the tender red flamed all over her face and neck. "Mother," said she.

How is imagery used to describe Nanny's face?

"What say?"

"I've been thinkin'—I don't see how we're goin' to have any—weddin' in this room. I'd be ashamed to have his folks come if we didn't have anybody else."

"Mebbe we can have some new paper before then; I can put it on. I guess you won't have no call to be ashamed of your belongin's."

---

pathos (PAY thos) an element in experience evoking pity
obstinate (OB stuh nut) stubborn
halloos (huh LOOZ) shouts; yells; calls
aureole (AWR ee ohl) a halo
porcelain (PAWR suh lin) china

Here is another example of foreshadowing. You are given a plot clue about what will happen later. Do you have any ideas?

"We might have the weddin' in the new barn," said Nanny, with gentle pettishness. "Why, Mother, what makes you look so?"

Mrs. Penn had started, and was staring at her with a curious expression. She turned again to her work, and spread out a pattern carefully on the cloth. "Nothin'," said she.

Presently Adoniram clattered out of the yard in his two-wheeled dump cart, standing as proudly upright as a Roman charioteer. Mrs. Penn opened the door and stood there a minute looking out; the halloos of the men sounded louder.

It seemed to her all through the spring months that she heard nothing but the halloos and the noises of saws and hammers. The new barn grew fast. It was a fine edifice for this little village. Men came on pleasant Sundays, in their meeting suits and clean shirt bosoms, and stood around it admiringly. Mrs. Penn did not speak of it, and Adoniram did not mention it to her, although sometimes, upon a return from inspecting it, he bore himself with injured dignity.

Does this give you a clue to the theme?

"It's a strange thing how your mother feels about the new barn," he said, confidentially, to Sammy one day.

The plot is about to take an unexpected twist.

Sammy only grunted after an odd fashion for a boy; he had learned it from his father. The barn was all completed ready for use by the third week in July. Adoniram had planned to move his stock in on Wednesday; on Tuesday he received a letter which changed his plans. He came in with it early in the morning. "Sammy's been to the post-office," said he, "an' I've got a letter from Hiram." Hiram was Mrs. Penn's brother, who lived in Vermont.

"Well," said Mrs. Penn, "what does he say about the folks?"

The new plot event is revealed. What plot question does this raise?

"I guess they're all right. He says he thinks if I come up country right off there's a chance to buy jest the kind of a horse I want." He stared reflectively out of the window at the new barn.

Mrs. Penn was making pies. She went on clapping the rolling-pin into the crust, although she was very pale, and her heart beat loudly.

"I dunno' but what I'd better go," said Adoniram. "I hate to go off jest now, right in the midst of hayin', but the ten-acre lot's cut, an' I guess Rufus an' the others can git along without me three or

edifice (ED uh fis) a large structure

four days. I can't get a horse round here to suit me, nohow, an' I've got to have another for all that wood-haulin' in the fall. I told Hiram to watch out, an' if he got wind of a good horse to let me know. I guess I'd better go."

"I'll get out your clean shirt an' collar," said Mrs. Penn calmly.

She laid out Adoniram's Sunday suit and his clean clothes on the bed in the little bedroom. She got his shaving-water and razor ready. At last she buttoned on his collar and fastened his black cravat.

Adoniram never wore his collar and cravat except on extra occasions. He held his head high, with a rasped dignity. When he was all ready, with his coat and hat brushed, and a lunch of pie and cheese in a paper bag, he hesitated on the threshold of the door. He looked at his wife, and his manner was defiantly apologetic. "*If* them cows come today, Sammy can drive 'em into the new barn," said he; "an' when they bring the hay up, they can pitch it in there."

"Well," replied Mrs. Penn.

Adoniram set his shaven face ahead and started. When he had cleared the door-step, he turned and looked back with a kind of nervous solemnity. "I shall be back by Saturday if nothin' happens," said he.

"Do be careful, Father," returned his wife.

She stood in the door with Nanny at her elbow and watched him out of sight. Her eyes had a strange, doubtful expression in them; her peaceful forehead was contracted. She went in, and about her baking again. Nanny sat sewing. Her wedding day was drawing nearer, and she was getting pale and thin with her steady sewing. Her mother kept glancing at her.

"Have you got that pain in your side this mornin'?" she asked.

"A little."

Mrs. Penn's face, as she worked, changed, her perplexed forehead smoothed, her eyes were steady, her lips firmly set. She formed a maxim for herself, although incoherently with her

A new plot question: What does Sarah have in mind?

---

cravat (kruh VAT) a necktie; scarf
maxim (MAK sim) a statement of a general truth
incoherently (in koh HIR unt lee) not logically; disjointedly

unlettered thoughts. "Unsolicited opportunities are the guide-posts of the Lord to the new roads of life," she repeated in effect, and she made up her mind to her course of action.

"S'posin' I *had* wrote to Hiram," she muttered once, when she was in the pantry—"s'posin' I had wrote, an' asked him if he knew of any horse? But I didn't, an' Father's goin' wa'n't none of my doin'. It looks like a providence." Her voice rang out quite loud at the last.

"What you talkin' about, Mother?" called Nanny.

"Nothin'."

Mrs. Penn hurried her baking; at eleven o'clock it was all done. The load of hay from the west field came slowly down the cart track, and drew up at the new barn. Mrs. Penn ran out. "Stop!" she screamed—"stop!"

The men stopped and looked; Sammy upreared from the top of the load, and stared at his mother.

"Stop!" she cried out again. "Don't you put the hay in that barn; put it in the old one."

This is a brief description of a stereotyped, secondary character. Would this character be considered round or flat?

"Why, he said to put it in here," returned one of the haymakers, wonderingly. He was a young man, a neighbor's son, whom Adoniram hired by the year to help on the farm.

"Don't you put the hay in the new barn; there's room enough in the old one, ain't there?" said Mrs. Penn.

"Room enough," returned the hired man, in his thick, rustic tones. "Didn't need the new barn, nohow, far as room's concerned. Well, I s'pose he changed his mind." He took hold of the horses' bridles.

Mrs. Penn went back to the house. Soon the kitchen windows were darkened, and a fragrance like warm honey came into the room.

Nanny laid down her work. "I thought Father wanted them to put the hay into the new barn?" she said, wonderingly.

"It's all right," replied her mother.

Sammy slid down from the load of hay, and came in to see if dinner was ready.

"I ain't goin' to get a regular dinner today, as long as Father's

---

rustic (RUS tik) of or living in the country, rural; simple, plain; rough, awkward

Homestead of Ellsworth Ball, detail, Sallie Cover. Private Collection

gone," said his mother. "I've let the fire go out. You can have some bread an' milk an' pie. I thought we could get along." She set out some bowls of milk, some bread, and a pie on the kitchen table. "You'd better eat your dinner now," said she. "You might jest as well get through with it. I want you to help me afterward."

Nanny and Sammy stared at each other. There was something strange in their mother's manner. Mrs. Penn did not eat anything herself. She went into the pantry, and they heard her moving dishes while they ate. Presently she came out with a pile of plates. She got the clothes-basket out of the shed, and packed them in it. Nanny and Sammy watched. She brought out cups and saucers, and put them in with the plates.

"What you goin' to do, Mother?" inquired Nanny, in a timid voice. A sense of something unusual made her tremble, as if it were a ghost. Sammy rolled his eyes over his pie.

"You'll see what I'm goin' to do," replied Mrs. Penn. "If you're through, Nanny, I want you to go upstairs an' pack up your things; an' I want you, Sammy, to help me take down the bed in the bedroom."

"Oh, Mother, what for?" gasped Nanny.

"You'll see."

Some imagery that may be unfamiliar is explained.

During the next few hours a feat was performed by this simple, pious New England mother which was equal in its way to Wolfe's storming of the Heights of Abraham. It took no more genius and audacity of bravery for Wolfe to cheer his wondering soldiers up those steep precipices, under the sleeping eyes of the enemy, than for Sarah Penn, at the head of her children, to move all their little household goods into the new barn while her husband was away.

Nanny and Sammy followed their mother's instructions without a murmur; indeed, they were overawed. There is a certain uncanny and superhuman quality about all such purely original undertakings as their mother's was to them. Nanny went back and forth with her light loads, and Sammy tugged with sober energy.

Do you think this is the climax of the plot?

At five o'clock in the afternoon the little house in which the Penns had lived for forty years had emptied itself into the new barn.

Every builder builds somewhat for unknown purposes, and is in a measure a prophet. The architect of Adoniram Penn's barn, while he designed it for the comfort of four-footed animals, had planned better than he knew for the comfort of humans. Sarah Penn saw at a glance its possibilities. Those great box-stalls, with quilts hung before them, would make better bedrooms than the one she had occupied for forty years, and there was a tight carriage-room. The harness-room, with its chimney and shelves, would make a kitchen of her dreams. The great middle space would make a parlor, by-and-by, fit for a palace. Up stairs there was as much room as down. With partitions and windows, what a house would there be! Sarah looked at the row of stanchions before the allotted space for cows, and reflected that she would have her front entry there.

---

precipices (PRES uh pis iz) steep cliffs; vertical or hanging rock faces
stanchions (STAN chunz) upright bars, beams or posts used as support

At six o'clock the stove was up in the harness-room, the kettle was boiling, and the table set for tea. It looked almost as home-like as the abandoned house across the yard had ever done. The young hired man milked, and Sarah directed him calmly to bring the milk to the new barn. He came gaping, dropping little blots of foam from the brimming pails on the grass. Before the next morning he had spread the story of Adoniram Penn's wife moving into the new barn all over the little village. Men assembled in the store and talked it over, women with shawls over their heads scuttled into each other's houses before their work was done. Any deviation from the ordinary course of life in this quiet town was enough to stop all progress in it. Everybody paused to look at the staid, independent figure on the side track. There was a difference of opinion with regard to her. Some held her to be insane; some, of a lawless and rebellious spirit.

Friday the minister went to see her. It was in the forenoon, and she was at the barn door shelling pease for dinner. She looked up and returned his salutation with dignity, then she went on with her work. She did not invite him in. The saintly expression of her face remained fixed, but there was an angry flush over it.

The minister stood awkwardly before her, and talked. She handled the pease as if they were bullets. At last she looked up, and her eyes showed the spirit that her meek front had covered for a lifetime.

"There ain't no use talkin', Mr. Hersey," said she. "I've thought it all over an' over, an' I believe I'm doin' what's right. I've made it the subject of prayer, an' it's betwixt me an' the Lord an' Adoniram. There ain't no call for nobody else to worry about it."

> Could this be another theme clue?

"Well, of course, if you have brought it to the Lord in prayer, and feel satisfied that you are doing right, Mrs. Penn," said the minister, helplessly. His thin gray-bearded face was pathetic. He was a sickly man; his youthful confidence had cooled; he had to scourge himself up to some of his pastoral duties as relentlessly as a Catholic ascetic, and then he was prostrated by the smart.

"I think it's right jest as much as I think it was right for our forefathers to come over from the old country 'cause they didn't have what belonged to 'em," said Mrs. Penn. She arose.

---

scourge (SKURJ) to whip; to chastise, punish
prostrated (PROS trayt id) laid low; completely overcome

Symbolism is used here. Plymouth Rock symbolizes the start of a new life in a new environment for the Penn family, just as it did for the Pilgrims.

The barn threshold might have been Plymouth Rock from her bearing. "I don't doubt you mean well, Mr. Hersey," said she, "but there are things people hadn't ought to interfere with. I've been a member of the church for over forty year. I've got my own mind an' my own feet, an' I'm goin' to think my own thoughts an' go my own ways, an' nobody but the Lord is goin' to dictate to me unless I've a mind to have him. Won't you come in an' set down? How is Mis' Hersey?"

"She is well, I thank you," replied the minister. He added some more perplexed apologetic remarks; then he retreated.

He could expound the intricacies of every character study in the Scriptures, he was competent to grasp the Pilgrim Fathers and all historical innovators, but Sarah Penn was beyond him. He could deal with primal cases, but parallel ones worsted him. But, after all, although it was aside from his province, he wondered more how Adoniram Penn would deal with his wife than how the Lord would. Everybody shared the wonder. When Adoniram's four new cows arrived, Sarah ordered three to be put in the old barn, the other in the house shed where the cooking-stove had stood. That added to the excitement. It was whispered that all four cows were domiciled in the house.

Toward sunset on Saturday, when Adoniram was expected home, there was a knot of men in the road near the new barn. The hired man had milked, but he still hung around the premises. Sarah Penn had supper all ready. There were brown-bread and baked beans and a custard pie; it was the supper that Adoniram loved on a Saturday night. She had on a clean calico, and she bore herself imperturbably. Nanny and Sammy kept close at her heels. Their eyes were large, and Nanny was full of nervous tremors. Still there was to them more pleasant excitement than anything else. An inborn confidence in their mother over their father asserted itself.

Is this rising action leading to the climax, or is it falling action headed toward resolution?

Sammy looked out of the harness-room window. "There he is," he announced, in an awed whisper. He and Nanny peeped around the casing. Mrs. Penn kept on about her work. The children

---

intricacies (IN trih kuh seez) complexities; complications
innovators (IN uh vayt urz) makers of changes; introducers of new methods
imperturbably (im pur TUR buh blee) in a manner that cannot be excited; impassively

watched Adoniram leave the new horse standing in the drive while he went to the house door. It was fastened. Then he went around to the shed. That door was seldom locked, even when the family was away. The thought how her father would be confronted by the cow flashed upon Nanny. There was a hysterical sob in her throat. Adoniram emerged from the shed and stood looking about in a dazed fashion. His lips moved; he was saying something, but they could not hear what it was. The hired man was peeping around a corner of the old barn, but nobody saw him.

Adoniram took the new horse by the bridle and led him across the yard to the new barn. Nanny and Sammy slunk close to their mother. The barn doors rolled back, and there stood Adoniram, with the long mild face of the great Canadian farm horse looking over his shoulder.

Nanny kept behind her mother, but Sammy stepped suddenly forward, and stood in front of her.

Adoniram stared at the group. "What on airth you all down here for?" said he. "What's the matter over to the house?"

"We've come here to live, Father," said Sammy. His shrill voice quavered out bravely.

"What"—Adoniram sniffed—"what is it smells like cookin'?" said he. He stepped forward and looked in the open door of the harness-room. Then he turned to his wife. His old bristling face was pale and frightened. "What on airth does this mean, Mother?" he gasped.

"You come in here, Father," said Sarah. She led the way into the harness-room and shut the door. "Now, Father," said she, "you needn't be scared. I ain't crazy. There ain't nothin' to be upset over. But we've come here to live, an' we're goin' to live here. We've got jest as good a right here as new horses an' cows. The house wa'n't fit for us to live in any longer, an' I made up my mind I wa'n't goin' to stay there. I've done my duty by you forty year, an' I'm goin' to do it now; but I'm goin' to live here. You've got to put in some windows and partitions; an' you'll have to buy some furniture."

"Why, Mother!" the old man gasped.

"You'd better take your coat off an' get washed—there's the wash-basin—an' then we'll have supper."

"Why, Mother!"

Do you think this is a plot clue, a theme clue, or both?

From Arkansas, 1943, Georges Schreiber

Sammy went past the window, leading the new horse to the old barn. The old man saw him, and shook his head speechlessly. He tried to take off his coat, but his arms seemed to lack the power. His wife helped him. She poured some water into the tin basin, and put in a piece of soap. She got the comb and brush, and smoothed his thin gray hair after he had washed. Then she put the beans, hot bread, and tea on the table. Sammy came in, and the family drew up. Adoniram sat looking dazedly at his plate, and they waited.

"Ain't you goin' to ask a blessin', Father?" said Sarah.

And the old man bent his head and mumbled.

All through the meal he stopped eating at intervals, and stared furtively at his wife; but he ate well. The home food tasted good to him, and his old frame was too sturdily healthy to be affected by his mind. But after supper he went out, and sat down on the step of the smaller door at the right of the barn, through which he had meant his Jerseys to pass in stately file, but which Sarah designed for her front house door, and he leaned his head on his hands.

After the supper dishes were cleared away and the milk-pans washed, Sarah went out to him. The twilight was deepening. There was a clear green glow in the sky. Before them stretched the smooth level of field; in the distance was a cluster of hay-stacks like the huts of a village; the air was very cool and calm and sweet. The landscape might have been an ideal one of peace.

Sarah bent over and touched her husband on one of his thin, sinewy shoulders. "Father!"

The old man's shoulders heaved: he was weeping.

"Why, don't do so, Father," said Sarah.

"I'll—put up the—partitions, an'—everything you—want, Mother."

Sarah put her apron up to her face; she was overcome by her own triumph.

Adoniram was like a fortress whose walls had no active resistance, and went down the instant the right besieging tools were used. "Why, Mother," he said, hoarsely, "I hadn't no idee you was so set on't as all this comes to."

The last plot question is answered. The conflict has been resolved. Do you think this is the climax, the resolution, or both?

Finally, the theme is made clear. Imagery is added to enhance the meaning.

---

besieging (bih SEEJ ing) hemming in with armed forces; closing in; overwhelming

The Revolt of Mother ■ 275

Review the Selection

Recall

1. In which season is the story set?

2. Why were the men digging?

3. How long had Sarah and Adoniram been married?

Infer

4. Why do you think Adoniram has never built a new house?

5. Discuss Sarah's attitude toward men.

6. Why do you think Sarah finally decides to act?

7. Why does Sarah not invite the minister in at first, and why does she later ask him in to sit down?

Apply

8. Give three examples to show why the old house was inadequate.

9. Select two setting descriptions that illustrate the type of housekeeper Sarah was.

10. What would have and have not happened if Adoniram did not receive the letter from Hiram when he did?

Respond to Literature
Do you think the lifestyle of the Penn family was unusual for that period in American history? Explain.

THINK ABOUT FICTION

It is the imagination of the author, rather than factual data, which forms the basis of any fictional work. This is not to say that fiction cannot include such things as historical events or the personal experiences of real people—including the author. These types of things can be woven into the story. However, the heart and soul of fictional literature remains the author's imagination.

1. Which element of setting—time or place—would you consider dominant in the story? Why?

2. Interpret the author's tone. What is her attitude toward the protagonist and antagonist?

3. Describe the type of conflict involved in the plot. Was there more than one type? Explain your answer.

4. What do you consider the climax or turning point of the plot? Is the resolution found in the climax or elsewhere? Explain your answer.

5. State in your own words what you consider to be the theme of the story.

DEVELOP YOUR VOCABULARY

A **dialect** is the form, or variety, of a spoken language used by members of a region, a community, or a social group. Each dialect has pronunciations, grammatical features, and vocabulary that are peculiar to it and different from those of other dialects.

In "The Revolt of Mother," the characters speak in dialect. The author shows that certain speech sounds are omitted by using an apostrophe in their place. She spells some words in the phonetic patterns used by the characters.

Rewrite each of these sentences from the story in standard English.

1. "You hadn't ought to judge Father, though."

2. "I ain't got nothin' to say about it, Mother; an' I ain't goin' to say nothin'."

3. "We ain't had no new paper on it for ten year."

4. "S'posin' I had wrote to Hiram."

5. "There ain't no call for nobody else to worry about it."

Learn About

Samuel L. Clemens (Mark Twain) and His Memories,
1880. The Granger Collection

READING FOCUS

Compare and Contrast You have learned that comparing means finding similarities and contrasting means finding differences. By highlighting the common and unique qualities of different stories, you can learn more about each.

In "How to Tell a Story," Mark Twain states that there are three different kinds of stories. As you read, pay attention to how he compares and contrasts the three. Think about why he finds one kind of story much funnier than the other two.

EXPOSITION

Exposition, along with narration, description, and persuasion, is one of the four forms of discourse. The purpose of exposition is to explain. It is the kind of writing done, for example, to interpret facts and opinions, to explain the nature of freedom, to outline the structure of a government, or to account for events in history. In short, it is the kind of writing in which an author gives information about a subject.

Authors have several ways of explaining a subject. They may **define** it—tell what it is and demonstrate its purpose. They may **compare and contrast** it with something else—show its likenesses and differences. They may **classify** it—put it in its type or class. They may **analyze** it—focus on its elements and their significance.

As you read this selection, ask yourself:
1. Which way or ways of explaining does Twain use in this work?
2. Which form of discourse did Twain use in the examples he gives?

WRITING CONNECTION

Choose an object, such as a favorite possession, and write a paragraph defining its nature and use.

Old Barn in Field of Asters, Henry Poor. Corbis Bettmann

from HOW TO TELL A STORY

by Mark Twain

I do not claim that I can tell a story as it ought to be told. I only claim to know how a story ought to be told, for I have been almost daily in the company of the most expert story-tellers for many years.

There are several kinds of stories, but only one difficult kind—the humorous. I will talk mainly about that one. The humorous story is American, the comic story is English, the witty story is French. The humorous story depends for its effect upon the *manner* of the telling; the comic story and the witty story upon the *matter*.

The humorous story may be spun out to great length, and may wander around as much as it pleases, and arrive nowhere in particular; but the comic and witty stories must be brief and end with a point. The humorous story bubbles gently along, the others burst.

The humorous story is strictly a work of art—high and delicate art—and only an artist can tell it; but no art is necessary in telling the comic and the witty story; anybody can do it. The art of telling a humorous story—understand, I mean by word of mouth, not print—was created in America, and has remained at home.

The humorous story is told gravely; the teller does his best to conceal the fact that he even dimly suspects that there is anything funny about it; but the teller of the comic story tells you beforehand that it is one of the funniest things he has ever heard, then tells it with eager delight, and is the first person to laugh when he gets through. And sometimes, if he has had good success, he is so glad and happy that he will repeat the "nub" of it and glance around from face to face, collecting applause, and then repeat it again. It is a pathetic thing to see.

Very often, of course, the rambling and disjointed humorous story finishes with a nub, point, snapper, or whatever you like to call it. Then the listener must be alert, for in many cases the teller will divert attention from that nub by dropping it in a carefully casual and indifferent way, with the pretense that he does not know it is a nub.

Artemus Ward used that trick a good deal; then when the belated audience presently caught the joke he would look up with innocent surprise, as if wondering what they had found to laugh at. Dan Setchell used it before him, Nye and Riley and others use it today.

But the teller of the comic story does not slur the nub; he shouts it at you—every time. And when he prints it, in England, France, Germany, and Italy, he italicizes it, puts some whopping exclamation-points after it, and sometimes explains it in a parenthesis. All of which is very depressing, and makes one want to renounce joking and lead a better life.

Let me set down an instance of the comic method, using an anecdote which has been popular all over the world for twelve or fifteen hundred years. The teller tells it in this way:

The Wounded Soldier

In the course of a certain battle a soldier whose leg had been shot off appealed to another soldier who was hurrying by to carry him to the rear, informing him at the same time of the loss which he had sustained; whereupon the generous son of Mars,[1] shouldering the unfortunate, proceeded to carry out his desire. The bullets and cannon-balls were flying in all directions, and presently one of the latter took the wounded man's head off—without, however, his deliverer being aware of it. In no long time he was hailed by an officer, who said:

"Where are you going with that carcass?"

"To the rear, sir—he's lost his leg!"

"His leg, forsooth?" responded the astonished officer; "you mean his head, you booby."

---

pathetic (puh THET ik) pitiful
divert (dih VURT) turn aside
slur (SLUR) make unclear; pass over carelessly
renounce (rih NOUNS) rejected; abandon with disgust
sustained (suh STAYND) experienced; suffered
carcass (KAHR kus) dead body, usually of an animal
forsooth (for SOOTH) archaic for *in truth;* indeed
booby (BOO bee) fool
[1]**son of Mars:** In ancient Roman mythology, Mars was the god of war.

Whereupon the soldier dispossessed himself of his burden, and stood looking down upon it in great perplexity. At length he said:

"It is true, sir, just as you have said." Then after a pause he added, "*But he* TOLD *me* IT WAS HIS LEG!!!!!"

Here the narrator bursts into explosion after explosion of thunderous horse-laughter, repeating that nub from time to time through his gaspings and shriekings and suffocatings.

It takes only a minute and a half to tell that in its comic-story form; and isn't worth the telling, after all. Put into the humorous-story form it takes ten minutes, and is about the funniest thing I have ever listened to—as James Whitcomb Riley[2] tells it.

He tells it in the character of a dull-witted old farmer who has just heard it for the first time, thinks it is unspeakably funny, and is trying to repeat it to a neighbor. But he can't remember it; so he gets all mixed up and wanders helplessly round and round, putting in tedious details that don't belong in the tale and only retard it; taking them out conscientiously and putting in others that are just as useless; making minor mistakes now and then and stopping to correct them and explain how he came to make them; remembering things which he forgot to put in in their proper place and going back to put them in there; stopping his narrative a good while in order to try to recall the name of the soldier that was hurt, and finally remembering that the soldier's name was not mentioned, and remarking placidly that the name is of no real importance, anyway—better, of course, if one knew it, but not essential, after all— and so on, and so on, and so on.

The teller is innocent and happy and pleased with himself, and has to stop every little while to hold himself in and keep from laughing outright; and does hold in, but his body quakes in a jelly-like way with interior chuckles; and at the end of the ten minutes the audience have laughed until they are exhausted, and the tears are running down their faces.

The simplicity and innocence and sincerity and unconsciousness of the old farmer are perfectly simulated, and the result is a performance which is thoroughly charming and delicious. This is art—and fine and beautiful, and only a master can compass it; but a machine could tell the other story.

To string incongruities and absurdities together in a wandering and sometimes purposeless way, and seem innocently unaware that they are absurdities, is the basis of the American art, if my position is correct. Another feature is the slurring of the point. A third is the dropping of a studied remark apparently without knowing it, as if one were thinking aloud. The fourth and last is the pause.

---

perplexity (pur PLEK sih tee) confusion; uncertainty
tedious (TEE dee us) boring; tiresome
incongruities (in kon GROO ih teez) things inconsistent or not in harmony
absurdities (ab SUR duh teez) ridiculous things
[2]**James Whitcomb Riley:** (1849–1916) a popular poet and speaker at the time

Artemus Ward dealt in numbers three and four a good deal. He would begin to tell with great animation something which he seemed to think was wonderful; then lose confidence, and after an apparently absent-minded pause add an incongruous remark in a soliloquizing way; and that was the remark intended to explode the mine—and it did.

For instance, he would say eagerly, excitedly, "I once knew a man in New Zealand who hadn't a tooth in his head"—here his animation would die out; a silent, reflective pause would follow, then he would say dreamily, and as if to himself, "and yet that man could beat a drum better than any man I ever saw."

The pause is an exceedingly important feature in any kind of story, and a frequently recurring feature, too. It is a dainty thing, and delicate, and also uncertain and treacherous; for it must be exactly the right length—no more and no less—or it fails of its purpose and makes trouble. If the pause is too short the impressive point is passed, and the audience have had time to divine that a surprise is intended—and then you can't surprise them, of course.

On the platform I used to tell a . . . ghost story that had a pause in front of the snapper on the end, and that pause was the most important thing in the whole story. If I got it the right length precisely, I could spring the finishing ejaculation with effect enough to make some impressible girl deliver a startled little yelp and jump out of her seat—and that was what I was after.

---

recurring (rih KUR ing) occurring again and again
ejaculation (ee jak yoo LAY shun) exclamation

Mark Twain (1835–1910)

"The difference between the right word and the almost right word," wrote Mark Twain, "is the difference between lightning and the lightning bug." Finding that *just-right* word was Mark Twain's specialty.

America's favorite humorist was born Samuel Langhorne Clemens in 1835. He grew up in Hannibal, Missouri, on the west bank of the Mississippi River. His father died when he was 12, and "Sam'l" quit school to go to work for a printer. That was the first of his four careers. In the late 1850s he became a steamboat pilot, and in the 1860s he turned to newspaper work. Sketches and stories written for newspapers soon made him known across the country.

While working on his famous book *The Adventures of Tom Sawyer*, he often wrote fifty pages a day. After that book, he went on to write such classics as *Life on the Mississippi* and *The Adventures of Huckleberry Finn*.

Twain had many friends and was a concerned family man. He traveled often to many parts of the world. He made, lost, and then remade a fortune in business. But the shock of his wife's death in 1904 left him a troubled man, and his last years were not happy ones. His birth in 1835 had coincided with the appearance of Halley's comet. Knowing that the comet's next visit was due in 1910, Twain told his friends that he would "go out with it," too.

Twain was right about his death. This self-educated genius, this "Lincoln of our literature," died peacefully on the night of April 21, 1910.

Review the Selection

UNDERSTAND THE SELECTION

Recall

1. What three types of stories does Mark Twain talk about?

2. Which of these is most difficult?

3. What country does he say is associated with this most difficult type?

Infer

4. Whom does Mark Twain respect more, a storyteller or a story writer?

5. How does he feel about comic stories?

6. How does Twain feel about America as compared to other countries?

Apply

7. Do you agree that this kind of story is more difficult to tell and therefore superior to the other kinds? Why?

Respond to Literature

Do you think writers today are more concerned with storytelling than they were in Twain's time? Why?

THINK ABOUT EXPOSITION

Defining, comparing and contrasting, classifying, and analyzing are techniques used in expository writing. **Exposition** is the form of discourse used to explain or inform. Expository works often begin with a **thesis statement**, a statement of what the author intends to explain in the work. Expository essays usually have a beginning, a middle, and an end.

1. Does Twain make a thesis statement? If so, what is it?

2. Which of the techniques of exposition do you see in Twain's essay? Support your ideas with examples.

3. What form of discourse other than exposition does Twain use?

4. For what purpose does he use this other form of discourse?

5. Does Twain's essay have a recognizable beginning, middle, and end?

READING FOCUS

Compare and Contrast Look at Twain's comparison and contrast of the three types of stories: comic, witty, and humorous. According to Twain, how are these three types of stories similar? How are they different?

DEVELOP YOUR VOCABULARY

A dictionary gives not only the correct spelling and definition of a word, but also shows how the word is divided into syllables. Consult a dictionary to review the meaning of the following words from the story. Also, rewrite each word in syllable form. Then identify the five words that contain four or more syllables. Show that you understand the meaning of these five words by using each of them in a short paragraph with a humorous tone.

1. pathetic
2. divert
3. slur
4. renounce
5. sustained
6. carcass
7. perplexity
8. tedious
9. incongruity
10. absurdity
11. recurring
12. dapper
13. salient
14. discrepancy
15. defunct
16. hearse

Learn About

SETTING

Setting refers to where and when a story takes place, as well as to the general background of the action. Authors often describe the setting in detail. The more important the place of the action is to the plot, the more important it is for the author to describe it.

The location of a story may be very specific—a particular room in a particular house, a dungeon in a castle, or a shack in the woods. Behind the specific location there is always some general location—mountains, the desert, the seashore, a region, a city, or a country. The time of a story may specify day or night, a season of the year, or an historical era. Sometimes the location is the more important element in the setting; at other times, the time period is dominant.

As you read the story, ask yourself:
1. How important is the setting to this story?
2. Is time or place the more important element in the story?

WRITING CONNECTION

Think back to an enjoyable experience you have had recently. In four or five lines, describe the setting—time and place—of this experience.

READING FOCUS

Predict Outcomes To predict means to make an educated guess about what will happen next. When you read a story, you can use details, foreshadowing, and various clues to predict the story's outcome or ending. As you read "To Build a Fire," think about the importance of the title. Pay attention to the role of the fire in the story, to the man's character, and to the dog's concerns. Try to use these clues to predict the outcome of the story.

To Build a Fire

by Jack London

Day had broken cold and gray, exceedingly cold and gray, when the man turned aside from the main Yukon trail and climbed the high earth-bank, where a dim and little-traveled trail led eastward through the fat spruce timberland. It was a steep bank, and he paused for breath at the top, excusing the act to himself by looking at his watch. It was nine o'clock. There was no sun nor hint of sun, though there was not a cloud in the sky. It was a clear day, and yet there seemed an intangible pall over the face of things, a subtle gloom that made the day dark, and that was due to the absence of sun. This fact did not worry the man. He was used to the lack of sun. It had been days since he had seen the sun, and he knew that a few more days must pass before that cheerful orb, due south, would just peep above the sky-line and dip immediately from view.

The man flung a look back along the way he had come. The Yukon lay a mile wide and hidden under three feet of ice. On top of this ice were as many feet of snow. It was all pure white, rolling in gentle undulations where the ice jams of the freeze-up had formed. North and south, as far as his eye could see, it was unbroken white, save for a dark hairline that curved and twisted from around the spruce-covered island to the south, and that curved and twisted away into the north, where it disappeared behind another spruce-covered island. This dark hairline was the trail—the main trail—that led south five hundred miles to the Chilcoot Pass, Dyea, and salt water; and that led north seventy miles to Dawson, and still on to the north a thousand miles to Nulato, and finally to St. Michael, on Bering Sea, a thousand miles and half a thousand more.

But all this—the mysterious, far-reaching hairline trail, the absence of sun from the sky, the tremendous cold, and the strangeness and weirdness of it all—made no impression on the man. It was not because he was long used to it. He was a newcomer in the land, a *chechaquo,*

---

orb (AWRB) round object
undulations (un juh LAY shunz) waves or wavy outlines
hairline (HAIR lyn) very thin line

and this was his first winter. The trouble with him was that he was without imagination. He was quick and alert in the things of life, but only in the things, and not in the significances. Fifty degrees below zero meant eighty-odd degrees of frost. Such fact impressed him as being cold and uncomfortable, and that was all. It did not lead him to meditate upon his frailty in general, able only to live within certain narrow limits of heat and cold; and from there on it did not lead him to the conjectural field of immortality and man's place in the universe. Fifty degrees below zero stood for a bite of frost that hurt and that must be guarded against by the use of mittens, ear flaps, warm moccasins, and thick socks. Fifty degrees below zero was to him just precisely fifty degrees below zero. That there should be anything more to it than that was a thought that never entered his head.

As he turned to go, he spat speculatively. There was a sharp, explosive crackle that startled him. He spat again. And again, in the air, before it could fall to the snow, the spittle crackled. He knew that at fifty below spittle crackled on the snow, but this spittle had crackled in the air. Undoubtedly it was colder than fifty below—how much colder he did not know. But the temperature did not matter. He was bound for the old claim on the left fork of Henderson Creek, where the boys were already. They had come over across the divide from the Indian Creek country, while he had come the roundabout way to take a look at the possibilities of getting out logs in the spring from the islands in the Yukon. He would be in to camp by six o'clock; a bit after dark, it was true, but the boys would be there, a fire would be going, and a hot supper would be ready. As for lunch, he pressed his hand against the protruding bundle under his jacket. It was also under his shirt, wrapped up in a handkerchief and lying against the naked skin. It was the only way to keep the biscuits from freezing. He smiled agreeably to himself as he thought of those biscuits, each cut open and sopped in bacon grease, and each enclosing a generous slice of fried bacon.

He plunged in among the big spruce trees. The trail was faint. A foot of snow had fallen since the last sled had passed over, and he was glad he was without a sled, traveling light. In fact, he carried nothing but the lunch wrapped in the handkerchief. He was surprised, however, at the cold. It certainly was cold, he concluded, as he rubbed his numb nose and cheekbones with his mittened hand. He was a warm-whiskered man, but the hair on his face did not protect the high cheekbones and the eager nose that thrust itself aggressively into the frosty air.

At the man's heels trotted a dog, a big native husky, the proper wolf dog, gray-coated and without any visible or temperamental difference from its brother, the wild wolf. The animal was depressed by the tremendous cold. It knew that it was no time for traveling. Its instinct told it a

---

meditate (MED uh tayt) think deeply; ponder
immortality (im aw TAL ih tee) unending life
speculatively (SPEK yuh luh tiv lee) thinking about possibilities
spittle (SPIT ul) saliva; what one spits

truer tale than was told to the man by the man's judgment. In reality, it was not merely colder than fifty below zero; it was colder than sixty below, than seventy below. It was seventy-five below zero. Since the freezing point is thirty-two above zero, it meant that one hundred and seven degrees of frost obtained. The dog did not know anything about thermometers. Possibly in its brain there was no sharp consciousness of a condition of very cold such as was in the man's brain. But the brute had its instinct. It experienced a vague but menacing apprehension that subdued it and made it slink along at the man's heels, and that made it question eagerly every unwonted movement of the man as if expecting him to go into camp or to seek shelter somewhere and build a fire. The dog had learned fire and it wanted fire, or else to burrow under the snow and cuddle its warmth away from the air.

The frozen moisture of its breathing had settled on its fur in a fine powder of frost, and especially were its jowls, muzzle, and eyelashes whitened by its crystalled breath. The man's red beard and mustache were likewise frosted, but more solidly, the deposit taking the form of ice and increasing with every warm, moist breath he exhaled. Also, the man was chewing tobacco and the muzzle of ice held his lips so rigidly that he was unable to clear his chin when he expelled the juice. The result was that a crystal beard of the color and solidity of amber was increasing its length on his chin. If he fell down it would shatter itself, like glass,

into brittle fragments. But he did not mind the appendage. It was the penalty all tobacco chewers paid in that country, and he had been out before in two cold snaps. They had not been so cold as this, he knew, but by the spirit thermometer at Sixty Mile he knew they had registered at fifty below and at fifty-five.

He held on through the level stretch of woods for several miles, crossed a wide flat. . ., and dropped down a bank to the frozen bed of a small stream. This was Henderson Creek, and he knew he was ten miles from the forks. He looked at his watch. It was ten o'clock. He was making four miles an hour, and he calculated that he would arrive at the forks at half-past twelve. He decided to celebrate that event by eating his lunch there.

The dog dropped in again at his heels, with a tail drooping discouragement, as the man swung along the creek bed. The furrow of the old sled trail was plainly visible, but a dozen inches of snow covered the marks of the last runners. In a month no man had come up or down that silent creek. The man held steadily on. He was not much given to thinking, and just then particularly he had nothing to think about save that he would eat lunch at the forks and that at six o'clock he would be in camp with the boys. There was nobody to talk to; and, had there been, speech would have been impossible because of the ice muzzle on his mouth. So he continued monotonously to chew tobacco and to increase the length of his amber beard.

---

apprehension (ap rih HEN shun) worry; fear of a coming event
muzzle (MUZ ul) mouth and nose of an animal

Trapper in the Wilderness, Sydney Laurence. The Shelburne Museum, Shelburne, VT

Once in a while the thought reiterated itself that it was very cold and that he had never experienced such cold. As he walked along he rubbed his cheekbones and nose with the back of his mittened hand. He did this automatically, now and again changing hands. But, rub as he would, the instant he stopped his cheekbones went numb, and the following instant the end of his nose went numb. He was sure to frost his cheeks; he knew that, and experienced a pang of regret that he had not devised a nose strap of the sort Bud wore in cold snaps. Such a strap passed across the cheeks, as well, and saved them. But it didn't matter much, after all. What were frosted cheeks? A bit painful, that was all; they were never serious.

Empty as the man's mind was of thoughts, he was keenly observant, and he noticed the changes in the creek, the

---

reiterated (ree IT uh rayt id) repeated tiresomely

curves and bends and timber jams, and always he sharply noted where he placed his feet. Once, coming around a bend, he shied abruptly, like a startled horse, curved away from the place where he had been walking, and retreated several paces back along the trail. The creek he knew was frozen clear to the bottom—no creek could contain water in that arctic winter—but he knew also that there were springs that bubbled out from the hillsides and ran along under the snow and on top the ice of the creek. He knew that the coldest snaps never froze these springs, and he knew likewise their danger. They were traps. They hid pools of water under the snow that might be three inches deep, or three feet. Sometimes a skin of ice half an inch thick covered them, and in turn was covered by the snow. Sometimes there were alternate layers of water and ice-skin, so that when one broke through he kept on breaking through for a while, sometimes wetting himself to the waist.

That was why he had shied in such panic. He had felt the give under his feet and heard the crackle of a snow-hidden ice-skin. And to get his feet wet in such a temperature meant trouble and danger. At the very least it meant delay, for he would be forced to stop and build a fire, and under its protection to bare his feet while he dried his socks and moccasins. He stood and studied the creek bed and its banks, and decided that the flow of water came from the right. He reflected awhile, rubbing his nose and cheeks,

then skirted to the left, stepping gingerly and testing the footing for each step. Once clear of the danger, he took a fresh chew of tobacco and swung along at his four-mile gait.

In the course of the next two hours he came upon several similar traps. Usually the snow above the hidden pools had a sunken, candied appearance that advertised the danger. Once again, however, he had a close call; and once, suspecting danger, he compelled the dog to go on in front. The dog did not want to go. It hung back until the man shoved it forward, and then it went quickly across the white, unbroken surface. Suddenly it broke through, floundered to one side, and got away to firmer footing. It had wet its forefeet and legs, and almost immediately the water that clung to it turned to ice. It made quick efforts to lick the ice off its legs, then dropped down in the snow and began to bite out the ice that had formed between the toes. This was a matter of instinct. To permit the ice to remain would mean sore feet. It did not know this. It merely obeyed the mysterious prompting that arose from the deep crypts of its being. But the man knew, having achieved a judgment on the subject, and he removed the mitten from his right hand and helped tear out the ice particles. He did not expose his fingers more than a minute, and was astonished at the swift numbness that smote them. It certainly was cold. He pulled on the mitten hastily, and beat the hand savagely across his chest.

---

shied (SHYD) drew back
reflected (ruh FLEK tid) thought
gait (GAYT) manner of walking or running

At twelve o'clock the day was at its brightest. Yet the sun was too far south on its winter journey to clear the horizon. The bulge of the earth intervened between it and Henderson Creek, where the man walked under a clear sky at noon and cast no shadow. At half-past twelve, to the minute, he arrived at the forks of the creek. He was pleased at the speed he had made. If he kept it up, he would certainly be with the boys by six. He unbuttoned his jacket and shirt and drew forth his lunch. The action consumed no more than a quarter of a minute, yet in that brief moment the numbness laid hold of the exposed fingers. He did not put the mitten on, but, instead, struck the fingers a dozen sharp smashes against his leg. Then he sat down on a snow-covered log to eat. The sting that followed upon the striking of his fingers against his leg ceased so quickly that he was startled. He had had no chance to take a bit of biscuit. He struck the fingers repeatedly and returned them to the mitten, baring the other hand for the purpose of eating. He tried to take a mouthful, but the ice muzzle prevented. He had forgotten to build a fire and thaw out. He chuckled at his foolishness, and as he chuckled he noted the numbness creeping into the exposed fingers. Also, he noted that the stinging which had first come to his toes when he sat down was already passing away. He wondered whether the toes were warm or numb. He moved them inside the moccasins and decided that they were numb.

He pulled the mitten on hurriedly and stood up. He was a bit frightened. He stamped up and down until the stinging returned into the feet. It certainly was cold, was his thought. That man from Sulphur Creek had spoken the truth when telling how cold it sometimes got in the country. And he had laughed at him at the time! That showed one must not be too sure of things. There was no mistake about it, it *was* cold. He strode up and down, stamping his feet and threshing his arms, until reassured by the returning warmth. Then he got out matches and proceeded to make a fire. From the undergrowth, where high water of the previous spring had lodged a supply of seasoned twigs, he got his firewood. Working carefully from a small beginning, he soon had a roaring fire, over which he thawed the ice from his face and in the protection of which he ate his biscuits. For the moment the cold of space was outwitted. The dog took satisfaction in the fire, stretching out close enough for warmth and far enough away to escape being singed.

When the man had finished, he filled his pipe and took his comfortable time over a smoke. Then he pulled on his mittens, settled the ear flaps of his cap firmly about his ears, and took the creek trail up the left fork. The dog was disappointed and yearned back toward the fire. The man did not know cold. Possibly all the generations of his ancestry had been ignorant of cold, of real cold, of cold one hundred and seven degrees below freezing point. But the dog knew; all its ancestry knew, and it had inherited the knowledge. And it knew that it was not good to walk abroad in such fearful cold. It was the time to lie snug in a hole in the snow and wait for a curtain of cloud to be drawn across the face of outer space whence this cold came. On the other hand, there was no keen intimacy between the dog and the man. The one was the toil slave of the other, and the only caresses it had ever received were the caresses of the whiplash and of harsh and menacing throat sounds that threatened the whiplash. So the dog made no effort to communicate its apprehension to the man. It was not concerned in the welfare of the man; it was for its own sake that it yearned back toward the fire. But the man whistled, and spoke to it with the sound of whiplashes, and the dog swung in at the man's heels and followed after.

The man took a chew of tobacco and proceeded to start a new amber beard. Also, his moist breath quickly powdered with white his mustache, eyebrows, and lashes. There did not seem to be so many springs on the left fork of the Henderson, and for half an hour the man saw no signs of any. And then it happened. At a place where there were no signs, where the soft, unbroken snow seemed to advertise solidity beneath, the man broke through. It was not deep. He wet himself halfway to the knees before he floundered out to the firm crust.

He was angry, and cursed his luck aloud. He had hoped to get into camp with the boys at six o'clock, and this would delay him an hour, for he would have to build a fire and dry out his footgear. This was imperative at that low temperature—for he knew that much; and he turned aside to the bank, which he climbed. On top, tangled in the under-brush about the trunks of several small spruce trees, was a high-water deposit of dry firewood—sticks and twigs, principally, but also larger portions of seasoned branches and fine, dry, last year's grasses. He threw down several large pieces on top of the snow. This served for a foundation and prevented the young flame from drowning itself in the snow it otherwise would melt. The flame he got by touching a match to a small shred of birch bark that he took from his pocket. This burned even more readily than paper. Placing it on the foundation, he fed the young flame with wisps of dry grass and with the tiniest dry twigs.

He worked slowly and carefully, keenly aware of his danger. Gradually, as the flame grew stronger, he increased the size of the twigs with which he fed it. He squatted in the snow, pulling the twigs out from their entanglement in the brush and feeding directly to the flame. He knew there must be no failure. When it is seventy-five below zero, a man must not fail in his first attempt to build a fire—that is, if his feet are wet. If his feet are dry, and he fails, he can run along the trail for half a mile and restore his circulation. But the circulation of wet and freezing feet cannot be restored by running when it is seventy-five below. No matter how fast he runs, the wet feet will freeze the harder.

All this the man knew. The old-timer on Sulphur Creek had told him about it the previous fall, and now he was appreciating the advice. Already all sensation had gone out of his feet. To build the fire

---

intimacy (IN tuh muh see) very close friendship, even love
imperative (im PER uh tiv) really necessary; essential

he had been forced to remove his mittens, and the fingers had quickly gone numb. His pace of four miles an hour had kept his heart pumping blood to the surface of his body and to all the extremities. But the instant he stopped, the action of the pump eased down. The cold of space smote the unprotected tip of the planet, and he, being on that unprotected tip, received the full force of the blow. The blood of his body recoiled before it. The blood was alive, like the dog, and like the dog it wanted to hide away and cover itself up from the fearful cold. So long as he walked four miles an hour, he pumped that blood, willy-nilly, to the surface; but now it ebbed away and sank down into the recesses of his body. The extremities were the first to feel its absence. His wet feet froze the faster, and his exposed fingers numbed the faster, though they had not yet begun to freeze. Nose and cheeks were already freezing, while the skin of all his body chilled as it lost its blood.

But he was safe. Toes and nose and cheeks would be only touched by the frost, for the fire was beginning to burn with strength. He was feeding it with twigs the size of his finger. In another minute he would be able to feed it with branches the size of his wrist, and then he could remove his wet footgear, and, while it dried, he could keep his naked feet warm by the fire, rubbing them at first, of course, with snow. The fire was a success. He was safe. He remembered the advice of the old-timer on Sulphur Creek, and smiled. The old-timer had been very serious in laying down the law that no man must travel alone in the Klondike[1] after fifty below. Well, here he was; he had had the accident; he was alone; and he had saved himself. Those old-timers were rather womanish, some of them, he thought. All a man had to do was to keep his head, and he was all right. Any man who was a man could travel alone. But it was surprising, the rapidity with which his cheeks and nose were freezing. And he had not thought his fingers could go lifeless in so short a time. Lifeless they were, for he could scarcely make them move together to grip a twig, and they seemed remote from his body and from him. When he touched a twig, he had to look and see whether or not he had hold of it. The wires were pretty well down between him and his finger ends.

All of which counted for little. There was the fire, snapping and crackling and promising life with every dancing flame. He started to untie his moccasins. They were coated with ice; the thick German socks were like sheaths of iron halfway to the knees; and the moccasin strings were like rods of steel all twisted and knotted as by some conflagration. For a moment he tugged with his numb fingers, then, realizing the folly of it, he drew his sheath knife.

---

extremities (ik STREM ih teez) hands and feet; parts farthest away
ebbed (EBD) flowed back or away
recesses (REE ses ez) interior places
sheaths (SHEETHZ) protective coverings
conflagration (kon fluh GRAY shun) huge fire
[1]**The Klondike:** an area in northern Canada, next to Alaska.

But before he could cut the strings, it happened. It was his own fault or, rather, his mistake. He should not have built the fire under the spruce tree. He should have built it in the open. But it had been easier to pull the twigs from the brush and drop them directly on the fire. Now the tree under which he had done this carried a weight of snow on its boughs. No wind had blown for weeks, and each bough was fully freighted. Each time he had pulled on a twig he had communicated a slight agitation to the tree—an imperceptible agitation, so far as he was concerned, but an agitation sufficient to bring about the disaster. High up in the tree one bough capsized its load of snow. This fell on the boughs beneath, capsizing them. This process continued, spreading out and involving the whole tree. It grew like an avalanche, and it descended without warning upon the man and the fire, and the fire was blotted out! Where it had burned was a mantle of fresh and disordered snow.

The man was shocked. It was as though he had just heard his own sentence of death. For a moment he sat and stared at the spot where the fire had been. Then he grew very calm. Perhaps the old-timer on Sulphur Creek was right. If he had only had a trail mate he would have been in no danger now. The trail mate could have built the fire. Well, it was up to him to build a fire over again, and this second time there must be no failure. Even if he succeeded, he would most likely lose some toes. His feet must be badly frozen by now, and there would be some time before the second fire was ready.

Such were his thoughts, but he did not sit and think them. He was busy all the time they were passing through his mind. He made a new foundation for a fire, this time in the open, where no treacherous tree could blot it out. Next, he gathered dry grasses and tiny twigs from the high-water flotsam. He could not bring his fingers together to pull them out, but he was able to gather them by the handful. In this way he got many rotten twigs and bits of green moss that were undesirable, but it was the best he could do. He worked methodically, even collecting an armful of the larger branches to be used later when the fire gathered strength. And all the while the dog sat and watched him, a certain yearning wistfulness in its eyes, for it looked upon him as the fire provider, and the fire was slow in coming.

When all was ready, the man reached in his pocket for a second piece of birch bark. He knew the bark was there, and, though he could not feel it with his fingers, he could hear its crisp rustling as he fumbled for it. Try as he would, he could not clutch hold of it. And all the time, in his consciousness, was the knowledge that each instant his feet were freezing. This thought tended to put him in a panic, but he fought against it and kept calm. He pulled on his mittens with his teeth, and threshed his arms back and forth, beating his hands with all his might against his sides. He did this sitting down, and he stood up to do it; and all the while the dog

---

mantle (MAN tul) something that covers
methodically (muh THOD ik lee) orderly; systematically

sat in the snow, its wolf brush of a tail curled around warmly over its forefeet, its sharp wolf ears pricked forward intently as it watched the man. And the man, as he beat and threshed with his arms and hands, felt a great surge of envy as he regarded the creature that was warm and secure in its natural covering.

After a time he was aware of the first faraway signals of sensation in his beaten fingers. The faint tingling grew stronger till it evolved into a stinging ache that was excruciating, but which the man hailed with satisfaction. He stripped the mitten from his right hand and fetched forth the birch bark. The exposed fingers were quickly going numb again. Next he brought out his bunch of sulphur matches. But the tremendous cold had already driven the life out of his fingers. In his effort to separate one match from the others, the whole bunch fell in the snow. He tried to pick it out of the snow, but failed. The dead fingers could neither touch nor clutch. He was very careful. He drove the thought of his freezing feet, and nose, and cheeks, out of his mind, devoting his whole soul to the matches. He watched, using the sense of vision in place of that of touch, and when he saw his fingers on each side the bunch, he closed them—that is, he willed to close them, for the wires were down, and the fingers did not obey. He pulled the mitten on the right hand, and beat it fiercely against his knee. Then, with both mittened hands, he scooped the bunch of matches, along with

much snow, into his lap. Yet he was no better off.

After some manipulation he managed to get the bunch between the heels of his mittened hands. In this fashion he carried it to his mouth. The ice crackled and snapped when by a violent effort he opened his mouth. He drew the lower jaw in, curled the upper lip out of the way, and scraped the bunch with his upper teeth in order to separate a match. He succeeded in getting one, which he dropped on his lap. He was no better off. He could not pick it up. Then he devised a way. He picked it up in his teeth and scratched it on his leg. Twenty times he scratched before he succeeded in lighting it. As if flamed he held it with his teeth to the birch bark. But the burning brimstone went up his nostrils and into his lungs, causing him to cough spasmodically. The match fell into the snow and went out.

The old-timer on Sulphur Creek was right, he thought in the moment of controlled despair that ensued: after fifty below, a man should travel with a partner. He beat his hands, but failed in exciting any sensation. Suddenly he bared both hands, removing the mittens with his teeth. He caught the whole bunch between the heels of his hands. His arm muscles not being frozen enabled him to press the hand heels tightly against the matches. Then he scratched the bunch along his leg. It flared into flame, seventy sulphur matches at once! There was no wind to blow them out. He kept his head

---

excruciating (ik SKROO shee ayt ing) very painful
spasmodically (spaz MOD ik lee) in sudden bursts

to one side to escape the strangling fumes, and held the blazing bundle to the birch bark. As he so held it, he became aware of sensation in his hand. His flesh was burning. He could smell it. Deep down below the surface he could feel it. The sensation developed into pain that grew acute. And still he endured it, holding the flame of the matches clumsily to the bark that would not light readily because his own burning hands were in the way, absorbing most of the flame.

At last, when he could endure no more, he jerked his hands apart. The blazing matches fell sizzling into the snow, but the birch bark was alight. He began laying dry grasses and the tiniest twigs on the flame. He could not pick and choose, for he had to lift the fuel between the heels of his hands. Small pieces of rotten wood and green moss clung to the twigs, and he bit them off as well as he could with his teeth. He cherished the flame carefully and awkwardly. It meant life, and it must not perish. The withdrawal of blood from the surface of his body now made him begin to shiver, and he grew more awkward. A large piece of green moss fell squarely on the little fire. He tried to poke it with his fingers, but his shivering frame made him poke too far, and he disrupted the nucleus of the little fire, the burning grasses and tiny twigs separating and scattering. He tried to poke them together again, but in spite of the tenseness of the effort, his shivering got away with him, and the twigs were hopelessly scattered. Each twig gushed a puff of

smoke and went out. The fire provider had failed. As he looked apathetically about him, his eyes chanced on the dog, sitting across the ruins of the fire from him, in the snow, making restless, hunching movements, slightly lifting one forefoot and then the other, shifting its weight back and forth on them with wistful eagerness.

The sight of the dog put a wild idea into his head. He remembered the tale of the man, caught in a blizzard, who killed a steer and crawled inside the carcass, and

---

apathetically (ap uh THET ik lee) with little or no feeling

so was saved. He would kill the dog and bury his hands in the warm body until the numbness went out of them. Then he could build another fire. He spoke to the dog, calling it to him; but in his voice was a strange note of fear that frightened the animal, who had never known the man to speak in such a way before. Something was the matter, and its suspicious nature sensed danger—it knew not what danger, but somewhere, somehow, in its brain arose an apprehension of the man. It flattened its ears down at the sound of the man's voice, and its restless, hunching movements and liftings and shiftings of its forefeet became more pronounced; but it would not come to the man. He got on his hands and knees and crawled toward the dog. This unusual posture again excited suspicion, and the animal sidled mincingly away.

The man sat up in the snow for a moment and struggled for calmness. Then he pulled on his mittens, by means of his teeth, and got upon his feet. He glanced down at first in order to assure himself that he was really standing up, for the absence of sensation in his feet left him unrelated to the earth. His erect position in itself started to drive the webs of suspicion from the dog's mind; and when he spoke peremptorily, with the sound of whiplashes in his voice, the dog rendered its customary allegiance and came to him. As it came within reaching distance, the man lost his control. His arms flashed out to the dog, and he experienced genuine surprise when he discovered that his hands could

not clutch, that there was neither bend nor feeling in the fingers. He had forgotten for the moment that they were frozen and that they were freezing more and more. All this happened quickly, and before the animal could get away, he encircled its body with his arms. He sat down in the snow, and in this fashion held the dog, while it snarled and whined and struggled.

But it was all he could do, hold its body encircled in his arms and sit there. He realized that he could not kill the dog. There was no way to do it. With his helpless hands he could neither draw nor hold his sheath knife nor throttle the animal. He released it, and it plunged wildly away, with tail between its legs, and still snarling. It halted forty feet away surveying him curiously, with ears sharply pricked forward. The man looked down at his hands in order to locate them, and found them hanging on the ends of his arms. It struck him as curious that one should have to use his eyes in order to find out where his hands were. He began threshing his arms back and forth, beating the mittened hands against his sides. He did this for five minutes, violently, and his heart pumped enough blood up to the surface to put a stop to his shivering. But no sensation was aroused in the hands. He had an impression that they hung like weights on the ends of his arms, but when he tried to run the impression down, he could not find it.

A certain fear of death, dull and oppressive, came to him. This fear quickly became poignant as he realized that it was

---

sidled (SYD uld) moved sideways; edged along slyly
poignant (POIN yunt) sharp; keenly felt

no longer a mere matter of freezing his fingers and toes, or of losing his hands and feet, but that it was a matter of life and death with the chances against him. This threw him into a panic, and he turned and ran up the creek bed along the old, dim trail. The dog joined in behind and kept up with him. He ran blindly, without intention, in fear such as he had never known in his life. Slowly, as he plowed and floundered through the snow, he began to see things again—the banks of the creek, the old timber jams, the leafless aspens, and the sky. The running made him feel better. He did not shiver. Maybe, if he ran on, his feet would thaw out; and, anyway, if he ran far enough, he would reach camp and the boys. Without doubt he would lose some fingers and toes and some of his face; but the boys would take care of him, and save the rest of him when he got there. And at the same time there was another thought in his mind that said he would never get to the camp and the boys; that it was too many miles away, that the freezing had too great a start on him, and that he would soon be stiff and dead. This thought he kept in the background and refused to consider. Sometimes it pushed itself forward and demanded to be heard, but he thrust it back and strove to think of other things.

It struck him as curious that he could run at all on feet so frozen that he could not feel them when they struck the earth and took the weight of his body. He seemed to himself to skim along above the surface, and to have no connection with the earth. Somewhere he had once seen a winged Mercury,[2] and he wondered if Mercury felt as he felt when skimming over the earth.

His theory of running until he reached camp and the boys had one flaw in it; he lacked the endurance. Several times he stumbled, and finally he tottered, crumpled up, and fell. When he tried to rise, he failed. He must sit and rest, he decided, and next time he would merely walk and keep on going. As he sat and regained his breath, he noted that he was feeling quite warm and comfortable. He was not shivering, and it even seemed that a warm glow had come to his chest and trunk. And yet, when he touched his nose or cheeks, there was no sensation. Running would not thaw them out. Nor would it thaw out his hands and feet. Then the thought came to him that the frozen portions of his body must be extending. He tried to keep this thought down, to forget it, to think of something else; he was aware of the panicky feeling that it caused, and he was afraid of the panic. But the thought asserted itself, and persisted, until it produced a vision of his body totally frozen. This was too much, and he made another wild run along the trail. Once he slowed down to a walk, but the thought of the freezing extending itself made him run again.

And all the time the dog ran with him, at his heels. When he fell down a second time, it curled its tail over its forefeet and sat in front of him, facing him, curiously

---

[2]**Mercury:** the ancient Roman god who served as messenger of the gods and is often pictured with wings on his heels

To Build a Fire ■ 299

eager and intent. The warmth and security of the animal angered him, and he cursed it till it flattened down its ears appeasingly. This time the shivering came more quickly upon the man. He was losing his battle with the frost. It was creeping into his body from all sides. The thought of it drove him on, but he ran no more than a hundred feet, when he staggered and pitched headlong. It was his last panic. When he had recovered his breath and control, he sat up and entertained in his mind the conception of meeting death with dignity. However, the conception did not come to him in such terms. His idea of it was that he had been making a fool of himself, running around like a chicken with its head cut off—such was the simile that occurred to him. Well, he was bound to freeze anyway, and he might as well take it decently. With this new-found peace of mind came the first glimmerings of drowsiness. A good idea, he thought, to sleep off to death. It was like taking an anesthetic. Freezing was not so bad as people thought. There were lots worse ways to die.

He pictured the boys finding his body next day. Suddenly he found himself with them, coming along the trail and looking for himself. And, still with them, he came around a turn in the trail and found himself lying in the snow. He did not belong with himself any more, for even then he was out of himself, standing with the boys and looking at himself in the snow. It certainly was cold, was his thought. When he got back to the States he could tell the folks what real cold was. He drifted on from this to a vision of the old-timer on Sulphur Creek. He could see him quite clearly, warm and comfortable, and smoking a pipe.

"You were right, old hoss; you were right," the man mumbled to the old-timer of Sulphur Creek.

Then the man drowsed off into what seemed to him the most comfortable and satisfying sleep he had ever known. The dog sat facing and waiting. The brief day drew to a close in a long, slow twilight. There were no signs of a fire to be made, and, besides, never in the dog's experience had it known a man to sit like that in the snow and make no fire. As the twilight drew on, its eager yearning for the fire mastered it, and with a great lifting and shifting of forefeet, it whined softly, then flattened its ears down in anticipation of being chidden by the man. But the man remained silent. Later the dog whined loudly. And still later it crept close to the man and caught the scent of death. This made the animal bristle and back away. A little longer it delayed, howling under the stars that leaped and danced and shone brightly in the cold sky. Then it turned and trotted up the trail in the direction of the camp it knew, where were the other food providers and fire providers.

---

appeasingly (uh PEEZ ing lee) in a manner to please or obey
anesthetic (an is THET ik) substance that lessens pain
chidden (CHY din) scolded

Jack London (1876–1916)

Jack London was born in San Francisco. He grew up there and in nearby Oakland. At fifteen he was a high-school dropout, a married man, and known as the "Prince of the Oyster Pirates." He worked in a canning factory and tramped around the United States. At seventeen he sailed the Pacific as a crew member on a sealing ship. At twenty-one he joined the gold rush in the Yukon, a region of northern Canada and the setting of "To Build a Fire." Like the characters in his stories and novels, London seemed always in motion.

However, London found the time to read a good deal. When he was about twenty, he decided to be a writer, and he thought a college education would be necessary. For three months he studied for hours every day to pass the entrance exams for the University of California. He succeeded—but then found college too slow for him. For the second time in his life he became a dropout.

London wrote about 150 short stories, selling his first one in 1899. In 1903, *The Call of the Wild*, a novel about a dog, made him famous. From then until his death, he averaged four books a year. He also served as a war reporter in the Far East and Mexico. He was the first American author to earn more than a million dollars from his writing, but he spent it quickly and finally suffered financial disaster while still a young man.

The brief biography you have just read gives several details about London's life before the age of twenty-one. In your opinion, in what way might these experiences have enriched his fiction?

Review the Selection

UNDERSTAND THE SELECTION

Recall

1. Where is "To Build a Fire" set?

2. What does the man eat for lunch?

3. Where is the man heading?

Infer

4. London writes that "he was without imagination." Why is this a problem?

5. Why does the dog think that "the man's ancestors had known nothing of cold"?

6. Explain the importance of the pieces of birch bark in the man's pocket.

7. Describe the relationship between the man and the dog.

Apply

8. How does London foreshadow the tragedy at the end of the story?

9. Predict what might have happened if the man had taken the advice of the old-timer from Sulphur Creek.

10. Would you have attempted what this man did? Why or why not?

Respond to Literature

Do you think the Gold Rush was the reason the man placed himself in this setting? Explain.

THINK ABOUT SETTING

Setting deals primarily with place and time. It also includes everything in the environment, such as objects that are important to the story.

1. How important is the setting to this story?

2. Which aspect of setting—time or place—is dominant in this story? Explain why.

3. Pick three sentences from the story that describe the different elements of nature that contribute to the setting. Explain their significance to the plot.

4. Do you consider the dog to be part of the setting or a character? Why?

5. The author does not give the man's name or any details of his background. Does this work? Explain.

READING FOCUS

Predict Outcomes As you read "To Build a Fire," you made predictions about the outcome of the story. Did you predict the outcome of the story correctly? If so, identify the clues in the story that helped you make your prediction. If not, identify the clues that suggested the ending you predicted.

The Inuit people of the far north, where "To Build a Fire" takes place, have contributed several words to English. *Inuit* is the preferred term for the people we used to call Eskimos. These people live near the Arctic Circle, where it is very cold. They have learned over generations how to keep warm in such a frozen climate.

Look in a dictionary that has word histories for the meaning of each of the following words. Then use each word in a sentence of your own. Tell how each object named might or might not have helped save the life of the main character of "To Build a Fire."

1. anorak   **4.** malamute
2. husky   **5.** mukluk
3. igloo   **6.** umiak

RHYME

Rhyme is the recurrence of the same or similar sounds at regular intervals in one or more lines of poetry. The sameness in rhyme is based on the sounds of the vowel and the consonant that follows it. For example, *fit* and *sit* have the same vowel sound followed by the same consonant sound. Only the consonant before the vowel is different. This kind of rhyme is called **perfect rhyme**.

The rhyme must also involve the accented syllable. For example, two words ending in *-ing* do not necessarily rhyme because the *-ing* syllable does not have the emphasis, or accent. Thus, *saying* and *playing* rhyme, but *looking* and *seeing* do not.

Most rhymes are **end rhymes**; that is, the words with the same sounds are at the end of the lines. However, poems may also have **internal rhymes**—two rhyming words within the same line.

As you read the selection, ask yourself:
1. Which are the rhyming words in the poem?
2. Does the author use end rhymes, internal rhymes, or both?

READING FOCUS

Support an Opinion It is important to support an opinion. Giving reasons for an opinion makes the opinion more convincing. As you read this poem, look for how the writer supports her opinion that America is beautiful.

WRITING CONNECTION

Write two lines that have end rhymes. Write two lines that have internal rhymes.

Mount Katahdin, Maine, 1853, Frederick Edwin Church. The Granger Collection

AMERICA
THE BEAUTIFUL

by Katharine Lee Bates

O beautiful for spacious skies,
For amber waves of grain,
For purple mountain majesties
Above the fruited plain!

Wheatfield Watercolor, Emil Nolde. Corbis Bettmann

5   America! America!
      God shed His grace on thee
    And crown thy good with brotherhood
       From sea to shining sea!

    O beautiful for pilgrim feet,
10   Whose stern, impassioned stress
    A thoroughfare for freedom beat
       Across the wilderness!
      America! America!
      God mend thine every flaw,
15   Confirm thy soul in self-control,
       Thy liberty in law!

    O beautiful for heroes proved
       In liberating strife,
  Who more than self their country loved,
20   And mercy more than life!
      America! America!
       May God thy gold refine,
  Till all success be nobleness
      And every gain divine!

25   O beautiful for patriot dream
      That sees beyond the years
   Thine alabaster cities gleam
       Undimmed by human tears!
      America! America!
30   God shed His grace on thee
    And crown thy good with brotherhood
       From sea to shining sea!

---

impassioned (im PASH und) determined; filled with
  passionate feeling
thoroughfare (THUR oh fair) passage; way through

Review the Selection

UNDERSTAND THE SELECTION

Recall

1. How many stanzas are there all together in "America the Beautiful"?

2. What colors are mentioned?

3. Is any part of the poem repeated? If so, which part?

Infer

4. What does "fruited plain" mean?

5. To what do you think "Confirm thy soul in self-control" refers?

6. To what does the reference "from sea to shining sea" refer?

7. What is "liberating strife"?

Apply

8. Would you say that "America the Beautiful" is a poem or a song—or both? Explain.

9. Do you see any relationship between stanzas in poetry and paragraphs in prose? Explain.

10. What kind of rhyming scheme can you notice? Is more than one pattern used? Explain.

Respond to Literature

Does the imagery in this poem apply to America today in the same way as when Katharine Lee Bates wrote it? Explain.

THINK ABOUT RHYME

Rhyme adds greatly to the beauty of much poetry, but have you thought about why this is so? One reason is that rhyme has a musical quality; the repetition of sounds has an echo-like quality that is pleasing to the ear. Rhyme also has a rhythmic function; it is a kind of "time-beater" since the rhyming words note the end of a **verse**, or line of poetry. It also helps to delineate divisions of the poem.

1. Which words in the first four lines of each stanza rhyme?

2. What are rhymes of this kind called?

3. What end rhymes are there in the second four lines of each stanza?

4. Are there any other rhymes in the second four lines of each stanza? If so, what are they called?

5. Are there imperfect rhymes in the poem? If so, what are they?

READING FOCUS

Support an Opinion How did Katharine Lee Bates support her opinion that America is beautiful in these areas?
- its physical beauty
- its history in becoming a country
- its struggles

Adjectives are words that describe. They are used to limit, or modify, the meaning of nouns. In her poem, Bates uses strong, vivid adjectives to create images for the reader. Some of these are *spacious*, *amber*, *purple*, *fruited*, *impassioned*, *liberating*, and *alabaster*. Notice that her choices include not only adjectives but participles used as adjectives.

Read the following sentences. Then change the italicized weak adjective in each into a more vivid one. You can use two or more adjectives for the italicized one, if you wish.

1. An *awful* rain fell all day.

2. The doorbell made a *funny* noise.

3. I had a *great* time at the picnic.

4. The day of our hike was *nice*.

5. We moved the *old* bed up to the attic.

RHYME SCHEME

Rhymes usually occur in the same places throughout a poem. This regularity is known as the **rhyme pattern** or **rhyme scheme**. You can detect a rhyme scheme by assigning letters to designate the words at the end of the lines. The same letter is used for words having the same sounds. Thus, a simple rhyme scheme would be *abcb*. This pattern shows that the words at the end of lines two and four rhyme, but that the words at the end of lines one and three do not.

There are many different kinds of rhyme schemes. They depend on the number of lines per stanza and on which lines rhyme. It is not necessary that every line rhyme with some other line.

As you read the poems by Teasdale, ask yourself:

1. Which are the rhyming words in each poem?
2. What is the rhyme scheme of each poem?

WRITING CONNECTION

Think of a four-line stanza of a poem that you know. If you can't think of a poem, think of a song or nursery rhyme. Write it down. Then, using the form shown above, write the rhyme scheme.

READING FOCUS

Recognize Figures of Speech A figure of speech is an imaginative statement rather than a statement of fact. Instead of saying "The sun was setting," a writer might say "The red sun was pasted in the sky like a wafer." The statement is not literally true; it is an imaginative way to make the reader see the sunset.

Look for figures of speech in Teasdale's poems. Examine the suggested meaning of the words in each figure of speech to help determine the picture the poet is trying to create.

BARTER

by Sara Teasdale

Life has loveliness to sell,
    All beautiful and splendid things,
Blue waves whitened on a cliff,
    Soaring fire that sways and sings,
5   And children's faces looking up
Holding wonder like a cup.

Life has loveliness to sell,
    Music like a curve of gold,
Scent of pine trees in the rain,
10   Eyes that love you, arms that hold,
And for your spirit's still delight,
Holy thoughts that star the night.

Spend all you have for loveliness,
    Buy it and never count the cost;
15   For one white singing hour of peace
    Count many a year of strife well lost,
And for a breath of ecstasy
Give all you have been, or could be.

---

barter (BAHRT ur) trade; exchanging one thing for another
soaring (SAWR ing) rising or gliding high into the air
wonder (WUN dur) feeling of surprise, admiration, awe, caused by something strange,
   unexpected, or incredible
star (STAHR) to mark or set with stars, as a decoration
strife (STRYF) troublesome conflict; quarreling
ecstasy (EK stuh see) a feeling of overpowering joy; great delight

The Northern Lights, Sydney Laurence. Shelburne Museum, Shelburne, VT

THE FALLING STAR

by Sara Teasdale

I saw a star slide down the sky,
Blinding the north as it went by,
Too burning and too quick to hold,
Too lovely to be bought or sold,
Good only to make wishes on
And then forever to be gone.

THE LONG HILL

by Sara Teasdale

I must have passed the crest a while ago
    And now I am going down—
Strange to have crossed the crest and not to know,
    But the brambles were always catching the hem of my gown.

5   All the morning I thought how proud I should be
    To stand there straight as a queen,
Wrapped in the wind and the sun with the world under me—
    But the air was dull, there was little I could have seen.

It was nearly level along the beaten track
10   And the brambles caught in my gown—
But it's no use now to think of turning back,
    The rest of the way will be only going down.

Southwest Wind, Childe Hassam. Corbis Bettmann

---

crest (KREST) the top of anything; summit; ridge
brambles (BRAM bulz) prickly shrubs

I SHALL NOT CARE

by Sara Teasdale

When I am dead and over me bright April
    Shakes out her rain-drenched hair,
Tho' you should lean above me broken-hearted,
    I shall not care.

I shall have peace, as leafy trees are peaceful
    When rain bends down the bough,
And I shall be more silent and cold-hearted
    Than you are now.

A Summer Night, 1890, Winslow Homer. The Granger Collection

---

drenched (DRENCHT) soaked; wet all over
bough (BOU) a large branch of a tree

Author Biography

Sara Teasdale (1884–1933)

Sara Teasdale, born in St. Louis, Missouri, in 1884, was homeschooled until she was nine because of her fragile health. She wrote poetry from an early age and contributed some sonnets to a literary monthly, *Wheel*. Later, she often visited Chicago where she became associated with the magazine *Poetry*.

One of the influences on Teasdale's poetry was her travels. After an initial trip in 1905, Teasdale became a frequent visitor to Europe. She went to New York in 1914 where she met many important writers of the day as well as a shoe manufacturer named Ernst Filsinger, who became her husband. After her marriage, she moved to New York City and made it her home for the remainder of her life. Unhappily, her marriage ended in divorce in 1929.

Teasdale published six volumes of poetry during her lifetime, the first when she was only twenty-three. Her third volume, titled *Love Songs*, won the Columbia University Poetry Society Prize (which became the Pulitzer Prize) and the Poetry Society of America Prize in 1918. A seventh volume, *Strange Victory*, often considered her best, was published shortly after her death in 1933.

In addition to her writing, Teasdale edited an anthology of love poems by women called *The Answering Voice* and a collection of poetry for children called *Rainbow Gold*. While writing a biography of English poet Christina Rossetti, whose work had influenced her poetry, Teasdale became ill with pneumonia. She overdosed on barbiturates and died in January of 1933.

Review the Selection

UNDERSTAND THE SELECTION

Recall

1. Which word in each stanza summarizes the theme of "Barter"?

2. In "The Falling Star," why can't you buy or sell a falling star?

3. In "The Long Hill," what has the speaker "passed" and "crossed"?

Infer

4. Of these four poems, which is the most positive or optimistic? Why?

5. What could "The Falling Star" symbolize?

6. What do the "hill" and the "crest" represent in "The Long Hill"?

7. In "I Shall Not Care," explain who "you" might be.

Apply

8. Select three things described in "Barter." Of what experiences does each remind you?

9. Is the mood of "The Falling Star" positive or negative? Explain.

10. Predict what the speaker is heading toward at the end of "The Long Hill."

Respond to Literature

By reading Teasdale's poems, could you tell when they were written? Explain.

THINK ABOUT RHYME SCHEME

Once a rhyme scheme has been established in the first stanza, it is usually followed in all subsequent stanzas. The pattern of the rhymes helps to give a certain form to each stanza and to the poem as a whole.

1. What is the rhyme scheme of "Barter"? What do you notice about the first and third lines of each stanza?

2. What is the rhyme scheme in "The Falling Star"?

3. What is the rhyme scheme of "The Long Hill"?

4. What is the rhyme scheme in "I Shall Not Care"? Does the poem contain internal rhymes as well as end rhymes?

5. Find three instances in these poems in which the rhyming words have different numbers of syllables.

READING FOCUS

Recognize Figures of Speech Choose one figure of speech from any of the four poems in this selection. Paraphrase it as a plain statement of fact and compare the two versions.

DEVELOP YOUR VOCABULARY

A noun names a person, a place, or a thing. A verb names an action or a state of being. Some words can be used as both nouns and verbs. Their part of speech depends on how they are used in a sentence. For example: Joe and Emma have to *look* for the book, You should have seen the *look* on his face. In these sentences, *look* is used first as a verb, then as a noun. The way in which any word is classified as a part of speech depends on the way it is used in a sentence.

Review the meaning of the following words in a dictionary. State which way each is used in the context of the poem. Then write two sentences for each of the words, using the word as a noun in one sentence and as a verb in the other. At the end of each sentence, tell how the word has been used.

1. barter
2. waves
3. wonder
4. star
5. cost
6. crest

Learn About

IRONY

Irony occurs when the intent or tone of the words used is exactly opposite of what the actual meaning of the words say. For example, if someone asks you if you mind having a flu shot, you may reply, "I can hardly wait!" Are you really eager to have the shot, or are you dreading it? Your words say you are eager, but your tone of voice expresses a feeling that is the opposite of eager. This example explains one kind of irony.

Another kind is called **irony of situation**. This term refers to events that turn out to be the opposite of what you expect or consider appropriate. Suppose, for example, that someone taunts you for some misfortune. If that person, without knowing it, is at that moment suffering the same misfortune, that is irony of situation.

As you read the poem, ask yourself:
1. Which type of irony does the poem tell about?
2. Does the author offer any comment about the events?

READING FOCUS

Make Inferences from Connotations Connotations suggest connections beyond a word's literal meaning. For example, you might describe a man's profile as "carved from flint." The phrase suggests a quality of hardness and harshness that the word *strong* does not convey. As you read "Richard Cory," think about the connotations of each word used to describe him. What inferences can you make about Richard Cory from these connotations?

WRITING CONNECTION

Assume that a friend has just broken a favorite possession of yours. Write what you would say that would show a contrast between what your words are and what you mean.

318 ■ **Unit 4**

RICHARD CORY

by Edwin Arlington Robinson

Whenever Richard Cory went down town,
We people on the pavement looked at him:
He was a gentleman from sole to crown,
Clean favored, and imperially slim.

5   And he was always quietly arrayed,
And he was always human when he talked;
But still he fluttered pulses when he said,
"Good-morning," and he glittered when he
    walked.

And he was rich—yes, richer than a king—
10   And admirably schooled in every grace:
In fine, we thought that he was everything
To make us wish that we were in his place.

So on we worked, and waited for the light,
And went without the meat, and cursed the
    bread;
15   And Richard Cory, one calm summer night,
Went home and put a bullet through his head.

---

favored (FAY vurd) featured
imperially (im PIR ee ul ee) supremely
arrayed (uh RAYD) dressed
admirably (AD mur uh blee) excellently
fine (FYN) summary; conclusion

Review the Selection

UNDERSTAND THE SELECTION

Recall

1. What type of physical build did Richard Cory have?

2. What are the only words he is quoted as saying in the poem?

3. In what season did he kill himself?

Infer

4. How do you think Richard Cory traveled about? Explain why you have this impression.

5. Paraphrase the expression "from sole to crown."

6. Why do you think he "fluttered pulses" when he spoke to people?

7. Why do you think people "cursed the bread"?

Apply

8. How do you think Cory would have treated you if you met? Why?

9. Select three adjectives to describe this man.

10. Why do you think Richard Cory killed himself?

Respond to Literature

Suppose that Richard Cory had lived in a country that had royalty. What do you think his position would have been?

THINK ABOUT IRONY

Irony is a common form of expression in literature—as in life. It is an effective way of contrasting the literal meaning of words with the opposite meaning behind those words. Irony of situation refers to events that are contrary to what the reader or characters in the literary work expect or believe to be appropriate.

1. Which sort of irony does Robinson use in his poem?

2. What characteristics of Richard Cory made him someone with whom people would like to change places?

3. Does the author have any comments to make about the ending of the poem? If so, what is his message?

4. What does Robinson mean when he says that Richard Cory "glittered when he walked"?

5. Does the poem suggest to you any general lessons about life? If so, what are they?

READING FOCUS

Make Inferences from Connotations List some of the words and phrases used to describe Richard Cory. Identify what these words and phrases connote beyond their literal definitions. Then explain what you infer about Cory from the language used to describe him.

Robinson creates some memorable images in "Richard Cory." Note particularly his choice of verbs. Cory wasn't merely *dressed*; he was *arrayed*. He didn't *make pulses skip a beat*; he *fluttered pulses*. Other people didn't *complain* about their lot; they *cursed* the bread.

Verbs are important in writing. Since they carry the action, strong, vivid verbs can make your writing lively.

Choose the most vivid verbs from the list in parentheses:

1. The thief (*walked*, *slunk*, *crept*, *went*) away in the night.

2. Alfonso (*tiptoed*, *moved*, *walked*) across the library.

3. My brother (*devoured*, *gobbled*, *ate*) the snacks eagerly.

4. The fire (*flamed*, *burned*, *blazed*) hotly in the fireplace.

5. The child (*pleaded*, *asked*, *requested*) not to be punished.

The Modern View

When all our hopes are sown on stony ground,
And we have yielded up the thought of gain,
Long after our last songs have lost their sound
We may come back, we may come back again.
                                        —Arna Bontemps

Janitor's Holiday, Paul Sample. The Metropolitan Museum of Art,
Arthur Hoppock Hearn Fund

CHARACTER

A **character** in literature is the representation in words of a person, or in some instances, an animal. Writers reveal the traits, or personality, of a character through description, dialogue, actions, and commentary. Often, writers present direct information about a character. This may include a description of a character's physical appearance. The words a character uses may clearly tell what he or she is thinking and feeling.

Writers also present less obvious, indirect information, called **character clues**. You can look closely at what a character does, says, feels, and thinks, and how other characters talk about and act toward that character, to make intelligent guesses about that character's personality.

As you read "A Day's Wait," ask yourself:

1. What kind of character is Schatz?
2. What actions does he take that reveal his character?

READING FOCUS

Identify Imagery Imagery consists of words that describe what you might feel, hear, see, taste, or smell if you were in the scene. Writers use imagery to make the readers feel as though they are experiencing the story or poem first-hand. Look for imagery as you read the story.

WRITING CONNECTION

Write a paragraph that reveals a strong character trait of a person you know well. Be sure to include enough specific information to help your reader decide what this person is really like.

A DAY'S WAIT

by Ernest Hemingway

He came into the room to shut the windows while we were still in bed and I saw he looked ill. He was shivering, his face was white, and he walked slowly as though it ached to move.

"What's the matter, Schatz?"

"I've got a headache."

"You better go back to bed."

"No. I'm all right."

"You go to bed. I'll see you when I'm dressed."

But when I came downstairs he was dressed, sitting by the fire, looking a very sick and miserable boy of nine years. When I put my hand on his forehead I knew he had a fever.

"You go up to bed," I said, "you're sick."

"I'm all right," he said.

When the doctor came he took the boy's temperature.

"What is it?" I asked him.

"One hundred and two."

Downstairs, the doctor left three different medicines in different colored capsules with instructions for giving them. One was to bring down the fever, another a purgative, the third to overcome an acid condition. The germs of influenza can only exist in an acid condition, he explained. He seemed to know all about influenza and said there was nothing to worry about if the fever did not go above one hundred and four degrees. This was a light epidemic of flu and there was no danger if you avoided pneumonia.

Back in the room I wrote the boy's temperature down and made a note of the time to give the various capsules.

---

purgative (PUR guh tiv) strong laxative
influenza (in floo EN zuh) disease usually called "flu"

"Do you want me to read to you?"

"All right. If you want to," said the boy. His face was very white and there were dark areas under his eyes. He lay still in the bed and seemed very detached from what was going on.

I read aloud from Howard Pyle's *Book of Pirates*; but I could see he was not following what I was reading.

"How do you feel, Schatz?" I asked him.

"Just the same, so far," he said.

I sat at the foot of the bed and read to myself while I waited for it to be time to give another capsule. It would have been natural for him to go to sleep, but when I looked up he was looking at the foot of the bed, looking very strangely.

"Why don't you try to go to sleep? I'll wake you up for the medicine."

"I'd rather stay awake."

After a while he said to me, "You don't have to stay in here with me, Papa, if it bothers you."

"It doesn't bother me."

"No, I mean you don't have to stay if it's going to bother you."

I thought perhaps he was a little lightheaded and after giving him the prescribed capsules at eleven o'clock I went out for a while.

It was a bright, cold day, the ground covered with a sleet that had frozen so that it seemed as if all the bare trees, the bushes, the cut brush and all the grass and the bare ground had been varnished with ice. I took the young Irish setter for a little walk up the road and along a frozen creek, but it was difficult to stand or walk on the glassy surface and the red dog slipped and slithered and I fell twice, hard, once dropping my gun and having it slide away over the ice.

We flushed a covey of quail under a high clay bank with overhanging brush and I killed two as they went out of sight over the top of the bank. Some of the covey lit in trees, but most of them scattered into brush piles and it was necessary to jump on the ice-coated mounds of brush several times before they would flush. Coming out while you were poised unsteadily on the icy, springy

---

slither (SLITH ur) slip and slide
flush (FLUSH) drive birds or animals from hiding place
covey (KUV ee) flock of birds

Adirondacks, Winslow Homer. Corbis Bettmann

brush they made difficult shooting and I killed two, missed five, and started back pleased to have found a covey close to the house and happy there were so many left to find on another day.

At the house they said the boy had refused to let anyone come into the room.

"You can't come in," he said. "You mustn't get what I have."

I went up to him and found him in exactly the position I had left him, white-faced, but with the tops of his cheeks flushed by the fever, staring still, as he had stared, at the foot of the bed.

I took his temperature.

"What is it?"

"Something like a hundred," I said. It was one hundred and two and four tenths.

"It was a hundred and two," he said.

"Who said so?"

"The doctor."

"Your temperature is all right," I said. "It's nothing to worry about."

"I don't worry," he said, "but I can't keep from thinking."

"Don't think," I said. "Just take it easy."

"I'm taking it easy," he said and looked straight ahead. He was evidently holding tight onto himself about something.

"Take this with water."

"Do you think it will do any good?"

"Of course it will."

I sat down and opened the *Pirate* book and commenced to read, but I could see he was not following, so I stopped.

"About what time do you think I'm going to die?" he asked.

"What?"

"About how long will it be before I die?"

"You aren't going to die. What's the matter with you?"

"Oh, yes, I am. I heard him say a hundred and two."

"People don't die with a fever of one hundred and two. That's a silly way to talk."

"I know they do. At school in France the boys told me you can't live with forty-four degrees. I've got a hundred and two."

He had been waiting to die all day, ever since nine o'clock in the morning.

"You poor Schatz," I said. "Poor old Schatz. It's like miles and kilometers. You aren't going to die. That's a different thermometer. On that thermometer thirty-seven is normal. On this kind it's ninety-eight."

"Are you sure?"

"Absolutely," I said. "It's like miles and kilometers. You know, like how many kilometers we make when we do seventy miles in the car?"

"Oh," he said.

But his gaze at the foot of the bed relaxed slowly. The hold over himself relaxed too, finally, and the next day it was very slack and he cried very easily at little things that were of no importance.

---

commence (kuh MENS) begin

Ernest Hemingway (1899–1961)

Quick! List three facts about a famous living American writer.

Could you do it? Maybe. But if you'd lived during the time of Ernest Hemingway, you probably could have done it easily. Wherever he went and whatever he did, Hemingway was always big news. His name was often in the headlines:

HEMINGWAY BREAKS NOSE IN BOXING RING

PLANE CRASH KILLS HEMINGWAY IN AFRICA

GOOD NEWS: HEMINGWAY ALIVE!

HEMINGWAY MARRIES FOR FOURTH TIME

HEMINGWAY YACHT IN U-BOAT CHASE

GUN ACCIDENT INJURES HEMINGWAY

A bear of a man, Hemingway photographed well. All America knew what he looked like. He seemed always in action: skiing in Switzerland, hunting in Africa, fishing from his private yacht, risking his life as a reporter on distant war fronts. Yet, somehow during his active life, he took the time to write the stories and novels that won him one of the highest honors a writer can earn, the Nobel Prize.

"All you have to do is, write one true sentence," Hemingway discovered when he was starting out. "Write the truest sentence you know." That one sentence, he found, would lead to another, to a paragraph, to a story. He disliked fancy writing; he wanted it pure and simple, lifelike and honest. Do you think any other author of our century has had a greater influence on modern American writers than Ernest Hemingway?

How did Hemingway differ from the stereotype you may have in mind of a "famous author"?

Review the Selection

UNDERSTAND THE SELECTION

Recall

1. Between what times of day does "A Day's Wait" take place?

2. At what object in his room does Schatz constantly gaze?

3. What is Schatz's temperature the second time it is taken?

Infer

4. What is the first clue that Schatz is worried about more than his fever?

5. Why does Schatz suggest to his father that he may leave the room?

6. How does the reader know when Schatz has stopped worrying?

7. Why does Schatz cry very easily the next day?

Apply

8. If you were Schatz, what thoughts would run through your mind?

9. What might have happened if Schatz had heard what the doctor really said?

10. Choose two other appropriate titles for "A Day's Wait."

Respond to Literature

What events in the early twentieth century might have prompted Hemingway to write this story of courage?

THINK ABOUT CHARACTER

A **character** is a person or animal in a story, poem, or drama. Readers infer what a character's words, actions, feelings, and thoughts really show about his or her personality. Readers may also learn about a character through the things other characters say about him or her.

1. What kind of a person is Schatz?

2. Writers usually describe a character's physical appearance. Yet, in the story, Hemingway only describes Schatz's face, and then, briefly. What other character clues help you to determine what Schatz is really like?

3. Select three of Schatz's statements and explain how each contributes to your understanding of his character. Explain what each statement revealed about him.

4. Understanding a character's personality allows you to predict how he or she may react to other events. When he is older, how might Schatz react to a physically dangerous fire or storm? Explain your answer.

READING FOCUS

Identify Imagery As you read, you were able to identify words that described sights, sounds, smells, tastes, and feelings of touch. Choose an example of imagery from the story that particularly appealed to you. Explain why you chose it.

DEVELOP YOUR VOCABULARY

A **synonym** is a word that has the same or nearly the same meaning as another word. For instance, Schatz is described as being *detached*—not really involved with what is going on in his room. The author might have used the words *distracted* or *preoccupied* as synonyms for *detached*.

Read the sentences below and choose the best synonym for the *italicized* word.

1. He could fall and *slither* across the frozen pond.
   a. pause
   b. glide
   c. relax
   d. listen
   e. stumble

2. Hunters often use dogs to *flush* their prey from hiding places.
   a. dislodge
   b. smell
   c. force
   d. recover
   e. convince

3. We were startled by a *covey* of pigeons . . .
   a. handful
   b. group
   c. feather
   d. line
   e. regiment

4. Each time that his father *commenced* reading, Schatz would turn away.
   a. halted
   b. interrupted
   c. started
   d. paused
   e. ended

Learn About

LYRIC POETRY

Of the many types of poetry written, the lyric is perhaps the most varied in structure, subject matter, and mood. Some characteristics that **lyric poems** have in common, however, are these: they are brief and imaginative; they have "melody;" they express the personal, emotional feelings and thoughts of a single speaker.

Lyric poems make use of many poetic techniques to achieve their musical quality. Two such techniques are repetition and alliteration. **Repetition**, using the same or similar words over again, may occur at regular or irregular places in the poem. Alliteration is also a device of repetition. In **alliteration**, it is the initial consonant (or sometimes vowel) sounds of nearby words that are repeated, as in *"Bend* the *bow;* let the *bolt burst* the *bubble* apart."

As you read the poems, ask yourself:
1. What unified emotional impression does each poem make?
2. What poetic devices are used in each poem?

READING FOCUS

Evaluate the Writer's Purpose Evaluating the writer's purpose means figuring out why the author wrote something. This will give you insight into the deeper meanings of the work. Also, as a reader you can evaluate whether you agree or disagree with the author's attitude toward the subject. As you read each of these poems, decide what the poet's purpose is and whether you agree with it.

WRITING CONNECTION

Using alliteration, write a four-line stanza in which at least two words in each line begin with the same sound.

Lament

by Edna St. Vincent Millay

My Family, Leopold Seyffert. The Brooklyn Museum

Listen, children:
Your father is dead.
From his old coats
I'll make you little jackets;
5   I'll make you little trousers
From his old pants.
There'll be in his pockets
Things he used to put there,
Keys and pennies
10   Covered with tobacco;
Dan shall have the pennies
To save in his bank;
Anne shall have the keys
To make a pretty noise with.
15   Life must go on,
And the dead be forgotten;
Life must go on,
Though good men die;
Anne, eat your breakfast;
20   Dan, take your medicine;
Life must go on;
I forget just why.

Afternoon on a Hill

by Edna St. Vincent Millay

I will be the gladdest thing
    Under the sun!
I will touch a hundred flowers
    And not pick one.
5   I will look at cliffs and clouds
      With quiet eyes,
Watch the wind bow down the grass,
    And the grass rise.
10   And when lights begin to show
    Up from the town,
I will mark which must be mine,
    And then start down!

Author Biography
Edna St. Vincent Millay (1892–1950)

Edna St. Vincent Millay was a writer who wanted to tell the truth about life and love from a woman's point of view. In the 1920s, Millay became a symbol of life, love, and a newfound freedom. She would start a poem:

> What lips my lips have kissed, and where, and why,
> I have forgotten . . .

In the 1920s, this was scandalous, but for many people delightfully so. Curious poetry lovers flocked to her poetry readings across the country. There they found a small, attractive young woman with golden red hair, a sensitive voice, and a dignified manner. They also found that Millay's reputation as a symbol of bright, adventurous youth was only part of the picture. Most of her best poems did not concern love at all, and she often spoke of sorrow, hardship, and loss. It is upon this reputation that her fame rests.

Hardship and loss were hardly strangers to the young poet. Her early life on the coast of Maine had been generally happy but far from easy. Her parents were divorced when she was a young girl, and for years her mother supported the family on what she could earn as a nurse. Although Millay was an active, prize-winning student in high school, there was no money for college. Accepting this loss as a fact of life, she continued to work at her poetry. A long poem called "Renascence," written when she was nineteen, brought her early fame. Then came college, success, years of travel, and a good marriage. Much of her later work reveals an inner anguish caused by what she saw as human injustice and stupidity. Her greatest regret was that even a perfect poem can do little to remake an imperfect world.

Why do you think Millay's poems were so shocking in the 1920s?

Review the Selection

UNDERSTAND THE SELECTION

Recall

1. What is the subject of "Lament"?

2. What items does the wife retrieve from her husband's pockets?

3. Identify the elements of nature mentioned in "Afternoon on a Hill."

Infer

4. How old do you think the two children in "Lament" are? Why?

5. Has the speaker in "Lament" accepted her husband's death? Explain.

6. Why is "Afternoon on a Hill" written in the future tense?

7. In "Afternoon on a Hill," what do you think "quiet eyes" means?

Apply

8. How would you characterize the mother in "Lament"?

9. On one level, "Afternoon on a Hill" is about someone thinking about spending an afternoon on a hill. What is another meaning of the poem?

10. Why will the speaker in "Lament" remember that life must go on?

Respond to Literature

How does the subject matter of "Lament" reflect the changing roles of women in U.S. society during the 1920s?

THINK ABOUT LYRIC POETRY

Lyric poems may have any of a number of rhythmic patterns and may be either rhymed or unrhymed. Sometimes rhythms can be varied by the kinds of consonants the poet chooses. For instance, consonants like *l*, *m*, *n*, and *r* can be drawn out to produce a smooth rhythm when spoken aloud. Consonants like *b*, *d*, *k*, *p*, and *t*, however, create a quickened or staccato rhythm.

1. What rhythmic devices can you find in the first poem you read, "Lament"?

2. What rhythmic devices do you find in the second poem "Afternoon on a Hill"?

3. How does the repetition of the sentence "Life must go on" in "Lament" contribute to the meaning of the poem?

4. Explain the sequence of events in "Afternoon on a Hill."

5. Who is the speaker in each poem?

READING FOCUS

Evaluate the Writer's Purpose What do you think the poet's purpose is in "Lament"? What is the poet's purpose in writing "Afternoon on a Hill"? Provide details from each poem to support your responses.

DEVELOP YOUR VOCABULARY

Figurative language is a way of putting words and phrases together to create a meaning that is different from the dictionary meaning of the individual words. For instance, in "The reader *jumped* to the wrong conclusion," the word *jump* is used figuratively to suggest that the reader assumed something too quickly.

Words or phrases that mean exactly what they say are called **literal language**. In "The track runner *jumped* the hurdles successfully," the words mean exactly, or literally, what they say.

For each pair of sentences below, determine which sentence uses figurative and which sentence uses literal language.

1. The substitute teacher *saddled* us with too much homework.

2. The cowboy *saddled* his spotted pony and began his journey.

3. The pianist *struck the right notes*.

4. The politician *struck the right notes* in her reelection speech.

Learn About

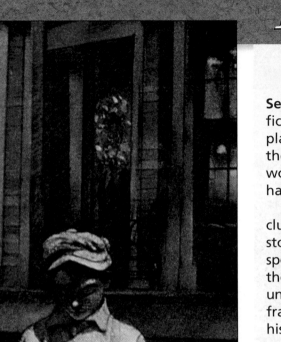

READING FOCUS

Recognize Implied Theme A theme is the message that a story is written to convey. An implied theme is one that you must infer from the work as a whole. As you read "home," think about the larger message the author may be sending.

SETTING

Setting is the time and place in which fiction, such as a short story, poem, or play, occurs. You can think of setting as the total environment, or the created world, in which a work of literature happens.

To determine setting, look for word clues that tell *where* and *when* the story takes place. For example, look for specific words and phrases that describe the location and scenery of the story. To understand the *when* of a story—its time frame—read for details that show the historical time period, season of year, and time of day. Remember, too, that story settings can change over time.

Setting is crucial because it can affect people and events in a story. Setting can force a character to act or feel in certain ways. For example, you would expect a person who is caught in a terrible snowstorm to behave differently than one who is relaxing on a warm, sunny beach.

As you read "home" ask yourself:
1. What is the setting of the story?
2. How does the setting affect the character's behavior?

WRITING CONNECTION

Writers use details to help the reader visualize a setting. Write a brief description of a favorite place and include vivid and specific details.

home

by Gwendolyn Brooks

What had been wanted was this always, this always to last, the talking softly on this porch, with the snake plant in the jardiniere in the southwest corner, and the obstinate slip from Aunt Eppie's magnificent Michigan fern at the left side of the friendly door. Mama, Maud Martha and Helen rocked slowly in their rocking chairs, and looked at the late afternoon light on the lawn, and at the emphatic iron of the fence and at the poplar tree. These things might soon be theirs no longer. Those shafts and pools of light, the tree, the graceful iron, might soon be viewed possessively by different eyes.

Papa was to have gone that noon, during his lunch hour, to the office of the Home Owners' Loan. If he had not succeeded in getting another extension, they would be leaving this house in which they had lived for more than fourteen years. There was little hope. The Home Owners' Loan was hard. They sat, making their plans.

"We'll be moving into a nice flat somewhere," said Mama. "Somewhere on South Park, or Michigan, or in Washington Park Court." Those flats, as the girls and Mama knew well, were burdens on wages twice the size of Papa's. This was not mentioned now.

"They're much prettier than this old house," said Helen. "I have friends I'd just as soon not bring here. And I have other friends that wouldn't come down this far for anything, unless they were in a taxi."

Yesterday, Maud Martha would have attacked her. Tomorrow she might. Today she said nothing. She merely gazed at a little hopping robin in the tree, her tree, and tried to keep the fronts of her eyes dry.

---

jardiniere (jahr duh NIR) a decorative flower pot or stand
obstinate (OB stuh nut) stubborn
emphatic (em FAT ik) very striking; definite
flat (FLAT) an apartment with rooms on one floor

"Well, I do know," said Mama, turning her hands over and over, "that I've been getting tireder and tireder of doing that firing. From October to April, there's firing to be done."

"But lately, we've been helping, Harry and I," said Maud Martha. "And sometimes in March and April and in October, and even in November, we could build a little fire in the fireplace. Sometimes the weather was just right for that."

She knew, from the way they looked at her, that this had been mistake. They did not want to cry.

But she felt that the little line of white, somewhat ridged with smoked purple, and all that cream-shot saffron, would never drift across any western sky except that in back of this house. The rain would drum with as sweet a dullness nowhere but here. The birds on South Park were mechanical birds, no better than the poor caught canaries in those "rich" women's sun parlors.

"It's just going to kill Papa!" burst out Maud Martha. "He loves this house! He *lives* for this house!"

"He lives for us," said Helen. "It's us he loves. He wouldn't want the house, except for us."

"And he'll have us," added Mama, "wherever."

"You know," Helen sighed, "if you want to know the truth, this is a relief. If this hadn't come up, we would have gone on, just dragged on, hanging out here forever."

"It might," allowed Mama, "be an act of God. God may just have reached down, and picked up the reins."

"Yes," Maud Martha cracked in, "that's what you always say—that God knows best."

Her mother looked at her quickly, decided the statement was not suspect, looked away.

Helen saw Papa coming. "There's Papa," said Helen.

They could not tell a thing from the way Papa was walking. It was that same dear little staccato walk, one shoulder down, then the other, then repeat, and repeat. They watched his progress. He passed the Kennedys', he passed the vacant lot, he passed Mrs. Blakemore's. They wanted to hurl themselves over the fence, into the street, and shake the truth out of his collar. He opened his gate—the gate—and still his stride and face told them nothing.

---

firing (FYR ing) to light a fire in a boiler
saffron (SAF run) bright, orange-yellow color
staccato (stuh KAHT oh) short, distinct movement

Oil Sketch for *American Gothic*, Grant Wood. Rinard Collection, Estate of Grant Wood/Licensed by VAGA, New York, NY

"Hello," he said.

Mama got up and followed him through the front door. The girls knew better than to go in too.

Presently Mama's head emerged. Her eyes were lamps turned on.

"It's all right," she exclaimed. "He got it. It's all over. Everything is all right."

The door slammed shut. Mama's footsteps hurried away.

"I think," said Helen, rocking rapidly, "I think I'll give a party. I haven't given a party since I was eleven. I'd like some of my friends to just casually see that we're homeowners."

---

presently (PREZ unt lee) in a little while

Review the Selection

UNDERSTAND THE SELECTION

Recall

1. Where does "home" take place?

2. For whom are the women waiting?

3. Would it cost the family the same, more, or less money to live in a flat?

Infer

4. Do you think the family could move into a nice flat? Why?

5. Do you think Helen is stating her real feelings about moving away?

6. Why does Maud Martha fear that her comment about "a little fire in the fireplace" will make the others cry?

7. Why does Helen decide to give a party at the conclusion of the story?

Apply

8. Defend or refute: "Characters always believe they have complete control over their lives."

9. Contrast Mama's attitude about leaving with Maud Martha's. Would you expect a mother to act this way?

10. Brooks tries to show people coping with disappointment. Is she successful? Explain.

Respond to Literature

How does "home" reflect the experience of many American families?

THINK ABOUT SETTING

Setting often contributes to a particular mood or atmosphere in a story, poem, or play. A large, comfortable front porch establishes one set of feelings, while a small, cramped apartment creates quite different feelings. Characters in a story are usually influenced by the setting.

1. Describe the setting that Gwendolyn Brooks created in "home."

2. What time of day does "home" take place?

3. How does the setting contribute to the mood or atmosphere of "home"?

4. Find two descriptions of the setting of "home" that you feel are especially powerful or vivid. What words does the author use to help you picture the setting?

5. The setting of "home" is perhaps the dominant element in the story. Should setting always be this important? Explain.

READING FOCUS

Recognize Implied Theme What was the implied theme in "home"? What clues in the story helped you to determine this?

DEVELOP YOUR VOCABULARY

You can often figure out the meaning of an unfamiliar word by looking closely at its **context**, that is, the words that surround it. For example, you may be unfamiliar with the meaning of *recluse* in "The old *recluse* lived alone, cut off from the rest of the world." By examining the words surrounding *recluse*, you should be able to guess that it means, "someone who lives alone, away from others."

Use context clues to determine the meaning of the italicized words below. Then, use all the italicized words in original sentences.

1. The *obstinate* teenager refused her parents' repeated requests to clean her room.

2. The grasshopper made short *staccato* hops across the corn field.

3. Her responsibility was *firing* the cold, unlit stove . . .

4. The vocabulary test would begin *presently*; I had about five minutes.

Self-Portrait, Marvin Gray Johnson.
National Museum of American Art

READING FOCUS

Evaluate the Poet's Style A poet's style is how the poet conveys a message. Does the poet use a particular poetry form, such as lyric or free verse? Does the poet use a particular type of speech—formal or informal? The style a poet chooses often greatly affects the meaning of his or her work. As you read these poems, look for a common style that would define the poetry of Langston Hughes.

CONFLICT

In literature, **conflict** is the struggle that occurs between opposite forces in a plot. As you know, there are two types of conflict. The first, **external conflict**, involves a person's struggle against an outside force, such as another person, nature, or even the society in which he or she lives.

Internal conflict, as you may suspect, involves an emotional or psychological struggle within a person's mind. In this type of conflict, an individual is divided by two opposing ideas or feelings.

It may help you to think of conflict as a battle, the fighting of which produces a certain tension. This tension excites our interest. We read further to see who wins a particular struggle and how the tension is released.

As you read the following poems by Langston Hughes, ask yourself:

1. What external and internal conflicts occur in the poems?
2. How, if ever, are these conflicts resolved?

WRITING CONNECTION

Write a short paragraph, or a four-line stanza, about an important conflict in your own life. Describe whether the struggle is external, internal, or both.

DREAM VARIATIONS

by Langston Hughes

To fling my arms wide
In some place of the sun,
To whirl and to dance
Till the white day is done.
5   Then rest at cool evening
Beneath a tall tree
While night comes on gently,
    Dark like me—
That is my dream!

10   To fling my arms wide
In the face of the sun,
Dance! Whirl! Whirl!
Till the quick day is done,
Rest at pale evening . . .
15   A tall, slim tree . . .
Night coming tenderly
    Black like me.

The Dress She Wore Was Blue, John Henry series
by Palmer Hayden. Museum of African American Art,
Palmer C. Hayden Collection

THEME FOR ENGLISH B

by Langston Hughes

The instructor said,

> *Go home and write*
> *a page tonight.*
> *And let that page come out of you—*
> *Then, it will be true.*

5

I wonder if it's that simple?

I am twenty-two, colored, born in Winston-Salem,[1]
I went to school there, then Durham,[2] then here
to this college on the hill above Harlem.[3]

10   I am the only colored student in my class.
The steps from the hill lead down into Harlem,
through a park, then I cross St. Nicholas,
Eighth Avenue, Seventh, and I come to the Y,
the Harlem Branch Y, where I take the elevator

15   up to my room, sit down, and write this page:

It's not easy to know what is true for you or me
at twenty-two, my age. But I guess I'm what
I feel and see and hear, Harlem, I hear you:
hear you, hear me—we two—you, me, talk on this page.

20   (I hear New York, too.) Me—who?
Well, I like to eat, sleep, drink, and be in love.
I like to work, read, learn, and understand life.
I like a pipe for a Christmas present,
or records—Bessie,[4] bop, or Bach.

---

bop (BOP) short for *bebop:* early modern jazz
[1]**Winston Salem:** city in North Carolina
[2]**Durham:** city in North Carolina
[3]**Harlem:** a section of New York City in the northern part of Manhattan
[4]**Bessie Smith:** a famous jazz singer

25   I guess being colored doesn't make me *not* like
      the same things other folks like who are other races.
      So will my page be colored that I write?
      Being me, it will not be white.
      But it will be
30   a part of you, instructor.
      You are white—
      yet a part of me, as I am a part of you.
      That's American.
      Sometimes perhaps you don't want to be a part of me.
35   Nor do I often want to be a part of you.
      But we are, that's true!
      As I learn from you,
      I guess you learn from me—
      although you're older—and white—
40   and somewhat more free.

      This is my page for English B.

from Montage of a Dream Deferred

by Langston Hughes

Dream Boogie

Good morning, daddy![1]
Ain't you heard
The boogie-woogie rumble
Of a dream deferred?

5   Listen closely:
You'll hear their feet
Beating out and beating out a—

> *You think*
> *It's a happy beat?*

10 Listen to it closely:
Ain't you heard
something underneath
like a—

> *What did I say?*

15 Sure,
I'm happy!
Take it away!

> *Hey, pop!*
> *Re-bop!*
20 *Mop!*

> *Y-e-a-h!*

---

montage (mon TAHZH) picture made up of a number of separate pictures
deferred (dih FURD) put off
[1]**daddy:** here slang for "friend" or "brother"

Warning

Daddy,
don't let your dog
curb you!

Tell Me

Why should it be *my* loneliness,
Why should it be *my* song,
Why should it be *my* dream
    deferred
      overlong?

Request

Gimme $25.00
and the change.
I'm going
where the morning
and the evening
won't bother me.

Argument

White is right,
Yellow mellow,
Black, get back!

    Do you believe that, Jack?

5   Sure do!

    Then you're a dope
    for which there ain't no hope.
    Black is fine!
    And, God knows,
10   *It's mine!*

Midsummer Night in Harlem, Palmer Hayden.
Museum of African American Art

Blues at Dawn

I don't dare start thinking in the morning.
I don't dare start thinking in the morning.
    If I thought thoughts in bed,
    Them thoughts would bust my head—
5   So I don't dare start thinking in the morning.

I don't dare remember in the morning
Don't dare remember in the morning.
    If I recall the day before,
    I wouldn't get up no more—
10 So I don't dare remember in the morning.

Harlem

What happens to a dream deferred?

    Does it dry up
    like a raisin in the sun?
    Or fester like a sore—
5   And then run?
    Does it stink like rotten meat?
    Or crust and sugar over—
    like a syrupy sweet?

    Maybe it just sags
10 like a heavy load.

Or does it explode?

Island

Between two rivers,
North of the park,
Like darker rivers
The streets are dark.

5   Black and white,
Gold and brown—
Chocolate-custard
Pie of a town.

Dream within a dream,
10 *Our dream deferred.*

Good morning, daddy!

Ain't you heard?

AUTHOR BIOGRAPHY
Langston Hughes (1902–1967)

Who are you, Langston Hughes? What do you stand for? Let's let the poet himself tell us:

> I play it cool
> And dig all jive.
> That's the reason
> I stay alive.
>
> My motto,
> As I live and learn,
>   is:
> *Dig and Be Dug*
> *In Return.*

The American people have "dug" the poetry of Langston Hughes for over seventy years. His language is direct and uncomplicated. He catches the rhythms of jazz and the soulful sounds of the blues. In his own words, he gives us the "music of a community."

Langston Hughes was born in Joplin, Missouri, in 1902. After high school he traveled, worked at odd jobs, and polished his writing in his spare time. His first book, *The Weary Blues*, came out in 1926. Soon after graduating from Lincoln University, in Pennsylvania in 1929, he settled down in the Harlem section of New York City. In addition to poetry, Hughes wrote stories, novels, plays, articles for magazines and newspapers, and even an autobiography. During his life his name appeared on the covers of about thirty books.

The short poem on the left is entitled "Motto." What do the last two lines mean? How is that meaning related to Langston Hughes's life and career?

Review the Selection

UNDERSTAND THE SELECTION

Recall

1. In "Theme for English B," where does the speaker live?

2. Identify three musical elements in *Montage*.

3. In "Harlem," what is compared to "a raisin in the sun" and "rotten meat"?

Infer

4. What is the "dream deferred"?

5. "Warning," is an example of figurative language. Explain what it means.

6. Why does the poet call his poem a "montage"? Explain.

7. In "Dream Variations," what is the speaker's real hope?

Apply

8. How would you characterize the speaker in "Theme for English B"?

9. What might Hughes have done if he hadn't become a poet?

10. In "Theme for English B," how might the instructor grade the poet's work?

THINK ABOUT CONFLICT

External conflict always involves a struggle between a person and an opposing force, such as another person, nature, or society. **Internal conflict**, however, concerns a struggle within a person's own mind. Conflict is not only an element in a plot, it can also become the theme—the central, or dominating, idea in an author's work.

1. What external or internal conflict does the speaker of "Blues at Dawn" experience?

2. What opposing thoughts or feelings does the speaker of "Theme for English B" reveal?

3. In "Argument," part of the speaker's ordeal involves an external or outside force. What is that force?

4. How is the tension that is expressed throughout "Dream Boogie," finally released?

5. A conflict is resolved when one side wins the "battle." Does "Montage" seem to end with any resolution? What gives you the feeling that the conflict will continue?

Respond to Literature

How are the themes of Hughes's poems consistent with developments in America during the early 20th century?

READING FOCUS

Evaluate the Poet's Style How would you describe Langston Hughes's style? How does his style of writing affect the meaning of the poems?

DEVELOP YOUR VOCABULARY

A **simile** is a direct comparison in which one thing is said to be similar to, or like, something else. The words *like* or *as* are used in a simile. In "He's as skinny as a rail," a person is compared to a rail to show how thin he is.

A **metaphor** is a comparison in which one thing is said to *be* something else. In "A blanket of snow covered our village," snow is compared to a blanket to create a visual picture of the spreading snow.

Read the sentences below and tell which contain a simile and which contain a metaphor. What is being compared?

1. The professional wrestler's body was as solid as a rock.

2. Their escape plan was a shining jewel, perfect in every way.

3. The tears from her eyes fell like tiny raindrops.

4. Pace yourself, for life is a long and winding road.

5. Always courageous, the comic book hero had nerves of steel.

MOOD

Whether reading a letter from a friend or listening to a favorite song, you are constantly responding to feelings suggested by words and phrases.

Works of literature, too, summon emotional responses. The feelings that a poem, play, or short story conveys are called its **mood**. The mood may be peaceful, gloomy, joyous, or mysterious. In other words, mood is the total atmosphere that a writer creates through his or her imaginative use of language.

Mood is suggested through setting, imagery, action, and the words of characters. For example, an autumn afternoon setting may establish an atmosphere of serenity. Conversely, startled deer, fleeing from a thunderstorm, can suggest a mood of uncertainty and fear.

When reading, look at how the descriptive words create a mood.

As you read "Fog," ask yourself:
1. What mood, or feeling, does this poem give you?
2. What sensory details contribute to this mood?

READING FOCUS

Recognize Figurative Language Figurative language is often used to compare things in literature and poetry. The comparison can be a metaphor in which one thing stands for something else. For example, "The star was a beacon." Read "Fog" to discover what metaphor Sandburg uses for fog.

WRITING CONNECTION

Write a four-sentence passage that describes the room in which you are sitting. Using sensory details, suggest the mood of the room.

FOG

by Carl Sandburg

The fog comes
on little cat feet.

It sits looking
over harbor and city
on silent haunches
and then moves on.

Savannah Nocturne, Eliot Clark. Telfair Museum of Art

Review the Selection

UNDERSTAND THE SELECTION

Recall

1. What is the poem's subject?

2. To what object does the poet compare this subject?

3. What is the setting of the poem?

Infer

4. To which sense does the poem most appeal?

5. Is the fog an invited guest?

6. What do you know about the sound of fog from this poem?

7. What do the phrases "comes on" and "moves on" suggest about the fog's visits?

Apply

8. The poet compares the fog to just one thing throughout the poem. Is this effective? Explain.

9. To what other animal might you compare fog? Explain.

10. Why do you think Sandburg chose to write a *poem* about fog, instead of a short story or nonfiction article?

Respond to Literature

Compare "Fog" to other poems you have read in this unit. What elements does it have in common with them? What elements differ?

THINK ABOUT MOOD

Mood is the feeling that a work of literature expresses to the reader. Mood is created through the author's choice of sensory words, setting details, actions, and words that characters speak. It also results from an author's use of such techniques as meter, rhyme (or no rhyme), alliteration, repetition, imagery, and symbolism. In short, mood is created by combinations and variations in the poetic and literary devices available to the writer.

1. Describe the mood of "Fog."

2. What descriptive words or phrases does the poet use to create this feeling?

3. What other words might you use to add to this particular mood?

4. The poet purposely selects certain traits of a cat and leaves out others. How would the mood of the poem change if the poet had compared the fog to a kitten? Would the poem be as successful?

5. The poet uses alliteration in the poem. What two sounds does he particularly repeat?

READING FOCUS

Recognize Figurative Language What metaphor is used for fog in this poem? Why do you think the poet uses this metaphor?

DEVELOP YOUR VOCABULARY

The **denotation** of a word is its usual meaning, or "dictionary definition." The **connotation** of a word is the feeling or thought that the word suggests. For instance, *beckon*, *invite*, and *summon* have similar denotations, or definitions, but their connotations are different. The word *beckon*, is somehow more mysterious or tantalizing than the more conventional word *invite*.

For each sentence below, choose the word with the more vivid connotation and explain your reasoning.

1. The stallion (*jumped*, *bounded*) over the wooden fence in one easy motion.

2. The (*musty*, *stale*) odor of the attic reminded me of a damp shoe.

3. A few crumbling bricks were all that was left of the (*old*, *ancient*) Greek temple.

4. Which soldier dared to follow the enemy down the dark (*cavity*, *hole*)?

5. This particular robbery case (*confused*, *baffled*) the detective.

6. The (*hungry*, *famished*) hikers frantically searched for something to eat.

Learn About

SYMBOLISM

A **symbol** is something that stands for, or represents, something else. In literature, a symbol is a person, place, object, or event that represents a particular idea or concept. For example, the Statue of Liberty is more than just a large object that stands in New York City's harbor. For people all over the world, the Statue of Liberty represents (or symbolizes) the freedom and justice that is found in the United States.

Writers use symbols to convey a deeper meaning than could be expressed by the **literal**, or exact meaning, of the words. If, for instance, the Statue of Liberty were mentioned several times in a poem about immigrants journeying to the United States, you might conclude that the poem was about freedom and justice.

As you read the following poems by Robert Frost, ask yourself:
1. What symbols does the poet use in his poems?
2. What ideas or concepts do these symbols represent?

Reading Focus

Make Inferences Making inferences means making logical guesses about information not stated directly in a story or poem. You can do this by paying attention to clues the author provides, or by applying your own knowledge and experiences. You can make inferences to connect ideas, to figure out a mystery, or to predict what might happen next. As you read these poems, make inferences about the situations presented.

WRITING CONNECTION

Many sports teams use animals or objects in their names. Think of the Chicago Bears and the Oakland Raiders. What is the name of your school's sports team? Explain briefly the idea symbolized by that name.

The Pasture

by Robert Frost

I'm going out to clean the pasture spring;
I'll only stop to rake the leaves away
(And wait to watch the water clear, I may):
I shan't be gone long.—You come too.

I'm going out to fetch the little calf
That's standing by the mother. It's so young
It totters when she licks it with her tongue.
I shan't be gone long.—You come too.

Evening Glow, The Old Red Cow, Albert Pinkham Ryder.
The Brooklyn Museum

---

fetch (FECH) get and bring back

The Road Not Taken

by Robert Frost

Two roads diverged in a yellow wood,
And sorry I could not travel both
And be one traveler, long I stood
And looked down one as far as I could
5   To where it bent in the undergrowth;

Then took the other, as just as fair,
And having perhaps the better claim,
Because it was grassy and wanted wear;
Though as for that, the passing there
10   Had worn them really about the same,

And both that morning equally lay
In leaves no step had trodden black.
Oh, I kept the first for another day!
Yet knowing how way leads on to way,
15   I doubted if I should ever come back.

I shall be telling this with a sigh
Somewhere ages and ages hence:
Two roads diverged in a wood, and I—
I took the one less traveled by,
20   And that has made all the difference.

---

diverge (dih VURJ) spread apart

Landscape, Ernest Lawson. The Brooklyn Museum

Woodland Repose, John F. Carlson. Toledo Museum of Art

Stopping by Woods on a Snowy Evening

by Robert Frost

Whose woods these are I think I know. a
His house is in the village though; a
He will not see me stopping here b
To watch his woods fill up with snow. a

5   My little horse must think it queer b
To stop without a farmhouse near b
Between the woods and frozen lake c
The darkest evening of the year. b

He gives his harness bells a shake c
10 To ask if there is some mistake. c
The only other sound's the sweep d
Of easy wind and downy flake. c

The woods are lovely, dark and deep. d
But I have promises to keep, e
15 And miles to go before I sleep, e
And miles to go before I sleep. e

Robert Frost (1874–1963)

One day in 1909 the State Superintendent of Schools in New Hampshire dropped into a small high school. His inspection included an English classroom—and a happy surprise. "A class of boys and girls were listening open-mouthed to the teacher," he wrote later. "Slumped down behind a desk at the front of the room was a young man who was talking to the students as he might talk to a group of friends around his own fireside." The inspector had discovered "the best teacher in New Hampshire."

Inspector Charles Silver couldn't have known, of course, that he had also discovered a talented young poet named Robert Frost. His visit was to mark a turning point in Frost's life. Up to that time, Frost had thought of himself as a failure. He had failed at college, dropping out after two years. He had failed as a chicken farmer. And most important to him, he had failed to get many of his poems printed.

Then the turning point arrived. With Silver's help, Frost found a job teaching in a New Hampshire school. He still wanted to write, however, and in 1912, he sold his farm and moved his family to England, an attempt to "get away from it all." In 1913, his first book of poems was accepted by a London publisher. At the age of 39, Frost was finally on his way. He decided to return to the United States after the beginning of World War I.

Before long, Robert Frost was able to live the life he wanted. He bought a small farm in New Hampshire. He taught and traveled a little. He published book after book and collected prize after prize. His hair slowly turned gray with age, and white with wisdom. "America's beloved poet" lived to be nearly 90.

Frost is often called a "nature poet," but he never liked the term. "I guess I'm just not a nature poet," he once said. "I have only written two poems without a human being in them." He might have added that his real subject was *human* nature.

Review the Selection

UNDERSTAND THE SELECTION

Recall

1. In "The Pasture" what two actions does the speaker plan to accomplish?

2. Where does "The Road Not Taken" take place?

3. What happens in "Stopping by Woods on a Snowy Evening"?

Infer

4. In which season does "The Road Not Taken" take place?

5. Why do you think the speaker in "The Road Not Taken" chooses the road that he or she does?

6. Do you think the horse in "Stopping by Woods on a Snowy Evening" shares the speaker's thoughts?

7. What does the speaker of "Stopping by Woods" feel?

Apply

8. Why might Frost have often begun his poetry readings with "The Pasture"?

9. Would the speaker of "The Road Not Taken" now choose the other road?

10. Where do you think the speaker in "Stopping by Woods" is going?

Respond to Literature

How does the poet's use of nature reflect one aspect of modern poetry?

THINK ABOUT SYMBOLISM

Writers use symbols to deepen and enrich the meaning of a work of literature. Symbols may or may not be simple, however. The image behind the symbol may consist of many ideas and attitudes. You might find it helpful to think of a **symbol** as something visible used to represent something invisible, such as an idea, concept, or hidden truth.

1. What symbols does the poet use in "The Road Not Taken"?

2. What do you think the two roads in "The Road Not Taken" represent? Explain your thinking.

3. In "Stopping by Woods on a Snowy Evening," what is the literal meaning of the word *miles*?

4. What idea or concept is conveyed by the poet's use of the word *miles*?

5. In the work of Robert Frost and many other poets water is a symbol of truth. Explain how this symbol contributes to your understanding of "The Pasture."

READING FOCUS

Make Inferences What inferences did you make about the farm and the two woods described in these poems? What personal experiences did you draw from to make these inferences?

DEVELOP YOUR VOCABULARY

The development of the English language falls into three historical periods. The oldest, the Old English (or Anglo-Saxon) period, began around A.D. 440, when northern European tribes invaded the British Isles. The blending of their languages produced what we now call Old English.

Over the centuries, Old English gave way to Middle English and then to Modern English. Many changes occurred. In addition, English acquired hundreds of thousands of words from other languages.

Robert Frost's poetic vocabulary is made up almost exclusively of words that trace back to Old English. Look up the following words in a dictionary that has word histories. Which words do not come from Old English. From what languages do they come?

1. rake
2. watch
3. tongue
4. pasture
5. yellow
6. both
7. morning
8. black
9. doubt
10. sigh
11. hence
12. house
13. stop
14. snow
15. farm
16. wind

Learn About

Summer at Campobello, New Brunswick, detail, Edward W. D. Hamilton. Museum of Fine Arts, Boston

READING FOCUS

Interpret Dialogue Dialogue is the words that characters speak in a story. As in real life, what the characters say may not be what they really feel or believe. You must use the context and tone of their words to interpret their real meanings. As you read this story, think about what the ladies mean when they speak, rather than concentrating on the actual words they say.

CHARACTER

You know from previous selections that writers create characters through description, dialogue, action, and the comments made about them by other characters in the story.

In literature, a character can be either flat or round. A **flat character** shows you only one side of his or her personality and is therefore not very true to life. A flat character usually represents a single idea or attitude. Many fairy tale characters are flat since they have only one of their personality traits exposed. An example would be a wicked stepmother.

A **round character** is someone you come to know from the inside out. A round character has many sides and is much more complex and lifelike. He or she is capable of responding to certain problems and situations in ways that may surprise you.

As you read "Lily Daw and the Three Ladies," ask yourself:
1. Which characters are uncomplicated, or flat?
2. Which characters do or say things that surprise you?

WRITING CONNECTION

Write a description of your favorite person. Include those specific qualities that make him or her a special, unique human being.

LILY DAW AND THE THREE LADIES

by Eudora Welty

Mrs. Watts and Mrs. Carson were both in the post office in Victory when the letter came from the Ellisville Institute for the Feeble Minded of Mississippi. Aimee Slocum, with her hand still full of mail, ran out in front and handed it straight to Mrs. Watts, and they all three read it together. Mrs. Watts held it taut between her pink hands, and Mrs. Carson underscored each line slowly with her thimbled finger. Everybody else in the post office wondered what was up now.

"What will Lily say," beamed Mrs. Carson at last, "when we tell her we're sending her to Ellisville!"

"She'll be tickled to death," said Mrs. Watts, and added in a guttural voice to a deaf lady, "Lily Daw's getting in at Ellisville!"

"Don't you all dare go off and tell Lily without me!" called Aimee Slocum, trotting back to finish putting up the mail.

"Do you suppose they'll look after her down there?" Mrs. Carson began to carry on a conversation with a group of Baptist ladies waiting in the post office. She was the Baptist preacher's wife.

"I've always heard it was lovely down there, but crowded," said one.

"Lily lets people walk over her so," said another.

"Last night at the tent show—" said another, and then popped her hand over her mouth.

"Don't mind me, I know there are such things in the world," said Mrs. Carson, looking down and fingering the tape measure which hung over her bosom.

"Oh, Mrs. Carson. Well, anyway, last night at the tent show, why, the man was just before making Lily buy a ticket to get in."

"A ticket!"

"Till my husband went up and explained she wasn't bright, and so did everybody else."

The ladies all clucked their tongues.

"Oh, it was a very nice show," said the

---

feeble minded (FEE buhl MIN dihd) an out-of-date expression for a person with a weak or slow mind
taut (TAWT) stretched tightly
underscored (UN dur skawrd) underlined
thimbled (THIM buld) wearing a small, protective cap used in sewing
gutteral (GUT ur ul) harsh or growling sound

Lily Daw and the Three Ladies ■ 367

Summer at Campobello, New Brunswick, Edward W. D. Hamilton. Museum of Fine Arts, Boston

lady who had gone. "And Lily acted so nice. She was a perfect lady—just set in her seat and stared."

"Oh, she can be a lady—she can be," said Mrs. Carson, shaking her head and turning her eyes up. "That's just what breaks your heart."

"Yes'm, she kept her eyes on—what's that thing makes all the commotion? The xylophone," said the lady. "Didn't turn her head to the right or to the left the whole time. Set in front of me."

"The point is, what did she do after the show?" asked Mrs. Watts practically. "Lily has gotten so she is very mature for her age."

"Oh, Etta!" protested Mrs. Carson, looking at her wildly for a moment.

"And that's how come we are sending her to Ellisville," finished Mrs. Watts.

"I'm ready, you all," said Aimee Slocum, running out with white powder all over her face. "Mail's up. I don't know how good it's up."

"Well, of course, I do hope it's for the best," said several of the other ladies. They did not go at once to take their mail out of their boxes; they felt a little left out.

The three women stood at the foot of the water tank.

"To find Lily is a different thing," said Aimee Slocum.

"Where in the wide world do you suppose she'd be?" It was Mrs. Watts who was carrying the letter.

"I don't see a sign of her either on this side of the street or on the other side," Mrs. Carson declared as they walked along.

Ed Newton was stringing Redbird school tablets on the wire across the store.

"If you're after Lily, she come in here while ago and tole me she was fixin' to git married," he said.

"Ed Newton!" cried the ladies all together, clutching one another. Mrs. Watts began to fan herself at once with the letter from Ellisville. She wore widow's black, and the least thing made her hot.

"Why she is not. She's going to Ellisville, Ed," said Mrs. Carson gently. "Mrs. Watts and I and Aimee Slocum are paying her way out of our own pockets. Besides, the boys of Victory are on their honor. Lily's not going to get married, that's just an idea she's got in her head."

"More power to you, ladies," said Ed Newton, spanking himself with a tablet.

---

commotion (kuh MOH shun) noisy confusion

When they came to the bridge over the railroad tracks, there was Estelle Mabers, sitting on a rail. She was slowly drinking an orange Ne-Hi.

"Have you seen Lily?" they asked her.

"I'm supposed to be out here watching for her now," said the Mabers girl, as though she weren't there yet. "But for Jewel—Jewel says Lily come in the store while ago and picked out a two-ninety-eight hat and wore it off. Jewel wants to swap her something else for it."

"Oh, Estelle, Lily says she's going to get married!" cried Aimee Slocum.

"Well I declare," said Estelle; she never understood anything.

Loralee Adkins came riding by in her Willys-Knight,[1] tooting the horn to find out what they were talking about.

Aimee threw up her hands and ran out into the street. "Loralee, Loralee, you got to ride us up to Lily Daw's. She's up yonder fixing to get married!"

"Hop in, my land!"

"Well, that just goes to show you right now," said Mrs. Watts, groaning as she was helped into the back seat. "What we've got to do is persuade Lily it will be nicer to go to Ellisville."

"Just to think!"

While they rode around the corner Mrs. Carson was going on in her sad voice, sad as the soft noises in the henhouse at twilight. "We buried Lily's poor defenseless mother. We gave Lily all her food and kindling and every stitch she had on. Sent her to Sunday school to learn the Lord's teachings, had her baptized a Baptist. And when her old father commenced beating her and tried to cut her head off with the butcher knife, why, we went and took her away from him and gave her a place to stay."

The paintless frame house with all the weather vanes was three stories high in places and had yellow and violet stained-glass windows in front and gingerbread around the porch. It leaned steeply to one side, toward the railroad, and the front steps were gone. The car full of ladies drew up under the cedar tree.

"Now Lily's almost grown up," Mrs. Carson continued. "In fact, she's grown," she concluded, getting out.

"Talking about getting married," said Mrs. Watts disgustedly. "Thanks, Loralee, you run on home."

They climbed over the dusty zinnias onto the porch and walked through the open door without knocking.

"There certainly is always a funny smell in this house. I say it every time I come," said Aimee Slocum.

Lily was there, in the dark of the hall, kneeling on the floor by a small open trunk.

When she saw them she put a zinnia in her mouth, and held still.

"Hello, Lily," said Mrs. Carson reproachfully.

"Hello," said Lily. In a minute she gave a suck on the zinnia stem that sounded

---

kindling (KIND ling) small pieces of dry firewood
stitch (STICH) slang for clothing
reproachfully (rih PROHCH fuh lee) scolding; blaming
[1]**Willys-Knight:** type of car made in this period

exactly like a jay bird. There she sat, wearing a petticoat for a dress, one of the things Mrs. Carson kept after her about. Her milky-yellow hair streamed freely down from under a new hat. You could see the wavy scar on her throat if you knew it was there.

Mrs. Carson and Mrs. Watts, the two fattest, sat in the double rocker. Aimee Slocum sat on the wire chair donated from the drugstore that burned.

"Well, what are you doing, Lily?" asked Mrs. Watts, who led the rocking.

Lily smiled.

The trunk was old and lined with yellow and brown paper, with an asterisk pattern showing in darker circles and rings. Mutely the ladies indicated to each other that they did not know where in the world it had come from. It was empty except for two bars of soap and a green washcloth, which Lily was now trying to arrange in the bottom.

"Go on and tell us what you're doing, Lily," said Aimee Slocum.

"Packing, silly," said Lily.

"Where are you going?"

"Going to get married, and I bet you wish you was me now," said Lily. But shyness overcame her suddenly, and she popped the zinnia back into her mouth.

"Talk to me, dear," said Mrs. Carson. "Tell old Mrs. Carson why you want to get married."

"No," said Lily, after a moment's hesitation.

"Well, we've thought of something that will be so much nicer," said Mrs. Carson. "Why don't you go to Ellisville!"

"Won't that be lovely?" said Mrs. Watts. "Goodness, yes."

"It's a lovely place," said Aimee Slocum uncertainly.

"You've got bumps on your face," said Lily.

"Aimee, dear, you stay out of this, if you don't mind," said Mrs. Carson anxiously. "I don't know what it is comes over Lily when you come around her."

Lily stared at Aimee Slocum meditatively.

"There! Wouldn't you like to go to Ellisville now?" asked Mrs. Carson.

"No'm," said Lily.

"Why not?" All the ladies leaned down toward her in impressive astonishment.

"'Cause I'm goin' to get married," said Lily.

"Well, and who are you going to marry, dear?" asked Mrs. Watts. She knew how to pin people down and make them deny what they'd already said.

Lily bit her lip and began to smile. She reached into the trunk and held up both cakes of soap and wagged them.

"Tell us," challenged Mrs. Watts. "Who you're going to marry, now."

"A man last night."

There was a gasp from each lady. The possible reality of a lover descended suddenly like a summer hail over their heads. Mrs. Watts stood up and balanced herself.

---

petticoat (PET ee koht) type of woman's underskirt
asterisk (AS tur isk) star-shaped sign or symbol
mutely (MYOOT lee) silently
meditatively (MED uh tayt iv lee) thinking quietly

"One of those show fellows! A musician!" she cried.

Lily looked up in admiration.

"Did he—did he do anything to you?" In the long run, it was still only Mrs. Watts who could take charge.

"Oh, yes'm," said Lily. She patted the cakes of soap fastidiously with the tips of her small fingers and tucked them in with the washcloth.

"What?" demanded Aimee Slocum, rising up and tottering before her scream. "What?" she called out in the hall.

"Don't ask her what," said Mrs. Carson, coming up behind. "Tell me, Lily—just yes or no—are you the same as you were?"

"He had a red coat," said Lily graciously. "He took little sticks and went *ping-pong! ding-gong!*"

"Oh, I think I'm going to faint," said Aimee Slocum, but they said, "No, you're not."

"The xylophone!" cried Mrs. Watts. "The xylophone player! Why, the coward, he ought to be run out of town on a rail!"

"Out of town? He is out of town, by now," cried Aimee. "Can't you read—the sign in the cafe—Victory on the ninth, Como on the tenth? He's in Como. Como!"

"All right! We'll bring him back!" cried Mrs. Watts. "He can't get away from me!"

"Hush," said Mrs. Carson. "I don't think it's any use following that line of reasoning at all. It's better in the long run

for him to be gone out of our lives for good and all. That kind of a man. He was after Lily's body alone and he wouldn't ever in this world make the poor little thing happy, even if we went out and forced him to marry her like he ought—at the point of a gun."

"Still—" began Aimee, her eyes widening.

"Shut up," said Mrs. Watts. "Mrs. Carson, you're right, I expect."

"This is my hope chest[2]—see?" said Lily politely in the pause that followed. "You haven't even looked at it. I've already got soap and a washrag. And I have my hat—on. What are you all going to give me?"

"Lily," said Mrs. Watts, starting over, "we'll give you lots of gorgeous things if you'll only go to Ellisville instead of getting married."

"What will you give me?" asked Lily.

"I'll give you a pair of hemstitched pillowcases," said Mrs. Carson.

"I'll give you a big caramel cake," said Mrs. Watts.

"I'll give you a souvenir from Jackson—a little toy bank," said Aimee Slocum. "Now will you go?"

"No," said Lily.

"I'll give you a pretty little Bible with your name on it in real gold," said Mrs. Carson.

"What if I was to give you a pink crape de chine brassiere with adjustable shoulder straps?" asked Mrs. Watts grimly.

"Oh, Etta."

---

fastidiously (fa STID ee us lee) very sensitive; dainty
[2]**hope chest:** box in which a woman collects linen and clothing before being married

"Well, she needs it," said Mrs. Watts. "What would they think if she ran all over Ellisville in a petticoat looking like a Fiji?"

"I wish *I* could go to Ellisville," said Aimee Slocum luringly.

"What will they have for me down there?" asked Lily softly.

"Oh! lots of things. You'll have baskets to weave, I expect. . . ." Mrs. Carson looked vaguely at the others.

"Oh, yes indeed, they will let you make all sorts of baskets," said Mrs. Watts; then her voice too trailed off.

"No'm, I'd rather get married," said Lily.

"Lily Daw! Now that's just plain stubbornness!" cried Mrs. Watts. "You almost said you'd go and then you took it back!"

"We've all asked God, Lily," said Mrs. Carson finally, "and God seemed to tell us—Mr. Carson, too—that the place where you ought to be, so as to be happy, was Ellisville."

Lily looked reverent, but still stubborn.

"We've really just got to get her there—now!" screamed Aimee Slocum all at once. "Suppose—! She can't stay here!"

"Oh no, no, no," said Mrs. Carson hurriedly. "We mustn't think that."

They sat sunken in despair.

"Could I take my hope chest—to go to Ellisville?" asked Lily shyly, looking at them sidewise.

"Why, yes," said Mrs. Carson blankly.

Silently they rose once more to their feet.

"Oh, if I could just take my hope chest!"

"All the time it was just her hope chest," Aimee whispered.

Mrs. Watts struck her palms together. "It's settled!"

"Praise the fathers," murmured Mrs. Carson.

Lily looked up at them, and her eyes gleamed. She cocked her head and spoke out in a proud imitation of someone—someone utterly unknown.

"O.K.—Toots!"

The ladies had been nodding and smiling and backing away toward the door.

"I think I'd better stay," said Mrs. Carson, stopping in her tracks. "Where—where could she have learned that terrible expression?"

"Pack up," said Mrs. Watts. "Lily Daw is leaving for Ellisville on Number One."

In the station the train was puffing. Nearly everyone in Victory was hanging around waiting for it to leave. The Victory Civic Band had assembled without any orders and was scattered through the crowd. Ed Newton gave false signals to start on his bass horn. A crate full of baby chickens got loose on the platform. Everybody wanted to see Lily all dressed up, but Mrs. Carson and Mrs. Watts had sneaked her into the train from the other side of the tracks.

The two ladies were going to travel as far as Jackson to help Lily change trains and be sure she went in the right direction.

Lily sat between them on the plush

---

luringly (LUUR ing lee) to tempt or attract

Lady in a Black Hat, J. Alden Weir. The Brooklyn Museum

seat with her hair combed and pinned up into a knot under a small blue hat which was Jewel's exchange for the pretty one. She wore a traveling dress made out of part of Mrs. Watts's last summer's mourning. Pink straps glowed through. She had a purse and a Bible and a warm cake in a box, all in her lap.

Aimee Slocum had been getting the outgoing mail stamped and bundled. She stood in the aisle of the coach now, tears shaking from her eyes.

"Good-by, Lily," she said. She was the one who felt things.

"Good-by, silly," said Lily.

"Oh, dear, I hope they get our telegram to meet her in Ellisville!" Aimee cried sorrowfully, as she thought how far away it was. "And it was so hard to get it all in ten words, too."

"Get off, Aimee, before the train starts and you break your neck," said Mrs. Watts, all settled and waving her dressy fan gaily. "I declare, it's so hot, as soon as we get a few miles out of town I'm going to slip my corset down."

"Oh, Lily, don't cry down there. Just be good, and do what they tell you—it's all because they love you." Aimee drew her mouth down. She was backing away, down the aisle.

Lily laughed. She pointed across Mrs. Carson's bosom out the window toward a man. He had stepped off the train and just stood there, by himself. He was a stranger and wore a cap.

"Look," she said, laughing softly through her fingers.

"Don't—look," said Mrs. Carson very distinctly, as if, out of all she had ever spoken, she would impress these two solemn words upon Lily's soft little brain. She added, "Don't look at anything till you get to Ellisville."

Outside, Aimee Slocum was crying so hard she almost ran into the stranger. He wore a cap and was short and seemed to have on perfume, if such a thing could be.

"Could you tell me, madam," he said, "where a little lady lives in this burg[3] name of Miss Lily Daw?" He lifted his cap—and he had red hair.

"What do you want to know for?" Aimee asked before she knew it.

"Talk louder," said the stranger. He almost whispered, himself.

---

[3]**burg:** slang for small town

"She's gone away—she's gone to Ellisville!"

"Gone?"

"Gone to Ellisville!"

"Well, I like that!" The man stuck out his bottom lip and puffed till his hair jumped.

"What business did you have with Lily?" cried Aimee suddenly.

"We was only going to get married, that's all," said the man.

Aimee Slocum started to scream in front of all those people. She almost pointed to the long black box she saw lying on the ground at the man's feet. Then she jumped back in fright.

"The xylophone! The xylophone!" she cried, looking back and forth from the man to the hissing train. Which was more terrible? The bell began to ring hollowly, and the man was talking.

"Did you say Ellisville? That in the state of Mississippi?" Like lightning he had pulled out a red notebook entitled, "Permanent Facts & Data." He wrote down something. "I don't hear well."

Aimee nodded her head up and down, and circled around him.

Under "Ellis-Ville Miss" he was drawing a line; now he was flicking it with two little marks. "Maybe she didn't say she would. Maybe she said she wouldn't." He suddenly laughed very loudly, after the way he had whispered. Aimee jumped back. "Women!—Well, if we play anywheres near Ellisville, Miss., in the future I may look her up and I may not," he said.

The bass horn sounded the true signal for the band to begin. White steam rushed out of the engine. Usually the train stopped for only a minute in Victory, but the engineer knew Lily from waving at her, and he knew this was her big day.

"Wait!" Aimee Slocum did scream. "Wait, mister! I can get her for you. Wait, Mister Engineer! Don't go!"

Then there she was back on the train, screaming in Mrs. Carson's and Mrs. Watts's faces.

"The xylophone player! The xylophone player to marry her! Yonder he is!"

"Nonsense," murmured Mrs. Watts, peering over the others to look where Aimee pointed. "If he's there I don't see him. Where is he? You're looking at One-Eye Beasley."

"The little man with the cap—no, with the red hair! Hurry!"

"Is that really him?" Mrs. Carson asked Mrs. Watts in wonder. "Mercy! He's small, isn't he?"

"Never saw him before in my life!" cried Mrs. Watts. But suddenly she shut up her fan.

"Come on! This is a train we're on!" cried Aimee Slocum. Her nerves were all unstrung.

"All right, don't have a conniption fit, girl," said Mrs. Watts. "Come on," she said thickly to Mrs. Carson.

"Where are we going now?" asked Lily as they struggled down the aisle.

"We're taking you to get married," said Mrs. Watts. "Mrs. Carson, you'd better phone up your husband right there in the station."

"But I don't want to git married," said Lily, beginning to whimper. "I'm going to Ellisville."

"Hush, and we'll all have some ice-cream cones later," whispered Mrs. Carson.

The Coming Train, Edward Lamson Henry. Toledo Museum of Art

Just as they climbed down the steps at the back end of the train, the band went into "Independence March."

The xylophone player was still there, patting his foot. He came up and said, "Hello, Toots. What's up—tricks?" and kissed Lily with a smack, after which she hung her head.

"So you're the young man we've heard so much about," said Mrs. Watts. Her smile was brilliant. "Here's your little Lily."

"What say?" asked the xylophone player.

"My husband happens to be the Baptist preacher of Victory," said Mrs. Carson in a loud, clear voice. "Isn't that lucky? I can get him here in five minutes: I know exactly where he is."

They were in a circle around the xylophone player, all going into the white waiting room.

"Oh, I feel just like crying, at a time like this," said Aimee Slocum. She looked back and saw the train moving slowly away, going under the bridge at Main Street. Then it disappeared around the curve.

"Oh, the hope chest!" Aimee cried in a stricken voice.

"And whom have we the pleasure of addressing?" Mrs. Watts was shouting, while Mrs. Carson was ringing up the telephone.

The band went on playing. Some of the people thought Lily was on the train, and some swore she wasn't. Everybody cheered, though, and a straw hat was thrown into the telephone wires.

Review the Selection

UNDERSTAND THE SELECTION

Recall

1. Where does the story take place?

2. How have the three ladies helped Lily Daw in the past?

3. Where do they want to send her?

Infer

4. Who, among the three ladies, is employed? What is her job?

5. Who is the leader? Explain.

6. Would Lily have been happy at Ellisville? Explain.

7. Why are the three ladies so anxious to get Lily Daw on the first train?

Apply

8. Select a passage that shows Lily is not as "feeble-minded" as the ladies want to believe.

9. Were the three ladies acting in Lily's best interest when they decided not to send her to Ellisville?

10. If you were the xylophone player, would you be surprised by the end of the story?

Respond to Literature

Discuss which changes in U.S. society during the 1920s and 1930s gave Eudora Welty the opportunity to explore women's characters.

THINK ABOUT CHARACTER

Although flat characters are usually less complex and lifelike than round characters, they still serve an important purpose. Often, writers create a variety of simple, or flat, characters to give you a vivid impression about the different kinds of people who live in a particular place.

1. What kind of characters are Ed Newton, Estelle Mabers, and Loralee Adkins? How do you know?

2. Briefly characterize Aimee Slocum.

3. What does their last-minute decision to make Lily marry the xylophone player reveal about the three ladies?

4. Describe what the author thinks about Mrs. Carson in the sentence, "Mrs. Carson was going on in her sad voice, sad as the soft noises in the henhouse at twilight."

5. What does Lily Daw do or say in the story that surprises you?

READING FOCUS

Interpret Dialogue In the story, whose dialogue was the easiest to interpret? Why do you think this is so?

DEVELOP YOUR VOCABULARY

Adjectives are words that modify nouns and pronouns. For instance, *talented* writer, *several* typewriters, *plastic* cup. **Adverbs** are words that modify adjectives, verbs, and other adverbs. For instance, spoke *loudly*, *reasonably* correct, ran *quickly*.

You can often form adverbs from adjectives by adding the suffix *-ly* to the adjective. For instance, "The children's problem was most *unfortunate*." "*Unfortunately*, the children's problem was never solved."

Copy the adjectives below on a separate sheet of paper and write an original sentence for each. Then add *-ly* to each adjective and write a sentence that shows your understanding of the newly formed adverb.

1. mute
2. fastidious
3. anxious
4. eager

5. hesitant
6. dangerous
7. serious
8. bright

Learn About

Humor

In literature, humor is any writing that produces an amused response. As you explore humor, you will develop the ability to distinguish between the different techniques that writers use to make you laugh.

Much of what we find funny, or humorous, comes from the comic reactions of characters to a particular problem or situation. When a character makes sharp, clever remarks about a situation, we may laugh at his wit. When someone behaves in a way that is entirely unexpected, or "out of character," we often find that person's actions amusing.

Humor often comes from the difference between what you think will happen in a situation, and what actually occurs. An example of this **irony of situation** is when a tragic or seemingly dangerous event turns out to be quite funny.

As you read *The Still Alarm*, ask yourself:

1. Which dialogue or actions in the play are humorous?
2. What makes them humorous?

Think about the last time you laughed, and write a brief paragraph that explains what made you think the statement, action, or event to which you reacted was funny.

READING FOCUS

Understand Cause and Effect In many works of literature an author first creates an event—the cause. Then the author shows a logical effect to demonstrate that the events are related. However, sometimes the effect is unexpected, and that makes the story or play funny. Look for unexpected effects as you read *The Still Alarm*. Think about how these unexpected events add humor to the play.

THE STILL ALARM

by George S. Kaufman

(Vital Note: It is important that the entire play be acted calmly and politely, in the manner of an English drawing-room[1] comedy. No actor ever raises his voice; every line must be read as though it were an invitation to a cup of tea. If this direction is disregarded, the play has no point at all.)

The scene is a hotel bedroom. Two windows are in the rear wall with a bed between them. A telephone stand is at one end of the bed and a dresser is near the other. In the right wall is a door leading to the hall with a chair nearby. In the left wall is a door to another room; near it is a small table and two chairs. ED *and* BOB *are on the stage.* ED *is getting into his overcoat as the curtain rises. Both are at the hall door.*

ED: Well, Bob, it's certainly been nice to see you again.

BOB: It was nice to see *you.*

ED: You come to town so seldom, I hardly ever get the chance to—

BOB: Well, you know how it is. A business trip is always more or less of a bore.

ED: Next time you've got to come out to the house.

BOB: I want to come out. I just had to stick around the hotel this trip.

ED: Oh, I understand. Well, give my best to Edith.

BOB (*remembering something*): Oh, I say, Ed. Wait a minute.

ED: What's the matter?

BOB: I knew I wanted to show you something. (*Crosses to table. Gets roll of blueprints from drawer.*) Did you know I'm going to build?

---

[1]**drawing room:** formal living room or parlor. A "drawing room comedy" is a humorous play acted out in a dignified, serious manner.

ED (*follows to table*): A house?

BOB: You bet it's a house! (*Knock on hall door.*) Come in! (*Spreads plans.*) I just got these yesterday.

ED (*sits*): Well, that's fine! (*The knock is repeated—louder. Both men now give full attention to the door.*)

BOB: Come! Come in!

BELLBOY (*enters*): Mr. Barclay?

BOB: Well?

BELLBOY: I've a message from the clerk, sir. For Mr. Barclay personally.

BOB (*crosses to* BOY): I'm Mr. Barclay. What is the message?

BELLBOY: The hotel is on fire, sir.

BOB: What's that?

BELLBOY: The hotel is on fire.

ED: This hotel?

BELLBOY: Yes, sir.

BOB: Well—is it bad?

BELLBOY: It looks pretty bad, sir.

ED: You mean it's going to burn down?

BELLBOY: We think so—yes, sir.

BOB (*a low whistle of surprise*): Well! We'd better leave.

BELLBOY: Yes, sir.

BOB: Going to burn down, huh?

BELLBOY: Yes, sir. If you'll step to the window you'll see. (BOB *goes to a window.*)

BOB: Yes, that is pretty bad. H'm (*to* ED). I say, you really ought to see this—

ED (*crosses to window, peers out*): It's reached the floor right underneath.

BELLBOY: Yes, sir. The lower part of the hotel is about gone, sir.

BOB (*still looking out—looks up*): Still all right up above, though. (*Turns to* BOY.) Have they notified the Fire Department?

BELLBOY: I wouldn't know, sir. I'm only the bellboy.

BOB: Well, that's the thing to do, obviously—(*Nods head to each one as if the previous line was a bright idea.*)—notify the Fire Department. Just call them up, give them the name of the hotel—

ED: Wait a minute. I can do better than that for you. (*To the* BOY.) Ring through to the Chief, and tell him that Ed Jamison told you to telephone him. (*To* BOB.) We went to school together, you know.

BOB: That's fine. (*To the* BOY) Now, get that right. Tell the Chief that Mr. Jamison said to ring him.

ED: *Ed* Jamison.

BOB: Yes, *Ed* Jamison.

BELLBOY: Yes, sir. (*Turns to go.*)

BOB: Oh! Boy! (*Pulls out handful of change; picks out a coin.*) Here you are.

BELLBOY: Thank you, sir. (*Exit* BELLBOY.)

(ED *sits at table, lights cigarette, and throws match on floor, then steps on it. There is a moment's pause.*)

BOB: Well! (*Crosses and looks out window.*) Say, we'll have to get out of here pretty soon.

ED (*going to window*): How is it—no better?

BOB: Worse, if anything. It'll be up here in a few moments.

ED: What floor *is* this?

BOB: Eleventh.

ED: Eleven. We couldn't jump, then.

BOB: Oh, no. You never could jump. (*Comes away from window to dresser.*) Well, I've got to get my things together. (*Pulls out suitcase.*)

ED (*smoothing out the plans*): Who made these for you?

BOB: A fellow here—Rawlins. (*Turns a shirt in his hand.*) I ought to call one of the other hotels for a room.

ED: Oh, you can get in.

BOB: They're pretty crowded. (*Feels something on the sole of his foot; inspects it.*) Say, the floor's getting hot.

ED: I know it. It's getting stuffy in the room, too. Phew! (*He looks around, then goes to the phone.*) Hello. Ice water in eleven eighteen. (*Crosses to table.*)

BOB (*at bed*): That's the stuff. (*Packs.*) You know, if I move to another hotel I'll never get my mail. Everybody thinks I'm stopping here.

ED (*studying the plans*): Say, this isn't bad.

BOB (*eagerly*): Do you like it? (*Remembers his plight.*) Suppose I go to another hotel and there's a fire there, too!

ED: You've got to take *some* chance.

BOB: I know, but here I'm sure. (*Phone rings.*) Oh, answer that, will you, Ed? (*To dresser and back.*)

ED (*crosses to phone*): Sure. (*At phone.*) Hello— Oh, that's good. Fine. What? Oh! Well, wait a minute. (*To* BOB.) The firemen are downstairs and some of them want to come up to this room.

BOB: Tell them, of course.

ED (*at phone*): All right. Come right up. (*Hangs up, crosses, and sits at table.*) Now we'll get some action.

BOB (*looks out of window*): Say, there's an awful crowd of people on the street.

ED (*absently, as he pores over the plans*): Maybe there's been some kind of accident.

---

plight (PLYT) bad condition or problem
absently (AB sunt lee) with attention elsewhere
pore over (PAWR OH vur) study carefully

BOB (*peering out, suitcase in hand*): No. More likely they heard about the fire. (*A knock at the door.*) Come in.

BELLBOY (*enters*): I beg pardon, Mr. Barclay, the firemen have arrived.

BOB: Show them in. (*Crosses to door.*)

(*The door opens. In the doorway appear two* FIREMEN *in full regalia. The* FIRST FIREMAN *carries a hose and rubber coat; the* SECOND *has a violin case.*)

FIRST FIREMAN (*very apologetically*): Mr. Barclay.

BOB: I'm Mr. Barclay.

FIRST FIREMAN: We're the firemen, Mr. Barclay. (*They remove their hats.*)

BOB: How de do?

ED: How de do?

BOB: A great pleasure, I assure you. Really must apologize for the condition of this room, but—

FIRST FIREMAN: Oh, that's all right. I know how it is at home.

BOB: May I present a friend of mine, Mr. Ed Jamison—

FIRST FIREMAN: How are you?

ED: How are you, boys? (SECOND FIREMAN *nods.*) I know your Chief.

FIRST FIREMAN: Oh, is that so? He knows the Chief—dear old Chiefie. (SECOND FIREMAN *giggles.*)

BOB (*embarrassed*): Well, I guess you boys want to get to work, don't you?

FIRST FIREMAN: Well, if you don't mind. We would like to spray around a little bit.

BOB: May I help you?

FIRST FIREMAN: Yes, if you please. (BOB *helps him into his rubber coat. At the same time the* SECOND FIREMAN, *without a word, lays the violin case on the bed, opens it, takes out the violin, and begins tuning it.*)

BOB (*watching him*): I don't think I understand.

FIRST FIREMAN: Well, you see, Sid doesn't get much chance to practice at home. Sometimes, at a fire, while we're waiting for a wall to fall or something, why, a fireman doesn't really have anything to do, and personally I like to see him improve himself symphonically. I hope you don't resent it. You're not antisymphonic?

---

regalia (rih GAYL yuh) signs of royalty, such as special dress (here used ironically)
antisymphonic (an tih sim FON ik) against music

BOB: Of course not—(BOB *and* ED *nod understandingly; the* SECOND FIREMAN *is now waxing the bow.*)

FIRST FIREMAN: Well, if you'll excuse me—(*To window. Turns with decision toward the window. You feel that he is about to get down to business.*)

BOB: Charming personalities.

ED (*follows over to the window*): How is the fire?

FIRST FIREMAN (*feels the wall*): It's pretty bad right now. This wall will go pretty soon now, but it'll fall out that way, so it's all right. (*Peers out.*) That next room is the place to fight it from. (*Crosses to door in left wall.* BOB *shows ties as* ED *crosses.*)

ED (*sees ties*): Oh! Aren't those gorgeous!

FIRST FIREMAN (*to* BOB): Have you the key for this room?

BOB: Why, no. I've nothing to do with that room. I've just got this one. (*Folding a shirt as he talks.*)

ED: Oh, it's very comfortable.

FIRST FIREMAN: That's too bad. I had something up my sleeve, if I could have gotten in there. Oh, well, may I use your phone?

BOB: Please do. (*To* ED) Do you think you might hold this? (*Indicates the hose.*)

ED: How?

FIRST FIREMAN: Just crawl under it. (*As he does that.*) Thanks. (*At phone.*) Hello. Let me have the clerk, please. (*To* SECOND FIREMAN.) Give us that little thing you played the night the Equitable Building burned down. (*Back to phone.*) Are you there? This is one of the firemen. Oh, *you* know. I'm in room—ah—(*Looks at* BOB.)

BOB: Eleven-eighteen.

FIRST FIREMAN: Eleven-eighteen, and I want to get into the next room—Oh, goody. Will you send someone up with the key? There's no one in there? Oh, super-goody! Right away. (*Hangs up.*)

BOB: That's fine. (*To* FIREMEN.) Won't you sit down?

FIRST FIREMAN: Thanks.

ED: Have a cigar?

FIRST FIREMAN (*takes it*): Much obliged.

BOB: A light?

FIRST FIREMAN: If you please.

ED (*failing to find a match*): Bob, have you a match?

BOB (*crosses to table*): I thought there were some here. (*Hands in pockets.*)

FIRST FIREMAN: Oh, never mind. (*He goes to a window, leans out, and emerges with cigar lighted.* BOB *crosses to dresser, slams drawer. The* SECOND FIREMAN *taps violin with bow.*)

FIRST FIREMAN: Mr. Barclay, I think he's ready now.

BOB: Pardon me.

(*They all sit. The* SECOND FIREMAN *takes center of stage, with all the manner of a concert violinist. He goes into "Keep the Home Fires Burning." BOB, ED, and* FIRST FIREMAN *wipe brow as lights dim to red on closing eight bars.*)

---

emerge (ih MURJ) come out into view

Review the Selection

UNDERSTAND THE SELECTION

Recall

1. On which floor of the hotel does the play take place?

2. What instrument does the Second Fireman play?

3. What song is played at the end?

Infer

4. How do you know that Bob is from out of town?

5. What is the name of Bob's wife? How do you know?

6. How does the First Fireman light his cigar?

7. Why is Ed's reaction to the crowd in the street so unusual?

Apply

8. Compare and contrast the behavior of the firemen in *The Still Alarm* to the actions of real firefighters.

9. If you were in the hotel, what would you do?

10. Discuss why the blueprints for Bob's new house make an excellent subject for conversation in this play.

Respond to Literature

Explain why an American audience in the 1930s might be entertained by *The Still Alarm*.

THINK ABOUT HUMOR

Sometimes an author will share with you an important secret that the characters in the play, poem, or short story don't know. This technique, called **dramatic irony**, can help you appreciate the humorous aspects of a problem or situation that the characters do not even know is funny.

1. How do Bob and Ed react when they first learn of the fire?

2. What do you know that the two characters fail to understand?

3. Playing a violin during a fire is an allusion, or reference, to a famous historical event. The Roman Emperor Nero was said to have played the violin while he watched Rome burn. How does this allusion contribute to the humor of the play?

4. Why is it essential that *The Still Alarm* be acted in a dignified, serious manner?

READING FOCUS

Understand Cause and Effect Identify a cause and effect relationship in the play. Is it humorous? Explain why or why not.

Nouns are words that name people, places, objects, or ideas. In the sentence, "The committee met secretly," *committee* is the noun. **Verbs** are words that express action or a state of being. In the sentence, "He sprinted for the bus," *sprinted* is the verb.

Read each of the sentences below and decide whether the italicized word is used as a noun or a verb. You may consult a dictionary to learn how each word is used in the sentence.

1. The batter slammed the *pitch* against the outfield wall.
   Pitch in and we'll finish the job today.

2. This inflatable bag will *cushion* the stuntwoman's fall.
   I sat down on the soft *cushion*.

3. Our new quarterback just may *spark* this team to victory.
   We need a small *spark* to light this fire.

4. A small *shudder* passed through him.
   I *shudder* to think of the hard work ahead.

Focus on Drama

A drama, or play, is a work of literature intended to be spoken or acted out. While drama shares many elements (or essential parts) with poetry, fiction, and nonfiction, it also has qualities which make it unique. Studying how the elements of drama work together can help you better understand a particular play.

Character   In literature a character is the representation of a person or animal. A playwright—the author—creates action and personalities through the dialogue spoken between characters. These characters reveal themselves by the way they speak.

Sometimes a character will speak directly to the audience. During this **soliloquy**, the character tells us directly about his or her hopes, fears, dreams, and intentions.

In a play, many of the minor, or less important characters, are flat, and the major, or main, characters are round. **Flat characters** show only one side, or aspect, of their personality, and usually represent a single idea or attitude. **Round characters** are more complete human beings whose reactions to certain problems and events may surprise you.

Setting   Setting is the time and place in which a play, poem, or story occurs. Stage plays are usually limited to three or four **sets**, or locations, while radio, television, and movie plays can take place in an unlimited number of settings.

To determine the *when* of a setting, you should look for clues that tell the historical time period, time of day, season of year, or passage of time. The *where* of a play is its location, scenery, even natural events, such as the weather.

While reading a play, you should pay attention to the **stage directions**. These are instructions that tell how characters should talk and move, and help you visualize the setting.

Plot   In literature, plot is the sequence of related events that make up a story. In drama, plot is established through connected **scenes**, or incidents, that usually take place in one location, and focus on a single conversation or event.

Plot begins with exposition, which gives you the background information you need to understand the action. Exposition is followed by complication. As the plot becomes more complicated, you approach the climax, or turning point, of the play. After the climax, you know how the drama will end. In the final part of the play, called the resolution, the conflict is resolved.

The plot of a drama may be moved along by a narrator, or announcer. You may think of this character as a storyteller who provides you with information not spoken by the characters.

Plot does not have to flow in chronological order. Sometimes, a writer will use **foreshadowing** to give you hints about events that are going to happen. Writers also use **flashbacks** to go back in time and tell you about something important that happened.

Conflict

To figure out the plot, you should think about the *conflicts* that the characters experience. **External conflict** is a struggle with an outside force, such as another person, nature, or society. **Internal conflict** is the emotional or psychological battle that takes place within a character.

Symbolism and Allegory

Often, a writer may use a person, place, object, or event that represents, or **symbolizes** a special idea, concept, or hidden truth. When an entire play or story is symbolic, we call it an **allegory**. Allegories are often used for explaining moral principles.

Theme

The central message, or main point, of a play, poem, or story is called its theme. Understanding the relationship between characters, events, and their outcomes, helps you figure out the basic idea about human experience, or theme.

As you read *Invasion from Mars*, ask yourself:
1. What characters are introduced?
2. When does the play take place? How many different settings are described?
3. What are the conflicts? How is the main conflict resolved?
4. Does the play have a theme? What is it?

Invasion from Mars

ADAPTED   *by Howard Koch*

CHARACTERS

THREE ANNOUNCERS
ORSON WELLES
CARL PHILLIPS, *radio commentator*
PROFESSOR RICHARD PIERSON, *astronomer*
A POLICEMAN
MR. WILMUTH, *a farmer*
BRIGADIER GENERAL MONTGOMERY SMITH
HARRY McDONALD
CAPTAIN LANSING
SECRETARY OF THE INTERIOR
SOLDIERS OF THE 22ND FIELD ARTILLERY: *An officer, a gunner, and an observer*
LIEUTENANT VOGHT, *commander of an Army bomber plane*
FIVE RADIO OPERATORS
A STRANGER

COLUMBIA BROADCASTING SYSTEM
ORSON WELLES AND MERCURY THEATRE
ON THE AIR
SUNDAY, OCTOBER 30, 1938
8:00 TO 9:00 P.M.

ANNOUNCER: The Columbia Broadcasting System and its associated stations present Orson Welles and the Mercury Theatre on the Air in a radio play by Howard Koch suggested by the H. G. Wells novel *The War of the Worlds.* (*Mercury Theatre Musical Theme*)

ANNOUNCER: Ladies and gentlemen: the director of the Mercury Theatre and star of these broadcasts, Orson Welles . . .

ORSON WELLES: We know now that in the early years of the twentieth century this world was being watched closely by

FOCUS ON DRAMA
STUDY HINTS

Notice the fore-shadowing here. What event are you being prepared for?

intelligences greater than man's and yet as mortal as his own. We know now that as human beings busied themselves about their various concerns they were scrutinized and studied, perhaps almost as narrowly as a man with a microscope might scrutinize the transient creatures that swarm and multiply in a drop of water. With infinite complacence people went to and fro over the earth about their little affairs, serene in the assurance of their rule over this small spinning fragment of solar driftwood which by chance or design man has inherited out of the dark mystery of Time and Space. Yet across an immense ethereal gulf, minds that are to our minds as ours are to the beasts in the jungle, intellects vast, cool and unsympathetic, regarded this earth with envious eyes and slowly and surely drew their plans against us. In the thirty-ninth year of the twentieth century came the great disillusionment.

It was near the end of October. Business was better. The war scare was over. More men were back at work. Sales were picking up. On this particular evening, October 30, the Crossley service[1] estimated that thirty-two million people were listening in on radios.

ANNOUNCER: . . . for the next twenty-four hours not much change in temperature. A slight atmospheric disturbance of undetermined origin is reported over Nova Scotia,[2] causing a low pressure area to move down rather rapidly over the northeastern states, bringing a forecast of rain, accompanied by winds of light gale force. Maximum temperature 66; minimum 48. This weather report comes to you from the Government Weather Bureau.

. . . We now take you to the Meridian Room in the Hotel Park Plaza in downtown New York, where you will be entertained by the music of Ramon Raquello and his orchestra.

(Spanish theme song . . . fades.)

---

mortal (MAWR tul) subject to death
transient (TRAN shunt) not permanent; passing quickly
complacence (kum PLAY sens) smug satisfaction; feeling of security
ethereal (ih THIR ee uhl) of the upper regions of space
[1]**Crossley service:** a service that estimated the size of radio audiences as the Nielsen rating service estimates the size of television audiences today
[2]**Nova Scotia:** a southeastern province of Canada

Note the new setting. Observe how frequently the setting begins to change.

ANNOUNCER THREE: Good evening, ladies and gentlemen. From the Meridian Room in the Park Plaza in New York City, we bring you the music of Ramon Raquello and his orchestra. With a touch of the Spanish, Ramon Raquello leads off with "La Cumparsita."

(Piece starts playing.)

Here is the first hint of the problem, or conflict.

ANNOUNCER TWO: Ladies and gentlemen, we interrupt our program of dance music to bring you a special bulletin from the Intercontinental Radio News. At twenty minutes before eight, central time, Professor Farrell of the Mount Jennings Observatory, Chicago, Illinois, reports observing several explosions of flaming gas, occurring at regular intervals on the planet Mars.

The spectroscope indicates the gas to be hydrogen and moving toward the earth with enormous velocity. Professor Pierson of the observatory at Princeton[3] confirms Farrell's observation, and describes the phenomenon as (quote) like a jet of blue flame shot from a gun (unquote). We now return you to the music of Ramon Raquello, playing for you in the Meridian Room of the Park Plaza Hotel, situated in downtown New York.

(Music plays for a few moments until piece ends . . . sound of applause)

Now a tune that never loses favor, the ever-popular "Stardust." Ramon Raquello and his orchestra . . .

(Music)

ANNOUNCER TWO: Ladies and gentlemen, following on the news given in our bulletin a moment ago, the Government Meteorological Bureau has requested the large observatories of the country to keep an astronomical watch on any further disturbances occurring on the planet Mars. Due to the unusual nature of this occurrence, we have arranged an interview with the noted astronomer, Professor Pierson, who will give us his

---

spectroscope (SPEK truh skohp) a scientific instrument used to identify substances
phenomenon (fih NOM uh non) a fact or event that can be described in a scientific way
[3]**Princeton:** a university in New Jersey

views on this event. In a few moments we will take you to the Princeton Observatory at Princeton, New Jersey. We return you until then to the music of Ramon Raquello and his orchestra.

(*music . . .*)

ANNOUNCER TWO: We are ready now to take you to the Princeton Observatory at Princeton where Carl Phillips, our commentator, will interview Professor Richard Pierson, famous astronomer. We take you now to Princeton, New Jersey.

The main character or protagonist, is introduced.

(*Echo chamber*)

PHILLIPS: Good evening, ladies and gentlemen. This is Carl Phillips, speaking to you from the observatory at Princeton. I am standing in a large semi-circular room, pitch black except for an oblong split in the ceiling. Through this opening I can see a sprinkling of stars that cast a kind of frosty glow over the intricate mechanism of the huge telescope. The ticking sound you hear is the vibration of the clockwork. Professor Pierson stands directly above me on a small platform, peering through the giant lens. I ask you to be patient, ladies and gentlemen, during any delay that may arise during our interview. Beside his ceaseless watch of the heavens, Professor Pierson may be interrupted by telephone or other communications. During this period he is in constant touch with the astronomical centers of the world . . . Professor, may I begin our questions?

PIERSON: At any time, Mr. Phillips.

PHILLIPS: Professor, would you please tell our radio audience exactly what you see as you observe the planet Mars through your telescope?

PIERSON: Nothing unusual at the moment, Mr. Phillips. A red disk swimming in a blue sea. Transverse stripes across the disk. Quite distinct now because Mars happens to be at the point nearest the earth . . . in opposition, as we call it.

Why is this information important to the plot development?

PHILLIPS: In your opinion, what do these transverse stripes signify, Professor Pierson?

PIERSON: Not canals, I can assure you, Mr. Phillips, although

---

transverse (trans VURS) crossing from side to side

that's the popular conjecture of those who imagine Mars to be inhabited. From a scientific viewpoint the stripes are merely the result of the planet's atmospheric conditions.

PHILLIPS: Then you're quite convinced as a scientist that living intelligence as we know it does not exist on Mars?

PIERSON: I should say the chances against it are a thousand to one.

PHILLIPS: And yet how do you account for these gas eruptions occurring on the surface of the planet at regular intervals?

PIERSON: Mr. Phillips, I cannot account for it.

PHILLIPS: By the way, Professor, for the benefit of our listeners, how far is Mars from the earth?

PIERSON: Approximately forty million miles.

PHILLIPS: Well, that seems a safe enough distance.

PHILLIPS: Just a moment, ladies and gentlemen, someone has just handed Professor Pierson a message. While he reads it, let me remind you that we are speaking to you from the observatory in Princeton, New Jersey, where we are interviewing the world-famous astronomer, Professor Pierson . . . One moment, please. Professor Pierson has passed me a message which he has just received . . . Professor, may I read the message to the listening audience?

PIERSON: Certainly, Mr. Phillips.

PHILLIPS: Ladies and gentlemen, I shall read you a wire addressed to Professor Pierson from Dr. Gray of the National History Museum, New York. "9:15 P.M. Eastern Standard Time. Seismograph registered shock of almost earthquake intensity occurring within a radius of twenty miles of Princeton. Please investigate. Signed, Lloyd Gray, Chief of Astronomical Division." . . . Professor Pierson, could this occurrence possibly have something to do with the disturbances observed on the planet Mars?

PIERSON: Hardly, Mr. Phillips. This is probably a meteorite of unusual size and its arrival at this particular time is merely a

Here, the plot begins to build. Does Professor Pierson see any relationship between the disturbances on Mars and these earthquake shocks?

---

conjecture (kun JEK chur) an opinion formed without facts but based on pertinent knowledge or experience; guess

seismograph (SYZ muh graf) an instrument that records the intensity and duration of earthquakes

meteorite (MEET ee uh ryt) part of a heavenly body that passes through the atmosphere and falls to the earth's surface as a piece of matter

coincidence. However, we shall conduct a search, as soon as daylight permits.

PHILLIPS: Thank you, Professor. Ladies and gentlemen, for the past ten minutes we've been speaking to you from the observatory at Princeton, bringing you a special interview with Professor Pierson, noted astronomer. This is Carl Phillips speaking. We now return you to our New York studio.

(*Fade in piano playing*)

ANNOUNCER TWO: Ladies and gentlemen, here is the latest bulletin from the Intercontinental Radio News. Montreal, Canada: Professor Morse of McGill University reports observing a total of three explosions on the planet Mars, between the hours of 7:45 P.M. and 9:20 P.M., Eastern Standard Time. This confirms earlier reports received from American observatories. Now, nearer home, comes a special announcement from Trenton,[4] New Jersey. It is reported that at 8:50 P.M. a huge, flaming object, believed to be a meteorite, fell on a farm in the neighborhood of Grovers Mill, New Jersey, twenty-two miles from Trenton. The flash in the sky was visible for several hundred miles and the noise of the impact was heard as far north as Elizabeth.

We have sent a special mobile unit to the scene, and will have our commentator, Mr. Phillips, give you a word description as soon as he can reach there from Princeton. In the meantime, we take you to the Hotel Martinet in Brooklyn, where Bobby Millette and his orchestra are offering a program of dance music.

(*Swing band for twenty seconds . . . then cut*)

ANNOUNCER TWO: We take you now to Grovers Mill, New Jersey. (*Crowd noises . . . police sirens*)

PHILLIPS: Ladies and gentlemen, this is Carl Phillips again, at the Wilmuth farm, Grovers Mill, New Jersey. Professor Pierson and myself made the eleven miles from Princeton in ten minutes. Well, I . . . I hardly know where to begin, to paint for you a word picture of the strange scene before my eyes, like

Note how the change of setting adds a certain reality, or truth, to the broadcast.

---

[4]**Trenton:** the capital of New Jersey

Notice the descriptive words that help you visualize this new setting.

something out of a modern *Arabian Nights*.[5] Well, I just got here. I haven't had a chance to look around yet. I guess that's it. Yes, I guess that's the . . . thing, directly in front of me, half buried in a vast pit. Must have struck with terrific force. The ground is covered with splinters of a tree it must have struck on its way down. What I can see of the . . . object itself doesn't look very much like a meteor, at least not the meteors I've seen. It looks more like a huge cylinder. It has a diameter of . . . what would you say, Professor Pierson?

PIERSON (*off*): About thirty yards.

PHILLIPS: About thirty yards . . . The metal on the sheath is . . . well, I've never seen anything like it. The color is sort of yellowish-white. Curious spectators now are pressing close to the object in spite of the efforts of the police to keep them back. They're getting in front of my line of vision. Would you mind standing on one side, please?

POLICEMAN: One side, there, one side.

PHILLIPS: While the policemen are pushing the crowd back, here's Mr. Wilmuth, owner of the farm here. He may have

---

sheath (SHEETH) a case or covering
[5]***Arabian Nights:*** a collection of tales from Arabia, India, and Persia.

some interesting facts to add . . . . Mr. Wilmuth, would you please tell the radio audience as much as you remember of this rather unusual visitor that dropped in your backyard? Step closer, please. Ladies and gentlemen, this is Mr. Wilmuth.

WILMUTH: I was listenin' to the radio.

PHILLIPS: Closer and louder, please.

WILMUTH: Pardon me!

PHILLIPS: Louder, please, and closer.

WILMUTH: Yes, sir—while I was listening to the radio and kinda drowsin', that Professor fellow was talkin' about Mars, so I was half dozin' and half . . .

PHILLIPS: Yes, Mr. Wilmuth. Then what happened?

WILMUTH: As I was sayin', I was listenin' to the radio kinda halfways . . .

PHILLIPS: Yes, Mr. Wilmuth, and then you saw something?

WILMUTH: Not first off. I heard something.

PHILLIPS: And what did you hear?

WILMUTH: A hissing sound. Like this: sssssss . . . kinda like a Fourt'-of-July rocket.

PHILLIPS: Then what?

Notice that Mr. Wilmuth says he was listening to the radio program. Why does the writer have him make this remark?

Tell briefly whether Mr. Wilmuth is a flat or round character.

WILMUTH: Turned my head out the window and would have swore I was asleep and dreamin'.

PHILLIPS: Yes?

WILMUTH: I seen a kinda greenish streak and then zingo! Somethin' smacked the ground. Knocked me clear out of my chair!

PHILLIPS: Well, were you frightened, Mr. Wilmuth?

WILMUTH: Well, I—I ain't quite sure. I reckon I—I was kinda riled.

PHILLIPS: Thank you, Mr. Wilmuth. Thank you.

WILMUTH: Want me to tell you some more?

PHILLIPS: No . . . That's quite all right, that's plenty.

PHILLIPS: Ladies and gentlemen, you've just heard Mr. Wilmuth, owner of the farm where this thing has fallen. I wish I could convey the atmosphere . . . the background of this . . . fantastic scene. Hundreds of cars are parked in a field in back of us. Police are trying to rope off the roadway leading into the farm. But it's no use. They're breaking right through. Their headlights throw an enormous spotlight on the pit where the object's half buried. Some of the more daring souls are venturing near the edge. Their silhouettes stand out against the metal sheen.

Here Mr. Phillips helps you picture the setting in your mind.

(*Faint humming sound*)

To what sense does Mr. Phillips' description appeal?

One man wants to touch the thing . . . he's having an argument with a policeman. The policeman wins . . . Now, ladies and gentlemen, there's something I haven't mentioned in all this excitement, but it's becoming more distinct. Perhaps you've caught it already on your radio. Listen: (*Long pause*) . . . Do you hear it? It is a curious humming sound that seems to come from inside the object. I'll move the microphone nearer. Here. (*Pause*) Now we're not more than twenty-five feet away. Can you hear it now? Oh, Professor Pierson!

PIERSON: Yes, Mr. Phillips?

PHILLIPS: Can you tell us the meaning of that scraping noise inside the thing?

PIERSON: Possibly the unequal cooling of its surface.

PHILLIPS: Do you still think it's a meteor, Professor?

---

riled (RYLD) irritated; angered

PIERSON: I don't know what to think. The metal casing is definitely extraterrestrial . . . not found on this earth. Friction with the earth's atmosphere usually tears holes in a meteor. This thing is smooth and, as you can see, of a cylindrical shape.

How has Professor Pierson's attitude changed?

PHILLIPS: Just a minute! Something's happening! Ladies and gentlemen, this is terrific! This end of the thing is beginning to flake off! The top is beginning to rotate like a screw! The thing must be hollow!

Here the plot begins to build faster.

VOICES: She's a movin'!

Look, the darn thing's unscrewing!

Keep back, there! Keep back, I tell you!

Maybe there's men in it trying to escape!

It's red hot, they'll burn to a cinder!

Keep back there. Keep those idiots back!

What feelings do the shouting background voices convey?

(*Suddenly the clanking sound of a huge piece of falling metal*)

VOICES: She's off! The top's loose!

Look out there! Stand back!

PHILLIPS: Ladies and gentlemen, this is the most terrifying thing I have ever witnessed . . . Wait a minute! *Someone's crawling out of the hollow top.* Someone or . . . something. I can see peering out of that black hole two luminous disks . . . are they eyes? It might be a face. It might be . . .

(*Shout of awe from the crowd*)

PHILLIPS: Good heavens, something's wriggling out of the shadow like a gray snake. Now it's another one, and another. They look like tentacles to me. There, I can see the thing's body. It's large as a bear and it glistens like wet leather. But that face. It . . . it's indescribable. I can hardly force myself to keep looking at it. The eyes are black and gleam like a serpent. The mouth is V-shaped with saliva dripping from its rimless lips that seem to quiver and pulsate. The monster or whatever it is can hardly move. It seems weighed down by . . . possibly gravity or something. The thing's raising up. The crowd falls back. They've seen enough. This is the most extraordinary experience. I can't find words . . . I'm pulling this

Here, an alien character is introduced. What do Mr. Phillips's sensory words suggest about the visitor?

---

pulsate (PUL sayt) throb in a regular rhythm

microphone with me as I talk. I'll have to stop the description until I've taken a new position. Hold on, will you please, I'll be back in a minute.

(*Fade into piano*)

ANNOUNCER TWO: We are bringing you an eyewitness account of what's happening on the Wilmuth farm, Grovers Mill, New Jersey. (*More piano*) We now return you to Carl Phillips at Grovers Mill.

PHILLIPS: Ladies and gentlemen (Am I on?). Ladies and gentlemen, here I am, in back of a stone wall that adjoins Mr. Wilmuth's garden. From here I get a sweep of the whole scene. I'll give you every detail as long as I can talk. As long as I can see. More state police have arrived. They're drawing up a cordon in front of the pit, about thirty of them. No need to push the crowd back now. They're willing to keep their distance. The captain is speaking with someone. We can't quite see who. Oh yes, I believe it's Professor Pierson. Yes, it is. Now they've parted. The professor moves around one side, studying the object, while the captain and two policemen advance with something in their hands. I can see it now. It's a white handkerchief tied to a pole . . . a flag of truce. If those creatures know what that means . . . what anything means! . . . *Wait!* Something's happening!

(*Hissing sound followed by a humming that increases in intensity.*)

A humped shape is rising out of the pit. I can make out a small beam of light against a mirror. What's that? There's a jet of flame springing from that mirror, and it leaps right at the advancing men. It strikes them head on! Good Lord, they're turning into flame!

(*Screams and unearthly shrieks*)

Now the whole field's caught fire. (*Explosion*) The woods . . . the barns . . . the gas tanks of automobiles . . . it's spreading everywhere. It's coming this way. About twenty yards to my right . . .

Notice the continuing use of foreshadowing.

Would you expect visitors from another planet to understand our symbol for surrender?

Is the conflict external or internal?

---

cordon (KAWR dun) a line or circle of police stationed around an area to guard it

(Crash of microphone . . . then dead silence)

ANNOUNCER TWO: Ladies and gentlemen, due to circumstances beyond our control, we are unable to continue the broadcast from Grovers Mill. Evidently there's some difficulty with our field transmission. However, we will return to that point at the earliest opportunity. In the meantime, we have a late bulletin from San Diego, California. Professor Indellkoffer, speaking at a dinner of the California Astronomical Society, expressed the opinion that the explosions on Mars are undoubtedly nothing more than severe volcanic disturbances on

What do the explosions on the surface of Mars really represent?

the surface of the planet. We continue now with our piano interlude.

(*Piano . . . then cut*)

Ladies and gentlemen, I have just been handed a message that came in from Grovers Mill by telephone. Just a moment. At least forty people, including six state troopers lie dead in a field east of the village of Grovers Mill, their bodies burned and twisted beyond all possible recognition. The next voice you hear will be that of Brigadier General Montgomery Smith, commander of the state militia at Trenton, New Jersey.

SMITH: I have been requested by the governor of New Jersey to place the counties of Mercer and Middlesex as far west as Princeton, and east to Jamesburg, under martial law. No one will be permitted to enter this area except by special pass issued by state or military authorities. Four companies of state militia are proceeding from Trenton to Grovers Mill, and will aid in the evacuation of homes within the range of military operations. Thank you.

Notice how the tension *appears* to be resolved. Do you think the Martians will decide to seek peace?

ANNOUNCER: You have just been listening to General Montgomery Smith, commanding the state militia at Trenton. In the meantime, further details of the disaster at Grovers Mill are coming in. The strange creatures, after unleashing their deadly assault, crawled back in their pit and made no attempt to prevent the efforts of the firemen to recover the bodies and extinguish the fire. Combined fire departments of Mercer County are fighting the flames which threaten the entire countryside.

We have been unable to establish any contact with our mobile unit at Grovers Mill, but we hope to be able to return you there at the earliest possible moment. In the meantime we take you—uh, just one moment please.

(*Long pause*)

Notice that the Announcer has lowered his voice. Why does he do this?

(*Whisper*) Ladies and gentlemen, I have just been informed that we have finally established communication with an

---

interlude (IN tur lood) musical performance between the acts of a play
martial law (MAHR shul LAW) temporary rule by the military authorities
militia (muh LISH uh) an army of citizens rather than professional soldiers, called out in time of emergency

eyewitness of the tragedy. Professor Pierson has been located at a farmhouse near Grovers Mill where he has established an emergency observation post. As a scientist, he will give you his explanation of the calamity. The next voice you hear will be that of Professor Pierson, brought to you by direct wire. Professor Pierson.

PIERSON: Of the creatures in the rocket cylinder at Grovers Mill, I can give you no reliable information—either as to their nature, their origin, or their purposes here on earth. Of their destructive instrument I might venture some conjectural explanation. For want of a better term, I shall refer to the mysterious weapon as a heat ray. It's all too evident that these creatures have scientific knowledge far in advance of our own. It is my guess that in some way they are able to generate an intense heat in a chamber of practically absolute nonconductivity. This intense heat they project in a parallel beam against any object they choose, by means of a polished parabolic mirror of unknown composition, much as the mirror of a lighthouse projects a beam of light. That is my conjecture of the origin of the heat ray . . .

How do the words that Professor Pierson uses make him sound like a scientist?

ANNOUNCER TWO: Thank you, Professor Pierson. Ladies and gentlemen, here is a bulletin from Trenton. It is a brief statement informing us that the burnt body of Carl Phillips has been identified in a Trenton hospital. Now here's another bulletin from Washington, D.C.

Office of the director of the National Red Cross reports ten units of Red Cross emergency workers have been assigned to the headquarters of the state militia stationed outside of Grovers Mill, New Jersey. Here's a bulletin from state police, Princeton Junction: The fires at Grovers Mill and vicinity are now under control. Scouts report all quiet in the pit, and no sign of life appearing from the mouth of the cylinder . . . And now, ladies and gentlemen, we have a special statement from Mr. Harry McDonald, vice-president in charge of operations.

McDONALD: We have received a request from the militia at Trenton

---

nonconductivity (non kon duk TIV uh tee) the ability to contain and not transmit heat
parabolic (par uh BOL ik) bowl shaped

to place at their disposal our entire broadcasting facilities. In view of the gravity of the situation, and believing that radio has a definite responsibility to serve in the public interest at all times, we are turning over our facilities to the state militia at Trenton.

ANNOUNCER: We take you now to the field headquarters of the state militia near Grovers Mill, New Jersey.

Do you think the conflict has been resolved?

CAPTAIN: This is Captain Lansing of the signal corps,[6] attached to the state militia now engaged in military operations in the vicinity of Grovers Mill. Situation arising from the reported presence of certain individuals of unidentified nature is now under complete control.

What do the Captain's words suggest about his abilities as a commander?

The cylindrical object which lies in a pit directly below our position is surrounded on all sides by eight battalions of infantry, without heavy fieldpieces, but adequately armed with rifles and machine guns. All cause for alarm, if such cause ever existed, is now entirely unjustified. The things, whatever they are, do not even venture to poke their heads above the pit. I can see their hiding place plainly in the glare of the searchlights here. With all their reported resources, these creatures can scarcely stand up against heavy machine-gun fire. Anyway, it's an interesting outing for the troops. I can make out their khaki uniforms, crossing back and forth in front of the lights. It looks almost like a real war. There appears to be some slight smoke in the woods bordering the Millstone River. Probably fire started by campers. Well, we ought to see some action soon. One of the companies is deploying on the left side. A quick thrust and it will all be over. Now wait a minute! I see something on top of the cylinder. No, it's nothing but a shadow. Now the troops are on the edge of the Wilmuth farm. Seven thousand armed men closing in on an old metal tube. Wait, that wasn't a shadow! It's something moving . . . solid metal . . . kind of a shieldlike affair rising up out of the cylinder . . . It's going higher and higher. Why, it's standing on legs . . . actually rearing up on a sort of metal framework. Now it's reaching above the trees and the searchlights are on it! Hold on!

---

fieldpieces (FEELD pees iz) mobile artillery
deploying (dih PLOI ing) spreading out
[6]**signal corps:** the part of the army in charge of communications

ANNOUNCER: Ladies and gentlemen, I have a grave announcement to make. Incredible as it may seem, both the observations of science and the evidence of our eyes lead to the inescapable assumption that those strange beings who landed in the Jersey farmlands tonight are the vanguard of an invading army from the planet Mars. The battle which took place tonight at Grovers Mill has ended in one of the most startling defeats ever suffered by an army in modern times; seven thousand men armed with rifles and machine guns set against a single fighting machine of the invaders from Mars. One hundred and twenty known survivors. The rest are strewn over the battle area from Grovers Mill to Plainsboro crushed and trampled to death under the metal feet of the monster, or burned to cinders by its heat ray. The monster is now in control of the middle section of New Jersey and has effectively cut the state through its center. Communication lines are down from Pennsylvania to the Atlantic Ocean. Railroad tracks are torn and service from New York to Philadelphia discontinued except routing some of the trains through Allentown and Phoenixville.[7] Highways to the north, south, and west are clogged with frantic human traffic. Police and army reserves are unable to control the mad rush. By morning the fugitives will have swelled Philadelphia, Camden and Trenton, it is estimated, to twice their normal population.

At this time, martial law prevails throughout New Jersey and eastern Pennsylvania. We take you now to Washington for a special broadcast on the National Emergency . . . the Secretary of the Interior . . .

SECRETARY: Citizens of the nation: I shall not try to conceal the gravity of the situation that confronts the country, nor the concern of your government in protecting the lives and property of its people. However, I wish to impress upon you—private citizens and public officials, all of you—the urgent need of calm and resourceful action. Fortunately, this formidable enemy is still confined to a comparatively small area, and we

Note the outcome of the battle between the Martians and the army. Predict what the Martians will do next.

Describe the reactions of people in New Jersey and Pennsylvania.

What is the Secretary of Interior really feeling? Is he optimistic?

---

vanguard (VAN gahrd) the part of an army that goes ahead of the main body in an advance
[7]**Allentown and Phoenixville:** cities in eastern Pennsylvania

may place our faith in the military forces to keep them there. In the meantime, placing our faith in God, we must continue the performance of our duties each and every one of us, so that we may confront this destructive enemy with a nation united, courageous, and consecrated to the preservation of human supremacy on this earth. I thank you.

ANNOUNCER: You have just heard the Secretary of the Interior speaking from Washington. Bulletins too numerous to read are piling up in the studio here. We are informed that the central portion of New Jersey is blacked out from radio communication due to the effect of the heat ray upon power lines and electrical equipment. Here is a special bulletin from New York. Cables received from English, French, German scientific organizations offering assistance. Astronomers report continued gas outbursts at regular intervals on planet Mars. Majority voice opinion that enemy will be reinforced by additional rocket machines. There have been several attempts made to locate Professor Pierson of Princeton, who has observed Martians at close range. It is feared he was lost in recent battle. Langham Field, Virginia: Scouting planes report three Martian machines visible above treetops, moving north toward Somerville with population fleeing ahead of them. Heat ray not in use; although advancing at express-train speed, invaders pick their way carefully. They seem to be making conscious effort to avoid destruction of cities and countryside. However, they stop to uproot power lines, bridges, and railroad tracks. Their apparent objective is to crush resistance, paralyze communication, and disorganize human society.

Here is a bulletin from Basking Ridge, New Jersey: Raccoon hunters have stumbled on a second cylinder similar to the first lying in the great swamp twenty miles south of Morristown. U.S. army fieldpieces are proceeding from Newark to blow up second invading unit before cylinder can be opened and the fighting machine rigged. They are taking up position in the foothills of Watchung Mountains.[8] Another bulletin from Langham Field, Virginia: Scouting planes report enemy machines, now three in number, increasing speed northward

How do you know that so far, the Martians have only landed in the United States?

Notice the increasing number of bulletins. How do they contribute to the growing tension in the drama?

---

consecrated (KON sih krayt id) dedicated
[8]**Watchung Mountains:** a range of low mountains in New Jersey

kicking over houses and trees in their evident haste to unite with their allies south of Morristown. Machines also sighted by telephone operator east of Middlesex within ten miles of Plainfield. Here's a bulletin from Winston Field, Long Island. Fleet of army bombers carrying heavy explosives flying north in pursuit of enemy. Scouting planes act as guides. They keep speeding enemy in sight. Just a moment please. Ladies and gentlemen, we've run special wires to the artillery line in adjacent villages to give you direct reports in the zone of the advancing enemy. First we take you to the battery of the 22nd Field Artillery, located in the Watchung Mountains.

Is this new development a genuine cause for hope?

OFFICER: Range, thirty-two meters.

GUNNER: Thirty-two meters.

OFFICER: Projection, thirty-nine degrees.

GUNNER: Thirty-nine degrees.

OFFICER: Fire! (*Boom of heavy gun . . . pause*)

OBSERVER: One hundred and forty yards to the right, sir.

OFFICER: Shift range . . . thirty-one meters.

GUNNER: Thirty-one meters.

OFFICER: Projection . . . thirty-seven degrees.

GUNNER: Thirty-seven degrees.

OFFICER: Fire! (*Boom of heavy gun . . . pause*)

OBSERVER: A hit, sir! We got the tripod of one of them. They've stopped. The others are trying to repair it.

OFFICER: Quick, get the range! Shift thirty meters.

GUNNER: Thirty meters.

OFFICER: Projection . . . twenty-seven degrees.

GUNNER: Twenty-seven degrees.

OFFICER: Fire! (*Boom of heavy gun . . . pause*)

OBSERVER: Can't see the shell land, sir. They're letting off a smoke.

OFFICER: What is it?

OBSERVER: A black smoke, sir. Moving this way. Lying close to the ground. It's moving fast.

OFFICER: Put on gas masks. (*Pause*) Get ready to fire. Shift to twenty-four meters.

GUNNER: Twenty-four meters.

Describe the conflict in this scene.

---

tripod (TRY pod) three legged support

Invasion from Mars ■ **407**

OFFICER: Fire! (*Boom*)

GUNNER: Still can't see, sir. The smoke's coming nearer.

OFFICER: Get the range. (*Coughs*)

OBSERVER: Twenty-three meters. (*Coughs*)

OFFICER: Twenty-three meters. (*Coughs*)

GUNNER: Twenty-three meters. (*Coughs*)

OBSERVER: Projection, twenty-two degrees. (*Coughing*)

OFFICER: Twenty-two degrees. (*Fade in coughing*)

(*Fading in . . . sound of airplane motor*)

COMMANDER: Army bombing plane, V-8-43, off Bayonne, New Jersey, Lieutenant Voght, commanding eight bombers. Reporting to Commander Fairfax, Langham Field . . . This is Voght, reporting to Commander Fairfax, Langham Field . . . Enemy tripod machines now in sight. Reinforced by three machines from the Morristown cylinder . . . six altogether. One machine partially crippled. Believed hit by shell from army gun in Watchung Mountains. Guns now appear silent. A heavy black fog hanging close to the earth . . . of extreme density, nature unknown. No sign of heat ray. Enemy now turns east, crossing Passaic River into the Jersey marshes. Another straddles the Pulaski Skyway.[9] Evident objective is New York City. They're pushing down a high tension power station. The machines are close together now, and we're ready to attack. Planes circling, ready to strike. A thousand yards and we'll be over the first—eight hundred yards . . . six hundred . . . four hundred . . . two hundred . . . There they go! The giant arm raised . . . Green flash! They're spraying us with flame! Two thousand feet. Engines are giving out. No chance to release bombs. Only one thing left . . . drop on them, plane and all. We're diving on the first one. Now the engine's gone! Eight . . .

OPERATOR ONE: This is Bayonne, New Jersey, calling Langham Field . . .

This is Bayonne, New Jersey, calling Langham Field. Come in, please . . . Come in, please. . .

OPERATOR TWO: This is Langham Field . . . go ahead . . .

OPERATOR ONE: Eight army bombers in battle with enemy tripod

---

[9]**Pulaski Skyway:** an elevated highway in eastern New Jersey

What happens to the soldiers?

Where are the Martians now heading?

Notice the rising level of tension in the Commander's voice. What does his final action tell about the Commander's character?

machines over Jersey marshlands. Engines disabled by heat ray. All crashed. One enemy machine destroyed. Enemy now discharging heavy black smoke in direction of—

OPERATOR THREE: This is Newark, New Jersey . . .

This is Newark, New Jersey . . .

Warning! Poisonous black smoke pouring in from Jersey marshes. Reaches South Street. Gas masks useless. Urge population to move into open spaces . . . automobiles use Routes 7, 23, 24 . . . Avoid congested areas. Smoke now spreading over Raymond Boulevard . . .

How powerful is the Martian's poison gas?

OPERATOR FOUR: 2X2L . . . calling CQ . . .

2X2L . . . calling CQ . . .   2X2L . . . calling 8X3R . . .

Come in, please . . .

OPERATOR FIVE: This is 8X3R . . . coming back at 2X2L.

OPERATOR FOUR: How's reception? How's reception? K, please. Where are you, 8X3R?

What's the matter? Where are you?

(Bells ringing over city gradually diminishing)

ANNOUNCER: I'm speaking from the roof of Broadcasting Building, New York City. The bells you hear are ringing to warn the people to evacuate the city as the Martians approach. Estimated in last two hours three million people have moved out along the roads to the north. Hutchison River Parkway still kept open for motor traffic. Avoid bridges to Long Island . . . hopelessly jammed. All communication with Jersey shore closed ten minutes ago. No more defenses. Our army wiped out . . . artillery, air force, everything wiped out. This may be the last broadcast. We'll stay here to the end . . . People are holding service below us . . . in the cathedral.

(Voices singing hymn)

Now I look down the harbor. All manner of boats, overloaded with fleeing population, pulling out from docks.

(Sound of boat whistles)

Streets are all jammed. Noise in crowds is like New Year's Eve in the city. Wait a minute . . . Enemy now in sight above the Palisades.[10] Five great machines. First one is crossing river. I can see it from here, wading the Hudson like a man wading through a brook . . . A bulletin's handed me . . . Martian cylinders are falling all over the country. One outside Buffalo, one in Chicago, St. Louis . . . seem to be timed and spaced . . . Now the first machine reaches the shore. He stands watching, looking over the city. His steel, cowlish head is even with the skyscrapers. He waits for the others. They rise like a line of new towers on the city's west side . . . Now they're lifting their metal hands. This is the end now. Smoke comes out . . . black smoke, drifting over the city. People in the streets see it now. They're running toward the East River . . . thousands of them, dropping in like rats. Now the smoke's spreading faster.

It's reached Times Square. People trying to run away from it, but it's no use. They're falling like flies. Now the smoke's crossing Sixth Avenue . . . Fifth Avenue . . . one hundred yards away . . . it's fifty feet . . .

OPERATOR FOUR: 2X2L calling CQ . . .
2X2L calling CQ . . .
2X2L calling CQ . . . New York.
Isn't there anyone on the air?
Isn't there anyone . . .
2X2L—

ANNOUNCER: You are listening to a CBS presentation of Orson Welles and the Mercury Theatre on the Air in a original dramatization of *The War of the Worlds* by H. G. Wells. The performance will continue after a brief intermission.
This is the Columbia . . . Broadcasting System.

(*Music*)

PIERSON: As I set down these notes on paper, I'm consumed by the thought that I may be the last living man on earth. I have been hiding in this empty house near Grovers Mill—a small island of daylight cut off by the black smoke from the rest of the world. All that happened before the arrival of these monstrous creatures in the world now seems part of another life

---

cowlish (KOUL ish) hood shaped
[10]**Palisades:** the line of steep cliffs in northeastern New Jersey and southeastern New York on the west shore of the Hudson River

. . . a life that has no continuity with the present, furtive existence of the lonely derelict who pencils these words on the back of some astronomical notes bearing the signature of Richard Pierson. I look down, at my blackened hands, my torn shoes, my tattered clothes, and I try to connect them with a professor who lives at Princeton, and who on the night of October 30, glimpsed through his telescope an orange splash of light on a distant planet. My wife, my colleagues, my students, my books, my observatory, my . . . my world . . . where are they? Did they ever exist? Am I Richard Pierson? What day is it? Do days exist without calendars? Does time pass when there are no human hands left to wind the clocks? . . . In writing down my daily life I tell myself I shall preserve human history between the dark covers of this little book that was meant to record the movements of the stars . . . But to write I must live, and to live I must eat . . . I find moldy bread in the kitchen, and an orange not too spoiled to swallow. I keep watch at the window. From time to time I catch sight of a Martian above the black smoke.

The smoke still holds the house in its black coil . . . But at length there is a hissing sound and suddenly I see a Martian mounted on his machine, spraying the air with a jet of steam, as if to dissipate the smoke. I watch in a corner as his huge metal legs nearly brush against the house. Exhausted by terror, I fall asleep . . . It's morning. Sun streams in the window. The black cloud of gas has lifted, and the scorched meadows to the north look as though a black snowstorm has passed over them. I venture from the house. I make my way to a road. No traffic. Here and there a wrecked car, baggage overturned, a blackened skeleton. I push on north. For some reason I feel safer trailing these monsters than running away from them. And I keep a careful watch. I have seen the Martians feed. Should one of their machines appear over the top of trees, I am ready to fling myself flat on the earth. I come to a chestnut tree. October, chestnuts are ripe. I fill my pockets. I must keep alive. Two days I wander in a vague northerly direction through a barren world. Finally I notice a living creature . . . a small red squirrel in a beech tree. I stare at him, and wonder. He stares back at me.

Notice the plot development. Can Professor Pierson believe what has happened to him?

What does Professor Pierson seem to be questioning?

Imagine what it might be like to think you were the last person on Earth. How would you feel?

---

furtive (FUR tiv) sneaky, secretive
dissipate (DIS uh payt) scatter; clear away

I believe at that moment the animal and I shared the same emotion . . . the joy of finding another living being . . . I push on north. I find dead cows in a brackish field. Beyond, the charred ruins of a dairy. The silo remains standing guard over the wasteland like a lighthouse deserted by the sea. Astride the silo perches a weathervane. The arrow points north.

Notice Professor Pierson's use of flashback. What might this suggest about the outcome of his story?

Next day I came to a city vaguely familiar in its contours, yet its buildings strangely dwarfed and leveled off, as if a giant had sliced off its highest towers with a capricious sweep of his hand. I reached the outskirts. I found Newark, undemolished, but humbled by some whim of the advancing Martians. Presently, with an odd feeling of being watched, I caught sight of something crouching in a doorway. I made a step toward it, and it rose up and became a man—a man, armed with a large knife.

Here, a new conflict begins to develop.

STRANGER: Stop . . . Where did you come from?

PIERSON: I come from . . . many places. A long time ago from Princeton.

STRANGER: Princeton, huh? That's near Grovers Mill!

PIERSON: Yes.

What do his comments suggest about the Stranger's character?

STRANGER: Grovers Mill . . . (*Laughs as at a great joke, then sounds angry*) There's no food here. This is my country . . . all this end of town down to the river. There's only food for me . . . Which way are you going?

PIERSON: I don't know. I guess I'm looking for—for people.

STRANGER: (*nervously*) What was that? Did you hear something just then?

PIERSON: Only a bird (*marvels*) . . . A live bird!

STRANGER: You get to know that birds have shadows these days . . . Say, we're in the open here. Let's crawl into this doorway and talk.

PIERSON: Have you seen any Martians?

STRANGER: They've gone over to New York. At night the sky is alive with their lights. Just as if people were still living in it. By daylight you can't see them. Five days ago a couple of them carried something big across the flats from the airport. I believe they're learning how to fly.

---

brackish (BRAK ish) salty and marshy
capricious (kuh PRISH us) without apparent reason

PIERSON: Fly!

STRANGER: Yeah, fly.

PIERSON: Then it's all over with humanity. Stranger, there's still you and I. Two of us left.

STRANGER: They got themselves in solid; they wrecked the greatest country in the world. Those green stars, they're probably falling somewhere every night. They've only lost one machine. There isn't anything to do. We're done. We're licked.

PIERSON: Where were you? You're in a uniform.

STRANGER: What's left of it. I was in the militia—National Guard . . . That's good! Wasn't any war any more than there is between men and ants.

PIERSON: And we're edible ants. I found that out . . . What will they do to us?

STRANGER: I've thought it all out. Right now we're caught as we're wanted. The Martian only has to go a few miles to get a crowd on the run. But they won't keep doing that. They'll begin catching us systematic like—keeping the best and storing us in cages and things. They haven't begun on us yet!

PIERSON: Not begun!

STRANGER: Not begun. All that's happened so far is because we don't have sense enough to keep quiet . . . bothering them with guns and such stuff and losing our heads and rushing off in crowds. Now instead of our rushing around blind we've got to fix ourselves up according to the way things are now. Cities, nations, civilization, progress . . . done.

PIERSON: But if that's so, what is there to live for?

STRANGER: There won't be any more concerts for a million years or so, and no nice little dinners at restaurants. If it's amusement you're after, I guess the game's up.

PIERSON: And what is there left?

STRANGER: Life . . . that's what! I want to live. And so do you! We're not going to be exterminated. And I don't mean to be caught, either, and tamed, and fattened and bred like an ox.

PIERSON: What are you going to do?

STRANGER: I'm going on . . . right under their feet. I gotta plan. We humans as humans are finished. We don't know enough. We gotta learn plenty before we've got a chance. And we've got to live and keep free while we learn. I've thought it all out, see.

If you were listening to this radio drama in 1938, would this statement have caused you to jump up and look outside your windows?

Does the Stranger feel the participants in the war were evenly matched?

Does the Stranger see the Martian invasion the same way as Professor Pierson?

PIERSON: Tell me the rest.

STRANGER: Well, it isn't all of us that are made for wild beasts, and that's what it's got to be. That's why I watched you. All these little office workers that used to live in these houses—they'd be no good. They haven't any stuff to 'em. They just used to run off to work. I've seen hundreds of 'em, running wild to catch their commuters' train in the morning for fear that they'd get canned if they didn't; running back at night afraid they won't be in time for dinner. Lives insured and a little invested in case of accidents. And on Sundays, worried about the hereafter. The Martians will be a blessing for those guys. Nice roomy cages, good food, careful breeding, no worries. After a week or so chasing about the fields on empty stomachs they'll come and be glad to be caught.

PIERSON: You've thought it all out, haven't you?

STRANGER: You bet I have! And that isn't all. These Martians will make pets of some of them, train 'em to do tricks. Who knows? Get sentimental over the pet boy who grew up and had to be killed. And some, maybe, they'll train to hunt us.

PIERSON: No, that's impossible. No human being . . .

STRANGER: Yes, they will. There's people who'll do it gladly. If one of them ever comes after me . . .

PIERSON: In the meantime, you and I and others like us . . . where are we to live when the Martians own the Earth?

STRANGER: I've got it all figured out. We'll live underground. I've been thinking about the sewers. Under New York are miles and miles of 'em. The main ones are big enough for anybody. Then there's cellars, vaults, underground storerooms, railway tunnels, subways. You begin to see, eh? And we'll get a bunch of strong people together. No weak ones, that garbage, out.

PIERSON: And you meant me to go?

STRANGER: Well, I gave you a chance, didn't I?

PIERSON: We won't quarrel about that. Go on.

STRANGER: And we've got to make safe places for us to stay in, see, and get all the books we can—science books. That's where people like you come in, see? We'll raid the museums, we'll even spy on the Martians. It may not be so much we have to learn before—just imagine this: four or five of their own fighting machines suddenly start off—heat rays right and left

What does the Stranger think about the way that most people used to live?

What is the Stranger's view of human beings?

Do Professor Pierson and the Stranger seek the same human qualities in each other?

and not a Martian in 'em. Not a Martian in 'em. But humans—humans who have learned the way how. It may even be in our time. Gee! Imagine having one of them lovely things with its heat ray wide and free! We'd turn it on Martians, we'd turn it on people. We'd bring everybody down to their knees.

PIERSON: That's your plan?

STRANGER: You and me and a few more of us we'd own the world.

PIERSON: I see.

STRANGER: Say, what's the matter? Where are you going?

PIERSON: Not to your world . . . Good-bye, stranger . . .

PIERSON: After parting with the artilleryman, I came at last to the Holland Tunnel.[11] I entered that silent tube anxious to know the fate of the great city on the other side of the Hudson. Cautiously I came out of the tunnel and made my way up Canal Street.

I reached Fourteenth Street, and there again were black powder and several bodies, and an evil ominous smell from the gratings of the cellars of some of the houses. I wandered up through the Thirties and Forties;[12] I stood alone on Times Square.[13] I caught sight of a lean dog running down Seventh Avenue with a piece of dark brown meat in his jaws, and a pack of starving mongrels at his heels. He made a wide circle around me, as though he feared I might prove a fresh competitor. I walked up Broadway in the direction of that strange powder—past silent shop windows, displaying their quiet wares to empty sidewalks—past the Capitol Theater, silent, dark—past a shooting gallery, where a row of empty guns faced a halted line of wooden ducks. Near Columbus Circle I noticed models of 1939 motorcars in the showrooms facing empty streets. From over the top of the General Motors Building, I watched a flock of black birds circling in the sky. I hurried on. Suddenly I caught sight of the hood of a Martian machine, standing somewhere in Central Park, gleaming in the late afternoon sun. An insane idea! I rushed recklessly across

What is the Stranger's goal?

What does "world" mean in this phrase?

What sensory words does the author use to help you visualize the remains of New York City?

Note the foreshadowing; when do birds usually "circle in the sky"?

---

ominous (OM uh nus) threatening; sinister
[11]**Holland Tunnel:** a tunnel under the Hudson River between New York and New Jersey
[12]**Thirties and Forties:** numbered streets across Manhattan
[13]**Times Square:** the center of the theater district in New York City

Columbus Circle and into the Park. I climbed a small hill above the pond at Sixtieth Street. From there I could see, standing in a silent row along the mall, nineteen of those great metal Titans, their cowls empty, their steel arms hanging limp by their sides. I looked in vain for the monsters that inhabit those machines.

What conflict is finally resolved in this climax?

Suddenly, my eyes were attracted to the immense flock of black birds that hovered directly below me. They circled to the ground, and there before my eyes, stark and silent, lay the Martians, with the hungry birds pecking and tearing brown shreds of flesh from their dead bodies. Later when their bodies were examined in laboratories, it was found that they were killed by the putrefactive and disease bacteria against which their systems were unprepared . . . slain, after all man's defenses had failed, by the humblest thing that God in His wisdom put upon this earth.

Before the cylinder fell there was a general belief that through all the deep of space no life existed beyond the petty

---

Titans (TYT unz) giants
putrefactive (pyoo truh FAK tiv) rotting; decomposing

surface of our minute sphere. Now we see further. Dim and wonderful is the vision I have conjured up in my mind of life spreading slowly from this little seedbed of the solar system throughout the inanimate vastness of space. But that is a remote dream. It may be that the destruction of the Martians is only a reprieve. To them, and not to us, is the future ordained perhaps.

Here, the author gives you a hint about the theme of the radio drama.

Strange it now seems to sit in my peaceful study at Princeton writing down this last chapter of the record begun at a deserted farm in Grovers Mill. Strange to see from my window the university spires dim and blue through an April haze. Strange to watch children playing in the streets. Strange to see young people strolling on the green, where the new spring grass heals the last black scars of a bruised earth. Strange to watch the sightseers enter the museum where the disassembled parts of a Martian machine are kept on public view. Strange when I recall the time when I first saw it, bright and clean-cut, hard and silent, under the dawn of that last great day.

Notice that the action has shifted to the present time.

(*Music*)

This is Orson Welles, ladies and gentlemen, out of character to assure you that *The War of the Worlds* has no further significance than as the holiday offering it was intended to be. The Mercury Theatre's own radio version of dressing up in a sheet and jumping out of a bush and saying Boo! Starting now, we couldn't soap all your windows and steal all your garden gates, by tomorrow night . . . so we did the next best thing. We annihilated the world before your very ears, and utterly destroyed the Columbia Broadcasting System. You will be relieved, I hope, to learn that we didn't mean it, and that both institutions are still open for business. So good-bye everybody, and remember, please, for the next day or so, the terrible lesson you learned tonight. That grinning, glowing, globular invader of your living room is an inhabitant of the pumpkin patch, and if your doorbell rings and nobody's there, that was no Martian . . . it's Hallowe'en.

To what event does the narrator compare the radio drama, "Invasion from Mars"?

Who is this invader?

---

reprieve (rih PREEV) postponement
globular (GLOB yuh lur) rounded

Review the Selection

UNDERSTAND THE SELECTION

Recall

1. Where do the Martians first land?

2. Where does Pierson work?

3. Identify the Martians' primary objective.

Infer

4. Describe the reactions of most New Yorkers to the Martian invasion.

5. Why is the Martians' final defeat ironic? Explain your answer.

6. Why does the original announcer interrupt the radio play?

7. Why do you think Professor Pierson decides not to join the Stranger?

Apply

8. Briefly characterize the Martians. Support your answer with specific words and phrases from the play.

9. Compare and contrast the play with a real emergency broadcast.

10. Imagine you were listening to the radio in New Jersey on the night of October 30, 1938. How would you have responded?

Respond to Literature

What technological changes in the United States during the 1930s gave *Invasion from Mars* such a large audience?

THINK ABOUT DRAMA

Once a drama is written, the finished **script** is performed by actors, who make the printed words come alive.

The **characters** include the people, animals, or even Martians in a drama. Their personalities are revealed by actions and **dialogue**. Characters are often affected by their **setting**, the time and place in which their stories take place. The sequence of actions, events, and conflicts that characters experience is called the **plot**. The principal, or main, message of a play is called its **theme**.

1. Describe in detail two settings from *Invasion from Mars*.

2. Reread the dialogue on pages 411 through 413. What kind of man is Professor Pierson?

3. What is the central conflict?

4. What kind of conflict does Pierson face? What choice does he make?

5. What is the theme of the drama?

DEVELOP YOUR VOCABULARY

Jargon refers to the particular words and phrases, or special language, used by a group of people who share the same job, profession, hobby, or interest. When musicians talk about playing a *gig*, or hiring *roadies*, for example, they are using jargon to talk about their next concert or performance, and the people who handle their musical equipment when they are touring on the road.

Jargon is usually understood by people who are part of the group. Those outside the group, however, may be unfamiliar with the unusual words and terms.

Use a dictionary or encyclopedia to determine the meaning of each of the following "space" jargon words, and write original sentences using six of them. If you choose, you may suggest additional space jargon words.

1. booster   **5.** Mach

2. G-suit   **6.** touchdown

3. pitch   **7.** glitch

4. dry run   **8.** LEM

Learn About

TONE

In literature, **tone** is a writer's emotional attitude toward his or her subject. Tone is expressed through a writer's choice of words and details, and the way that he or she describes characters and events.

You may find it helpful to think of tone as a writer's way of "speaking." If, for example, a writer feels pleasantly amused or happy about a particular subject, he or she might "speak" with descriptive words, such as *gleeful*, *delighted*, or *thrilled*.

As you read, pay close attention to the words and phrases that a writer uses to reveal his or her particular attitude. Ask yourself whether these words suggest a tone of anger, sadness, joy, amazement, or some other emotion.

As you read "Futility," ask yourself:

1. What is the tone, or author's attitude, in this poem?
2. What words or phrases help you to determine this attitude?

READING FOCUS

Evaluate the Poet's Purpose Knowing the writer's purpose, or reason for writing a piece, helps the reader know how to react to it. Think about the poet's purpose as you read "Futility."

WRITING CONNECTION

On a piece of paper, write the words "Nice outfit." Say the words out loud. What attitude do they suggest? Now, write the various meanings you might achieve if you pronounced this phrase in different tones of voice.

FUTILITY

by Mary S. Hawling

I try to capture rhythm with
The make-shift words that limit me:
The wind has more success than I
By simply bending down a tree.

5   I seek for color, and must be
Content with some cold, distant name:
Yet swiftly, as the night walks near,
The sky is surging bronze and flame.

I struggle for a single line
10   To measure an emotion by:
A wild bird, effortless, takes wing
And writes a poem across the sky.

---

futility (fyoo TIL ih tee) lack of success; uselessness
make-shift or **makeshift** (MAYK shift) substitute; temporary

Review the Selection

UNDERSTAND THE SELECTION

Recall

1. What has more success than the speaker at capturing rhythm?

2. According to the speaker, what colors light the night sky?

3. To what does the speaker compare a wild bird?

Infer

4. Do you think the speaker of the poem finds writing difficult? Explain.

5. Explain the meaning of *name* in "Content with some cold distant name."

6. What do the last two lines of the poem mean to you?

7. What do you think the speaker is saying about writing a poem?

Apply

8. Compare and contrast the poet's efforts with the efforts of nature.

9. Do you think the author is successful in communicating beauty?

10. Choose two new titles for the poem.

Respond to Literature

Do you think "Futility" is an appropriate choice to conclude this unit? What events in the early 20th century might be characterized as futile?

THINK ABOUT TONE

When we talk about the sarcastic tone of a cutting remark or the friendly tone of a personal letter, we mean the specific attitude that is expressed by the speaker or writer. Another way to understand a writer's **tone**, is to think of it as his or her tone of voice. Just as you speak harshly when you are angry, an angry writer will use descriptive words that convey that feeling. A writer who is trying to convey a sympathetic tone will use words that express sympathy.

1. Does the title of the poem suggest that it will have a certain tone?

2. Does your reading of the poem support the view?

3. What word details help you to determine the tone of the poem?

4. What words would you use to change this tone?

5. The author says that writing a poem is an exercise in futility. Do you agree with her attitude? Explain the reasons for your opinion.

READING FOCUS

Evaluate the Poet's Purpose What do you think the poet's purpose was in writing "Futility"? Why do you think she expressed these thoughts in a poem? How did you react, knowing her purpose?

DEVELOP YOUR VOCABULARY

Antonyms are words that have opposite, or nearly opposite, meanings. For example, *reprimand* means "to scold harshly." An antonym for *reprimand* is *praise*. Understanding antonyms helps you to figure out contrasting ideas or statements.

Read each sentence below and choose the correct antonym for each italicized word. You may consult a dictionary.

1. The teacher *deferred* our test until next week.
   a. postponed   **c.** rushed
   b. delayed   **d.** moved

2. Preparing for the debate had put him in a *pensive* mood.
   a. thoughtful   **c.** tired
   b. silly   **d.** cultured

3. The *tumult* from the cheering crowd drowned out the announcer's voice.
   a. disturbance   **c.** silence
   b. uproar   **d.** screaming

4. Lost in a pleasant *reverie*, she didn't hear the doorbell ring.
   a. distraction   **c.** daydream
   b. concentration   **d.** diversion

The Contemporary Perspective

Wish for nothing larger
Than your own small heart
Or greater than a star.
—Alice Walker

Christina's World, Andrew Wyeth, 1948. Tempera on gessoed panel, 32¼" × 47¾" (81.9 × 121.3 cm). Collection, The Museum of Modern Art, New York. Purchase. Photograph ©2000 The Museum of Modern Art, New York

Learn About

POETIC FORM

A poem can be written in many different ways. A poem can read like a speech or like someone talking to you. How a poem affects you as you read it depends partly on its form, the way the poem is organized. Nothing about a poem is accidental; its words and the way they are organized are carefully considered.

There are different ways a poem can be organized; one basic way is by stanza. A **stanza** is simply two or more lines of poetry grouped together. A stanza may consist of one thought, action, image, or emotion, or more than one. Stanzas can be arranged by the passage of time, by subject, or as part of a series, one leading to the next. A stanza may have meaning by itself; some stanzas must be read together to have meaning.

As you read "The Secret," ask yourself:
1. How does one stanza lead to another?
2. How could the poem be organized differently?

WRITING CONNECTION

The form of a poem can make its meaning clearer or more difficult. Rewrite the poem in sentence form to see if the effect is different.

READING FOCUS

Summarize Text When you summarize text, you condense it to its most important points. Even a short poem can be summarized in a sentence or two that express the main idea or ideas of the poem. After you read the next selection, reread it and try writing a summary of its meaning. Notice how doing this improves your understanding of the main idea.

THE SECRET

by Denise Levertov

Two girls discover
the secret of life
in a sudden line of
poetry.

5 I who don't know the
secret wrote
the line. They
told me

(through a third person)
10 they had found it
but not what it was
not even

what line it was. No doubt
by now, more than a week
15 later, they have forgotten
the secret,

the line, the name of
the poem. I love them
for finding what
20 I can't find,

and for loving me
for the line I wrote,
and for forgetting it
so that

25 a thousand times, till death
finds them, they may
discover it again, in other
lines

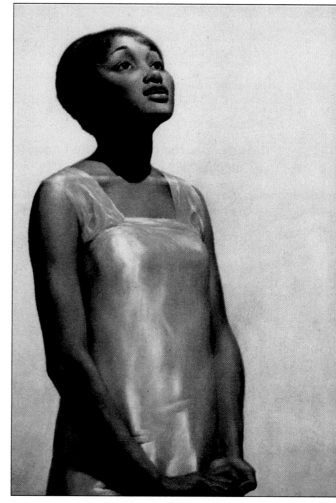

Ruby Green Singing, James Chapin.
Norton Museum of Art, West Palm Beach, FL.
Bequest of R.H. Norton

in other
30 happenings. And for
wanting to know it,
for

assuming there is
such a secret, yes,
35 for that
most of all.

Review the Selection

UNDERSTAND THE SELECTION

Recall

1. Where is the secret of "The Secret" discovered?

2. Why does the poet love the two girls "most of all"?

3. Explain how the poet knew the girls discovered the secret.

Infer

4. How did the two girls discover the secret?

5. The girls forgot the secret—why isn't that important?

6. Name several other places the secret might be found.

7. Why is the line of poetry described as sudden?

Apply

8. Imagine you discovered the secret of life. What do you think it is? How would you know when you found it? What might make you forget it?

9. Where would you look for the secret of life?

10. Write another title for the poem.

Respond to Literature

This poem says that the secret of life is ours to discover. Why is it important that we do?

THINK ABOUT POETIC FORM

The division of a poem into stanzas is only one aspect of poetic form. Each aspect, or element, of the poem except the **substance**—what the poem is about—contributes to the form. Rhythms fall into forms, as do meters. Rhyme scheme, if there is one, is a matter of form. So are length of line, length of poem, each individual image, and the relationship of one image to another. In short, **form** concerns the pattern, or structure, that is used to give expression to what the author wishes to say—to the content, or substance, of the poem.

1. Describe the form of the stanzas in "The Secret."

2. Where is the most important thought of the poem located?

3. Does each stanza contain a single thought or emotion?

4. What is the poet explaining in lines 21 to 35?

5. How would the effect of the poem be changed if the lines were grouped into one long stanza?

READING FOCUS

Summarize Text After you read "The Secret," you summarized it. In one sentence, state the main idea. How did summarizing the poem help you understand its meaning?

DEVELOP YOUR VOCABULARY

What do the words *foreign* and *alien* have in common? They are **synonyms**, meaning that they share the same, or almost the same, meaning.

In daily usage, however, synonyms can carry meanings that are quite different. Consider the noun *speech*, meaning "a talk or address given in public." Synonyms for *speech* include *address*, *oration*, *lecture*, *talk*, and *sermon*. Each of these synonyms means more than the general definition of *speech*. You would expect to hear a lecture in a classroom or a speech at a political meeting, but not in a church, where a sermon might be expected instead.

1. Which of the following are synonyms for *happening*?
   a. schedule
   b. occurrence
   c. location
   d. event

2. Which of the following words are synonyms for *beautiful*?
   a. pretty
   b. lovely
   c. wealthy
   d. abundant

Figurative language is language that departs from the original, exact, or literal meaning of words in order to achieve a fresh way of expressing an idea or image. Some types of figurative language are listed below.

Personification is a figure of speech in which inanimate things or abstract ideas are given human qualities or sensibilities.

Onomatopoeia is the use of words whose sounds suggest their meaning. Some examples are *buzz*, *jingle*, *bang*, and *pop*.

Simile is a figure of speech in which one thing is specifically likened to a dissimilar thing; the words *like* or *as* are used in the comparison.

Metaphor is a figure of speech in which two dissimilar things are likened to each other directly, as if one were the other.

As you read the poems, ask yourself:
1. What figures of speech are used in the poems?
2. What fresh impressions do you get from reading the poems?

READING FOCUS

Paraphrase Poetry When you paraphrase, you restate the speaker's experiences and feelings in your own words. Restating the lines or stanzas of a poem will help you to clarify their meanings. As you read the next three poems, practice paraphrasing the lines of each one.

WRITING CONNECTION

Write four sentences, using a different figure of speech in each.

SNOW

by Dorothy Aldis

The fenceposts wear marshmallow hats
On a snowy day;
Bushes in their night gowns
Are kneeling down to pray—
And all the trees have silver skirts
And want to dance away.

December Snow, C. E. Burchfield. Kennedy Galleries, Inc.

UMBILICAL

by Eve Merriam

You can take away my mother,
you can take away my sister,
but don't take away
my little transistor.

5 I can do without sunshine,
I can do without Spring,
but I can't do without
my ear to that thing.

I can live without water,
10 in a hole in the ground,
but I can't live without
that sound that sound that sound that sOWnd.

Still Life Radio Tube, Stuart Davis.
The Bettmann Archive

---

umbilical (um BIL ih kul) here, necessary for life; from "umbilical cord,"
   which keeps an unborn baby alive
transistor (tran ZIS tur) here, it means a transistor radio

Cloud World, Maynard Dixon. Arizona West Galleries

Cumulus Clouds

by Sheryl Nelms

a gallon of
rich
country cream

hand-whipped
5   into stiff
peaks

flung
from the beater

into dollops
10   across a blue oilcloth

---

cumulus (KYOO myuh lus) a type of rounded, fluffy cloud
dollops (DOL ups) mounds
oilcloth (OIL klawth) waterproofed cloth

Review the Selection

Recall

1. What is described in "Snow"?

2. How is the sky described in "Cumulus Clouds"?

3. What is most important to the speaker in "Umbilical"?

Infer

4. What general image does Dorothy Aldis use for snow?

5. What color are the clouds in "Cumulus Clouds"?

6. Why are the bushes described as kneeling in "Snow"?

7. Why do you think the last word in "Umbilical" is spelled "sOWnd"?

Apply

8. Imagine a snow-covered field. What is an everyday household object to which you could compare it?

9. Write another title for "Umbilical." Be sure it expresses the poem's meaning.

10. Why do you think the speaker of "Umbilical" says "you can take away my mother" and "sister"?

Respond to Literature

We live in a high-tech society; what does the poem "Umbilical" say about the effect of technology on our lives?

THINK ABOUT FIGURES OF SPEECH

Figures of speech help to clarify and illustrate ideas. They make writing more vivid and give life to inanimate objects. They aid readers in making new associations. A figure of speech is sometimes so essential to a poem that to remove it would destroy the poem.

1. When Aldis says that fenceposts wear hats she is using what figure of speech? Name two other examples of this figure of speech in her poem.

2. The title "Umbilical" is an example of which figure of speech? What comparison is implied in the title?

3. Why does the poet spell the last sound in "Umbilical" as sOWnd?

4. The entire third poem is an extended metaphor for what two things?

5. Are there any similes in the three poems? If so, where are they?

READING FOCUS

Paraphrase Poetry You have paraphrased the poems you just read. In your own words, state how paraphrasing helped to clarify the poems' meanings for you.

DEVELOP YOUR VOCABULARY

There are many ways in which the vocabulary of English has expanded. One way is by the addition of new words to the language. Another is by adding new meanings to existing words. Many words have gained new meanings by way of **metaphor**. The process is simple: a word used in one context is applied, by its similarity, to an object in another context. This is how names of parts of the body came to be applied to so many other things. Examples are the *arms* and *legs* of a chair, the *hands* and *face* of a clock, or the *eye* of a potato.

In the following sentences, all of the items *except one* are correct. Which item in each sentence is the incorrect one?

1. *Saws*, *rakes*, *gears*, and *rivers* have teeth.

2. A *drum*, *beet*, *hammer*, and a *pin* have a head.

3. A *bottle*, *violin*, *bale of hay*, and a *person* have a neck.

4. A *laundry bag*, *bed*, *book page*, and a *hill* have a foot.

Learn About

CHARACTERS' MOTIVES

A **motive** is an emotion or reason that causes a character to behave in a certain way. A motive may also cause an action to occur. There may even be more than one motive behind a character's actions.

The motive may come about as a result of outside forces. It may be a deep impulse within a person.

An author does not always clearly state characters' motives. Often you must read between the lines to identify them. As you read this selection, ask yourself:

1. Why is the character behaving as she does?
2. What are the results of her behavior?

WRITING CONNECTION

Write a short paragraph describing how you behaved in a specific social situation. What external or internal motives caused your behavior?

READING FOCUS

Use Word Identification What do you do when you encounter a word you do not understand? A dictionary may not always be close at hand. Therefore, it is helpful to know how to figure out word meanings. To do this, break the word down into prefixes, suffixes, roots, and other words with which you are familiar. As you encounter unfamiliar words, ask yourself:

1. Which parts of this word look familiar?
2. What are the meanings of the recognizable word parts?
3. What can I infer is the meaning of the whole word?

TWO KINDS
from The Joy Luck Club

by Amy Tan

My mother believed you could be anything you wanted to be in America. You could open a restaurant. You could work for the government and get good retirement. You could buy a house with almost no money down. You could become rich. You could become instantly famous.

"Of course you can be prodigy, too," my mother told me when I was nine. "You can be best anything. What does Auntie Lindo know? Her daughter, she is only best tricky."

America was where all my mother's hopes lay. She had come here in 1949 after losing everything in China: her mother and father, her family home, her first husband, and two daughters, twin baby girls. But she never looked back with regret. There were so many ways for things to get better.

We didn't immediately pick the right kind of prodigy. At first my mother thought I could be a Chinese Shirley Temple. We'd watch Shirley's old movies on TV as though they were training films. My mother would poke my arm and say, *"Ni kan"* — You watch. And I would see Shirley tapping her feet, or singing a sailor song, or pursing her lips into a very round O while saying, "Oh my goodness."

"Ni kan," said my mother as Shirley's eyes flooded with tears. "You already know how. Don't need talent for crying!"

Soon after my mother got this idea about Shirley Temple, she took me to a beauty training school in the Mission district and put me in the hands of a student who could barely hold the scissors without shaking. Instead of getting big fat curls, I emerged with an uneven mass of crinkly black fuzz. My mother dragged me off to the bathroom and tried to wet down my hair.

"You look like Negro Chinese," she lamented, as if I had done this on purpose.

The instructor of the beauty training school had to lop off these soggy clumps to make my hair even again. "Peter Pan is very popular these days," the instructor assured my mother. I now had hair the length of a boy's, with straight-across bangs that hung at a slant two inches above my eyebrows. I liked the haircut and it made me actually look forward to my future fame.

In fact, in the beginning, I was just as excited as my mother, maybe even more so.

---

prodigy (PRAHD uh jee) a child remarkably bright in some way

I pictured this prodigy part of me as many different images, trying each one on for size. I was a dainty ballerina girl standing by the curtains waiting to hear the right music that would send me floating on my tiptoes. I was like the Christ child lifted out of the straw manger, crying with holy indignity. I was Cinderella stepping from her pumpkin carriage with sparkly cartoon music filling the air.

In all of my imaginings, I was filled with a sense that I would soon become *perfect*. My mother and father would adore me. I would be beyond reproach. I would never feel the need to sulk for anything.

But sometimes the prodigy in me became impatient. "If you don't hurry up and get me out here, I'm disappearing for good," it warned. "And then you'll always be nothing."

Every night after dinner, my mother and I would sit at the Formica kitchen table. She would present new tests, taking her examples from stories of amazing children she had read in *Ripley's Believe It or Not*, or *Good Housekeeping*, *Reader's Digest*, and a dozen other magazines she kept in a pile in our bathroom. My mother got these magazines from people whose houses she cleaned. And since she cleaned many houses each week, we had a great assortment. She would look through them all, searching for stories about remarkable children.

The first night she brought out a story about a three-year-old boy who knew the capitals of all the states and even most of the European countries. A teacher was quoted as saying the little boy could also pronounce the names of the foreign cities correctly.

"What's the capital of Finland?" my mother asked me, looking at the magazine story.

All I knew was the capital of California, because Sacramento was the name of the street we lived on in Chinatown. "Nairobi!" I guessed, saying the most foreign word I could think of. She checked to see if that was possibly one way to pronounce "Helsinki" before showing me the answer.

The tests got harder—multiplying numbers in my head, finding the queen of hearts in a deck of cards, trying to stand on my head without using my hands, predicting the daily temperatures in Los Angeles, New York, and London.

One night I had to look at a page from the Bible for three minutes and then report everything I could remember. "Now Jehoshaphat had riches and honor in abundance and . . . that's all I remember, Ma," I said.

And after seeing my mother's disappointed face once again, something inside of me began to die. I hated the tests, the raised hopes and failed expectations. Before going to bed that night, I looked in the mirror above the bathroom sink and when I saw only my face staring back— and that it would always be this ordinary face—I began to cry. Such a sad, ugly girl! I made high-pitched noises like a crazed animal, trying to scratch out the face in the mirror.

Formica (for MY kuh) trade name for heat-resistant plastic

And then I saw what seemed to be the prodigy side of me—because I had never seen that face before. I looked at my reflection, blinking so I could see more clearly. The girl staring back at me was angry, powerful. This girl and I were the same. I had new thoughts, willful thoughts, or rather thoughts filled with lots of won'ts. I won't let her change me, I promised myself. I won't be what I'm not.

So now on nights when my mother presented her tests, I performed listlessly, my head propped on one arm. I pretended to be bored. And I was. I got so bored I started counting bellows of the foghorns out on the bay while my mother drilled me in other areas. The sound was comforting and reminded me of the cow jumping over the moon. And the next day, I played a game with myself, seeing if my mother would give up on me before eight bellows. After a while I usually counted only one, maybe two bellows at most. At last she was beginning to give up hope.

Two or three months had gone by without any mention of my being a prodigy again. And then one day my mother was watching *The Ed Sullivan Show* on TV. The TV was old and the sound kept shorting out. Every time my mother got halfway up from the sofa to adjust the set, the sound would go back on and Ed would be talking. As soon as she sat down, Ed would go silent again. She got up, the TV broke into loud piano music. She sat down. Silence. Up and down, back and forth, quiet and loud. It was like a stiff embraceless dance between her and the TV set. Finally she stood by the set with her hand on the sound dial.

She seemed entranced by the music, a little frenzied piano piece with this mesmerizing quality, sort of quick passages and then teasing lilting ones before it returned to the quick playful parts.

"*Ni kan,*" my mother said, calling me over with hurried hand gestures, "Look here."

I could see why my mother was fascinated by the music. It was being pounded out by a little Chinese girl, about nine years old, with a Peter Pan haircut. The girl had the sauciness of Shirley Temple. She was proudly modest like a proper Chinese child. And she also did this fancy sweep of a curtsy, so that the fluffy skirt of her white dress cascaded slowly to the floor like the petals of a large carnation.

In spite of these warning signs, I wasn't worried. Our family had no piano and we couldn't afford to buy one, let alone reams of sheet music and piano lessons. So I could be generous in my comments when my mother bad-mouthed the little girl on TV.

"Play note right, but doesn't sound good! No singing sound," complained my mother.

"What are you picking on her for?" I said carelessly. "She's pretty good. Maybe she's not the best, but she's trying hard." I knew almost immediately I would be sorry I said that.

---

bellows (BEHL ohz) roars; loud noises
mesmerizing (MEHZ muh ry zing) hypotizing; casting a spell
sauciness (SAH see nuhs) state of being bold or rude
cascaded (kas KAY dihd) flowed down like a small waterfall

"Just like you," she said. "Not the best. Because you not trying." She gave a little huff as she let go of the sound dial and sat down on the sofa.

The little Chinese girl sat down also to play an encore of "Anitra's Dance" by Grieg. I remember the song, because later on I had to learn how to play it.

Three days after watching *The Ed Sullivan Show*, my mother told me what my schedule would be for piano lessons and piano practice. She had talked to Mr. Chong, who lived on the first floor of our apartment building. Mr. Chong was a retired piano teacher and my mother had traded housecleaning services for weekly lessons and a piano for me to practice on every day, two hours a day, from four to six.

When my mother told me this, I felt as though I had been sent to hell. I whined and then kicked my foot a little when I couldn't stand it anymore.

"Why don't you like me the way I am? I'm *not* a genius! I can't play the piano. And even if I could, I wouldn't go on TV if you paid me a million dollars!" I cried.

My mother slapped me. "Who ask you be genius?" she shouted. "Only ask you be your best. For your sake. You think I want you be genius? Hnnh! What for! Who ask you!"

"So ungrateful," I heard her mutter in Chinese. "If she had as much talent as she has temper, she would be famous now."

Mr. Chong, whom I secretly nicknamed Old Chong, was very strange, always tapping his fingers to the silent music of an invisible orchestra. He looked ancient in my eyes. He had lost most of his hair on top of his head and he wore thick glasses and had eyes that always looked tired and sleepy. But he must have been younger than I thought, since he lived with his mother and was not yet married.

I met Old Lady Chong once and that was enough. She had this peculiar smell like a baby that had done something in its pants. And her fingers felt like a dead person's, like an old peach I once found in the back of the refrigerator; the skin just slid off the meat when I picked it up.

I soon found out why Old Chong had retired from teaching piano. He was deaf. "Like Beethoven!" he shouted to me. "We're both listening only in our head!" And he would start to conduct his frantic silent sonatas.

Our lessons went like this. He would open the book and point to the different things, explaining their purpose: "Key! Treble! Bass! No sharps or flats! So this is C major! Listen now and play after me!"

And then he would play the C scale a few times, a simple chord, and then, as if inspired by an old, unreachable itch, he gradually added more notes and running trills and a pounding bass until the music was really something quite grand.

I would play after him, the simple scale, the simple chord, and then I played some nonsense that sounded like a cat running up and down on top of garbage cans.

---

sonatas (suh NAH tuhs) compositions for one or two musical instruments

Old Chong smiled and applauded and then said, "Very good! But now you must learn to keep time!"

So that's how I discovered that Old Chong's eyes were too slow to keep up with the wrong notes I was playing. He went through the motions in half-time. To help me keep rhythm, he stood behind me, pushing down on my right shoulder for every beat. He balanced pennies on top of my wrists so I would keep them still as I slowly played scales and arpeggios. He had me curve my hand around an apple and keep that shape when playing chords. He marched stiffly to show me how to make each finger dance up and down, staccato like an obedient little soldier.

He taught me all of these things, and that was how I also learned I could be lazy and get away with mistakes, lots of mistakes. If I hit the wrong notes because I hadn't practiced enough, I never corrected myself. I just kept playing in rhythm. And Old Chong kept conducting his own private reverie.

So maybe I never really gave myself a fair chance. I did pick up the basics pretty quickly, and I might have become a good pianist at that young age. But I was so determined not to try, not to be anybody different that I learned to play only the most ear-splitting preludes, the most discordant hymns.

Over the next year, I practiced like this, dutifully in my own way. And then one day I heard my mother and her friend Lindo Jong both talking in a loud bragging tone of voice so others could hear. It was after church, and I was leaning against the brick wall wearing a dress with stiff white petticoats. Auntie Lindo's daughter, Waverly, who was about my age, was standing farther down the wall about five feet away. We had grown up together and shared all the closeness of two sisters squabbling over crayons and dolls. In other words, for the most part, we hated each other. I thought she was snotty. Waverly Jong had gained a certain amount of fame as "Chinatown's little Chinese Chess Champion."

"She bring home too many trophy," lamented Auntie Lindo that Sunday. "All day she play chess. All day I have no time do nothing but dust off her winnings." She threw a scolding look at Waverly, who pretended not to see her.

"You lucky you don't have this problem," said Aunt Lindo with a sigh to my mother.

And my mother squared her shoulders and bragged: "Our problem worser than yours. If we ask Jing-mei wash dish, she hear nothing but music. It's like you can't stop this natural talent."

And right then, I was determined to put a stop to her foolish pride.

A few weeks later, Old Chong and my mother conspired to have me play in a talent show which would be held in the

---

arpeggios (ahr PEHJ ee ohz) notes in a chord played in quick succession
staccato (stuh KAHT oh) music played with distinct breaks between notes
reverie (REHV uh ree) dreamy thoughts of pleasant things
petticoats (PEHT ee kohts) lace or ruffles on the bottom of a skirt

church hall. By then, my parents had saved up enough to buy me a secondhand piano, a black Wurlitzer spinet with a scarred bench. It was the showpiece of our living room.

For the talent show, I was to play a piece called "Pleading Child" from Schumann's *Scenes from Childhood*. It was a simple, moody piece that sounded more difficult than it was. I was supposed to memorize the whole thing, playing the repeat parts twice to make the piece sound longer. But I dawdled over it, playing a few bars and then cheating, looking up to see what notes followed. I never really listened to what I was playing. I daydreamed about being somewhere else, about being someone else.

The part I liked to practice best was the fancy curtsy: right foot out, touch the rose on the carpet with a pointed foot, sweep to the side, left leg bends, look up and smile.

My parents invited all the couples from the Joy Luck Club to witness my debut. Auntie Lindo and Uncle Tin were there. Waverly and her two older brothers had also come. The first two rows were filled with children both younger and older than I was. The littlest ones got to go first. They recited simple nursery rhymes, squawked out tunes on miniature violins, twirled Hula Hoops, pranced in pink ballet tutus, and when they bowed or curtsied, the audience would sigh in unison, "Awww," and then clap enthusiastically.

When my turn came, I was very confident. I remember my childish excitement.

It was as if I knew, without a doubt, that the prodigy side of me really did exist. I had no fear whatsoever, no nervousness. I remember thinking to myself, This is it! This is it! I looked out over the audience, at my mother's blank face, my father's yawn, Auntie Lindo's stiff-lipped smile, Waverly's sulky expression. I had on a white dress layered with sheets of lace, and a pink bow in my Peter Pan haircut. As I sat down I envisioned people jumping to their feet and Ed Sullivan rushing up to introduce me to everyone on TV.

And I started to play. It was so beautiful. I was so caught up in how lovely I looked at first I didn't worry how I would sound. So it was a surprise to me when I hit the first wrong note and I realized something didn't sound quite right. And then I hit another and another followed that. A chill started at the top of my head and began to trickle down. Yet I couldn't stop playing, as though my hands were bewitched. I kept thinking my fingers would adjust themselves back, like a train switching to the right track. I played this strange jumble through two repeats, the sour notes staying with me all the way to the end.

When I stood up, I discovered my legs were shaking. Maybe I had just been nervous and the audience, like Old Chong, had seen me go through the right motions and had not heard anything wrong at all. I swept my foot out, went down on my knee, looked up and smiled. The room was quiet, except for Old Chong, who was beaming and shouting,

---

spinet (SPIHN it) small piano
Joy Luck Club (JOY LUK KLUB) a group of women who met to play games and tell stories

"Bravo! Bravo! Well done!" But then I saw my mother's face, her stricken face. The audience clapped weakly, and as I walked back to my chair, with my whole face quivering as I tried not to cry, I heard a little boy whisper loudly to his mother, "That was awful," and the mother whispered back, "Well, she certainly tried."

And now I realized how many people were in the audience, the whole world it seemed. I was aware of eyes burning into my back. I felt the shame of my mother and father as they sat stiffly throughout the rest of the show.

We could have escaped during intermission. Pride and some strange sense of honor must have anchored my parents to their chairs. And so we watched it all: the eighteen-year-old boy with a fake mustache who did a magic show and juggled flaming hoops while riding a unicycle. The breasted girl with white makeup who sang from *Madama Butterfly* and got honorable mention. And the eleven-year-old boy who won first prize playing a tricky violin song that sounded like a busy bee.

After the show, the Hsus, the Jongs, and the St. Clairs from the Joy Luck Club came up to my mother and father.

"Lots of talented kids," Auntie Lindo said vaguely, smiling broadly.

"That was somethin' else," said my father, and I wondered if he was referring to me in a humorous way, or whether he even remembered what I had done.

Waverly looked at me and shrugged her shoulders. "You aren't a genius like me," she said matter-of-factly. And if I hadn't felt so bad, I would have pulled her braids and punched her stomach.

But my mother's expression was what devastated me: a quiet, blank look that said she had lost everything. I felt the same way, and it seemed as if everybody were now coming up, like gawkers at the scene of an accident, to see what parts were actually missing. When we got on the bus to go home, my father was humming the busy-bee tune and my mother was silent. I kept thinking she wanted to wait until we got home before shouting at me. But when my father unlocked the door to our apartment, my mother walked in and then went to the back, into the bedroom. No accusations. No blame. And in a way, I felt disappointed, I had been waiting for her to start shouting, so I could shout back and cry and blame her for all my misery.

I assumed the talent-show fiasco meant I never had to play the piano again. But two days later, after school, my mother came out of the kitchen and saw me watching TV.

"Four clock," she reminded me as if it were any other day. I was stunned, as though she were asking me to go through the talent-show torture again. I wedged myself more tightly in front of the TV.

"Turn off TV," she called from the kitchen five minutes later.

I didn't budge. And then I decided. I didn't have to do what my mother said

---

accusations (AK yoo ZAY shuhnz) charges of wrongdoing
fiasco (fee AS koh) a humiliating failure

anymore. I wasn't her slave. This wasn't China. I had listened to her before and look what happened. She was the stupid one.

She came out of the kitchen and stood in the arched entryway of the living room. "Four clock," she said once again, louder.

"I'm not going to play anymore," I said nonchalantly. "Why should I? I'm not a genius."

She walked over and stood in front of the TV. I saw her chest was heaving up and down in an angry way.

"No!" I said, and I now felt stronger, as if my true self had finally emerged. So this was what had been inside me all along.

"No! I won't!" I screamed.

She yanked me by the arm, pulled me off the floor, snapped off the TV. She was frighteningly strong, half pulling, half carrying me toward the piano as I kicked the throw rugs under my feet. She lifted me up onto the hard bench. I was sobbing now, looking at her bitterly. Her chest was heaving even more and her mouth was open, smiling crazily as if she were pleased I was crying.

"You want me to be someone that I'm not!" I sobbed. "I'll never be the kind of daughter you want me to be!"

"Only two kinds of daughters," she shouted in Chinese. "Those who are obedient and those who follow their own mind! Only one kind of daughter can live in this house. Obedient daughter!"

"Then I wish I wasn't your daughter. I wish you weren't my mother," I shouted. As I said these things I got scared. It felt like worms and toads and slimy things crawling out of my chest, but it also felt

good, as if this awful side of me had surfaced, at last.

"Too late change this," said my mother shrilly.

And I could sense her anger rising to its breaking point. I wanted to see it spill over. And that's when I remembered the babies she had lost in China, the ones we never talked about. "Then I wish I'd never been born!" I shouted. "I wish I were dead! Like them."

It was as if I had said the magic words. Alakazam!—and her face went blank, her mouth closed, her arms went slack, and she backed out of the room, stunned, as if she were blowing away like a small brown leaf, thin, brittle, lifeless.

It was not the only disappointment my mother felt in me. In the years that followed, I failed her so many times, each time asserting my own will, my right to fall short of expectations. I didn't get straight A's. I didn't become class president. I didn't get into Stanford. I dropped out of college.

For unlike my mother, I did not believe I could be anything I wanted to be. I could only be me.

And for all those years, we never talked about the disaster at the recital or my terrible accusations afterward at the piano bench. All that remained unchecked, like a betrayal that was now unspeakable. So I never found a way to ask her why she had hoped for something so large that failure was inevitable.

And even worse, I never asked her what frightened me the most: Why had she given up hope?

For after our struggle at the piano, she never mentioned my playing again. The lessons stopped. The lid to the piano was closed, shutting out the dust, my misery, and her dreams.

So she surprised me. A few years ago, she offered to give me the piano, for my thirtieth birthday. I had not played in all those years. I saw the offer as a sign of forgiveness, a tremendous burden removed.

"Are you sure?" I asked shyly. "I mean, won't you and Dad miss it?"

"No, this is your piano," she said firmly. "Always your piano. You only one can play."

"Well, I probably can't play anymore," I said. "It's been years."

"You pick up fast," said my mother, as if she knew this was certain. "You have a natural talent. You could be genius if you want to."

"No I couldn't."

"You just not trying," said my mother. And she was neither angry nor sad. She said it as to announce a fact that could never be disproved. "Take it," she said.

But I didn't at first. It was enough that she offered it to me. And after that, every time I saw it in my parents' living room, standing in front of the bay windows, it made me feel proud, as if it were a shiny trophy I had won back.

Last week I sent a tuner over to my parents' apartment and had the piano reconditioned, for purely sentimental reasons. My mother had died a few months before and I had been getting things in order for my father, a little bit at a time. I put the jewelry in special silk pouches. The sweaters she had knitted in yellow, pink, bright orange—all the colors I hated—I put those in moth-proof boxes. I found some old Chinese silk dresses, the kind with little slits up the sides. I rubbed the old silk against my skin, then wrapped them in tissue and decided to take them home with me.

After I had the piano tuned, I opened the lid and touched the keys. It sounded even richer than I remembered. Really, it was a very good piano. Inside the bench were the same exercise notes with handwritten scales, the same secondhand music books with their covers held together with yellow tape.

I opened up the Schumann book to the dark little piece I had played at the recital. It was on the left-hand side of the page, "Pleading Child." It looked more difficult than I remembered. I played a few bars, surprised at how easily the notes came back to me.

And for the first time, or so it seemed, I noticed the piece on the right-hand side. It was called "Perfectly Contented." I tried to play this one as well. It had a lighter melody but the same flowing rhythm and turned out to be quite easy. "Pleading Child" was shorter but slower; "Perfectly Contented" was longer, but faster. And after I played them both a few times, I realized they were two halves of the same song.

---

disproved (dis PROOVD) shown to be incorrect or false

Review the Selection

UNDERSTAND THE SELECTION

Recall

1. How did the mother pay for her daughter's piano lessons?

2. What did the narrator call her piano teacher?

3. Describe the mother's reaction to her daughter's performance.

Infer

4. How are the mother's hopes for her daughter a reflection of her attitude toward the United States?

5. What is the narrator's attitude toward Mr. Chong? How do you know?

6. In the mother's opinion, what kind of daughter is the narrator?

7. Was the father involved in his daughter's life? Explain.

Apply

8. When someone has high expectations for you, are you motivated to do your best or to give up?

9. What are some common conflicts that arise between young people and their parents or guardians?

10. What are two qualities of a good mother? A good daughter?

Respond to Literature

What causes tension between the mother and daughter in "Two Kinds"?

THINK ABOUT MOTIVE

Writers reveal characters' motives as a means of creating round, more complete characters. Identifying and analyzing these motives help the reader gain insight into the character's personality.

1. What are the mother's motives for wanting her daughter to be a prodigy?

2. What do these motives reveal about the mother's personality?

3. What is the narrator's motive for refusing to master the piano?

4. What does her refusal to play the piano reveal about her personality?

5. Is the daughter driven by outside forces, or does a deeper impulse explain her behavior? Explain.

READING FOCUS

Use Word Identification Choose two words from the selection that were unfamiliar to you. List and define the word parts. Then define the complete word. Next, use each word in a sentence about the story.

DEVELOP YOUR VOCABULARY

A suffix is a word part added to the end of a base word to make a new word. By adding a suffix to a root, or base, word, you can change the meaning. For example, the word *care* means "to feel an interest or worry." When you add the suffix *–less* to the root word to make *careless*, the meaning is the opposite, or "done without care." More than one suffix can be added to the same word, such as *careful*, *careless*, *carelessly*.

The words below come from the story. Identify and define each root word within the longer word. Then identify the suffix or suffixes and meaning of the longer word. Use the longer word in an original sentence.

Suffixes	Meaning
-ful	full of
-ly	in a certain way
-ness	the condition that is

1. carelessly
2. enthusiastically
3. nervousness
4. frighteningly
5. instantly
6. powerful

Learn About

READING FOCUS

Understand Levels of Meaning Many writers—and especially poets—write on more than one level of meaning. You can take their words literally, but there is also a deeper meaning. For example, the story of the three little pigs can be enjoyed just as it is told, but may also be taken as a lesson about the results of acting foolishly. In the poem on the next page, the first three stanzas have two levels of meaning. After reading the poem a few times, write down the deeper meaning that you find.

TONE

No matter what its subject is, every work of literature carries with it its own, individual **tone**. Tone can be defined as the author's attitude toward the subject of his or her work. Tone is also defined as the author's attitude toward the audience reading his or her work.

As you read a poem ask yourself how the poet feels about his or her subject. Tone can be any number of different attitudes toward the subject of the work: formal, serious, informal, playful, intimate, sarcastic or doubtful, to name a few. A subject important to the writer may be treated solemnly or seriously. The writer will treat the subject seriously if he or she wants you to take it seriously.

As you read the poem, ask yourself:
1. How does the poet feel about her subject?
2. How does the poet want the reader to feel about the subject?

WRITING CONNECTION

Writers use tone to reveal their attitude toward a subject. Think of an activity you like and one that you do not like. Write a paragraph about each, telling your reader why you like or do not like the activity. Compare the tone of each paragraph with that of the other.

The World Is Not a Pleasant Place to Be

by Nikki Giovanni

the world is not a pleasant place
to be without
someone to hold and be held by

5 a river would stop
its flow if only
a stream were there
to receive it

an ocean would never laugh
10 if clouds weren't there
to kiss her tears

the world is not
a pleasant place to be without
someone

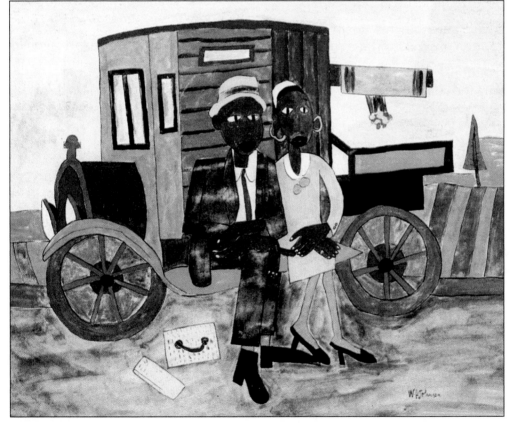

Honeymooners, William H. Johnson. The Aaron Douglas Collection of The Amistad Research Center, Tulane University

Review the Selection

UNDERSTAND THE SELECTION

Recall

1. How often is the title repeated?

2. What do we need to make the world a pleasant place?

3. What elements of nature are mentioned in the poem?

Infer

4. Why do you think the river in this poem would stop by a stream?

5. How do you think the ocean feels?

6. Would you describe this poem as a question? an answer? a statement?

7. What natural event could be represented by the image of a cloud kissing the ocean's tears?

Apply

8. How else could you define "someone to hold and be held by"?

9. What do the images of nature all have in common?

10. What other moment in nature can illustrate the theme of this poem?

Respond to Literature

In this poem, Giovanni describes a need that all people share. What must people have in order to survive? What is most important to you? Explain.

THINK ABOUT TONE

Tone may be described as a common ground between the author and the reader, reached when both understand what the author is trying to create. If the reader misunderstands a writer's tone, he or she will miss a great deal of the meaning of the work.

1. The poem "The World Is Not a Pleasant Place to Be" gives two examples illustrating its main idea. Where are they?

2. How did you feel after you read the poem?

3. What emotions are expressed in the poem?

4. Characterize the tone of the poem.

5. What does the image of "to kiss her tears" suggest to you?

READING FOCUS

Understand Levels of Meaning As you read "The World Is Not a Pleasant Place to Be," you thought about the levels of meaning in the poem. What deeper meaning beyond the literal did you find in the first three stanzas? Write down the literal meaning and the deeper meaning of each stanza.

Homophones are words that sound alike but are different in spelling, meaning, and origin. Read this sentence, for example: The Smiths' party was a *boar*, *accept* for *there* food. The writer has incorrectly used homophones for the three italicized words in the sentence. Corrected, the sentence would read: The Smiths' party was a *bore*, *except* for *their* food.

Using a homophone in place of the correct word in a sentence can confuse the reader and make nonsense of your writing. If you are not sure of which homophone to use, check in a dictionary.

Look at the poem to find a homophone for each of these words.

1. floe	**5.** bee
2. wood	**6.** two
3. knot	**7.** buy
4. plaice	**8.** tiers

Nichols Canyon Road, David Hockney. Art Resource

READING FOCUS

Make Inferences When you make an inference, you come to your own conclusion based on information you have received. For example, a detective who knows that a criminal is heading to the airport with a bag of stolen money infers that the crook is about to leave town. Active readers are like detectives. They use information from the text to infer something that is not directly stated. As you read the next selection, ask yourself questions that begin with *Why* or *How*. Then, use clues in the selection to infer the answers.

POINT OF VIEW

Point of view refers to the vantage point from which an author views the events of a fictional story. Sometimes an author takes the position of an all-knowing observer who can describe the events and thoughts of all characters in the story. This point of view, called the **omniscient point of view**, is written in the third person. An author may write in the third person but present the story as seen by only one character. This is called the **limited point of view**.

At other times a single character tells the story as he or she experienced it. Such a character may be the main character, a minor one, or a mere bystander. In any case, the character, called a **first-person narrator**, tells the story in the first person.

It is very rare that any story is told in the second person. Second-person point of view means the author places you, the reader, as the character experiencing the events.

As you read the story, ask yourself:
1. Who is telling the story?
2. In what person is the story told?

WRITING CONNECTION

Write a paragraph in the first person, telling a brief story. Rewrite the paragraph, using the third person. Compare the two.

JOURNEY

by Joyce Carol Oates

You begin your journey on so high an elevation that your destination is already in sight—a city that you have visited many times and that, moreover, is indicated on a traveler's map you have carefully folded up to take along with you. You are a lover of maps, and you have already committed this map to memory, but you bring it with you just the same.

The highway down from the mountains is broad and handsome, constructed after many years of ingenious blasting and leveling and paving. Engineers from all over the country aided in the construction of this famous highway. Its cost is so excessive that many rumors have circulated about it—you take no interest in such things, sensing that you will never learn the true cost anyway, and that this will make no difference to your journey.

After several hours on this excellent highway, where the sun shines ceaselessly and where there is a moderate amount of traffic, cars like your own at a safe distance from you, as if to assure you that there are other people in the world, you become sleepy from the monotony and wonder if perhaps there is another, less

---

elevation (el uh VAY shun) a high place
ingenious (in JEEN yus) clever, resourceful
excessive (ik SES iv) going beyond what's right or usual
moderate (MOD ur it) within reasonable limits; not excessive
monotony (muh NOT un ee) tiresome sameness

perfect road parallel to this. You discover on the map a smaller road, not exactly parallel to the highway and not as direct, but one that leads to the same city.

You turn onto this road, which winds among foothills and forests and goes through several small villages. You sense by the attitude of the villagers that traffic on this road is infrequent but nothing to draw special attention. At some curves the road shrinks, but you are fortunate enough to meet no oncoming traffic.

The road leads deep into a forest, always descending in small cramped turns. Your turning from left to right and from right to left, in a slow hypnotic passage, makes it impossible for you to look out at the forest. You discover that for some time you have not been able to see the city you are headed for, though you know it is still somewhere ahead of you.

By mid-afternoon you are tired of this road, though it has served you well, and you come upon a smaller, unpaved road that evidently leads to your city, though in a convoluted way. After only a moment's pause you turn onto this road, and immediately your automobile registers the change—the chassis bounces, something begins to vibrate, something begins to rattle. This noise is disturbing, but after a while you forget about it in your interest in the beautiful countryside. Here the trees are enormous. There are no villages or houses. For a while the dirt road runs alongside a small river, dangerously close to the river's steep bank, and you begin to feel apprehension. It is necessary for you to drive very slowly. At times your speedometer registers less than five miles an hour. You will not get to the city before dark.

The road narrows until it is hardly more than a lane. Grass has begun to grow in its center. As the river twists and turns, so does the road twist and turn, curving around hills that consist of enormous boulders, bare of all trees and plants, covered only in patches by a dull, brown lichen that is unfamiliar to you. Along one stretch, rocks of varying sizes have fallen down onto the road, so that you are forced to drive around them with great caution.

---

hypnotic (hip NOT ik) causing sleep
convoluted (KON vuh loot id) twisting; indirect
chassis (CHAS ee) a car's frame
apprehension (ap rih HEN shun) fear; dread
lichen (LY kun) a mosslike plant which grows on rocks and trees

Stone City, Iowa, Grant Wood. Joslyn Art Museum, Omaha, Nebraska. Estate of Grant Wood/Licensed by VAGA, New York, NY

Navigating these blind turns, you tap your horn to give warning in case someone should be approaching. But it is all unnecessary, since you come upon no other travelers.

Late in the afternoon, your foot numb from its constant pressure on the accelerator, your body jolted by the constant bumps and vibrations of the car, you decide to make the rest of your journey on foot, since you must be close to your destination by now.

A faint path leads through a tumble of rocks and bushes and trees, and you follow it enthusiastically. You descend a hill, slipping a little, so that a small rockslide is released; but you are able to keep your balance. At the back of your head is the precise location of your parked car, and behind that the curving dirt road,

---

navigating (NAV uh gayt ing) steering
enthusiastically (en thoo zee AS tik lee) eagerly

and behind that the other road, and then the magnificent highway itself: you understand that it would be no difficult feat to make your way back to any of these roads, should you decide that going by foot is unwise. But the path, though overgrown, is through a lovely forest, and then through a meadow in which yellow flowers are blooming, and you feel no inclination to turn back.

By evening you are still in the wilderness and you wonder if perhaps you have made a mistake. You are exhausted, your body aches, your eyes are seared by the need to stare so intently at everything around you. Now that the sun has nearly set, it is getting cold; evenings here in the mountains are always chilly.

You find yourself standing at the edge of a forest, staring ahead into the dark. Is that a field ahead, or a forest of small trees? Your path has long since given way to wild grass. Clouds obscure the moon, which should give you some light by which to make your way, and you wonder if you dare continue without this light.

Suddenly you remember the map you left back in the car, but you remember it as a blank sheet of paper.

You resist telling yourself you are lost. In fact, though you are exhausted and it is almost night, you are not lost. You have begun to shiver, but it is only with cold, not with fear. You are really satisfied with yourself. You are not lost. Though you can remember your map only as a blank sheet of paper, which can tell you nothing, you are not really lost.

If you had the day to begin again, on that highway which was so wide and clear, you would not have varied your journey in any way: in this is your triumph.

---

feat (FEET) accomplishment
inclination (in kluh NAY shun) preference
seared (SIRD) scorched; burned
obscure (ub SKYOOR) darken; dim; hide from sight

Joyce Carol Oates (1938–)

"If you are a writer, you locate yourself behind a wall of silence, and no matter what you are doing, driving a car or walking or doing housework, which I love, you can still be writing, because you have that space."

This remark by Joyce Carol Oates may explain why she is one of the most productive and versatile writers today. To her, writing is mostly daydreaming. When the idea is all set in her mind, she just sits down and writes it.

Oates has been creating fictional worlds all her life, which began in Lockport, New York, and continued in a rural area of Erie County. She submitted her first novel to a publisher at the age of fifteen. It was rejected for being too depressing, but this slight did not stop her. She entered Syracuse University in 1956, and she wrote a novel each semester. She went on to become co-winner of the *Mademoiselle* college fiction award in 1959 for her short story "In the Old World." In addition to writing, upon graduation in 1960, she was elected to the Phi Beta Kappa honor society and was valedictorian of her class.

Joyce Carol Oates does not spend all of her time writing. In addition to her one to four volumes a year, she involves herself in a parallel career in teaching. From 1962 to 1967, she taught at the University of Detroit and from 1967 to 1978 at the University of Windsor in Ontario. In 1978, she joined the faculty of Princeton University. Her books have won many awards, and her talent seems to continue to grow. She has earned a reputation as one of America's finest and best-known writers.

Oates says that she locates herself behind a "wall of silence" to write her stories. Why do you suppose that such a "wall of silence" is necessary for a writer?

Review the Selection

Recall

1. How much traffic is on the highway?

2. What is the destination?

3. When does the journey end?

Infer

4. Why do you think the broad highway is famous?

5. Why do you think you turn off onto a smaller road?

6. Why do you think your destination must be close as you start walking on the path?

7. Why does the day end in triumph?

Apply

8. Predict what might have happened if you had not turned off the broad highway.

9. What might have happened if you had not left the map in the car?

10. What do you think this journey represents?

Respond to Literature

Think about the freedom you have to make important decisions in your life. Different people choose different roads to follow. Why do you think it is important that choices and the freedom to choose are available to everyone?

THINK ABOUT POINT OF VIEW

Point of view is very important in fiction because it governs how the writer tells the story. If, for example, the first-person narrator tells the story, only his or her thoughts can be recorded, and only actions that he or she views can be told.

1. The grammatical person used in this story is unusual. Who is it?

2. Some people would think that "you" in the story is not really "the person being spoken to" but a substitute for "I." Do you agree? Why or why not?

3. How did the author's use of *you* make you feel as you read the story?

4. Do you think "you" should have been more concerned about "your" plight as the way became more and more difficult? Why or why not?

5. Do you think the end of the strange journey was indeed a triumph for "you"?

READING FOCUS

Make Inferences Write a few of the *Why* and *How* questions you asked yourself as you read "Journey." For each question, state the inferences you made and provide details from the story that helped you make it.

DEVELOP YOUR VOCABULARY

An **antonym** is a word whose meaning is the opposite of that of another word. *Happy* and *sad* are common examples.

Words are sometimes antonyms in one context but not in another. The adjectives *fast* and *slow* are usually antonyms. In the sentence "The carrots are *fast* in the ground," however, *fast* means "firmly fixed." The opposite of *fast* in this sentence is not *slow*, but *loose*.

The *italicized* words below are from "Journey." Choose the word that is the better antonym in the context given.

1. an *excessive* explanation:
   a. moderate   **b.** insufficient

2. *ingenious* blasting:
   a. stupid   **b.** unskillful

3. *convoluted* roadway:
   a. straight   **b.** simple

4. follow the path *enthusiastically*:
   a. unwillingly   **b.** soberly

Learn About

Slum Child, Margaret Burroughs. Collection of the artist

READING FOCUS

Understand Meaning Through Context
When you come upon an unfamiliar word as you read, you might be able to figure out what the word means by looking at the rest of the sentence or the paragraph it is in. As you read the excerpt from *Black Boy*, jot down each unfamiliar word. Then write what you think it means, based on the context of the sentence or sentences around it.

PURPOSE

Authors write to inform, to describe, to entertain or amuse, or to persuade. Any one or more of these may serve as an author's reason for giving readers a unified impression of his or her character, personality, and thoughts.

Autobiography can be defined as a narrative of an author's life written by him- or herself. What might motivate a person to write his or her own life story? Perhaps the author was a part of historical events or movements that would make his or her life inherently interesting.

An author may know, too, that his or her life experience and philosophy are so special that they may help or inspire others. The mere process of exploring one's own personality may result in insights that the author knows will interest the reader.

As you read the incident from Wright's boyhood, ask yourself:
1. Why did Wright tell the incident?
2. What did he want to accomplish by telling it?

WRITING CONNECTION

Write a short paragraph telling of an incident from your life. Then write another telling why you chose that incident.

from
BLACK BOY

by Richard Wright

Hunger stole upon me so slowly that at first I was not aware of what hunger really meant. Hunger had always been more or less at my elbow when I played, but now I began to wake up at night to find hunger standing at my bedside, staring at me gauntly. The hunger I had known before this had been no grim, hostile stranger; it had been a normal hunger that had made me beg constantly for bread, and when I ate a crust or two I was satisfied. But this new hunger baffled me, scared me, made me angry and insistent. Whenever I begged for food now my mother would pour me a cup of tea which would still the clamor in my stomach for a moment or two; but a little later I would feel hunger nudging my ribs, twisting my empty guts until they ached. I would grow dizzy and my vision would dim. I became less active in my play, and for the first time in my life I had to pause and think of what was happening to me.

"Mama, I'm hungry," I complained one afternoon.

"Jump up and catch a kungry," she said, trying to make me laugh and forget.

"What's a *kungry*?"

"It's what little boys eat when they get hungry," she said.

"What does it taste like?"

---

gauntly (GAWNT lee) in the manner of a thin bony person
grim (GRIM) very serious
still (STIL) make calm and quiet
clamor (KLAM ur) noise; excitement

"I don't know."

"Then why do you tell me to catch one?"

"Because you said that you were hungry," she said, smiling.

I sensed that she was teasing me and it made me angry.

"But I'm hungry. I want to eat."

"You'll have to wait."

"But I want to eat now."

"But there's nothing to eat," she told me.

"Why?"

"Just because there's none," she explained.

"But I want to eat," I said, beginning to cry.

"You'll just have to wait," she said again.

"But why?"

"For God to send some food."

"When is He going to send it?"

"I don't know."

"But I'm hungry!"

She was ironing and she paused and looked at me with tears in her eyes.

"Where's your father?" she asked me.

I stared in bewilderment. Yes, it was true that my father had not come home to sleep for many days now and I could make as much noise as I wanted. Though I had not known why he was absent, I had been glad that he was not there to shout his restrictions at me. But it had never occurred to me that his absence would mean that there would be no food.

"I don't know," I said.

"Who brings food into the house?" my mother asked me.

"Papa," I said. "He always brought food."

"Well, your father isn't here now," she said.

"Where is he?"

"I don't know," she said.

"But I'm hungry," I whimpered, stomping my feet.

"You'll have to wait until I get a job and buy food," she said.

As the days slid past the image of my father became associated with my pangs of hunger, and whenever I felt hunger I thought of him with a deep biological bitterness.

---

image (IM ij) mental picture
pangs (PANGZ) sharp pains

Martial Memory, Philip Guston. Eliza McMillan Fund, The Saint Louis Art Museum

My mother finally went to work as a cook and left me and my brother alone in the flat each day with a loaf of bread and a pot of tea. When she returned at evening she would be tired and dispirited and would cry a lot. Sometimes, when she was in despair, she would call us to her and talk to us for hours, telling us that we now had no father, that our lives would be different from those of other children, that we must learn as soon as possible to take care of ourselves, to dress ourselves, to prepare our own food; that we must take upon ourselves the responsibility of the flat while she worked. Half frightened, we would promise solemnly. We did not understand what had happened between our father and our mother and the most that these long talks did to us was to make us feel a vague dread. Whenever we asked why father had left, she would tell us that we were too young to know.

One evening my mother told me that thereafter I would have to do the shopping for food. She took me to the corner store to show me the way. I was proud; I felt like a grownup. The next afternoon I looped the basket over my arm and went down the pavement toward the store. When I reached the corner, a gang of boys grabbed me, knocked me down, snatched the basket, took the money, and sent me running home in panic. That evening I told my mother what had happened, but she made no comment; she sat down at once, wrote another note, gave me more money, and sent me out to the grocery again. I crept down the steps and saw the same gang of boys playing down the street. I ran back into the house.

"What's the matter?" my mother asked.

"It's those same boys," I said. "They'll beat me."

"You've got to get over that," she said. "Now, go on."

"I'm scared," I said.

"Go on and don't pay any attention to them," she said.

I went out of the door and walked briskly down the sidewalk, praying that the gang would not molest me. But when I came abreast of them someone shouted.

"There he is!"

They came toward me and I broke into a wild run toward home. They overtook me and flung me to the pavement. I yelled,

---

flat (FLAT) apartment
dispirited (dih SPIR it id) discouraged; low in spirits
molest (muh LEST) bother, annoy

pleaded, kicked, but they wrenched the money out of my hand. They yanked me to my feet, gave me a few slaps, and sent me home sobbing. My mother met me at the door.

"They b-beat m-me," I gasped. "They t-t-took the m-money."

I started up the steps, seeking the shelter of the house.

"Don't you come in here," my mother warned me.

I froze in my tracks and stared at her.

"But they're coming after me," I said.

"You just stay right where you are," she said in a deadly tone. "I'm going to teach you this night to stand up and fight for yourself."

She went into the house and I waited, terrified, wondering what she was about. Presently she returned with more money and another note; she also had a long heavy stick.

"Take this money, this note, and this stick," she said. "Go to the store and buy those groceries. If those boys bother you, then fight."

I was baffled. My mother was telling me to fight, a thing that she had never done before.

"But I'm scared," I said.

"Don't you come into this house until you've gotten those groceries," she said.

"They'll beat me; they'll beat me," I said.

"Then stay in the streets; don't come back here!"

I ran up the steps and tried to force my way past her into the house. A stinging slap came on my jaw. I stood on the sidewalk, crying.

"Please, let me wait until tomorrow," I begged.

"No," she said. "Go now! If you come back into this house without those groceries, I'll whip you!"

She slammed the door and I heard the key turn in the lock. I shook with fright. I was alone upon the dark, hostile streets and gangs were after me. I had the choice of being beaten at home or away from home. I clutched the stick, crying, trying to reason. If I were beaten at home, there was absolutely nothing that I could do about it; but if I were beaten in the streets, I had a chance to fight and defend myself. I walked slowly down the sidewalk, coming closer to the gang of boys, holding the stick tightly. I was so full of fear that I could scarcely breathe. I was almost upon them now.

---

wrench (RENCH) twist

"There he is again!" the cry went up.

They surrounded me quickly and began to grab for my hand. "I'll kill you!" I threatened.

They closed in. In blind fear I let the stick fly, feeling it crack against a boy's skull. I swung again, lamming another skull, then another. Realizing that they would retaliate if I let up for but a second, I fought to lay them low, to knock them cold, to kill them so that they could not strike back at me. I flayed with tears in my eyes, teeth clenched, stark fear making me throw every ounce of my strength behind each blow. I hit again and again, dropping the money and the grocery list. The boys scattered, yelling, nursing their heads, staring at me in utter disbelief. They had never seen such frenzy. I stood panting, egging them on, taunting them to come on and fight. When they refused, I ran after them and they tore out for their homes, screaming. The parents of the boys rushed into the streets and threatened me, and for the first time in my life I shouted at grownups, telling them that I would give them the same if they bothered me. I finally found my grocery list and the money and went to the store. On my way back I kept my stick poised for instant use, but there was not a single boy in sight. That night I won the right to the streets of Memphis.

---

lamming (LAM ing) striking
retaliate (rih TAL ee ayt) strike back
stark (STAHRK) complete; downright
utter (UT ur) complete
frenzy (FREN zee) madness; rage
egging (EG ing) urging
taunting (TAWNT ing) daring; teasing
poised (POIZD) set and ready

Richard Wright (1908–1960)

If the previous selection appeals to you, you might try looking for the book in a library. It is from *Black Boy*, the first volume of Richard Wright's autobiography, published in 1945. The book is powerful. The life Wright led as a child was a tough one, indeed.

Wright was born on a farm near Natchez, Mississippi, in 1908. His family moved here and there, at last settling in Memphis, Tennessee. When his parents separated, his mother had to work long hours to support the family. Wright hung out on the streets and in vacant lots. He learned to amuse the customers in bars by drinking liquor. "I was a drunkard in my sixth year," he tells us, "before I had begun school." Then his mother became very ill, and he spent some time in an orphanage. He quit school after the ninth grade and worked at several low-paying jobs. Always interested in books, he read more and more. He learned that life *could* be different. He began to believe that maybe he *did* have a chance at a happier life, after all. *Black Boy* ends as he leaves the South in 1927, to start a new life in Chicago.

But sadly, there was prejudice in the North, too. Wright still found that he was thought of as an African American first, a person second. After the success of *Black Boy* in 1945, he decided to move to Europe. He spent his last years in France and died in Paris in 1960. The second volume of his autobiography, *American Hunger*, written in the 1940s, was published in 1977.

Richard Wright had an interest that gave his life a turn for the better. What was this interest? How did it help him?

Review the Selection

UNDERSTAND THE SELECTION

Recall

1. In what way does hunger affect the boy physically?

2. What does his mother give him to defend himself with?

3. Where does the boy live?

Infer

4. What does the absence of the father mean for the family?

5. Why does the boy's mother keep sending him to the store?

6. What is the turning point in the story?

7. Why does the boy shout at the grownups, too?

Apply

8. Do you think the boy's mother did the right thing? Why do you think so?

9. Predict what might happen the next time the boy goes to the store.

10. Describe what kind of person the boy will be after his experience on the street.

Respond to Literature

Describe something that happened to you which you considered to be a turning point in your life.

THINK ABOUT PURPOSE

People are innately curious about other people's lives. When these lives have impacted history, autobiographies may reveal new insights into events. The author may interpret facts and demonstrate his or her character or habit of mind.

1. What is Wright's purpose(s) in telling this incident—to inform, describe, entertain, or persuade?

2. What do you think the incident relayed in this excerpt represented to Wright?

3. What did Wright want to accomplish by telling this incident?

4. Why do you think Wright did not try to use the incident to "teach" readers how to raise children?

5. The incident is from Wright's autobiography. Why do you think he chose to write his life story?

READING FOCUS

Understand Meaning Through Context
As you read the excerpt from *Black Boy*, you guessed the meaning of unfamiliar words by looking for clues in the text. Choose four words that can be understood by looking at context. Then write the phrase or sentence that helped you understand each word.

DEVELOP YOUR VOCABULARY

At one point in the autobiographical incident, Wright admits that the gang of boys sent him "running home in panic." The word *panic* has an interesting history. It comes from Pan, Greek god of the fields, forests, flocks, and shepherds, who frightened people as they were traveling through the woods. An unreasonable fear is still called a *panic*.

The English language contains a number of words whose roots can be traced back to characters from Greek and Roman mythology. Look up the following words in a dictionary that has word histories. Give the meaning and origin of each word.

1. narcissus
2. martial
3. titan
4. jovial
5. atlas

6. Saturday
7. volcano
8. museum
9. tantalize
10. cereal

Focus ON NONFICTION

*T*o understand what an autobiography is, look at the word itself. It breaks down into three parts: *auto-*, *bio-* and *-graphy*. The dictionary will tell you that *auto-* means "self," *bio-* means "life," and *-graphy* means "a process, a manner or a method of writing."

When the three parts are combined, you can see that *autobiography* means "a self-written life story," or the story of a person's life written by himself or herself.

An autobiography can take one of several forms. There is the autobiography itself, a written story. There is also the journal, the diary, letters, and memoirs. These are all autobiographical works.

The first three, journals, diaries, and letters, are not usually intended for publication by the writer. They may serve the writer as a basis or as sources for the autobiography. Memoirs focus on the writer's involvement in public events and relationships with notable people.

Four elements are important in an autobiography. They are narrative style, point of view, purpose, and introspection. It is important to remember that autobiography, like all nonfiction, is based on fact. It consists of real events that happened to real people.

Narrative Style An autobiography is written in narrative style, that is, it tells a story. The narrative consists of events in the writer's life. A writer will organize the narrative in one of several ways. The most obvious—and the most common—is chronological. **Chronological** means "in time order." A chronological narrative is one that describes the events in the order in which they occurred.

Another method is to begin the autobiography with an event that the writer sees as most important in his or her life. The rest of the autobiography is then organized around this primary event.

Point of View In literature, point of view means the position from which the work is presented. In autobiography, since the writer is also the main character, the point of view is always first-person. The clues that tell the reader that the story is written from a first-person point of view are the words *I*, *me*, *my*, and *mine*.

The first-person point of view allows the reader to see the world through the eyes of the author. The reader gains a new perspective on events and other people. It seems as if the reader is inside the writer's mind, listening to his or her internal dialogue—the debate with self.

Purpose When you read an autobiography, consider the purpose of the writer. Was it to inform, describe, entertain, or persuade? More specifically, was it to glorify the writer? Was the purpose to make a point or proclaim a message? Was it to moralize about aspects of life? Was the purpose to satisfy the reader's curiosity about a personality?

An autobiography may be written for one of these purposes or a combination of them. There is always a reason why a writer decides to write his or her autobiography.

Introspection Introspection is an important element of autobiography. Introspection is the observation and analysis of oneself. An introspective person is one who closely and thoughtfully examines his or her own feelings, thoughts, and reactions.

Introspection can help the writer to analyze the role of self in a given situation. It thus adds another dimension to autobiography. It gives the reader a more complete portrait of the writer. It may also give the reader a chance to find something in common with his or her own life—something that every person shares. Reading an autobiography may tell the reader how different people are from each other, and in some ways, how much alike.

As you read "Little Things Are Big," examine the story to identify the elements of autobiography. Ask yourself these questions:

1. What form of autobiography is this story?
2. What is the point of view of the writer?
3. What do you think Colón's purpose was in writing this story?

Little Things Are BIG

by Jesús Colón

"I've been thinking; you know, sometimes one thing happens to change your life, how you look at things, how you look at yourself. I remember one particular event. It was when? 1955 or '56 . . . a long time ago. Anyway, I had been working at night. I wrote for the newspaper and, you know, we had deadlines. It was late after midnight on the night before Memorial Day. I had to catch the train back to Brooklyn; the West side IRT. This lady got on to the subway at 34th and Penn Station, a nice looking white lady in her early twenties. Somehow she managed to push herself in with a baby on her right arm and a big suitcase in her left hand. Two children, a boy and a girl about three and five years old trailed after her.

Anyway, at Nevins Street I saw her preparing to get off at the next station, Atlantic Avenue. That's where I was getting off too. It was going to be a problem for her to get off; two small children, a baby in her arm, and a suitcase in her hand. And there I was also preparing to get off at Atlantic Avenue. I couldn't help but imagine the steep, long concrete stairs going down to the Long Island Railroad and up to the street. Should I offer my help? Should I take care of the girl and the boy, take them by their hands until they reach the end of that steep long concrete stairs?

Courtesy is important to us Puerto Ricans. And here I was, hours past midnight, and the white lady with the baby in her arm, a suitcase and two white children badly needing someone to help her.

I remember thinking; I'm a Negro and a Puerto Rican. Suppose I approach this white lady in this deserted subway station late at night? What would she say? What would be the first reaction of

this white American woman? Would she say: 'Yes, of course you may help me,' or would she think I was trying to get too familiar or would she think worse? What would I do if she screamed when I went to offer my help? I hesitated. And then I pushed by her like I saw nothing as if I were insensitive to her needs. I was like a rude animal walking on two legs just moving on, half running along the long subway platform, leaving the children and the suitcase and the woman with the baby in her arms. I ran up the steps of that long concrete stairs in twos and when I reached the street, the cold air slapped my warm face.

Perhaps the lady was not prejudiced after all. If you were not that prejudiced, I failed you, dear lady. If you were not that prejudiced I failed you; I failed you too, children. I failed myself. I buried my courtesy early on Memorial Day morning.

So, here is the promise I made to myself back then: if I am ever faced with an occasion like that again, I am going to offer my help regardless of how the offer is going to be received. Then I will have my courtesy with me again."

Review the Selection

UNDERSTAND THE SELECTION

Recall

1. When does the story take place?

2. Which is the narrator's subway stop?

3. How many children did the woman have with her?

Infer

4. Why do you think that the narrator feels he should help the woman?

5. Why might the woman be afraid of the narrator?

6. Why did the narrator decide not to help the woman?

7. Explain how the narrator felt after he passed the woman.

Apply

8. Predict what might have happened if the narrator had offered to help the woman.

9. Is the narrator prejudiced? Explain.

10. What is your opinion of the narrator's decision? If he had decided to help the woman, how could he have approached her?

Respond to Literature

How does the narrator's awareness of prejudice in the United States affect his actions? Is this a positive or negative effect?

THINK ABOUT AUTOBIOGRAPHY

Autobiography is a true story in which the narrator/writer is the main character. Events in the life story of the writer are told from his or her point of view. The narrator also describes his or her emotions, reactions, and thoughts.

1. Describe Colón's instinctive reaction when he sees the woman and her children.

2. List several ways the narrator describes himself.

3. What reactions does the incident cause in the narrator?

4. What lesson does Colón tell you he has learned?

DEVELOP YOUR VOCABULARY

Colón asks if he *misjudged* the woman in the subway. Perhaps, he mused, she was not *prejudiced* after all. Both italicized words in the preceding two sentences come from the Latin word part *jus* or *juris*, meaning "law." Some Latin and Greek word parts are at the core of whole families of English words. *Jus* and *juris* are the core part of a word family that includes all the words below.

Look up the meaning of each word in the list below. Do they all have something to do with law today? Think about their meanings. Then use each word in a sentence of your own.

1. just
2. injury
3. jurisdiction
4. jurisprudence
5. adjust
6. jury
7. justice
8. perjury
9. judge
10. jurist

Learn About

FREE VERSE

Poetry that does not depend on rhyme or a regular meter is known as **free verse**. For its effectiveness, free verse depends on a variety of natural rhythms and the repetition of images and phrases.

In conversation, people naturally emphasize or accent certain words. Their tone varies, their voices rise at the end of a question or fall at the end of a statement. Unlike other types of poetry, free verse is characterized by these natural rhythms. The rhythmical unit to note is the stanza, not the foot or line.

Certain words or whole lines of free verse are repeated for emphasis. A line may not be repeated word for word, but may be varied to enrich the emotion it expresses.

As you read "Where Have You Gone," ask yourself:
1. What does the poet repeat?
2. Does reading the poem aloud help you to understand it better?

WRITING CONNECTION

Some verse can be read as if one person is talking to another. Write a short conversation with one person asking questions, and the other person answering. Then try casting the conversation in poetic units.

READING FOCUS

Interpret Character All good writers give clues about the personalities of their characters. Active readers use these clues to form an impression of each character. As you read the next selection, think about the two characters: the speaker and the one being spoken of. What clues can you find to help you understand their personalities?

WHERE HAVE YOU GONE

by Mari Evans

Alta, Aaron Douglas. Collection of Fisk University Art Museum

Where have you gone

with your confident
walk with
your crooked smile

5   why did you leave
me
when you took your
laughter
and departed

10 are you aware that
with you
went the sun
all light
and what few stars
15 there were?

where have you gone
with your confident
walk your
crooked smile the
20 rent money
in one pocket and
my heart
in another. . .

Review the Selection

UNDERSTAND THE SELECTION

Recall

1. In the second stanza, what does the speaker say has been taken?

2. How is "you" described?

3. What was in the pockets of the "you" in the poem?

Infer

4. To whom is the speaker speaking?

5. What does "the sun," "all light," and "what few stars there were" imply?

6. How does the speaker feel about "you" in the poem?

7. What kind of person do you think "you" is?

Apply

8. Do you think that the speaker of the poem knew that "you" was going to leave? Why do you think so?

9. Do you think that the speaker is "blindly" in love with "you"? Why do you think so?

10. Predict how the speaker might feel if "you" returned.

Respond to Literature

What emotions does the speaker express in "Where Have You Gone"? What situations in your life have made you feel the same way?

THINK ABOUT FREE VERSE

Rhymes are not required in free verse. In this poem phrases are repeated in varying ways to create a poem. The poem is organized into stanzas and expresses an emotion, an opinion, or an idea. Because it is not bound by strict rules of rhyme or meter, free verse often reads like the natural rhythms of speech.

1. What is the main emotion expressed by the poem?

2. List the verbs in the poem that suggest that feeling.

3. The title of the poem is in the form of a question. Keeping that in mind, describe the content of the poem itself.

4. List all of the lines or phrases that literally, or with variations, are repetitions of the poem's title.

5. Why is "the/ rent money/ in one pocket and my heart/ in another" such a startling comparison?

READING FOCUS

Interpret Character As you read "Where Have You Gone" you looked for clues about the personalities of the speaker and the one being spoken to. What did you decide? Write a paragraph telling what you think each character is like, and tell what clues make you think so.

"I always *vote* in the election; I know my *vote* makes a difference."

The *italicized* words in the sentence look like the same word, but they are different from each other. How do they differ? The first time the word *vote* is used, it is used as a verb. The second time *vote* is used, it is used as a noun. **Nouns** are words that name a person, place, idea, or object. **Verbs** are words that express an action or a state of being.

Look at the italicized words in the following sentences and write down whether they are nouns or verbs.

1. Let's go for a *walk*.

2. Did you *label* the package?

3. The explorers hope to *land* safely in a friendly country.

4. We saw a *play* performed at the theater.

5. Shall I *paint* the ceiling white?

Learn About

THEME

The central idea of a literary work is called the **theme**. In nonfiction, the general topic of discussion is the theme. The writer takes a position on the topic and proves or supports that position.

The fiction writer, the poet and the dramatist have a variety of ways to express the theme of a work. It may be expressed through the character, through the action and events, or through the images the author uses. The theme is not the "moral of the story," however. It is a truth about life. It presents no rule to live by, but makes a statement about the way people behave. Sometimes the theme is not specified. Readers may have to draw their own conclusions about what it is.

As you read "Everyday Use" ask yourself:

1. What is the theme of "Everyday Use"?
2. Is the theme made clear in the story? If so, how?

WRITING CONNECTION

Write a five–sentence paragraph about a fictional person whose actions demonstrate or express some particular attitude toward patriotism.

READING FOCUS

Compare and Contrast When you compare two things, you look at how they are the same. When you contrast, you look at differences. One way to do this is to use a simple graphic organizer, with one column to note things that are the same and one column for differences. The next selection describes two sisters. Divide your paper in half. Write *Same* at the top of one half and *Different* at the top of the other. As you read about the two sisters, jot down your observations about how they are the same and how they are different.

Everyday Use

by Alice Walker

I will wait for her in the yard that Maggie and I made so clean and wavy yesterday afternoon. A yard like this is more comfortable than most people know. It is not just a yard. It is like an extended living room. When the hard clay is swept clean as a floor and the fine sand around the edges lined with tiny, irregular grooves, anyone can come and sit and look up into the elm tree and wait for the breezes that never come inside the house.

Maggie will be nervous until after her sister goes: she will stand hopelessly in corners, homely and ashamed of the burn scars down her arms and legs, eying her sister with a mixture of envy and awe. She thinks her sister has held life always in the palm of one hand, that "no" is a word the world never learned to say to her.

You've no doubt seen those TV shows where the child who has "made it" is confronted, as a surprise, by her own mother and father, tottering in weakly from backstage. (A pleasant surprise, of course: What would they do if parent and child came on the show only to curse out and insult each other?) On TV mother and child embrace and smile into each other's faces. Sometimes the mother and father weep, the child wraps them in her arms and leans across the table to tell how she would not have made it without their help. I have seen these programs.

Sometimes I dream a dream in which Dee and I are suddenly brought together on a TV program of this sort. Out of a dark and soft-seated limousine I am ushered into a bright room filled with many people. There I meet a smiling, gray, sporty man like Johnny Carson who shakes my hand and tells me what a fine girl I have. Then we are on the stage and Dee is embracing me with tears in her eyes. She pins on my dress a large orchid, even though she has told me once that she thinks orchids are tacky flowers.

---

awe (AW) wonderment; admiration
confronted (kun FRUNT id) set face to face
tacky (TAK ee) too showy; not fashionable

In real life I am a large, big-boned woman with rough, man-working hands. In the winter I wear flannel nightgowns to bed and overalls during the day. I can kill and clean a hog as mercilessly as a man. My fat keeps me hot in zero weather. I can work outside all day, breaking ice to get water for washing; I can eat pork liver cooked over the open fire minutes after it comes steaming from the hog. One winter I knocked a bull calf straight in the brain between the eyes with a sledge hammer and had the meat hung up to chill before nightfall. But of course all this does not show on television. I am the way my daughter would want me to be: a hundred pounds lighter, my skin like an uncooked barley pancake. My hair glistens in the hot bright lights. Johnny Carson has much to do to keep up with my quick and witty tongue.

But that is a mistake. I know even before I wake up. Who ever knew a Johnson with a quick tongue? Who can even imagine me looking a strange white man in the eye? It seems to me I have talked to them always with one foot raised in flight, with my head turned in whichever way is farthest from them. Dee, though. She would always look anyone in the eye. Hesitation was no part of her nature.

"How do I look, Mama?" Maggie says, showing just enough of her thin body enveloped in pink skirt and red blouse for me to know she's there, almost hidden by the door.

"Come out into the yard," I say.

Have you ever seen a lame animal, perhaps a dog run over by some careless person rich enough to own a car, sidle up to someone who is ignorant enough to be kind to him? That is the way my Maggie walks. She has been like this, chin on chest, eyes on ground, feet in shuffle, ever since the fire that burned the other house to the ground.

Dee is lighter than Maggie, with nicer hair and a fuller figure. She's a woman now, though sometimes I forget. How long ago was it that the other house burned? Ten, twelve years? Sometimes I can still hear the flames and feel Maggie's arms sticking to me, her hair smoking and her dress falling off her in little black papery flakes. Her eyes seemed stretched open, blazed open by the flames reflected in them. And Dee. I see her standing off under the sweet gum tree she used to dig gum out of; a look of concentration on her face as she watched the last dingy gray board of the house fall in toward the red-hot brick chimney. Why don't you do a dance around the ashes? I'd wanted to ask her. She had hated the house that much.

I used to think she hated Maggie, too. But that was before we raised the money, the church and me, to send her to Augusta to school. She used to read to us without pity; forcing words, lies, other folks' habits, whole lives upon us two, sitting trapped and ignorant underneath her voice. She washed us in a river of make-believe, burned us with a lot of knowledge we didn't necessarily need to know.

---

sidle (SYD ul) move sideways; edge along slyly

Family, Charles H. Alston. Whitney Museum of American Art

Pressed us to her with the serious way she read, to shove us away at just the moment, like dimwits, we seemed about to understand.

Dee wanted nice things. A yellow organdy dress to wear to her graduation from high school; black pumps to match a green suit she'd made from an old suit somebody gave me. She was determined to stare down any disaster in her efforts. Her eyelids would not flicker for minutes at a time. Often I fought off the temptation to shake her. At sixteen she had a style of her own: and knew what style was.

I never had an education myself. After second grade the school was closed down. Don't ask me why: in 1927 colored asked fewer questions than they do now. Sometimes Maggie reads to me. She stumbles along good-naturedly but can't see well. She knows she is not bright. Like good looks and money, quickness passed her by. She will marry John Thomas (who has mossy teeth in an earnest face) and then I'll be free to sit here and I guess just sing church songs to myself. Although I never was a good singer. Never could carry a tune. I was always better at a man's job. I used to love to milk till I was hooked in the side in '49. Cows are soothing and slow and don't bother you, unless you try to milk them the wrong way.

I have deliberately turned my back on the house. It is three rooms, just like the one that burned, except the roof is tin; they don't make shingle roofs anymore. There are no real windows, just some holes cut in the sides, like the portholes in a ship, but not round and not square, with rawhide holding the shutters up on the outside. This house is in a pasture, too, like the other one. No doubt when Dee sees it she will want to tear it down. She wrote me once that no matter where we "choose" to live, she will manage to come see us. But she will never bring her friends. Maggie and I thought about this and Maggie asked me, "Mama, when did Dee ever *have* any friends?"

She had a few. Furtive boys in pink shirts hanging about on washday after school. Nervous girls who never laughed. Impressed with her, they worshiped the well-turned phrase, the cute shape, the scalding humor that erupted like bubbles in lye. She read to them.

When she was courting Jimmy T she didn't have much time to pay to us, but turned all her faultfinding power on him. He *flew* to marry a cheap city girl from a family of ignorant flashy people. She hardly had time to recompose herself.

When she comes I will meet—but there they are!

Maggie attempts to make a dash for the house, in her shuffling way, but I stay her with my hand. "Come back here," I say. And she stops and tries to dig a well in the sand with her toe.

---

organdy (AWR gun dee) kind of thin crisp cotton cloth
pumps (PUMPS) kind of low cut shoes for women
furtive (FUR tiv) sly; shifty
recompose (ree kum POHZ) pulls oneself together; become calm again

It is hard to see them clearly through the strong sun. But even the first glimpse of leg out of the car tells me it is Dee. Her feet were always neat-looking, as if God himself had shaped them with a certain style. From the other side of the car comes a short, stocky man. Hair is all over his head a foot long and hanging from his chin like a kinky mule tail. I hear Maggie suck in her breath. "Uhnnnh," is what it sounds like. Like when you see the wriggling end of a snake just in front of your foot on the road. "Uhnnnh."

Dee next. A dress down to the ground, in this hot weather. A dress so loud it hurts my eyes. There are yellows and oranges enough to throw back the light of the sun. I feel my whole face warming from the heat waves it throws out. Earrings gold, too, and hanging down to her shoulders. Bracelets dangling and making noises when she moves her arm up to shake the folds of the dress out of her armpits. The dress is loose and flows, and as she walks closer, I like it. I hear Maggie go "Uhnnnh" again. It is her sister's hair. It stands straight up like the wool on a sheep. It is black as night and around the edges are two long pigtails that rope about like small lizards disappearing behind her ears.

"Wa-su-zo-Tean-o!" she says, coming on in that gliding way the dress makes her move. The short stocky fellow with the hair to his navel is all grinning and he follows up with "Asalamalakim, my mother and sister!" He moves to hug Maggie but she falls back, right up against the back of my chair. I feel her trembling there and when I look up I see the perspiration falling off her chin.

"Don't get up," says Dee. Since I am stout it takes something of a push. You can see me trying to move a second or two before I make it. She turns, showing white heels through her sandals, and goes back to the car. Out she peeks next with a Polaroid. She stoops down quickly and lines up picture after picture of me sitting there in front of the house with Maggie cowering behind me. She never takes a shot without making sure the house is included. When a cow comes nibbling around the edge of the yard she snaps it and me and Maggie *and* the house. Then she puts the Polaroid in the back seat of the car, and comes up and kisses me on the forehead.

Meanwhile Asalamalakim is going through motions with Maggie's hand. Maggie's hand is as limp as a fish, and probably as cold, despite the sweat, and she keeps trying to pull it back. It looks like Asalamalakim wants to shake hands but wants to do it fancy. Or maybe he don't know how people shake hands. Anyhow, he soon gives up on Maggie.

"Well," I say. "Dee."

"No, Mama," she says. "Not 'Dee,' Wangero Leewanika Kemanjo!"

"What happened to 'Dee'?" I wanted to know.

"She's dead," Wangero said. "I couldn't bear it any longer, being named after the people who oppress me."

---

cowering (KOU ur ing) crouching in fear

"You know as well as me you was named after your aunt Dicie," I said. Dicie is my sister. She named Dee. We called her "Big Dee" after Dee was born.

"But who was *she* named after?" asked Wangero.

"I guess after Grandma Dee," I said.

"And who was she named after?" asked Wangero.

"Her mother," I said, and saw Wangero was getting tired. "That's about as far back as I can trace it," I said. Though, in fact, I probably could have carried it back beyond the Civil War through the branches.

"Well," said Asalamalakim, "there you are."

"Uhnnnh," I heard Maggie say.

"There I was not," I said, "before 'Dicie' cropped up in our family, so why should I try to trace it that far back?"

He just stood there grinning, looking down on me like somebody inspecting a Model A car. Every once in a while he and Wangero sent eye signals over my head.

"How do you pronounce this name?" I asked.

"You don't have to call me by it if you don't want to," said Wangero.

"Why shouldn't I?" I asked. "If that's what you want us to call you, we'll call you."

"I know it might sound awkward at first," said Wangero.

"I'll get used to it," I said. "Ream it out again."

---

ream (REEM) enlarge; open up (here used figuratively)

Well, soon we got the name out of the way. Asalamalakim had a name twice as long and three times as hard. After I tripped over it two or three times he told me to just call him Hakim-a-barber. I wanted to ask him was he a barber, but I didn't really think he was, so I didn't ask.

"You must belong to those beef-cattle peoples down the road," I said. They said "Asalamalakim" when they met you, too, but they didn't shake hands. Always too busy: feeding the cattle, fixing the fences, putting up salt-lick shelters, throwing down hay. When the white folks poisoned some of the herd the men stayed up all night with rifles in their hands. I walked a mile and a half just to see the sight.

Hakim-a-barber said, "I accept some of their doctrines, but farming and raising cattle is not my style." (They didn't tell me, and I didn't ask, whether Wangero (Dee) had really gone and married him.)

We sat down to eat and right away he said he didn't eat collards and pork was unclean. Wangero, though, went on through the chitlins and corn bread, the greens and everything else. She talked a blue streak over the sweet potatoes. Everything delighted her. Even the fact that we still used the benches her daddy made for the table when we couldn't afford to buy chairs.

"Oh, Mama!" she cried. Then turned to Hakim-a-barber. "I never knew how lovely these benches are. You can feel the rump prints," she said, running her hands underneath her and along the bench. Then she gave a sigh and her hand closed over Grandma Dee's butter dish. "That's it!" she said. "I knew there was something I wanted to ask you if I could have." She jumped up from the table and went over in the corner where the churn stood, the milk in it clabber by now. She looked at the churn and looked at it.

"This churn top is what I need," she said. "Didn't Uncle Buddy whittle it out of a tree you all used to have?"

"Yes," I said.

"Uh huh," she said happily. "And I want the dasher, too."

"Uncle Buddy whittle that, too?" asked the barber.

Dee (Wangero) looked up at me.

"Aunt Dee's first husband whittled the dash," said Maggie so low you almost couldn't hear her. "His name was Henry, but they called him Stash."

"Maggie's brain is like an elephant's," Wangero said, laughing. "I can use the churn top as a centerpiece for the alcove table," she said, sliding a plate over the churn, "and I'll think of something artistic to do with the dasher."

When she finished wrapping the dasher the handle stuck out. I took it for a

---

doctrine (DOK trin) belief, theory
collards (KOL urdz) kind of green vegetable
chitlins (CHIT linz) hog intestines used as food
clabber (KLAB ur) sour, thick milk
dasher (DASH ur) plunger with paddles for stirring
alcove (AL kohv) opening off a room

moment in my hands. You didn't even have to look close to see where hands pushing the dasher up and down to make butter had left a kind of sink in the wood. In fact, there were a lot of small sinks; you could see where thumbs and fingers had sunk into the wood. It was beautiful light yellow wood, from a tree that grew in the yard where Big Dee and Stash had lived.

After dinner Dee (Wangero) went to the trunk at the foot of my bed and started rifling through it. Maggie hung back in the kitchen over the dishpan. Out came Wangero with two quilts. They had been pieced by Grandma Dee and then Big Dee and me had hung them on the quilt frames on the front porch and quilted them. One was in the Lone Star pattern. The other was Walk Around the Mountain. In both of them were scraps of dresses Grandma Dee had worn fifty and more years ago. Bits and pieces of Grandpa Jarrell's Paisley shirts. And one teeny faded blue piece, about the size of a penny matchbox, that was from Great Grandpa Ezra's uniform that he wore in the Civil War.

"Mama," Wangero said sweet as a bird. "Can I have these old quilts?"

I heard something fall in the kitchen, and a minute later the kitchen door slammed.

"Why don't you take one or two of the others?" I asked. "These old things was just done by me and Big Dee from some tops your grandma pieced before she died."

"No," said Wangero. "I don't want those. They are stitched around the borders by machine."

"That'll make them last better," I said.

"That's not the point," said Wangero. "These are all pieces of dresses Grandma used to wear. She did all this stitching by hand. Imagine!" She held the quilts securely in her arms, stroking them.

"Some of the pieces, like those lavender ones, come from old clothes her mother handed down to her," I said, moving up to touch the quilts. Dee (Wangero) moved back just enough so that I couldn't reach the quilts. They already belonged to her.

"Imagine!" she breathed again, clutching them closely to her bosom.

"The truth is," I said, "I promised to give them quilts to Maggie, for when she marries John Thomas."

She gasped like a bee had stung her.

"Maggie can't appreciate these quilts!" she said. "She'd probably be backward enough to put them to everyday use."

"I reckon she would," I said. "God knows I been saving 'em for long enough with nobody using 'em. I hope she will!" I didn't want to bring up how I had offered Dee (Wangero) a quilt when she went away to college. Then she had told me they were old-fashioned, out of style.

"But they're *priceless*!" she was saying now, furiously; for she has a temper. "Maggie would put them on the bed and in five years they'd be in rags. Less than that!"

"She can always make some more," I said. "Maggie knows how to quilt."

---

rifling (RY fling) searching; going through hurriedly

Dee (Wangero) looked at me with hatred. "You just will not understand. The point is these quilts, *these* quilts!"

"Well," I said, stumped. "What would *you* do with them?"

"Hang them," she said. As if that was the only thing you could do with quilts.

Maggie by now was standing in the door. I could almost hear the sound her feet made as they scraped over each other.

"She can have them, Mama," she said, like somebody used to never winning anything, or having anything reserved for her. "I can 'member Grandma Dee without the quilts."

I looked at her hard. She had filled her bottom lip with checkerberry snuff and it gave her face a kind of dopey, hangdog look. It was Grandma Dee and Big Dee who taught her how to quilt herself. She stood there with her scarred hands hidden in the folds of her skirt. She looked at her sister with something like fear but she wasn't mad at her. This was Maggie's portion. This was the way she knew God to work.

When I looked at her like that something hit me in the top of my head and ran down to the soles of my feet. Just like when I'm in church and the spirit of God touches me and I get happy and shout.

I did something I never had done before: hugged Maggie to me, then dragged her on into the room, snatched the quilts out of Miss Wangero's hands and dumped them into Maggie's lap. Maggie just sat there on my bed with her mouth open.

"Take one or two of the others," I said to Dee.

But she turned without a word and went out to Hakim-a-barber.

"You just don't understand," she said, as Maggie and I came out to the car.

"What don't I understand?" I wanted to know.

"Your heritage," she said. And then she turned to Maggie, kissed her, and said, "You ought to try to make something of yourself, too, Maggie. It's really a new day for us. But from the way you and Mama still live you'd never know it."

She put on some sunglasses that hid everything above the tip of her nose and her chin.

Maggie smiled; maybe at the sunglasses. But a real smile, not scared. After we watched the car dust settle I asked Maggie to bring me a dip of snuff. And then the two of us sat there just enjoying, until it was time to go in the house and go to bed.

---

checkerberry (CHEK ur ber ee) kind of small red berry (wintergreen)

Alice Walker (1944–   )

Alice Walker, winner of both the Pulitzer Prize and the National Book Award, became a writer at age eight. Her story is an interesting one.

One day in Georgia in 1952, an eight-year-old Alice was shot accidentally in the right eye with a BB gun by one of her brothers. The family had little money, and the best medical attention was not available. She went blind in that eye. The pain ceased after a few days, but the scar tissue remained.

Ironically, the loss of an eye enabled the girl to "see." She soon found herself writing down thoughts and impressions in a notebook, and she discovered that the writing made her feel better. She also started to read a great deal.

Writing and reading helped erase the mental scars, but the scarred eye remained until Alice was 14, when an operation removed the disfigurement. Other changes followed fast. By graduation time she was not only class valedictorian but also voted "Most Popular." Her partial blindness, as well as her ability, qualified her for a special scholarship for the handicapped to Spelman College. She later transferred to Sarah Lawrence College, graduating in 1965.

Walker continued to write in notebooks at Sarah Lawrence and soon found herself writing poetry at a furious pace. She showed the poems to one of her teachers, the poet Muriel Rukeyser. With Rukeyser's help and encouragement, the poems became Alice Walker's first book, *Once* (1968).

Author of poems, novels, short stories, and works of nonfiction, Alice Walker is recognized today as one of America's leading writers. Her most famous work is probably *The Color Purple*, which also became a well-known film. Of general interest are a book of essays, *In Search of Our Mothers' Gardens*, and a biography of her "spirit helper," *Langston Hughes: American Poet*.

Review the Selection

UNDERSTAND THE SELECTION

Recall

1. How are the three women in the story related to each other?

2. Where does the narrator live?

3. What is Dee's "new" name?

Infer

4. Why does the narrator describe her hands as "rough, man-working hands"?

5. Why did Dee change her name?

6. Name three other details that tell you that Dee has changed.

7. What do the quilts symbolize?

Apply

8. How does the story make you feel about Dee and why?

9. Name two qualities in the mother that you admire.

10. What do you think Dee represents as compared to her sister and her mother?

Respond to Literature

The women in the story share a heritage, but they value objects from that heritage for different reasons. Why does Dee value the objects? Why do Maggie and her mother value them?

THINK ABOUT THEME

The **theme** of a work is its main, or central, idea. If you are stating the theme of a work, the wording should point out some general truth, or idea, about life. Some people confuse the theme of a literary work with a "lesson about life." Fables, like those of Aesop, always end with a **moral**, a lesson about how to conduct one's behavior. The theme statement observes a truth but makes no rules to imply it, leaving the reader to discover it by thought.

1. What is the theme of "Everyday Use"?

2. Why did Dee rename herself?

3. Why did the mother snatch the quilts away from Dee and give them to Maggie?

4. Do you think that Walker is making a moral statement about heritage? If so, what is it?

READING FOCUS

Compare and Contrast As you read "Everyday Use," you compared and contrasted aspects of the two sisters. Write one paragraph that describes their similarities and another paragraph that describes their differences.

DEVELOP YOUR VOCABULARY

Adverbs are words that modify verbs, adjectives, and other adverbs. To *modify* means "to limit or restrict in meaning." Many adverbs end in *-ly*; these adverbs usually tell *how*. **Adjectives** are words that modify nouns or pronouns. Descriptive adjectives tell *what kind*. Some of these adjectives also end in *-ly*.

Look at this sentence from "Everyday Use": "she will stand hopelessly in corners, homely and ashamed. . . ." *Hopelessly* modifies the verb *stand* and is an adverb. *Homely* modifies the pronoun *she* and is an adjective.

Tell whether the *italicized* word is an adjective or an adverb.

1. "She held the quilts *securely* in her arms. . . ."

2. "I can kill and clean a hog as *mercilessly* as a man."

3. "I never knew how *lovely* these benches are."

4. "She stumbles along *good-naturedly* but can't see well."

Learn About

CHARACTER

In literature, a character is simply a person in a story. In fiction, characters are imaginary people who spring from the mind of the writer. In nonfiction, the writer describes a real person.

There are three basic methods of revealing character in writing. In the first, the writer provides a clear and comprehensive description of the person. In the second, the writer shows the person in action. The personality is defined by what the individual does. In the third method, the writer tells the person's thoughts, emotions, and reactions to events. The third method, of course, is impossible for the nonfiction writer unless he or she learns about the inner life of the individual from interviews or close personal relationships. Even then, the writer must use his or her imagination.

As you read this personal recollection, ask yourself:

1. How does the writer show the personality of the main character?
2. Is the main character believable?

READING FOCUS

Understand Sequence of Events Story events are usually told in chronological, or time, order. The author describes the first happening, then the second, and so on. Sometimes, signal words such as *first*, *next*, or *finally* are used to indicate time order; sometimes there are no signal words, and you rely on story context. As you read the next selection, pay attention to the sequence of events. Jot down any signal words you notice.

WRITING CONNECTION

Write a short paragraph describing someone you know. Provide a clear and complete description of the person.

from
THE
WOMAN WARRIOR

by Maxine Hong Kingston

When she was about sixty-eight years old, Brave Orchid took a day off to wait at San Francisco International Airport for the plane that was bringing her sister to the United States. She had not seen Moon Orchid for thirty years. She had begun this waiting at home, getting up a half-hour before Moon Orchid's plane took off in Hong Kong. Brave Orchid would add her will power to the forces that keep an airplane up. Her head hurt with the concentration. The plane had to be light, so no matter how tired she felt, she dared not rest her spirit on a wing but continuously and gently pushed up on the plane's belly. She had already been waiting at the airport for nine hours. She was wakeful.

Next to Brave Orchid sat Moon Orchid's only daughter, who was helping her aunt wait. Brave Orchid had made two of her own children come too because they

could drive, but they had been lured away by the magazine racks and the gift shops and coffee shops. Her American children could not sit for very long. They did not understand sitting; they had wandering feet. She hoped they would get back from the pay t.v.'s or the pay toilets or wherever they were spending their money before the plane arrived. If they did not come back soon, she would go look for them. If her son thought he could hide in the men's room, he was wrong.

"Are you all right, Aunt?" asked her niece.

"No, this chair hurts me. Help me pull some chairs together so I can put my feet up."

She unbundled a blanket and spread it out to make a bed for herself. On the floor she had two shopping bags full of canned peaches, real peaches, beans wrapped in taro leaves, cookies, Thermos bottles, enough food for everybody, though only her niece would eat with her. Her bad boy and bad girl were probably sneaking hamburgers, wasting their money. She would scold them.

Many soldiers and sailors sat about, oddly calm, like little boys in cowboy uniforms. (She thought "cowboy" was what you would call a Boy Scout.) They should have been crying hysterically on their way to Vietnam. "If I see one that looks Chinese," she thought, "I'll go over and give him some advice." She sat up suddenly; she had forgotten about her own son, who was even now in Vietnam. Carefully she split her attention, beaming half of it to the ocean, into the water to keep him afloat. He was on a ship. He was in Vietnamese waters. She was sure of it. He and the other children were lying to her. They had said he was in Japan, and then they said he was in the Philippines. But when she sent him her help, she could feel that he was on a ship in Da Nang. Also she had seen the children hide the envelopes that his letters came in.

"Do you think my son is in Vietnam?" she asked her niece, who was dutifully eating.

"No. Didn't your children say he was in the Philippines?"

"Have you ever seen any of his letters with Philippine stamps on them?"

"Oh, yes. Your children showed me one."

"I wouldn't put it past them to send the letters to some Filipino they know. He puts Manila postmarks on them to fool me."

"Yes, I can imagine them doing that. But don't worry. Your son can take care of himself. All your children can take care of themselves."

"Not him. He's not like other people. Not normal at all. He sticks erasers in his ears, and the erasers are still attached to the pencil stubs. The captain will say, 'Abandon ship,' or, 'Watch out for bombs,' and he won't hear. He doesn't listen to orders. I told him to flee to Canada, but he wouldn't go."

She closed her eyes. After a short while, plane and ship under control, she looked again at the children in uniforms. Some of the blond ones looked like baby chicks, their crew cuts like the downy yellow on baby chicks. You had to feel sorry for them even though they were Army and Navy Ghosts.

Suddenly her son and daughter came running. "Come, Mother. The plane's landed early. She's here already." They hurried, folding up their mother's encampment. She was glad her children were not useless. They must have known what this trip to San Francisco was about then. "It's a good thing I made you come early," she said.

---

taro (TAHR oh) kind of tropical plant used for food
Filipino (fil uh PEE noh) native of the Philippines
downy (DOU nee) soft; fluffy
encampment (en KAMP munt) camp and equipment

Brave Orchid pushed to the front of the crowd. She had to be in front. The passengers were separated from the people waiting for them by glass doors and walls. Immigration Ghosts were stamping papers. The travellers crowded along some conveyor belts to have their luggage searched. Brave Orchid did not see her sister anywhere. She stood watching for four hours. Her children left and came back. "Why don't you sit down?" they asked.

"The chairs are too far away," she said.

"Why don't you sit on the floor then?"

No, she would stand, as her sister was probably standing in a line she could not see from here. Her American children had no feelings and no memory.

To while away time, she and her niece talked about the Chinese passengers. These new immigrants had it easy. On Ellis Island[1] the people were thin after forty days at sea and had no fancy luggage.

"That one looks like her," Brave Orchid would say.

"No, that's not her."

Ellis Island had been made out of wood and iron. Here everything was new plastic, a ghost trick to lure immigrants into feeling safe and spilling their secrets. Then the Alien Office could send them right back. Otherwise, why did they lock her out, not letting her help her sister answer questions and spell her name? At Ellis Island when the ghost asked Brave Orchid what year her husband had cut off his pigtail, a Chinese who was crouching on the floor motioned her not to talk. "I don't know," she had said. If it weren't for that Chinese man, she might not be here today, or her husband either. She hoped some Chinese, a janitor or a clerk, would look out for Moon Orchid. Luggage conveyors fooled immigrants into thinking the Gold Mountain was going to be easy.

Brave Orchid felt her heart jump— Moon Orchid. "There she is," she shouted. But her niece saw it was not her mother at all. And it shocked her to discover the woman her aunt was pointing out. This was a young woman, younger than herself, no older than Moon Orchid the day the sisters parted. "Moon Orchid will have changed a little, of course," Brave Orchid was saying. "She will have learned to wear western clothes." The woman wore a navy blue suit with a bunch of dark cherries at the shoulder.

"No, Aunt," said the niece. "That's not my mother."

"Perhaps not. It's been so many years. Yes, it is your mother. It must be. Let her come closer, and we can tell. Do you think she's too far away for me to tell, or is it my eyes getting bad?"

"It's too many years gone by," said the niece.

---

conveyor (belt) (kun VAY ur) endless moving belt or platform
  for carrying objects short distances
[1]**Ellis Island:** an island in New York harbor that served for years
  as an immigration examination center.
alien (AY lee un *or* AYL yun) non-citizen; foreigner

Brave Orchid turned suddenly—another Moon Orchid, this one a neat little woman with a bun. She was laughing at something the person ahead of her in line said. Moon Orchid was just like that, laughing at nothing. "I would be able to tell the difference if one of them would only come closer," Brave Orchid said with tears, which she did not wipe. Two children met the woman with the cherries, and she shook their hands. The other woman was met by a young man. They looked at each other gladly, then walked away side by side.

Up close neither one of those women looked like Moon Orchid at all. "Don't worry, Aunt," said the niece, "I'll know her."

"I'll know her too. I knew her before you did."

The niece said nothing, although she had seen her mother only five years ago. Her aunt liked having the last word.

Finally Brave Orchid's children quit wandering and drooped on a railing. Who knew what they were thinking? At last the niece called out, "I see her! I see her! Mother! Mother!" Whenever the doors parted, she shouted, probably embarrassing the American cousins, but she didn't care. She called out, "Mama! Mama!" until the crack in the sliding doors became too small to let in her voice. "Mama!" What a strange word in an adult voice. Many people turned to see what adult was calling, "Mama!" like a child. Brave Orchid saw an old, old woman jerk her head up, her little eyes blinking confusedly, a woman whose nerves leapt toward the sound anytime she heard "Mama!" Then she relaxed to her own business again. She was a tiny, tiny lady, very thin, with little fluttering hands, and her hair was in a gray knot. She was dressed in a gray wool suit; she wore pearls around her neck and in her earlobes. Moon Orchid *would* travel with her jewels showing. Brave Orchid momentarily saw, like a larger, younger outline around this old woman, the sister she had been waiting for. The familiar dim halo faded, leaving the woman so old, so gray. So old. Brave Orchid pressed against the glass. That old lady? Yes, that old lady facing the ghost who stamped her papers without questioning her was her sister. Then, without noticing her family, Moon Orchid walked smiling over to the Suitcase Inspector Ghost, who took her boxes apart, pulling out puffs of tissue. From where she was, Brave Orchid could not see what her sister had chosen to carry across the ocean. She wished her sister would look her way. Brave Orchid thought that if *she* were entering a new country, she would be at the windows. Instead Moon Orchid hovered over the unwrapping, surprised at each reappearance as if she were opening presents after a birthday party.

"Mama!" Moon Orchid's daughter kept calling. Brave Orchid said to her children, "Why don't you call your aunt too?

---

hover (HUV ur) stay nearby; linger about

Maybe she'll hear us if all of you call out together." But her children slunk away. Maybe that shame-face they so often wore was American politeness.

"Mama!" Moon Orchid's daughter called again, and this time her mother looked right at her. She left her bundles in a heap and came running. "Hey!" the Customs Ghost yelled at her. She went back to clear up her mess, talking inaudibly to her daughter all the while. Her daughter pointed toward Brave Orchid. And at last Moon Orchid looked at her—two old women with faces like mirrors.

Their hands reached out as if to touch the other's face, then returned to their own, the fingers checking the grooves in the forehead and along the sides of the mouth. Moon Orchid, who never understood the gravity of things, started smiling and laughing, pointing at Brave Orchid. Finally Moon Orchid gathered up her stuff, strings hanging and papers loose, and met her sister at the door, where they shook hands, oblivious to blocking the way.

"You're an old woman," said Brave Orchid.

"Aiaa. *You're* an old woman."

"But you are really old. Surely, you can't say that about me. I'm not old the way you're old."

"But *you* really are old. You're one year older than I am."

"Your hair is white and your face all wrinkled."

"You're so skinny."

"You're so fat."

"Fat women are more beautiful than skinny women."

The children pulled them out of the doorway. One of Brave Orchid's children brought the car from the parking lot, and the other heaved the luggage into the trunk. They put the two old ladies and the niece in the back seat. All the way home—across the Bay Bridge, over the Diablo hills, across the San Joaquin River to the valley, the valley moon so white at dusk—all the way home, the two sisters exclaimed every time they turned to look at each other, "Aiaa! How old!"

Brave Orchid forgot that she got sick in cars, that all vehicles but palanquins made her dizzy. "You're so old," she kept saying. "How did you get so old?"

Brave Orchid had tears in her eyes. But Moon Orchid said, "You look older than I. You *are* older than I," and again she'd laugh. "You're wearing an old mask to tease me." It surprised Brave Orchid that after thirty years she could still get annoyed at her sister's silliness.

---

slunk (SLUNK) moved in a fearful or embarrassed way
inaudibly (in AW duh blee) not being heard
gravity (GRAV ih tee) dignity; seriousness
oblivious (uh BLIV ee us) unaware; unmindful
palanquin (pal un KEEN) carriage on poles that is carried on people's shoulders

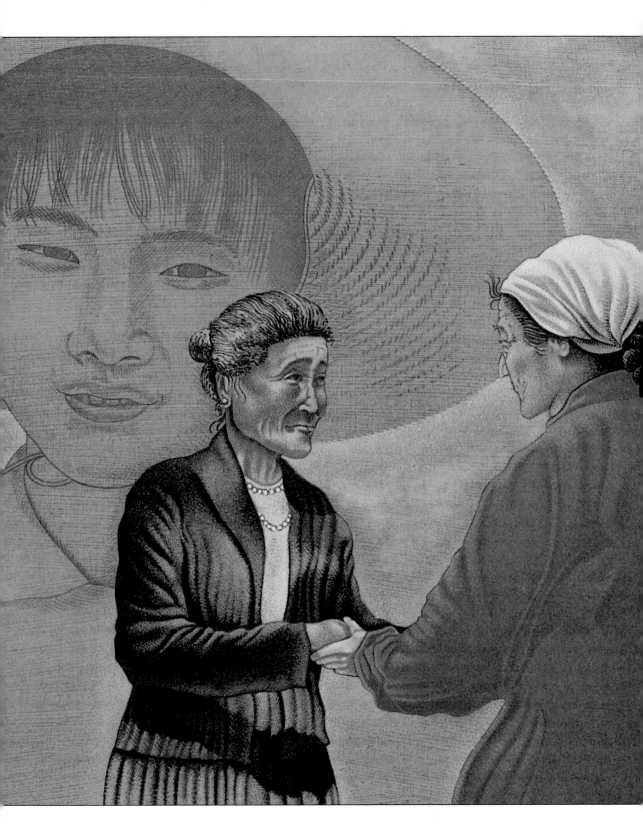

Review the Selection

UNDERSTAND THE SELECTION

Recall

1. How old is Brave Orchid?

2. When had she last seen her sister?

3. How many children does Moon Orchid have?

Infer

4. Why is Brave Orchid worried about her son?

5. Why does Brave Orchid bring food to the airport?

6. Who are the people Brave Orchid calls "ghosts"?

7. Explain how Brave Orchid feels when she first sees her sister.

Apply

8. Suppose you are meeting a family member you haven't seen for many years. What emotions might you feel?

9. Do you think the sisters are very similar or very different? Why do you think so?

10. How would you characterize Brave Orchid?

Respond to Literature

Does Brave Orchid feel more Chinese than American? What examples of her Chinese identity are found in the story?

THINK ABOUT CHARACTER

In fiction, the characters are imaginary, created in the writer's mind. In nonfiction the people described are real. Both fiction and nonfiction writers strive to present fully rounded depictions of personalities. They may include extensive physical description, a many-sided view of personality traits, and the individual's actions, opinions, beliefs, ideas, and thoughts.

1. Who is the most memorable character in the selection? Explain why.

2. What clues are you given about the character of Moon Orchid?

3. Are Brave Orchid's children well-rounded characters? Explain.

4. What does Brave Orchid's decision to arrive early at the airport tell you about her?

5. What does the emotion expressed in the final sentence tell you about Brave Orchid?

READING FOCUS

Understand Sequence of Events List the signal words and phrases that helped you understand the sequence of events. Use some of these words in a brief summary of the story's events.

DEVELOP YOUR VOCABULARY

Base words are English words that have no letters or syllables added to them. Prefixes are word parts that can be added at the beginning of base words to change their meaning. For example, *un-* is a commonly used prefix. Add it to *smiling* or *wrap*, and you have formed *unsmiling* and *unwrap*, both of which mean the opposite of the original word. Here are some common prefixes and their meanings:

mis-: wrong, badly, incorrectly
un-: not, the opposite of
re-: back or again

Write the following words from the selection. Then add one or more prefixes from the list and tell the meaning of each new word.

1. spell
2. new
3. sure
4. faded
5. wrinkled
6. take
7. turned
8. known
9. easy
10. discover
11. understood
12. safe

Learn About

OPEN FORM

Form is the structure of a poem. One frequently used form is open form. **Open form** means that the poem is written in one long, continuous structure with no stanzas.

Open form is often called **free verse** because it does not have meter, rhyme, or stanzas. It does, however, have some pattern of organization. Open form, or free verse, uses the length of the line and the way words and phrases are grouped to tie ideas together and emphasize them. The white spaces that are left between lines and words also add emphasis. Sometimes the white spaces are placed between lines at regular intervals, such as every four lines. These white spaces may make the poem look as if it has stanzas.

Open form makes it possible for a poet to express thoughts in new ways.

As you read "This Is Just to Say" and "The Term," ask yourself:

1. What is the form of "This Is Just to Say"?
2. What is the form of "The Term"?

WRITING CONNECTION

Open form allows a poet freedom. Use open form to write a four-line poem about something familiar, such as an apple.

READING FOCUS

Compare and Contrast When you compare, you see how things are alike; when you contrast, you look at their differences. The two poems on the next page are by the same author, William Carlos Williams. After you have read both poems several times, look for ways in which the poems are alike and ways in which they are different. Think about their form, the main idea of each, the use of figurative language, and their tone.

This Is Just to Say

by William Carlos Williams

I have eaten
the plums
that were in
the icebox

5   and which
you were probably
saving
for breakfast

Forgive me
10   they were delicious
so sweet
and so cold

The Term

by William Carlos Williams

A rumpled sheet
of brown paper
about the length

and apparent bulk
5   of a man was
rolling with the

wind slowly over
and over in
the street as

10   a car drove down
upon it and
crushed it to

the ground. Unlike
a man it rose
15   again rolling

with the wind over
and over to be as
it was before.

---

rumpled (RUM puld) wrinkled

Review the Selection

UNDERSTAND THE SELECTION

Recall

1. In "This Is Just to Say," what did the speaker eat?

2. In "The Term," how big was the brown paper?

3. What happened to the paper when the car drove over it?

Infer

4. Why did the speaker eat the plums?

5. Why did the poet write the poem "This Is Just To Say"?

6. What are two ways that the paper is like a man?

7. How is the paper unlike a man?

Apply

8. Why do you think the poet chose plums rather than apples, bananas, or oranges?

9. Why do you think the poet compared the paper to a man?

10. What would you compare a piece of paper to? A man to?

Respond to Literature

Why do people, like the speaker in "This Is Just to Say," take things they should not take? How would you explain taking something that you should not have?

THINK ABOUT POETIC FORM

Form refers to the shape, or pattern, of a poem. **Open form**, or free verse, does not have meter, rhyme, or stanzas. Using open form allows a poet greater freedom in presenting his or her ideas and emotions.

1. "This Is Just to Say" is written in open form. In what ways can this poem be called free verse?

2. Why are there spaces between every four lines?

3. What does the speaker tell about in the first four lines? In the next four? In the last four?

4. What is the form in "The Term"?

5. How many sentences are there in the poem?

6. Why are there open spaces every three lines?

READING FOCUS

Compare and Contrast As you read "This Is Just to Say" and "The Term," you compared and contrasted the poems. What is one way in which the poems are similar? What is one way in which they are different? Consider the form, the main idea, the use of figurative language, and the tone of each poem.

DEVELOP YOUR VOCABULARY

An **antonym** is a word that has the opposite or nearly the opposite meaning of another word. For example, *out* is an antonym for *in* because it has the opposite meaning.

1. Write antonyms for the following words.

   a. sweet   **e.** slowly
   b. cold   **f.** over
   c. rumpled   **g.** down
   d. man   **h.** to

2. Reread the two poems to find antonyms for the following words.

   a. like   **e.** tasteless
   b. blame   **f.** wasting
   c. fell   **g.** unseen
   d. after   **h.** without

3. Write an original sentence for each of the words that are antonyms for the words in question 2.

GLOSSARY

PRONUNCIATION KEY

Accent is the force or stress given to some words or syllables in speech. In this book, accent is indicated by the use of uppercase letters. One syllable words are always shown as accented. Thus, the pronunciation of *hand* is (HAND). In words of more than one syllable, the accented syllable is printed in uppercase letters. The other syllable or syllables are printed in lowercase letters. Thus, the pronunciation of *handbag* is (HAND bag).

Letter(s) in text words	Letter(s) used in respelling	Sample words	Phonetic respelling	Letter(s) in text words	Letter(s) used in respelling	Sample words	Phonetic respelling
a	a	bandit	(BAN dit)	i	uh	possible	(POS uh bul)
a	ay	makeup	(MAYK up)	o	o	bottle	(BOT ul)
a	air	daring	(DAIR ing)	o	u	gallon	(GAL un)
a	ah	dart	(DAHRT)	o	oh	open	(OH pun)
a	uh	about	(uh BOUT)	o	aw	horn	(HAWRN)
a	aw	ball	(BAWL)	oo	oo	move	(MOOV)
e	e	denim	(DEN im)	oo	uu	football	(FUUT bawl)
e	eh	ingest	(in JEHST)	oo	oo	pool	(POOL)
e	ih	delight	(dih LYT)	oi	oi	point	(POINT)
e	u	darken	(DAHR kun)	ou	ou	output	(OUT put)
e	ee	he	(HEE)	u	u	upshot	(UP shot)
i	i	mitten	(MIT un)	u	uh	support	(suh PAWRT)
i	ih	gravity	(GRAV ih tee)	u	oo	ruler	(ROO lur)
i	y	idle	(YD ul)	y	i	rhythm	(RITH um)
i	eye	idea	(eye DEE uh)	y	ee	lazy	(LAY zee)
i	ee	medium	(MEE dee um)	y	y	thyme	(TYM)

A

abbot (AB but) a man who is head of a monastery *p. 51*

abode (uh BOHD) home; residence *p. 173*

absently (AB sunt lee) with attention elsewhere *p. 382*

absurdities (ab SUR duh teez) ridiculous things *p. 281*

abyss (uh BIS) a thing too big for measurement *p. 144*

accusations (AK yoo ZAY shunz) charges of wrongdoing *p. 443*

acquiescence (ak we ESS cents) agreement; submission *p. 214*

acute (uh KYOOT) sharp, sensitive *p. 121*

admirably (AD mur uh blee) excellently *p. 319*

aft (AFT) to the rear of the boat *p. 209*

adversary (AD vur ser ee) opponent; enemy *p. 12*

agile (AJ ul) nimble; well-coordinated *p. 246*

ague (AY gyoo) violent fever *p. 30*

akin (uh KIN) related *p. 165*

alburnum (al BURN um) sapwood *p. 179*

alcove (AL kohv) opening off a room *p. 487*

alien (AY lee un or AYL yun) non-citizen; foreigner *p. 498*

anesthetic (an is THET ik) substance that lessens pain *p. 300*

annuities (un NOO uh teez) regular payments *p. 101*

anonymous (uh NON uh mus) written by a person whose name is withheld *p. 36*

antisymphonic (an tih sim FON ik) against music *p. 383*

anxiety (ang ZY uh tee) worry *p. 124*

apathetically (ap uh THET ik lee) with little or no feeling *p. 297*

appeasingly (uh PEEZ ing lee) in a manner to please or obey *p. 300*

appertaining (ap pur TAYn ing) belonging; fixed *p. 245*

apprehension (ap rih HEN shun) worry; fear of a coming event *p. 289*

apprehensions (ap rih HEN shunz) fears; dreads *pp. 130, 454*

apprentice (uh PREN tis) a person under legal agreement to work for a specified time under a master craftsperson in return for instruction and, formerly, support *p. 37*

ardent (AHR dunt) very eager; passionate *p. 250*

arpeggios (ahr PEHJ ee ohz) notes in a chord played in quick succession *p. 441*

arrant (AIR int) bare-faced; out-and-out *p. 89*

array (uh RAY) an orderly arrangement of troops *p. 12*

arrayed (uh RAYD) dressed *p. 319*

asterisk (AS tuh risk) star-shaped sign or symbol *p. 370*

asylum (uh SY lum) shelter *p. 188*

audacity (aw DAS uh tee) boldness; daring *p. 125*

aureole (AWR ee ohl) a halo *p. 265*

awe (AW) wonderment; admiration *p. 481*

awful (AW full) extreme; grave *p. 11*

B

barter (BAHRT ur) trade; exchanging one thing for another *p. 311*

becalm'd (bih KAHLMD) to make motionless from lack of wind *p. 35*

belfry (BEL free) bell tower *p. 161*

bellows (BEHL ohz) roars; loud noises *p. 439*

benediction (ben uh DIK shun) blessing *p. 166*

besieging (bih SEEJ ing) hemming in with armed forces; closing in; overwhelming *p. 275*

bigotry of purpose (BIG uh tree) singlemindedness *p. 209*

billet (BIL it) a brief letter *p. 31*

binnacle (BIN uh kuhl) wooden case holding the ship's compass *p. 209*

birthright (BURTH ryt) the rights that a person has because he/she was born in a certain family, nation, etc. *p. 72*

blade (BLAYD) dashing, jaunty, young man *p. 85*

bleating (BLEET ing) cry of sheep *p. 163*

bliss (BLIS) happiness; joy *p. 188*

blithe (BLYTH) happy; cheerful *p. 195*

boarded (BAWRD id) had rooms and meals provided regularly for pay *p. 35*

bobolink (BOB uh lingk) kind of songbird *p. 239*

bog (BOG) swamp; wet ground *p. 235*

booby (BOO bee) fool *p. 280*

bop (BOP) short for *bebop:* early modern jazz *p. 346*

Bornou land (BAWR noo) reference to homeland in Africa *p. 227*

bough (BOU) a large branch of a tree *p. 314*

brackish (BRAK ish) salty and marshy *p. 412*

brambles (BRAM bulz) prickly shrubs *p. 313*

brethren (BRETH run) brothers; fellow members of a group *p. 13*

bulk (BULK) object; shape *p. 162*

bulldozing (BUL dohz ing) bullying; threatening *p. 245*

bulwarks (BUL works) wall around the main deck *p. 209*

burthened (BURR thend) archaic word for *burdened p. 84*

C

cambric (KAM brik) very fine, thin linen or cotton *p. 261*

capricious (kuh PRISH us) without apparent reason *p. 412*

capstan (CAP stuhn) cylinder on which ropes are wound *p. 214*

carcass (KAHR kus) dead body, usually of an animal *p. 280*

Carrara (kuh RAHR uh) fine, white marble *p. 204*

cascade (kas KAYD) waterfall *p. 246*

cascaded (kas KAY dihd) flowed down like a small waterfall *p. 439*

censure (SEN shur) blame *p. 73*

chafed (CHAYFT) to have been worn away; eroded *p. 143*

chanticleer (CHAN tih klir) a rooster *pp. 84, 204*

chassis (CHAS ee) a car's frame *p. 454*

chastise (chas TYZ) punish *p. 133*

chastity (CHAS tuh tee) decency; modesty *p. 44*

chattel (CHAT ul) a moveable article of personal property; owned property *p. 68*

checkerberry (CHEK ur ber ee) kind of small red berry (wintergreen) *p. 490*

chid (CHYD) scolded *p. 35*

chidden (CHY din) scolded *p. 300*

chitlins (CHIT linz) hog intestines used as food *p. 487*

chorister (KAWR ih stur) singer in a choir *p. 239*

clabber (KLAB ur) sour, thick milk *p. 487*

clamor (KLAM ur) noise; excitement *p. 461*

cognomen (kog NOH men) name *p. 82*

cogwheel (KAHG hweel) a wheel with a rim notched into teeth, which mesh with those of another wheel to transmit or receive motion *p. 56*

collards (KOL urdz) kind of green vegetable *p. 487*

commence (kuh MENS) begin *p. 328*

commodious (kuh MOH dee us) spacious; roomy *p. 258*

commotion (kuh MOH shun) noisy confusion *p. 368*

complacence (kum PLAY sens) smug satisfaction; feeling of security *p. 391*

conceived (kun SEEVD) thought of; imagined *p. 121*

condescension (con duh SEN shun) snobbish behavior *p. 215*

conflagration (kon fluh GRAY shun) huge fire *p. 294*

conformity (kun FAWR muh tee) behavior that is in agreement with current rules *p. 176*

confronted (kun FRUNT id) set face to face *p. 481*

conjecture (kun JEK chur) an opinion formed without facts but based on pertinent knowledge or experience; guess *p. 394*

connate (CON ate) allied; existing together *p. 180*

consecrated (KON sih krayt id) dedicated *p. 406*

consolidate (kun SOL uh date) to unite *p. 22*

contrived (kun TRYVD) planned; devised *p. 187*

conveyor (belt) (kun VAY ur) endless moving belt or platform for carrying objects short distances *p. 498*

convoluted (KON vuh loot id) twisting; indirect *p. 454*

coquette (co KETT) flirt *p. 83*

cordial (CORD juhl) stimulating drink *p. 180*

cordon (KAWR dun) a line or circle of police stationed around an area to guard it *p. 400*

cot (KOT) cottage or small house *p. 29*

countenance (COUNT in ens) face *p. 187*

covet (KUV it) desire what belongs to another *p. 115*

covey (KUV ee) flock of birds *p. 326*

cowering (KOU ur ing) crouching in fear *p. 485*

cowlish (KOUL ish) hood shaped *p. 410*

cravat (kruh VAT) a necktie; scarf *p. 267*

credulity (kreh DOO lih tee) willingness to believe readily without proof; gullibility *p. 83*

crest (KREST) the top of anything; summit; ridge *p. 313*

crusty (KRUS tee) curt; rude *p. 172*

cultivated (KUL tuh vayt id) prepared and cared for the land on which plants grow *p. 171*

cumulus (KYOO myuh lus) a type of rounded, fluffy cloud *p. 433*

cunningly (KUN ing lee) slyly *p. 121*

curb stone (KURB stohn) stone or concrete edging of a sidewalk *p. 70*

D

dasher (DASH ur) plunger with paddles for stirring *p. 487*

dead reckoning (DED REK un ing) navigating without the assistance of stars *p. 175*

deferred (dih FURD) put off *p. 348*

delusive (dih LOO siv) misleading; unreal *p. 12*

demean'd (dih MEEND) lowered in status or character; degraded *p. 37*

departed (dih PAHRT id) dead *p. 187*

deploying (dih PLOI ing) spreading out *p. 404*

depreciate (duh PREE she ayt) devalue *p. 246*

descendant (dih SEN dunt) a person who is the offspring of a certain ancestor, family, group, etc. *p. 51*

deserts (dih ZURTS) reward or punishment; what is deserved *p. 99*

diadem (DY uh dem) crown (more like halo here) *p. 238*

discreet (dih SKREET) wisely careful *p. 249*

dispirited (dih SPIR it id) discouraged; low in spirits *p. 464*

disproved (dis PROOVD) shown to be incorrect or false *p. 445*

dissever (dih SEV ur) separate *p. 116*

dissipate (DIS uh payt) scatter; clear away *p. 411*

diverge (dih VURJ) spread apart *p. 360*

divert (dih VURT) turn aside *p. 280*

doctrine (DOK trin) belief, theory *p. 487*

doggedly (DAWG id lee) persistently; stubbornly *p. 258*

dollops (DOL ups) mounds *p. 433*

Dourra (DUUR uh) (usually spelled durra) a kind of grain grown in Northern Africa *p. 227*

downcast (DOUN kast) sad *p. 72*

downy (DOU nee) soft; fluffy *p. 496*

dreary (DRIR ee) dull; tiresome *p. 235*

drenched (DRENCHT) soaked; wet all over *p. 314*

E

ebbed (EBD) flowed back or away *p. 294*

ecstasy (EK stuh see) a feeling of overpowering joy; great delight *p. 311*

edifice (ED uh fis) a large structure *p. 266*

egging (EG ing) urging *p. 466*

ejaculation (ee jak you LAY shun) excitement *p. 282*

elevation (el uh VAY shun) a high place *p. 453*

emaciated (ih MAY see ayt id) abnormally lean *p. 137*

emerge (ih MURJ) come out into view *p. 385*

emphatic (em FAT ik) very striking; definite *p. 339*

encampment (en KAMP munt) camp and equipment *p. 496*

encroach (en KROHCH) to intrude upon the rights of others *p. 22*

enlightened (en LYT und) to have given the lights of knowledge to *p. 69*

enthusiastically (en thoo zee AS tik lee) eagerly *p. 455*

enveloped (en VEL upd) wrapped up *p. 124*

ermine (UR min) a weasel whose fur turns to white in the winter *p. 204*

errata (air RAH ta) a printer's term for "errors" *p. 39*

ethereal (ih THIR ee ul) of the upper regions of space *p. 391*

evitable (EH vuh tuh bul) avoidable *p. 175*

ewer (YOO er) pitcher *p. 215*

excessive (ik SES iv) going beyond what's right or usual *p. 453*

excruciating (ik SKROO shee ayt ing) very painful *p. 296*

extenuate (ik STEN yoo ayt) to lessen the seriousness of *p. 13*

extremities (ik STREM ih teez) hands and feet; parts farthest away *p. 294*

extricate (EK strih kayt) to set free; release; disentangle *p. 29*

exulting (ig ZULT ing) rejoicing; showing joy *p. 196*

F

fallow (FAL oh) land that is plowed, but not seeded *p. 171*

fan-tail (FAN tayl) spread the tail like a fan *p. 211*

fastidiously (fa STID ee us lee) very sensitively; daintily *p. 371*

favored (FAY vurd) featured *p. 319*

feat (FEET) accomplishment *p. 456*

feeble minded (FEE buhl MIN dihd) an out-of-date expression for a person with a weak or slow mind *p. 367*

fetch (FECH) get and bring back *p. 359*

fiasco (fee AS koh) a humiliating failure *p. 443*

fieldpieces (FEELD pees iz) mobile artillery *p. 404*

Filipino (fil uh PEE noh) native of the Philippines *p. 496*

fine (FYN) summary; conclusion *p. 319*

firing (FYR ing) to light a fire in a boiler *p. 340*

flat (FLAT) an apartment with rooms on one floor *pp. 339, 464*

fleet (FLEET) very fast *p. 162*

flotilla (floh TIL uh) a fleet of boats or small ships *p. 59*

fluently (FLOO unt lee) easily (of talking) *p. 125*

flush (FLUSH) drive birds or animals from hiding place *p. 326*

Formica (for MY kuh) trade name for a heat-resistant plastic *p. 438*

forsooth (for SOOTH) archaic for *in truth;* indeed *p. 280*

fowler (FOUL ur) hunter of wildfowl *p. 143*

frenzy (FREN zee) madness; rage *p. 466*

frugality (froo GAL uh tee) careful economy; thrift *p. 44*

furtive (FUR tiv) sly; shifty; sneaky; secretive *pp. 411, 484*

futility (fyoo TIL uh tee) lack of success; uselessness *p. 421*

G

gainsay (GAYN say) denying or opposing *p. 85*

gait (GAYT) manner of walking or running *p. 291*

Ganymede (GAN uh MEED) a beautiful young boy in Greek mythology *p. 152*

gauntly (GAWNT lee) in the manner of a thin bony person *p. 461*

Ghiblee (GIB lee) night wind that makes an eerie sound *p. 227*

girth (GURTH) strap that holds saddle on horse *p. 162*

gloaming (GLOHM ing) twilight *p. 204*

globular (GLOB yuh lur) rounded *p. 417*

grave (GRAYV) serious *p. 130*

gravity (GRAV ih tee) dignity; seriousness *p. 500*

grenadier (gren uh DIR) foot soldier *p. 162*

grim (GRIM) very serious *p. 461*

guttural (GUT ur ul) harsh or growling sound *p. 367*

H

habitable (HAB it uh bul) fit to be lived in *p. 31*

hairline (HAIR lyn) very thin line *p. 287*

halloos (huh LOOZ) shouts; yells; calls *p. 265*

hashed (HASHT) jumbled; all mixed up *p. 247*

hasty pudding (HAY stee PUUD ing) cornmeal mush *p. 35*

hatter (HAT ur) hat maker *p. 195*

heartfelt (HAHRT felt) sincere; meaningful *p. 166*

heather (HETH ur) low evergreen plant that often grows on moors *p. 237*

hideous (HID ee us) very ugly or frightening *p. 123*

high-born (HY bawrn) of noble birth *p. 115*

hillock (HIL uk) a small hill; mound *p. 259*

hover (HUV ur) stay nearby; linger about *p. 499*

hulk (HULK) old ship *p. 161*

humiliating (hyoo MIL ee ayt ing) lowering of pride or dignity *p. 67*

humility (hyoo MIL uh tee) humbleness; the absence of pride *p. 44*

husbandry (HUHZ buhn dree) farming; agriculture *p. 171*

hypnotic (hip NOT ik) causing sleep *p. 454*

hypocritical (hip uh KRIT ih kul) false; not sincere *p. 125*

I

illimitable (ih LIM ih tuh bul) endless *p. 143*

illuminated (ih LOO muh nayt id) made clear *p. 249*

image (IM ij) mental picture *p. 462*

immortality (im awr TAL ih tee) unending life *p. 288*

impassioned (im PASH und) determined; filled with passionate feeling *p. 307*

imperative (im PER uh tiv) really necessary; essential *p. 293*

imperially (im PIR ee ul ee) supremely *p. 319*

imperturbably (im pur TUR buh blee) in a manner that cannot be excited; impassively *p. 272*

impetuous (im PECH oo us) eager; violent *p. 162*

impudent (IM pyoo dunt) rude; insulting *p. 103*

imputation (IM pyoo TAY shun) a charge or attribution of guilt or fault; blame *p. 245*

inanimate (in AN uh mit) not living or moving *p. 260*

inaudibly (in AWD uh blee) not being heard *p. 500*

incidents (in suh DENTS) things that happen as the result of other things (here referring to the abuses of slavery) *p. 72*

inclination (in kluh NAY shun) a particular disposition or bent of mind; a liking or preference *pp. 18, 36, 456*

incoherently (in koh HIR unt lee) not logically; disjointedly *p. 267*

incompatible (in kum PAT uh bul) not in agreement *p. 69*

incongruities (in kon GROO ih teez) things inconsistent or not in harmony *p. 281*

inconsequential (in con suh KWEN shul) unimportant; trivial *p. 249*

indifference (in DIF ur uns) lack of interest *p. 186*

indissoluble (in duh SAHL u bul) incapable of coming apart; permanent *p. 216*

inevitable (in EV ih tuh bul) certain to happen *p. 13*

infest (in FEST) trouble; disturb *p. 166*

infinitesimal (in fin ih TES uh mul) too small to be measured *p. 258*

influenza (in floo EN zuh) disease usually called "flu" *p. 325*

ingenious (in JEEN yus) clever, resourceful *p. 453*

ingenuity (in juh NOO uh tee) cleverness; originality *p. 131*

innovators (IN uh vayt urz) makers of changes; introducers of new methods *p. 272*

inscrutable (in SCROO tuh bul) not able to be understood *p. 213*

instigates (IN stuh gaytz) brings about; stirs up *p. 245*

interlude (IN tur lood) musical performance between the acts of a play *p. 402*

interspersed (in tur SPURST) scattered among other things *p. 29*

intimacy (IN tuh muh see) very close friendship, even love *p. 293*

intolerable (in TOL ur uh bul) unbearable *p. 70*

intoxication (in tox ih KAY shun) great excitement *p. 247*

intricacies (IN trih kuh seez) complexities; complications *p. 272*

J

jardiniere (jahr duh NIR) a decorative flowerpot or stand *p. 339*

jockey (JOCK ee) cheater *p. 89*

Joy Luck Club (JOY LUK KLUB) a group of women who met to play games and tell stories *p. 442*

K

keel (KEEL) a piece of wood that runs along the centerline from the front of the boat to the back; "backbone" of a ship *pp. 196, 222*

kilter (KIL tur) good condition; proper order *p. 77*

kin (KIN) relatives *p. 136*

kindling (KIND ling) small pieces of dry firewood *p. 369*

kith (KITH) archaic word for friends *p. 136*

L

laboriously (luh BAWR ee us lee) with much labor and care *p. 249*

lamming (LAM ing) striking *p. 466*

lash (LASH) whip *p. 77*

lay (LAY) short song or story poem *p. 166*

leaden (LED un) dull, dark gray *p. 205*

leeward (LEE word) the direction toward which the wind blows downward *p. 217*

levee (LEV ee) a morning reception held by a person of high rank *p. 31*

libelling (LY bull ing) tending to expose a person to public ridicule in a written statement *p. 38*

lichen (LY kun) a mosslike plant which grows on rocks and trees *p. 454*

luringly (LUUR ing lee) to tempt or attract *p. 372*

M

Magi (MAY jy) the three wise men who, according to the biblical story, made the journey to Bethlehem to present gifts to the Christ child *p. 245*

magnitude (MAG nuh tood) importance; significance *p. 11*

make-shift (MAYK shift) substitute; temporary *p. 439*

maledictions (mal uh DIK shunz) curses *p. 216*

malice (MAL is) desire to inflict harm out of meanness; malevolence *pp. 213, 222*

manifold (MAN uh fohld) in many ways *p. 3*

man-of-war (man uv WAWR) warship *p. 161*

mantle (MAN tul) something that covers *p. 295*

marge (MAHRJ) edge or border *p. 143*

martial law (MAHR shul LAW) temporary rule by the military authorities *p. 402*

mason (MAY sun) stone worker *p. 195*

maxim (MAK sim) a statement of a general truth *p. 267*

meditate (MED uh tayt) think deeply; ponder *p. 288*

meditatively (MED uh tayt iv lee) thinking quietly *p. 370*

mendicancy (MEN dih CAN cee) beggary; poverty *p. 245*

mesmerizing (MEHZ muh ry zing) hypnotizing; casting a spell *p. 439*

meteorite (MEET ee uh ryt) part of a heavenly body that passes through the atmosphere and falls to the earth's surface as a piece of matter *p. 394*

methodically (muh THOD ik lee) orderly; systematically *p. 295*

militia (muh LISH uh) an army of citizens rather than professional soldiers, called out in time of emergency *p. 402*

mockery (MOK uh ree) person or thing made fun of *p. 125*

moderate (MOD ur it) within reasonable limits; not excessive *p. 453*

molest (muh LEST) bother, annoy *pp. 106, 464*

monotony (muh NOT un ee) tiresome sameness *p. 453*

montage (mon TAHZH) picture made up of a number of separate pictures *p. 348*

moor (MUUR) open wasteland *p. 237*

Moor (MUUR) referring to the African slave traders *p. 227*

moorings (MUUR ingz) ropes to fasten a ship *p. 161*

moral philosophy (MAWR ul fuh LOS uh fee) ethics; standards of conduct and moral judgment *p. 69*

mortal (MAWR tul) fatal; causing death; subject to death *pp. 122, 391*

mortification (MORE tih fih KAY shun) embarrassment; humiliation *p. 94*

muster (MUS tur) roll call *p. 162*

mutely (MYOOT lee) silently *p. 370*

muzzle (MUZ ul) mouth and nose of an animal *p. 289*

mystical (MIS tih kul) mysterious; having a hidden meaning *p. 198*

N

navigating (NAV uh gayt ing) steering *p. 455*

night-tide (NYT tyd) nighttime *p. 116*

nonconductivity (non kun duk TIV uh tee) the ability to contain and not transmit heat *p. 403*

nymphs (NIMFS) mythological spirits or fairies of the woods *p. 181*

O

object (OB jekt) purpose; goal *p. 197*

oblivious (uh BLIV ee us) unaware; unmindful *p. 500*

obscure (ub SKYOOR) darken; dim; hide from sight *p. 456*

obstinate (OB stuh nut) stubborn *pp. 265, 339*

occult (ah CULT) mysterious *p. 180*

oilcloth (OIL klawth) waterproofed cloth *p. 433*

ominous (OM uh nus) threatening; sinister *p. 415*

orb (AWRB) round object *p. 287*

organdy (AWR gun dee) kind of thin crisp cotton cloth *p. 484*

ought (AWT) anything (variation of aught) *p. 3*

outraged (OUT rayjd) insulted; made very angry *p. 104*

overshadowing (oh vur SHAD oh ing) hanging or looming over *p. 73*

P

palanquin (pal un KEEN) carriage on poles that is carried on people's shoulders *p. 500*

pangs (PANGZ) sharp pains *p. 462*

pantry (PAN tree) a small room or closet off the kitchen, where cooking ingredients and utensils, china, etc., are kept *p. 264*

parabolic (par uh BOL ik) bowl shaped *p. 403*

parmacetty (parm uh SHE tee) dialect for spermaceti, meaning a sperm whale *p. 211*

parsimony (PAR suh MOHN ee) stinginess *p. 245*

pathetic (puh THET ik) pitiful *p. 280*

pathos (PAY thos) an element in experience evoking pity *p. 265*

pedagogue (PED ah gog) teacher *p. 84*

peradventure (PURR ad VEN chur) archaic word for *perhaps p. 82*

perchance (pur CHANS) perhaps *p. 171*

perdition's (pur DIH shunz) Hell's *p. 212*

perplexity (pur PLEK sih tee) confusion; uncertainty *p. 281*

persever (pur SEV ur) continue to uphold; keep on trying (Today the word is spelled persevere and pronounced pur suh VEER.) *p. 3*

pertinaciously (pur tuh NAY shush ly) persistently; stubbornly *p. 220*

petitioned (puh TISH und) made a formal request of someone in authority *p. 12*

petticoat (PET ee koht) type of woman's underskirt *p. 370*

petticoats (PEHT ee kohts) lace or ruffles on the bottom of a skirt *p. 441*

phantom (FAN tum) something that seems real to the eye but does not exist; an unreal mental image *p. 12*

phenomenon (fih NOM uh non) a fact or event that can be described in a scientific way *p. 392*

pier-glass (PEER GLAS) mirror *p. 246*

pillions (PILL yons) cushions for a passenger behind the saddle *p. 89*

piqued (PEEKED) archaic meaning: *prided himself p. 84*

pitch (PICH) a black sticky substance formed from distilling of tar *p. 122*

placid (PLAS id) quiet *p. 131*

plashy (PLASH ee) marshy; wet *p. 143*

plight (PLYT) bad condition or problem *p. 382*

ploughed (PLOUD) plowed; made furrows in the soil *p. 77*

poignant (POIN yunt) sharp; keenly felt *p. 298*

poised (POIZD) set and ready *p. 466*

porcelain (PAWR suh lin) china *p. 265*

pore over (PAWR OH vur) study carefully *p. 382*

posterity (pos TERR i tee) descendants; succeeding generations *p. 51*

precept (PREE cept) rule of conduct; aphorism *p. 44*

precipices (PRES uh pis iz) steep cliffs; vertical or overhanging rock faces *p. 270*

prejudices (PREJ uh disses) judgments or opinions formed before the facts are known *p. 51*

presaging (pree SAYG ing) foreboding; warning *p. 214*

presently (PREZ unt lee) in a little while *p. 341*

principle (PRIN suh pul) a fundamental rule of conduct *p. 36*

procure (proh KYUUR) to obtain or secure *p. 31*

prodigy (PRAHD uh jee) a child remarkably bright in some way *p. 437*

profound (pruh FOUND) wise; intellectually deep *p. 122*

prostrated (PROS trayt id) laid low; completely overcome *p. 271*

prudence (PROOD uns) the quality of being cautious or discreet in conduct *p. 70*

pulsate (PUL sayt) throb in a regular rhythm *p. 399*

pumps (PUMPS) kind of low cut shoes for women *p. 484*

purgative (PUR guh tiv) strong laxative *p. 325*

putrefactive (pyoo truh FAK tiv) rotting; decomposing *p. 416*

Q

quarter (KWAR tur) mercy or indulgence *p. 84*

quench (KWENCH) satisfy thirst or other need *p. 3*

quiescent (kwee ES enct) quiet; motionless *p. 222*

R

rack (RAK) hardship; torture *p. 196*

ranged (RAYNJD) set forth; arranged *p. 198*

ransacking (RAN sak ing) searching furiously *p. 247*

rash (RASH) reckless; foolhardy *p. 103*

ream (REEM) enlarge; open up (here used figuratively) *p. 486*

recesses (REE ses ez) interior places *p. 294*

recompense (REHK um pens) repayment *p. 3*

recompose (ree kum POHZ) pull oneself together; become calm again *p. 484*

recourse (REE kawrs) a turning back for aid, safety, etc. *p. 31*

recurring (rih KUR ing) occurring again and again *p. 282*

reflected (rih FLEK tid) thought *p. 291*

regalia (rih GAYL yuh) signs of royalty, such as special dress (here used ironically) *p. 383*

reiterated (ree IT uh rayt id) repeated tiresomely *p. 290*

renounce (rih NOUNS) reject; abandon with disgust *p. 280*

repose (rih POHZ) rest *p. 190*

reprieve (rih PREEV) postponement *p. 417*

reproachfully (rih PROHCH fuh lee) scolding; blaming *p. 369*

repulsed (rih PULST) drove back; repelled *p. 107*

resolution (rez uh LOO shun) decision as to future action *p. 36*

resolved (rih ZOLVD) determined; decided *p. 107*

resounding (rih ZOUND ing) loud, echoing, or prolonged sound *p. 13*

restive (RES tiv) impatient; uneasy; stubborn *p. 263*

retaliate (rih TAL ee ayt) strike back *p. 466*

reverie (REHV uh ree) dreamy thoughts of pleasant things *p. 441*

rifling (RY fling) searching; going through hurriedly *p. 488*

riled (RYLD) irritated; angered *p. 398*

robust (roh BUST) strong; healthy *p. 195*

roistering (ROY stir ing) swaggering, unrestrained *p. 85*

rumpled (RUM puld) wrinkled *p. 505*

rustic (RUS tik) of or living in the country, rural; simple, plain; rough, awkward *p. 268*

rut (RUT) a track made by a wheeled vehicle *p. 238*

S

saffron (SAF run) bright, orange-yellow color *p. 340*

satyr (SA tyr) a literary work in which vices, stupidities, etc. are held up to ridicule and contempt *p. 38*

sauciness (SAH see nuhs) state of being bold or rude *p. 439*

scourge (SKURJ) to whip; to chastise, punish *p. 271*

seared (SIRD) scorched; burned *p. 456*

sedulous (SEJ uh lus) hard-working; diligent; persistent *p. 261*

seismograph (SYZ muyh graf) an instrument that records the intensity and duration of earthquakes *p. 394*

sepulcher (SEP ul kur) tomb; burial place *p. 115*

sequestered (suh QUEST erd) secluded; sheltered; withdrawn *p. 88*

seraph (SER uf) kind of heavenly being; winged angel *p. 115*

serenity (suh REN ih tee) peacefulness *p. 185*

sexton (SEKS tun) caretaker who rings the bells *p. 239*

sheaths (SHEETHZ) protective coverings or cases *pp. 294, 396*

shied (SHYD) drew back *p. 291*

shroud (SHROWD) group of ropes *p. 209*

shroud (SHROWD) something that hides or protects *p. 223*

sidled (SYD uld) moved sideways; edged along slyly *pp. 298, 482*

sinewing (SIN yoo ing) joining, like a tendon joins muscle to bone *p. 213*

siren (SY run) in Greek and Roman mythology, a sea nymph represented as part bird and part woman who lured sailors to their death by singing *p. 11*

slaughter (SLAWT ur) the killing of animals for food *p. 36*

sleepers (SLEE purz) railroad ties *p. 175*

slither (SLITH ur) slip and slide *p. 326*

slough (SLUF) shed skin *p. 180*

slunk (SLUNK) moved in a fearful or embarrassed way *p. 500*

slur (SLUR) make unclear; pass over carelessly *p. 280*

small-clothes (SMALL CLOTHZ) knee breeches *p. 93*

smites (SMYTS) inflicts a heavy blow; kills by striking *p. 227*

soaring (SAWR ing) rising or gliding high into the air *p. 311*

sociable (SOH shuh bul) enjoys the company of others *p. 41*

sombre (SOM bur) usually spelled somber; dark and gloomy *p. 162*

sonatas (suh NAH tuhs) compositions for one or two musical instruments *p. 440*

sounded (SOWND ed) dove deeply downward (by a whale or fish) *p. 218*

spar (SPAHR) pole attached to mast *p. 161*

Spartan-like (SPAHR tuhn-lyk) brave and frugal *p. 174*

spasmodically (spaz MOD ik lee) in sudden bursts *p. 296*

spectral (SPEK trul) ghostlike *p. 162*

spectroscope (SPEK truh skohp) a scientific instrument used to identify substances *p. 392*

speculatively (SPEK yuh luh tiv lee) thinking about possibilities *p. 288*

spinet (SPIHN it) small piano *p. 442*

spittle (SPIT ul) saliva; what one spits *p. 288*

spouse (SPOUS) husband or wife *p. 186*

staccato (stuh KAHT oh) short, distinct movement; music played with distinct breaks between notes *pp. 340, 441*

stanchions (STAN chunz) upright bars, beams, or posts used as support *p. 270*

star (STAHR) to mark or set with stars, as a decoration *p. 311*

stark (STAHRK) complete, downright *p. 466*

stifled (STY fuld) muffled, smothered *p. 122*

still (STIL) make calm and quiet *p. 461*

stitch (STICH) slang for clothing *p. 369*

stock (STOK) farm animals *p. 101*

stolid (STOL id) expressing little emotion *p. 263*

stomacher (STUM uhk ur) a decorated garment worn over the stomach and chest *p. 84*

strife (STRYF) troublesome conflict; quarreling *p. 311*

superfluity (SOO pur FLOO ih tee) excess feelings *p. 186*

superfluous (suu PUR floo us) beyond what is required *p. 175*

supernumerary (SOO per NOO mer AIRY) extra *p. 83*

surplice (SUR plis) loose-fitting garment worn by members of the clergy and choirs *p. 239*

suspension (suh SPEN shun) temporary stoppage *p. 56*

sustained (suh STAYND) experienced; suffered *p. 280*

swains (SWAYNS) suitors; boyfriends *p. 89*

T

tacit (TASS it) unspoken; understood *p. 214*

tacky (TAK ee) too showy; not fashionable *p. 481*

taro (TAHR oh) kind of tropical plant used for food *p. 496*

tarpaulins (TAR pul inz) sailors' hats made of canvas waterproofed with tar or wax *p. 211*

tart (TAHRT) small, filled pastry; small pie *p. 35*

taunting (TAWNT ing) daring; teasing *p. 466*

taut (TAWT) stretched tightly *p. 367*

tedious (TEE dee us) boring; tiresome *p. 281*

temperance (TEM pur uns) belief that no one should drink alcohol *p. 186*

temperance (TEM pur uns) self-restraint in conduct, appetite, etc. *pp. 35, 132*

tenement (TEN uh ment) archaic meaning: *residence* or *habitation p. 84*

tête-a-tête (TET ah TET) private conversation *p. 89*

thimbled (THIM buld) wearing a small, protective cap used in sewing *p. 367*

thoroughfare (THUR oh fair) passage; way through *p. 307*

thunderbird (THUN dur burd) in the mythology of certain North American Indians, an enormous bird supposed to produce thunder, lightning, and rain *p. 7*

tiara (tee AHR uh) crown *p. 215*

tinderbox (TIN dur BAHKS) formerly, a metal box for holding flint for starting a fire *p. 55*

Titans (TYT unz) giants *p. 416*

tramp (TRAMP) sound of a heavy footstep *p. 91*

tranquil (TRANG kwul) peaceful; at rest *p. 189*

tranquility (tran KWIL uh tee) calmness, peacefulness *pp. 20, 44*

transient (TRAN shunt) not permanent; passing quickly *p. 391*

transistor (tran ZIS tur) here, it means a transistor radio *p. 432*

transverse (trans VURS) crossing from side to side *p. 393*

tread (TRED) step; walk *p. 197*

tricked (TRIKT) dressed *p. 181*

trifles (TRY fulz) unimportant things *p. 125*

trill (TRIL) play music with a quivering sound *p. 197*

tripped (TRIPD) ran gracefully and lightly *p. 247*

tripod (TRY pod) three-legged support *p. 407*

tuft (TUFT) small bunch *p. 185*

U

umbilical (um BIL ih kul) here, necessary for life; from "umbilical cord," which keeps an unborn baby alive *p. 432*

unaccountable (un uh KOUNT uh bul) for no apparent reason *p. 198*

underscored (UN dur skawrd) underlined *p. 367*

undulations (un juh LAY shunz) waves or wavy outlines *p. 287*

unprovoked (un pruh VOHKT) not to stir up an action *p. 36*

usurpation (you sir PAY shun) illegal seizure; taking over *p. 22*

utter (UT ur) complete *p. 466*

utterance (UT ur uns) expressing by voice *p. 139*

V

vain (VAYN) without success; useless *p. 123*

vanguard (VAN gahrd) the part of an army that goes ahead of the main body in an advance *p. 405*

variable (VAIR ee ih bul) likely to change *p. 67*

venomous (VEN uh mus) poisonous; spiteful *p. 186*

vexed (VEKST) disturbed; annoyed; irritated *p. 122*

vicissitudes (vuh SIS uh toodz) ups and downs; changes *p. 185*

volition (voh LIH shun) will, determination *p. 221*

W

wafted (WAHFT id) blown along smoothly *p. 165*

wanton (WAHN tun) mischievous, unruly *p. 139*

weather (WETH ur) last through; endure *p. 196*

whetstone (HWET stohn) a stone used for sharpening tools *p. 214*

whither (HWITH ur) to what place, point, etc. *p. 143*

wight (WHYT) human being *p. 82*

will (WIL) wishes; desires *p. 197*

windward (WIND word) the direction from which the wind blows; a position of advantage *p. 217*

withe (WITH) flexible branch or twig *p. 82*

wonder (WUN dur) feeling of surprise, admiration, awe, caused by something strange, unexpected, or incredible *p. 311*

wont (WANT) habit *p. 209*

wrench (RENCH) twist *p. 465*

INDEX OF TITLES AND AUTHORS

INDEX OF SKILLS

End rhyme, 160, 304
English language
  eponymous words in, 183
  historical periods of, 365
  Inuit words in, 303
  Latin and Greek words used in, 475
  root words in, 141
  vocabulary expansion in, 435
  words borrowed from other languages in,
    201
  words with roots from Greek and Roman
    mythology in, 469
Eponymous words, 183
Essays, 182
  classification of, 170
  expository, 284
Etymology, 53
Exposition, 16, 17, 98, 112, 278, 284, 389
External conflict, 344, 352, 389

Facts
  recognizing, 10, 15
  use of exposition to interpret, 278
Falling action, 254
Fiction
  author's imagination and, 276
  characters in, 502
  defined, 140
  elements of, 128–129, 254–255
  forms of, 254
  importance of point of view in, 458
  role of suspense in, 120
  theme in, 129, 255
Figurative language, 202–203, 243, 255, 337,
    430
  recognizing, 354, 356
Figures of speech, 434
  recognizing, 310, 316
  understanding, 160, 168
First-person narrator, 452, 458
First-person point of view, 50, 129, 452,
    470–471
Flashbacks, 389
Flat characters, 128, 254, 366, 376, 388
Folklore, 54
Foreshadowing, 120, 126, 254, 389

Formal essays, 170
Form, poetic, 426, 428, 504, 506
Free verse, 476, 478, 504, 506

Generalizations, making, 34, 49

Homophones, 207, 451
Humor, 378, 386
  use of hyperbole for, 63
Hyperbole, 202–203
  defined, 63
  identifying, 80, 96

Idioms, 253
Imagery, 208, 224, 243, 255, 309, 321, 356
  identifying, 324, 330
  in poetry, 226, 230
  symbols and, 194
  understanding, 244, 252
  using specific words, 231
Inferences, making, 28, 33, 66, 74, 148, 156,
    234, 242, 358, 364, 452, 458
  from connotations, 318, 320
Informal essays, 170
Internal conflict, 129, 344, 352, 389
Internal rhyme, 160, 304
Introduction, in nonfiction, 17
Introspection, 471
Irony, 318, 320, 378
  dramatic, 386
Irony of situation, 318, 320, 378

Jargon, 157, 419

Language, changes in, 33
Legends, 54
Limited point of view, 452
Literal language, 243, 337, 358
Lyric poems, 142, 146, 336
  characteristics of, 332

Main idea and supporting details,
    recognizing, 54, 63
Meaning
  understanding levels of, 448, 450
  understanding, through context, 460, 468

Resolution, 208, 254, 389
  of conflict, 80, 140
  final, of plot, 80
Rhetoric, 15
Rhetorical questions, 15
Rhyme, 202, 308, 356
  end and internal, 160, 304
  perfect, 304
  poetry without, 506
  sounds of, 168
Rhyme pattern, 310
Rhyme scheme, 310, 316
Rhythm, 6, 114, 202, 206, 308, 336
Rising action, 254
Roots, 49, 436, 469
Root words, 49, 141
  adding suffixes to, 447
Round characters, 128, 254, 366, 376, 388

Scenes, 388
Scripts, 418
Second-person point of view, 50, 452
Sense impressions, 226, 230
Sequence of events, understanding, 98, 112,
    494, 502
Sets, 388
Setting, 254, 388
  components of, 286, 302
  contribution to mood of, 342
  in drama, 418
  in fiction, 128
Signal words, 494, 502
  identifying, 120, 126
Similes, 160, 168, 202–203, 255, 353, 430
Soliloquy, 388
Sound devices, poetic, 97, 160, 168, 203
Speaker, in poetry, 203
Specific words, 226, 231
Stage directions, 388
Stanzas, 202, 206, 310, 316, 426, 428, 478
  poetry without, 504, 506
Stereotypes, 128, 254
Style
  evaluating poet's, 344, 352
  narrative, 470

Suffixes, 49, 436, 447
  adjective-forming, 141, 377
  adverb-forming, 141, 377
  noun-forming, 141
Summarizing, of text, 426, 428
Supporting details, identifying, 170, 182
Suspense, 120, 126
Syllables, 285
Symbolism, 194, 200, 255, 356, 358, 364, 389
Symbols, 243
  images behind, 194, 364
  intangible, 200
  meanings conveyed by, 358
Synonyms, 9, 193, 331, 429

Tall tales, 54
Theme, 10, 480
  conflict as, 352
  confusion about, 492
  in drama, 418
  in exposition and persuasion, 17
  in fiction, 129, 255
  importance of understanding, 184, 192
  in nonfiction, 129
  recognizing implied, 342
  understanding relationships to figure out,
    389
Thesis statement, 10, 17, 284
Third-person limited point of view, 129
Third-person point of view, 50, 129
Tone, 2, 6, 255, 450
  defined, 448
  expression of, 420
  understanding writer's, 422

Verbs, 317, 321, 479
  defined, 387
  words used as nouns or, 27
Visualizing, 208, 224
Vocabulary development, 5, 9, 15, 27, 33,
    49, 53, 63, 75, 79, 97, 113, 127, 141, 147,
    157, 169, 183, 193, 201, 207, 225, 231,
    243, 253, 277, 285, 303, 309, 317, 321,
    331, 337, 343, 353, 357, 365, 377, 387,
    419, 423, 429, 435, 447, 451, 459, 469,
    475, 479, 493, 503, 507

INDEX OF FINE ART

ACKNOWLEDGMENTS

Unit 1: "Godasiyo, the Woman Chief" from *Teepee Tales of the American Indian*. Retold by Dee Brown. **Unit 3:** All Dickinson poetry reprinted by permission of the publishers and the Trustees of Amherst College from *The Poems of Emily Dickinson*, Ralph W. Franklin, ed., Cambridge, Mass: The Belknap Press of Harvard University Press. Copyright © 1998 by the President and Fellows of Harvard College. Copyright © 1951, 1955, 1979 by President and Fellows of Harvard College. "From Walden" from *The Writings of Henry David Thoreau, Walden*. Edited by: J. Lyndon Shanley. Copyright © 1971 renewed 1973 reprinted by permission of Princeton University Press. "from Nature" from *The Collected Works of Ralph Waldo Emerson*. Arranged by Alfred R. Ferguson. Harvard University Press. **Unit 4:** "I Shall Not Care." Reprinted with the permission of Scribner, a Division of Simon & Schuster from *The Collected Poems of Sara Teasdale*. Copyright © 1937 by Macmillan Publishing Company; copyright renewed © 1965 by Morgan Guaranty Trust Company of New York. "The Falling Star." Reprinted with the permission of Scribner, a Division of Simon & Schuster from *The Collected Poems of Sara Teasdale*. Copyright © 1937 by Macmillan Publishing Company; copyright renewed © 1965 by Morgan Guaranty Trust Company of New York. "The Long Hill." Reprinted with the permission of Scribner, a Division of Simon & Schuster from *The Collected Poems of Sara Teasdale*. Copyright © 1937 by Macmillan Publishing Company; copyright renewed © 1965 by Morgan Guaranty Trust Company of New York. "The Revolt of Mother" from *The Revolt of Mother & Other Stories* by Mary Wilkins. The Feminist Press. **Unit 5:** "Afternoon on a Hill" by Edna St. Vincent Millay. From *Collected Poems*, HarperCollins. Copyright © 1917, 1945 by Edna St. Vincent Millay. All rights reserved. Reprinted by permission of Elizabeth Barnett, literary executor. "Lament" by Edna St. Vincent Millay. From *Collected Poems*, HarperCollins. Copyright © 1921, 1948 by Edna St. Vincent Millay. All rights reserved. Reprinted by permission of Elizabeth Barnett, literary executor. "home" from *The World of Gwendolyn Brooks* by Gwendolyn Brooks. Copyright © 1971 by Gwendolyn Brooks Blakely. "Lily Daw & The Three Ladies" from *Selected Stories of Eudora Welty* by Eudora Welty. Copyright © 1936, 1937, 1938, 1939, 1941, 1943 by Eudora Welty. Harcourt, Inc. in the United States, Canada, and Open. Russell Volkening for British rights. "Fog" from *Carl Sandburg Selected Poems* Edited by: George Hendrick and Willene Hendricks. Copyright © 1996 by Maurice C. Greenbaum & Philip G. Carson as Trustees for the Carl Sandburg Farney Trust. "The Pasture" from *The Poetry of Robert Frost* edited by Edward Connery Lathem. Copyright © 1951 by Robert Frost, copyright 1923, 1939, 1967, 1969 by Henry Holt and Co. Reprinted by permission of Henry Holt and Company, LLC. "The Road Not Taken" from *The Poetry of Robert Frost* edited by Edward Connery Lathem. Copyright © 1951 by Robert Frost, copyright 1923, 1939, 1967, 1969 by Henry Holt and Co. Reprinted by permission of Henry Holt and Company, LLC. "Stopping by Woods on a Snowy Evening" from *The Poetry of Robert Frost* edited by Edward Connery Lathem. Copyright © 1951 by Robert Frost, copyright 1923, 1939 © 1967, 1969 by Henry, Holt and Co. Reprinted by permission of Henry Holt and Company, LLC. "Invasion From Mars" from *The Panic Broadcast* by Howard Koch. Copyright © 1940 by Hadley Cantril, © renewed 1967 by Howard Koch. "Theme for English B" from *Collected Poems* by Langston Hughes. Copyright © 1994 by the Estate of Langston Hughes. Reprinted by permission of Alfred A. Knopf, a Division of Random House Inc. "Harlem" from *Collected Poems* by Langston Hughes. Copyright © 1994 by the Estate of Langston Hughes. Reprinted by permission of Alfred A. Knopf, a Division of Random House Inc. "Dream Variations" from *Collected Poems* by Langston Hughes.

ART CREDITS

Illustrations

Unit 1: p. 34: Amanda Wilson; p. 47: Jeni Bassett; p. 58: Lonnie Knabel; **Unit 2:** p. 116: Ron De Felice; pp. 120, 123: Joe Ciardello; p. 151: Lisa Young; **Unit 3:** pp. 170, 172, 178: Den Schofield; p. 226: John Labbe; **Unit 4:** p. 239: Donna Day; p. 240: Guy Porfirio; pp. 244, 248, 250: Angelo Franco; p. 297: Bradford Brown; p. 318: Anthony Carnabuci; **Unit 5:** p. 354: Ruth Lozner/K. Hayes; p. 358: Laura Hartman-Maetro; pp. 396–397, 401: Paul Casale/Melissa Turk and the Artist Network; **Unit 6:** p. 426: Edward Blakeney; p. 430: Gary Underhill; p. 448: Eva Auchincloss; p. 473: William Ramos; p. 480: Cindy Spencer; pp. 494, 497, 501: Kye Carbone; p. 504: Marlies Merk-Najaka.

Photographs

Unit 1: p. 6: Stone; p. 10: Archive Photos; p. 30: Vanessa Vick/Photo Researchers, Inc.; p. 50: Dale Boyer/Photo Researchers, Inc.; p. 54: Westlight; p. 61: Courtesy of Dee Brown; **Unit 2:** p. 95: The Granger Collection; p. 111: Corbis Bettmann; p. 117: The Granger Collection; **Unit 3:** p. 160: The Granger Collection; p. 167: Corbis Bettmann; p. 184: Gavriel Jecon/Stone; p. 191: The Granger Collection; p. 199: The Granger Collection; p. 226: The Stock Market; **Unit 4:** p. 234: The Granger Collection; p. 237: Palmer Kane/The Stock Market; p. 241: J. Sommer Collection/Archive Photos; p. 251: The Granger Collection; p. 262: Randy Masser/International Stock; p. 283: Library of Congress/The Bridgeman Art Library; p. 286: Chip Porter/Alaska Stock Images; p. 301: Corbis Bettmann; p. 304: Rafael Macia/Photo Researchers, Inc.; p. 310: Willard Clay; p. 315: Corbis Bettmann; **Unit 5:** p. 324: Corbis Bettmann; p. 329: Corbis Bettmann; p. 332: Corbis Bettmann; p. 334: Lowell Georgia/Photo Researchers, Inc.; p. 335: The Granger Collection; p. 347 Courtesy of the Library of Congress; p. 351: The Granger Collection; p. 363: E. O. Hoppé/Corbis; p. 381: Corbis Bettmann; **Unit 6:** p. 436: Wayne Hoy/The Picture Cube, Inc.; p. 457: Bernard Gotfryd/Archive Photos; p. 467: Corbis Bettman; p. 491: Renato Rotolo/Corbis.

Note: Every effort has been made to locate the copyright owner of material reprinted in this book. Omissions brought to our attention will be corrected in subsequent editions.